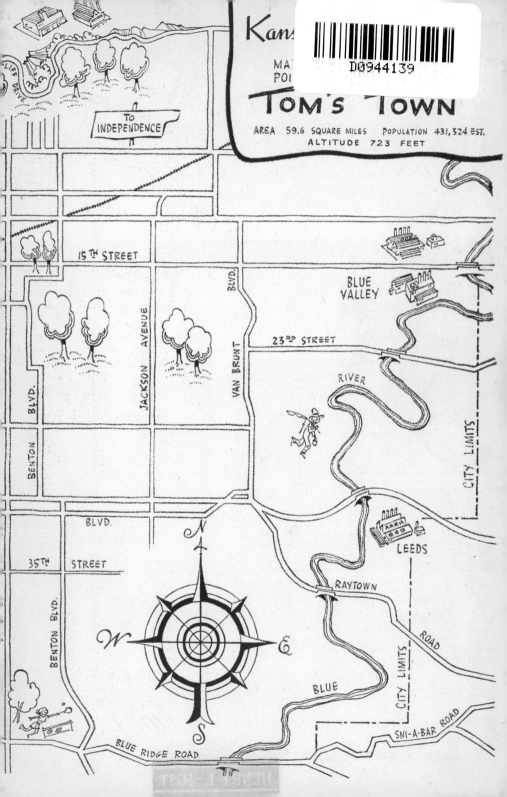

TOM'S TOWN

TOM'S TOWN

KANSAS CITY AND THE PENDERGAST LEGEND

by

WILLIAM M. REDDIG

J. B. LIPPINCOTT COMPANY

PHILADELPHIA AND NEW YORK

To J. P. G., who took me to the Old Town

Foreword

THE KANSAS CITY STORY

THIS IS A STORY of the House of Pendergast, the family that exerted a major influence on Kansas City, Missouri, politics for a half-century and finally established a dictatorial control that extended to the Missouri State Capitol and had important national ramifications.

This is also a story of a town, which for several interesting reasons calls itself the Heart of America. The two tales are really one and the spirit and substance of American politics are the things of which the whole narrative is made.

If one were seeking a complete pattern of the evolution of the boss system and municipal government in the industrial period—of the shape of American democracy at the seat of origin—one would not need to look farther than Kansas City in the years of Pendergast ascendency and decline. The design is perfectly clear, the details are complete, the local, state and national aspects in bold relief. A good deal of that is in this story.

This writer was impressed by the fact that the House of Pendergast rose to power and national notoriety in the home town of William Rockhill Nelson, one of the more vigorous, independent and highhanded newspaper publishers, who was dedicated to the anti-boss crusade and earned a seat among the giants of city building and progressive reform.

The Pendergasts and Nelson came on the Kansas City scene at approximately the same time, and prospered side by side despite each other. They were often at odds, their contests were vigorous and exciting and they had a profound effect on the character and experience of the

7

city which numbered around sixty thousand when they first saw it and which now numbers nearly one-half million inhabitants, not counting the one hundred and thirty-five thousand in the second Kansas City which is on the west or Kansas side of this metropolitan area on the Missouri-Kansas state line. The results of that struggle were reflected in various startling ways in the affairs of the main antagonists and that struggle continues today in the schemes and hopes of their successors.

Nelson, the supreme individualist and archenemy of the old party bosses, died shortly before the United States entered the First World War. The Pendergast machine rolled to oppressive power on the industrial and business boom tide of the postwar years, entrenched itself in the chaos of the depression years, grew fat and arrogant on the boodle from the spending spree that accompanied the national economic recovery. It fell apart in a fantastic series of crimes that disturbed the nation and were climaxed by the sending of Big Tom Pendergast to Federal prison in 1939.

The reckoning, which came when the nation was being aroused to prepare for another world war, was followed by an effort to make radical changes in municipal government and party organization, an effort that has continued in the 1940's and promises to produce more excitement. In a large measure this development represents a triumph for Baron Bill Nelson and the Fourth Estate over the old political boss, for most of the changes that have been accomplished are reforms which Nelson first espoused and the driving force behind the defeat of Pendergast and the rise of the new regime was Nelson's newspaper, the *Star,* no longer Nelson-owned but still directed by men who grew up under the founder.

Whether this Kansas City episode rounds out an era and defines a permanent forward step in good government are questions that only time and the experts may settle. Such findings are outside the province of the newspaperman who wrote this book in the first place because he knew some good stories of Alderman Jim Pendergast and Old Town, of Uncle Joe Shannon and Fifty-Fifty, of Big Tom Pendergast and the Free and Easy, of City Manager McElroy and Rabbi Mayerberg's crusade, of Senator Jim Reed's feud with Woodrow Wilson and Roosevelt, of Governor Stark and Emmet O'Malley's Missouri Compromise, of Harry S. Truman and the presidential destiny, and many others concerning various Goats, Rabbits, Republicans, North Side operators, South Side uplifters, Old Missouri revivalists and the remarkable, partisan Nonpartisans. They all belong in the book along with the solemn particulars of the business upon which politicians, their friends and victims expend an agonizing amount of attention.

In some ways this is a somber story but perhaps not a tragedy. For certain individuals concerned and for the masses whose main interests were at stake, it covers an interval that may have been the unhappiest time in American memory. But the politicians did their best to lighten the gloom and the Kansas Citians managed to be not too doleful through it all. In fact, they produced a surprising amount of laughter, which seemed genuine for it made a fine sound above the cries of anguish and the shouts of rage.

W. M. R.

Acknowledgments

The Starmen mentioned in this narrative are but a few of many staff members of the Kansas City Star *whose accounts were helpful in the writing of this story. For their excellent reporting; for the privilege of using* Kansas City Star's *admirable library facilities; for permission to quote from* Star *articles, interviews and editorials; for the loan of* Star *photographs reproduced in this book and for permission to reproduce cartoons by the* Star's *talented caricaturist, S. J. Ray, the writer takes this way of expressing his profound appreciation.*

Contents

Illustrations

(Halftones following page 192)

CARTOONS

TOM'S TOWN

1 *North Side, South Side*

KAWSMOUTH

VANDALS AND REFORMERS have conducted a long and not very successful campaign against the statue of Alderman Jim Pendergast which sits in Mulkey Square, near the west end of Twelfth Street, overlooking the industrial West Bottoms where the Pendergasts grew up with Kansas City. The statue of Boss Tom Pendergast's brother was placed there in 1913, paid for by popular subscription, unveiled before three thousand admirers of Alderman Jim, and was meant to stay. Consisting of three pieces—Alderman Jim and two cherubs—the memorial was designed and cast in bronze by the famous Chicago sculptor, Frederick C. Hibbard. It is esthetically satisfying to everyone except a bluenose Republican or a junk dealer, a fact that was painfully impressed on the loyal Democrats several years after the dedication ceremonies when the heavy bronze figures of Jim's two youthful and beautiful companions were stolen by a crew of despoilers whose identities were never learned, but who obviously were uncommonly desperate and physically powerful men. The outraged Democrats proceeded to order duplicates of the kidnaped young couple and saw to it that this art work was fastened down more securely.

The attack on the memorial of the saloonkeeper who founded the House of Pendergast continued for many years. Sum total of this earnest labor of defacement consists of three missing arms from the boy and girl who kneel beside Alderman Jim. The miscreants who made off with the arms must have been animated by a stronger sentiment than delight in destruction or the larcenous instinct, for it took several hours of painful toil with a hacksaw to cut through the metal, and the salvage value of each fragment was not more than fifty cents in the prewar market. It seemed obvious to all thoughtful citizens of the North Side that only a Republican would have the fanatical strength and determination to perform such a futile work.

An attempt to revive the anti-Pendergast movement in Mulkey Square was made not long ago at the height of the Nonpartisan reform when a virtuous leader of the Chamber of Commerce penned an impassioned appeal to the associated promoters, traders and herders who run the town. "I do not see," he declared, "why Kansas City should be disgraced any longer by having a bronze monument of a saloonkeeper on one of its most beautiful drives, and especially as that saloonkeeper bears the name of Pendergast, which has been such a great stigma to Kansas City."

The only effect produced by this agitation was a raucous laugh on Twelfth Street.

Old Jim is pretty durable, any way you take him. He sits in his alder-manic chair beside Kersey Coates Drive with a benign welcoming look and a proprietary air. He belongs in Mulkey Square. He was one of the promoters of the great industrial scene that spreads before him at Kaws-mouth, where the Kaw River and the Missouri, the West's "Big Muddy," have their confluence. He is the man most responsible for the fact that the district bounded on the south by Twelfth Street still is considered the Pendergast political domain, which another Jim, nephew of the old saloonkeeper, is directing.

The people who placed the statue were thoughtful enough to set it so that Alderman Jim looks directly over the ground where he operated the saloon and inn that established the family's fortune in business and politics. Twelfth Street at this point intersects Kersey Coates Drive and plunges west over a viaduct into a bottomland region of railroad tracks, warehouses, freight offices, factories, packing plants, stockyards, bridges and viaducts. Some six blocks west is the Kansas-Missouri state line and just beyond that boundary the Kaw or Kansas River winds to its im-minent meeting with the Missouri. Off to the right the great bend of the Missouri at Kawsmouth is clearly visible from the eminence on which the Pendergast memorial stands.

The view from Mulkey Square takes in the main part of the industrial congregation which has made Kansas City the butcher, miller and distributor of the Missouri Valley region and is a scene that is recommended to strangers who are confused when they are told that Kansas City is not in Kansas and was not named for that state. The enterprise got under way here thirty years before Kansas Territory was qualified for statehood and accepted into the Union in 1861. The Kansas plains were popularly known as the Great American Desert. That territory didn't seem to have a future until it was entered by reckless and headstrong promoters from New England, and the result was Bleeding Kansas, John Brown of Osawatomie, grasshoppers, Prohibition, Carrie Nation, cyclones, dust storms and, finally, Alf Landon.

On the other hand, the Show Me Land on the east side of the line was called the Great Blue Country by the early settlers. The blue skies, the blue waters in the springs and the streams that emptied into the Big Muddy, and the blue mist on the hills at sundown made the name right. Memory of that time survives in names like Blue Mills, Blue Mound, Blue Valley, Blue Springs, the Little Blue and the Big Blue rivers—all in Jackson County—and, somewhat less directly, in the Kansas City Blues, frequent occupants of the cellar position in the American Association of Baseball Clubs.

Kansas City probably would have been named Port Fonda if Abraham Fonda hadn't been feuding with Henry Jobe in 1838 when they and several other pioneer real estate developers got together to organize a townsite on 256 acres purchased for $4,200 from the estate of Gabriel Prudhomme, French fur trader and farmer. The democratic issue which was to trouble this community so greatly in subsequent years figured immediately in the original transaction, for Mr. Fonda listed himself as Abraham Fonda, Gentleman, and Henry Jobe belligerently identified himself as Henry Jobe, Carpenter, declaring that he would have nothing to do with a town that was named for a man who assumed the effete air of a gentleman. The Jobe faction voted consistently against Port Fonda and grew more eloquent as the jug was passed around. After long debate, the proprietors agreed to seek incorporation as the Town of Kansas, the name deriving from a festive Indian tribe * known as the

* The Kansas or Kaw Indians were famous for their feasting, dancing, speechmaking and gambling. A remnant of the tribe resides in Oklahoma.

Kanza or Kansas, which native poets have translated to mean People of
the South Wind. Although the compromise choice didn't have the hi-
falutin sound which most of the town's owners would have liked, it was
most appropriate, for their settlement owed its existence and its hope for
the future to the fact that it was situated just below the mouth of the Kaw
River.

Nature had favored this site as the gateway to the unexploited West
in every way except one—it didn't seem possible that men could push
back the towering river bluffs at this point to make room for a town of
any consequence, or that they would be able to cut trails through the
wooded hills so that passengers and freight from the Missouri River
steamboats could be moved to the Kansas plains for the long run west
by pack train and prairie schooner. That is, the prospect was dishearten-
ing to all except a few large investors in real estate. They were hustlers
and go-getters of immense purpose, men like John C. McCoy, son of a
famous Baptist missionary to the Indians and moving spirit in the organization of the two towns that grew into modern Kansas City.

McCoy started the promotion in the region of what is now Kansas
City's South Side even before there was a North Side. His first enterprise was Westport, four miles inland from the river landing, which he
established as a rival trail town to the original county-seat town of Independence. Popular legend has it that McCoy laid out Westport with
his wife's clothesline, but this has been discredited as a myth, probably
fostered by envious Independence merchants. The man who founded
Westport in 1833 was no bungler, and his town quickly eclipsed Independence as the head of the Santa Fe and Oregon trails. It was on the
west side of Jackson County, adjoining the Kansas line, while Independence lay on the east side and was isolated by several streams that
created fording problems for the travelers. After starting Westport on its
way, McCoy turned to the development of the river settlement near Kawsmouth, then known as Westport Landing and important only as the
place where the Missouri steamboats unloaded freight and people for
the short but difficult haul to Westport. Both enterprises were well
under way in time to catch the bulk of the outfitting business provided by the forty-niners and other wayfarers in the great migrations before the Civil War.

Promoter McCoy and associates were so certain that Westport Landing had a greater future than Westport that they called it the City of the Future. After purchasing the townsite and naming it the Town of Kansas, they had some difficulty with legal details and sales resistance, but by 1846 they had the boom started and it has been fairly constant in the succeeding century. Colonel Kersey Coates, prophet and builder who started the West Bluff phase of the development in the 1850's, estimated that the Kawsmouth project would grow into a community of a half-million residents. It absorbed old Westport at the turn of this century. Counting the Kansas Citians on both sides of the state line, the Colonel's prophecy now is out of date and a few years ago his daughter, Laura Coates Reed, upped the figure to two and possibly three millions.

All this came about in spite of the predictions of the people of the rival river towns of Lexington and St. Joseph, Missouri, Atchison and Leavenworth, Kansas, who thought that their towns were meant to be the City of the Future and were annoyed by the big talk of the early Kansas Citians. These scoffers admitted that ancient Rome made a good thing out of its seven hills, but what could be done with the seventy-and-seven hills of the Town of Kansas? They said that the Kansas City mountains were congenial only to strange types of men and animals. Among the beasts that inhabited this fearsome wilderness was a species of wild cattle with two long and two short legs on opposite sides rather than ends. The first permanent bluff dwellers were a few fearless characters like Old Pino, the pioneer fur trapper and mountain man, who came up the Missouri in 1815 with an expedition of the American Fur Company. Old Pino, a Frenchman whose real name was Jacques Fournais, lent a hand in Kansas City's first commercial activity at the trading post established in the Kawsmouth region by François Chouteau. After the big westward rush set in, Old Pino retired to a cabin on Kersey Coates's Hill to spend his last years, confident that he had found a place where civilization would never overtake him. He lived to be one hundred and twenty-four years old and it is said that the thing which hastened his end was his excitement at the sight of the first railroad locomotive chugging in the West Bottoms. The age of the mountain men finally ended in 1869 when the first bridge across the Big Muddy, a railroad structure—Octave Chanute's famous Hannibal Bridge for the Hannibal & St. Joseph Railroad—was built just below Kawsmouth and the Kansas Citians staged an enormous celebration in anticipation of the greatest traffic rush of all time.

The City of Kansas knew then that nothing could stop it, for it had survived floods, cholera, ague, border war, civil war and a multitude of lesser hazards. It had made the bluffs habitable by the expenditure of prodigious energy and by great fortitude. Reports circulating in envious neighboring towns indicated a large number of Kansas Citians were crippled in tumbles from the bluffs to the tops of buildings during the heroic excavating period. These accidents did not in the least dampen the enthusiasm of the pioneers, who were well fortified with mountain dew and the indomitable spirit of real estate agents.

When Jim Pendergast first saw the West Bottoms, the industrial development was just getting well under way and the West Bluff still retained some of the aspects of a jungle. Before he died the west face of the bluff was transformed into West Terrace Park, with stone walls and terraces giving the hill the appearance of a massive citadel. Behind this battlement the towers of downtown Kansas City rise.

The spectacular development at Kawsmouth requires poetic treatment to do it justice and that detail was attended to many years ago by a rugged Kansas poet, C. L. Edson, who was imported by Colonel Nelson's *Star* to celebrate the wonders and glories of the City on the Kaw. Charlie Edson produced numerous rousing items and achieved local immortality with his "Epic of Kansas City," a narrative of heroic quality, of which these verses are a good sample:

> The herders and the traders and the sod corn crew,
> They planted 'em a city when the world was new,
> They planted Kansas City and the darn thing grew.

> The bearcat killers and the Dan Boone clan,
> The boys that taught the panther his respect for man,
> They planted Kansas City where the bull trails ran.

> Ships made Carthage, gold made Nome,
> Grain built Babylon, the wars built Rome;
> Hogs made Chicago with their dying squeal,
> Up popped Pittsburgh at the birth of steel.

Come Kansas City, make your story brief:
Here stands a city built o' bread and beef.

This is Kansas City, where the tribe trails meet,
The rail head, the gateway, the West's Main Street,
The old tribal stamping ground to stamp your feet.*

Among the bearcat killers of Kawsmouth, Alderman Jim Pendergast
was certainly not the least and some day his home town may get around
to admitting that fact, and then do something about restoring the missing
pieces in the arms of the cherubs who attend him in Mulkey Square.

TRAVELERS' CHANCE

JAMES PENDERGAST was a young man with little education and no financial means whatever when he arrived in Kansas City in 1876. He found
himself in the midst of an international convention of traders, specu-
lators, prospectors, salesmen of gold bricks and snake oil, and sports.

In addition to the economic inducements, Kansas City had a cosmo-
politan flavor and a democratic spirit that made it appealing to widely
assorted tastes. It was not a Western city but had something of all four
points of the compass. The cattle range began just west of Kawsmouth
but the cowboys and stockmen who came in from Kansas were outnumbered by the Kentuckians and Tennesseans who were here first,
and they in turn were outnumbered by the men from the East and
North and the lands beyond the Atlantic. The census of 1870 gave Kansas
City a population of thirty-two thousand and revealed that about a
fourth of that number was foreign born. Blanketed Indians still strolled
in the square when Jim Pendergast first saw it, but these sons of the
original owners were outnumbered by large companies of Irishmen,
Germans, Englishmen, Canadians and Swedes who were competing
for the business with the Yankees and the native Missourians. Smaller
groups of Frenchmen, Hungarians, Norwegians, Austrians, Hollanders,
Scotsmen and Belgians joined the rivalry and quickly adapted themselves to the local customs. The Italians came along a little later to increase the pressure. Negroes made up a tenth of the population.

* By permission of the *Kansas City Star*.

The life of the town in this period centered in Market Square, near the Missouri River levee on the North Side. Horse and mule trading, farm-produce sales, political rallies, revival meetings, medicine shows and circuses went on simultaneously in various parts of the public forum, one part of which was occupied by the City Hall. Political activity came under the classification of popular entertainment and the party orators generated so much gas that the citizens were abnormally buoyant. The spirits of the partisans were revived by frequent visits to the dozen saloons lining the Main Street side of the square, appropriately designated Battle Row, which upheld its reputation for disturbance with or without the assistance of special squads of police.

Everybody but the Indians and the Negroes had a chance or labored under the illusion that tomorrow he would be able to retire in style. The promise of riches and the actual acquisition of sudden wealth in a considerable number of cases filled the fortune seekers with confidence and an overwhelming desire to prove their luck. They found uncommon encouragement in this line of endeavor, for the gambling industry attained a high state of development in Kansas City in the 1870's. The faro banks at Marble Hall and No. 3 Missouri Avenue were famous throughout the West. Scholarly gamblers like Canada Bill, who kept himself solvent betting on Webster's spelling and definition of words, and colorful plungers like Wild Bill Hickok, the two-gun marshal of Abilene, Kansas, made the town their headquarters. Jesse James found relaxation in the gambling halls during periods when he lived incognito in Kansas City, and was not molested. When they were not figuring on deals in lots, grain, hogs and cattle and other matters of commerce, the citizens exercised their financial genius at chuck-a-luck, faro, three-card monte, roulette, high five, keno, poker and, occasionally, craps. They bet on horse races, dog fights, free-for-alls with rats, cock fights and, in an extremity, they played fly-loo. This last game called for rare judgment, the players placing their money on common houseflies and guessing which one would move first, in what direction and how far.

A brief depression struck the happy Kansas City gamblers in 1881 when a Legislature controlled by farmers passed the Johnson anti-gambling law. The Kansas City protest against this interference with freedom was registered in melodramatic fashion by Bob Potee, the ele-

gant Virginia gentleman who was proprietor of the faro bank at No. 3
Missouri Avenue. Potee saw the Johnson law as the ominous dawn of
a new era and decided he didn't want to be around to witness all the
changes that were coming. One day he put on his high silk hat and
gloves, picked up his gold-headed cane and took a walk down to the
Missouri River. He kept walking majestically until the muddy waters
swirled over his head. His body was recovered and the town staged an
appropriate ceremony of farewell to a great man and his age. His funeral
service was held in a Grand Avenue church and the Reverend Samuel
Bookstaver Bell, a popular preacher of the day, delivered an impressive
sermon over his casket. Literally, as in the words of the "Cowboy's La-
ment," six tall gamblers bore the casket into the church and carried it
out for Bob Potee's last journey to his Virginia home.

The same year that Bob Potee prematurely decided that gambling had
no future, Jim Pendergast started up the road to success by backing his
judgment on a horse. A nag named Climax, a long shot, romped in
ahead of the field and Jim was riding on its nose with savings from his
wages as a puddler in the Jarboe Keystone iron foundry.

Pendergast used his winnings conservatively, setting himself up in
business as proprietor of an inn and a saloon in the West Bottoms. He
called his inn the American House, but it later became known as Pendergast House. His first saloon was named Climax, in tribute to the great
horse that paid off. The future political boss had entered a business with
a future. There were 220 retail groceries and 200 saloons in the city in
1880 and the expert opinion was that the latter trade was further from
being overcrowded than the former, as only the preachers and puritans
were irregular drinkers. Jim had a high regard for the saloonkeeping
profession and defended it warmly in later years when the puritans became more numerous and endeavored to suppress his kind. They moved
him to an expression of disgust when they introduced a bill in the Legislature to bar politicians from the saloon business.

"Well," he said, "there's some saloon men in politics whose word I'd
take before I'd take the word of some men in politics for whom there is
no room in the saloon business."

Pendergast's hotel and saloon were on St. Louis Avenue, just below
the West Bluff at Twelfth Street and just around the corner from roaring

Union Avenue, the short thoroughfare that carried traffic to the old Union Depot and served the basic needs of traveling America for more than thirty strenuous years.

Union Avenue society took a swashbuckling pride in a reputation for picturesque sordidness which was believed to compare favorably with the iniquity of New York's Bowery. Nothing was allowed to interfere with the business of making the transient's stopover at the midcontinent interchange point an interesting and instructive interval. At night the avenue leading from the depot became a midway blazing with light, tumultuous with the shouts of ballyhoo men and the cries of grays (the suckers of the day) being whisked out of sight. Booted cattlemen, silk-hatted gamblers, ticket scalpers, bunco artists, blanketed Indians, Kansas yokels and scented ladies, strolling by from Paris and New York, mingled in this boisterous democracy. Runners, barkers and cappers employed various irresistible devices to interest the travelers in the wonders of the hotels, burlesque shows, restaurants, saloons, museums, pawnshops and barbershops along the way. A simple matter of getting a haircut often turned into a strange and expensive adventure in this neighborhood. You could stroll along Union Avenue and avoid all the exciting experiences it offered, but not if you loitered, for cappers were ever vigilant, ready to seize you and hustle you inside for the full treatment.

Pendergast's establishment was one of the reputable places of the West Bottoms. Its genial host catered less to the traveling public than to the men who worked in the railroad yards and shops, the mills and the packing plants. His relationship with Union Avenue was primarily political. Within several years after he established himself on St. Louis Avenue, he won recognition as a figure in Democratic affairs by delivering a large number of West Bottoms votes to a successful candidate for mayor. He moved uptown to a larger saloon at 508 Main Street but retained his property on St. Louis Avenue. His popularity grew as he took the lead in opposing agitation for reform on Union Avenue and other lively spots in the West Bottoms.

The pressure for more decorum increased steadily, for Kansas City was growing up rapidly and beginning to settle down. On the crest of the West Bluff above Union Avenue was Kersey Coates's Quality Hill with his exclusive residential quarter and his Broadway with its luxury hotel and its Grand Opera House. The hotel, called the Coates House, had copper-roofed towers, a white marble swimming pool in the basement, and red plush, mirrors and marble in between. The Opera House was large and ornate, designed to accommodate the leading road shows from New York. Stage stars came to the theater and the hotel was filled with cattle barons, meat packers, capitalists from the East, gamblers and politicians. Guests looked out upon a cow pond and a Broadway alternately deep in dust or mud. One guest from the East, so the story goes, stepped outside the Coates House after a Missouri shower and was startled to see a man standing up to his chin in mud.

"My poor fellow," exclaimed the visitor, "let me help you."

"Oh, I'm all right, mister," said the man in the mud. "I'm standing on top of a hack. But mebbe you better do something for my passenger."

There were more cows, horses, mules, goats and dogs than people in the streets, and the bullfrogs in the cow ponds filled the night air with rustic sound, but the activity on the Hill and beyond to the east and southward made it plain that Kansas City was becoming a place of culture and refinement, with everything up to date.

The roar of industry in the West Bottoms also grew louder and Mr. Pendergast became a very busy man serving the social and political interests of the Kawsmouth toilers and businessmen. New industries crowded out the residences in this section, and work and recreation were equally strenuous. The entertainment activity reached its height on West Ninth Street near the Missouri-Kansas state line. The service there became so popular that it eventually produced the Wettest Block in the World. It had twenty-four buildings and twenty-three of them were saloons.

Jim Pendergast was instrumental in keeping the reform out of this hard-working, hard-drinking locality for many years. Then a crusading governor forced the police to interfere and they reduced the number of saloons in the wettest block to thirteen. That number was regarded as a bad omen by the saloonkeepers and gamblers, and their forebodings were borne out several years later when the building of Kansas City's present Union Station southeast of the Bottoms killed Union Avenue and threw a pall over the whole social life of the West Bottoms. The wake, held on Union Avenue on Halloween, 1914, was a carouse that inspired awed recollection for another twenty years, but the actual mourning was not prolonged. The change didn't come too soon, since industry needed the room for the expansion that fulfilled the famous prophecy of Senator Thomas Hart Benton, the Champion of the West and Hard Money. Standing on a Kansas City hill in 1852, he had called for fast action in the building of this "grand manufacturing and commercial community," where these rocky bluffs meet and turn aside the sweeping currents of the mighty Missouri.

KING OF THE FIRST

"I've got a lot of friends," said Jim Pendergast to a friendly newspaperman who liked his beer and conversation. "And, by the way, that's all there is to this boss business—friends. You can't coerce people into doing things for you—you can't make them vote for you. I never coerced anybody in my life. Whenever you see a man bulldozing anybody he doesn't last long. Still, I've been called a boss. All there is to it is having friends, doing things for people, and then later on they'll do things for you."

Jim Pendergast introduced the friendship-in-politics ideal on a scale never before known in Kansas City society. The mutual benefit principle acquired the force of doctrine in the Democratic faction which the saloonkeeper controlled. He honestly detested an ingrate and infused his followers with his own fanatical spirit of personal loyalty. Anyone accepted into his company was thereafter committed to work unswervingly for the common cause or suffer ostracism or worse.

Although the mercenary aspect of this movement was always pronounced, Pendergast was a genuinely friendly man. His round, ruddy face was a picture of Irish amiability and his heavy black mustache did not hide his easy smile. His voice was soft. He was usually at ease. The only sign he gave of anger was the swift vanishing of his smile. His angers were rare, but not light, affairs. His exceedingly agreeable manner covered but did not conceal a personality of uncommon forcefulness. The blend of sentiment and authority in his character made him a leader of the puddling gang before he became a landlord and a politician. He was twenty years old when he came down to Kansas City from the river town of St. Joseph, Missouri, where his parents had settled, when he was two years old, and reared a family of nine children. Jim, the second child, had been born in Gallipolis, Ohio.

"I'm from Gallipolis," he was fond of saying. "That name's a joke," he added, and his hearers laughed with him.

Puddler Jim became a sort of private banker for the workingmen in the West Bottoms and thereby he rose to power. In his saloon he established the system of cashing the paychecks of railroad men and packing-house workers. Greenbacks were scarce in those days. Jim installed a large safe and filled it, paydays, with silver and paper. The workers got into the habit of going to Jim's place to get their warrants and checks turned into spendable cash. They spent some of it across the bar but Jim did not make that a requisite. Men learned that he had an interest in humanity outside of business and that he could be trusted, and they returned the favor by patronizing his saloon and giving him their confidence.

The genial saloonkeeper spread harmony and Democratic unity over precincts that had been the hotly contested battleground of the Hickeys, the Kelleys, the Gaffneys and the Burnetts. Those Irish were notable exponents of packing-house election rules, which were based on the premise that the voter's life is necessarily hazardous and muscle must be employed to determine the will of the majority. Pendergast was versed in those rules, but he depended primarily on his popularity and his skill in trading favors and making alliances to promote his interests.

Expanding with the town, Pendergast opened his Main Street saloon, a block south of Market Square, a year before he became alderman from the First Ward. From his uptown seat he continued his helpful ways to the voting masses, but his saloon there was not a workingman's resort. It was a headquarters for businessmen, lawyers, contractors, boss gamblers and officeholders from the City Hall and Courthouse. Jim was as popular with these operators as he was with the leaders of shirtsleeve society in the West Bottoms.

After a decade devoted to doing favors for others, Jim asked for and received the public recognition that was his due. He stepped up to take his aldermanic seat in 1892, in a moment of great and unnatural peace, when the city was agitated by nothing more than the normal differences between Republicans and Democrats, and the Democrats felt that a new era of good feeling was dawning because their ticket in the city campaign was supported by the fiery Colonel Nelson of the *Star*. The truculent and meddlesome Colonel followed a line which he called "independent but not neutral," which was very confusing to the party leaders and often worked out to the disadvantage of the local Democrats. They won the *Star*'s approval in '92 by supporting charter amendments which the Colonel demanded, and by nominating for mayor a plausible individual named Will S. Cowherd, who later went on to Congress.

Pendergast strode on the stage as alderman and King of the First Ward at the very time that an ambitious effort was being made to discourage boss politicians through electoral reform. A month before the city election was held, the town approved a set of charter amendments, one of which provided that the parties nominate aldermen in each ward at a primary election, setting up machinery that was supposed to give the unorganized voter a voice in the selection of candidates. The prevailing method of making nominations was known as the "mob primary," which was simply a mass meeting managed by the party bosses, usually held in a beer garden or a hall next door to a saloon, and controlled by the faction with the huskiest and most impassioned ward heelers. One of the principal advocates of the electoral reform was Nelson's *Star*. Curiously enough, another was the boss of the First, Jim Pendergast. The new system depressed some of the old politicians, who depended on convention tricks and rushing tactics for their success, but it actually strengthened the position of Pendergast, who excelled in delivering votes.

Alderman Jim demonstrated more emphatically that he was the coming man in Kansas City Democracy two years later (1894) when he was one of the two Democratic candidates who survived the holocaust brought on by Colonel Nelson's disappointment with the Cowherd administration and the abrupt ending of Democratic factional peace. While the party debacle hurried to its climax, Alderman Jim stood serenely in the First Ward surrounded by his many friends. The rugged nature of the Kansas City political competition was displayed in several ways in this campaign, with the Republicans selecting the occasion to show that they could be tougher than the Democrats. The G.O.P. lined up with the notorious A.P.A. (American Protective Association), the Ku Kluxers of the period, who climaxed the campaign with a gun battle. The election-day massacre occurred in the Fifth Ward, a district usually controlled by Fighting Jim Pryor, a saloonkeeper and building contractor with a large Irish following. John Pryor, eighteen-year-old son of Fighting Jim and friend of young Tom Pendergast, and later one of his important business associates, set off hostilities when he converted a voter to the Democratic cause. His subject was an elderly German and the word got around that Big John Pryor had been so forceful in his electioneering that the old German was frightened into abandoning long-standing Republican convictions. The A.P.A. brigade, armed with deputy constable commissions and rifles, immediately set out to punish the Irish for this outrage, and soon captured John Pryor. The Fifth Ward boss's son was being hustled away to an uncertain fate when a bunch of the boys at Scanlan's saloon heard of his arrest and rushed joyously to the rescue. The two armies met on the Summit Street Bridge over the Belt Line. In their haste or because of overconfidence in their prowess in a free-for-all, the Irish neglected to supply themselves adequately with firearms, only one possessing a pistol. The A.P.A. men were well armed with Winchesters and when the smoke cleared one good Democrat lay dead and six were severely wounded. There was only one casualty on the other side.

When the votes were counted, the Republican ticket had a handsome majority except in two river wards controlled by Pendergast and his allies. This was the beginning of a six-year period of Republican domination of municipal affairs, a run of success which resulted, in considerable part, from the Democratic factional disputes. Alderman Pendergast continued to gain in prestige and influence throughout this lean time for his party in local affairs, producing majorities that startled veterans in the vote-getting trade. He finally was credited with carrying a thousand votes in his vest pocket, and Republican managers complained that hundreds of his followers crossed the state line from Kansas to vote for him on election day. He grew accustomed to hearing charges of intimidation of voters and ballot-box stuffing, and dismissed them with a smile and a shrug.

"I never needed a crooked vote," he told a *Star* reporter who interviewed him late in his career. "All I want is a chance for my friends to get to the polls."

Charges that he loaded the city payrolls with his friends and supporters and that he worked to turn city business to firms or individuals in the party's favor did not disturb him, for he regarded these spoils as the legitimate rewards of work for the Democratic cause. But he had a code of ethics which he observed rigorously and which excluded the boss himself from political boodle. He boasted proudly that he never took a cent in exchange for a political favor and not even his enemies challenged his reputation on that score.

The Pendergast command developed into an efficient team when Jim called his three brothers from St. Joseph—John, Mike and Tom. John was a quiet and steady man who was completely happy running the saloon on Main Street. Mike exhibited special adaptability as a rough-and-tumble man, as an organizer of ward clubs and a public jobholder. Tom exhibited exceptional talent for all phases of the Pendergast enterprises in politics and commerce.

Young Tom, sixteen years younger than the Alderman, attained voting age a year after Jim took office in the lower house of the City Council. He appeared on the scene after completing his schooling. He spent more time in school than any of the other brothers, going from a St. Joseph school to St. Mary's College in Kansas, where he distinguished himself as an athlete rather than a scholar. His baseball fielding and batting averages were so good that they attracted the attention of a professional league scout and he was offered a bush league contract. Family opposition kept him from becoming an early Babe Ruth.

The traits of character that peculiarly fitted Jim Pendergast for the role of political boss were intensified in Tom, but there were some marked differences. During his apprenticeship as an election worker, he was assigned to the toughest precincts and won the respect and friendship of the workingmen in the river wards. In the Pendergast saloons, where he worked as an efficient bookkeeper, he was a favorite among politicians, sportsmen and businessmen. The gamblers early admitted him to their fraternity and his special interest in horse racing, which later dominated his life and contributed largely to his ruin, probably was greatly stimulated during the period when he worked as cashier in a

Pendergast liquor concession at a race track. The effort to pick another Climax continued for almost a half-century before it rounded out the gambler's cycle.

The main difference between the brothers was suggested by their voices. Jim's light baritone was the voice of the mediator, the promoter of sociability and goodwill. Tom's heavy bass was the trumpet blast of a fighter. He was a blue-eyed, light-haired heavyweight who stood five feet nine inches, weighed around two hundred pounds and exuded energy from every pore. His head was planted on a short, thick neck which had the rugged look of an oak tree trunk. The impression of hugeness about him was emphasized by his face. It was a massive face—great jaw, large mouth and nose. He looked both formidable and engaging, for there was a humorous glint in his eyes, a jaunty air in his bearing and a sentimental quality in his expression along with the dominating impression of savage power. The total effect made him one of the most arresting figures ever observed in Kansas City. He drew attention wherever he went and men remembered him from one look.

The devastating force of Tom Pendergast's fists and his ferocity when crossed were early impressed on the citizens of the river wards. His skill and daring in the manly art of self-defense did not diminish his popularity with the men of the West Bottoms and Market Square, but brute force was secondary in the list of his qualifications for the work he had selected—the first was intelligence. Alderman Jim watched with approval while his young brother balanced the books in his saloons, made friends with the public and the important men, familiarized himself with the needs and interests of the North Side, and endeavored to emulate Jim in practising the ways of peace, compromise and self-control. It was early evident that he was being trained to take over the throne of the King of the First.

The Rabbits and the Goats

MIKE AND TOM PENDERGAST learned the political routine rapidly and found all aspects of the business both fascinating and stimulating to young men who hoped to get ahead in the world, but they soon saw that they were not getting the rewards of government to which they were entitled. They did not hold the public responsible for this lack of recognition. The trouble was Joe Shannon, who was building up a monopoly in the Courthouse and endeavoring to lower Pendergast prestige in the City Hall. Inasmuch as the more attractive prospects in jobs with fees, commissions and salaries were then in the Courthouse, something had to be done to reverse the Shannon, or Rabbit, trend.

The depth of the difference between the two principal Democratic factions in Jackson County was something an outsider could not readily appreciate, but it was suggested by the names of the rival groups—Rabbits and Goats. These popular designations were coined in the early days when the majority of the Pendergast following were Irish folk from the old sod who lived on the West Bluff in the laboring-class neighborhood that grew up around the residental quarter of the Quality Hill nabobs. Many of these Irish families kept goats, which had no respect for private property or class distinctions and made themselves a public nuisance. The Shannon workers lived over the Hill, in what was then the southeast part of the town and is now near the center of the downtown business section. Their homes were close to the wooded bottoms in the valley of O. K. Creek, where rabbits and other small game frolicked.

In the heat of a campaign an opposition orator called the Pendergast partisans Goats, after their numerous animal pets. Jim Pendergast liked goats and happily accepted them as a symbol of his faction's devotion to freedom and other liberal ideals. Leading his delegation on a march to a convention for a battle with the Shannon boys, he roared: "When we come over the hill like goats, they'll run like rabbits." When the contest was over the Goats had seized control of the City Hall, ousting the Shannon men from their easy jobs. It was a cold April day when winter lingered into spring and snow covered the ground. "What will become of the poor fellows who are losing their jobs?" some tenderhearted citizen asked. "They'll eat snow, like the rabbits," said a Goat.

The names were appropriate in many ways. The Pendergast Goats were rugged, combative, clannish and always hungry. The Shannon Rabbits were fleet, deceptive and prolific. The Rabbits also had large appetites. They ate snow no oftener than the Goats were compelled to subsist on tin cans.

The Daddy Rabbit, the Honorable Joseph B. Shannon, was ten years younger than the Chief Whiskers of the Goats but politically was quite as mature as the North Side boss. He made himself the Czar of the Ninth Ward while Pendergast was establishing himself as King of the First. The same year that Jim became an alderman, Joe went on the city payroll as market master. It was an appointive position, and a Republican revival limited Mr. Shannon's incumbency to one term. He wasn't able or inclined to match Alderman Jim's record for official connection with government in the early period, but he was on the political stage throughout Jim's time and held his stand there until the last days of the machine under Big Tom. He was sometimes down, frequently up, usually in the spotlight. He saw it all and had much to do with shaping the peculiar style and character of Jackson County politics. At the finish he served a twelve-year turn as a congressman—the Great Jeffersonian from Jackson County—and although he did not have much time left to live when the Kansas City machine fell apart, he stood around trying to pick up the pieces. When he finally shuffled off after a half-century in the hustings, he was a silver-haired, benevolent figure, full of practical wisdom, humor and sentiment—Uncle Joe to everyone, in or out of politics.

Like Jim Pendergast, Joe Shannon belonged to a large Irish family—there were eight Shannon children. Like so many of the individuals who figured in the Kansas City political and business life, he was traveling west when chance directed him to this bustling community at Kawsmouth. Joe's father was a railroad contractor and his death in a train collision in Kansas was the incident that brought about the family's move to Kansas City. The Widow Shannon and her eight children arrived at the Union Depot one night in 1879. She found friendly people who helped her to get established in the neighborhood of Fifteenth Street and Tracy Avenue. The Shannons were poor in everything except character and ingenuity. The older boys got jobs to provide a meager income for their mother. Joe quit school at twelve to contribute his small part toward the grocery bill. He and his brothers were good workers but the family's industriousness was less remarkable than its fighting quality and its political talent.

The Shannon boys discovered that they were living in the Ninth Ward and that it was the largest ward in the city, controlling one fifth of the delegates in conventions proportioned to the population. Long before he was of voting age, Joe was an experienced politician. The Shannon home became political headquarters for the Ninth Ward, and every time the family sat down for the evening meal there was a Democratic caucus. Their section of the city became known an Shannonville.

Joe Shannon inherited the family leadership upon the death of Frank, oldest of the brothers, a stonemason and a force in union politics. Under Joe's direction, Shannonville spread its influence over two wards in the city and extended its power into the county through alliances with party men in Independence, the old county seat.

Mr. Shannon made local politics a very involved and exciting business. He was as rugged a character as Jim Pendergast, almost as rugged as Tom. He endeavored to play the role of pacifier, like Alderman Jim, which was fortunate for the public peace as there was always more than enough disturbance in his domain. The respect he inspired in friend or foe was illustrated by an incident in the tumultuous election of '94, when Joe alone cowed an A.P.A. mob. An angry crowd gathered around a voting booth after someone circulated a report that the Shannon boys had broken open a ballot box and were stuffing it. When Joe Shannon appeared in the doorway, the would-be rioters abandoned their plan to raid the booth in favor of an investigation. He stood there, saying nothing and smiling coolly on the crowd until his commanding presence had tempered A.P.A. suspicions and indignation.

Mental and physical agility were nicely balanced in the person of the Rabbit leader. In one election he was arrested for exhibiting muscular dexterity in ejecting a Republican and a Populist watcher from a voting booth at the same moment. One of these individuals filed assault charges against Shannon in police court and Joe handled his own defense. He was educating himself to be a lawyer and was anxious to demonstrate his progress before his followers. His defense was that the complaining witness had picked a fight after Shannon gave him a friendly pat on the back. "Like this," said Joe, seizing the complainant and hurling him across the courtroom. The injured party bellowed with rage and charged at Shannon, the courtroom spectators roared with laughter and the police judge admitted that the Rabbit chief had proved his case, thereby escaping a five-hundred-dollar fine.

Joe Shannon was more versatile than either Jim or Tom Pendergast and, although he scattered his efforts when it seemed that he might have more profitably concentrated on organization matters, for a long time he threatened to overshadow his opponents from the North Side. His skill in planning coups was of a superior order and he delighted in intrigue. His plots and ambushes rather consistently advanced the Shannon cause although they frequently wrecked the Democratic Party.

The No. 1 Rabbit took the lead in promoting the long factional disorder which brought about the final collapse of the Combine, an outfit that had dominated things political for more than a decade. Both Shannon and Pendergast worked in and with the Combine, on occasion, in the years when they were rising to the command, and their disagreement with that early machine had nothing to do with reform sentiment but grew out of the struggle for power. Dissolution of the Combine marked an important step in the evolution of boss politics. From the wreckage Shannon and Pendergast emerged with enhanced power and prestige.

Once the stage was cleared for the main bout between the Goats and the Rabbits, the political struggle grew in intensity, with many interesting variations being introduced by Jim Pendergast's brothers, Mike and Tom, and many complications provided by Colonel Nelson of the *Star*.

BARON BILL

WHEN the Nonpartisan reform wrecked the Pendergast machine in 1940, few of the earnest workers in the cause paused to note that it had taken a half-century of vast agitation to bring about this event, and none thought to pay tribute to the man chiefly responsible for it. The movement that unhorsed Big Tom actually got under way a short time after William Rockhill Nelson arrived in Kansas City and it was operating vigorously in 1894, in the same election that eliminated the Combine and marked the emergence of Jim Pendergast and Joe Shannon as bosses of a new order. In that campaign the candidate representing the Nelson-supported Nonpartisan ticket finished third. Colonel Nelson was not in the least dismayed by the defeat of his independent champion. Instead he was moved to issue an optimistic prophecy. Vindication of the non-

partisan idea "does not depend on the result of one canvass," he declared
in his newspaper. "It will succeed in the end because it is right and because it is an odious reflection upon the honesty and intelligence of the
people to assume that they will long continue to favor a system which
eliminates the business idea from municipal government."

The Nelson doctrine that "municipal government is purely a business
affair" was such a hateful expression of the commercial spirit to both
Alderman Pendergast and Shannon that they eventually banded together
to oppose the spread of this philosophy. Their evangelism for pure Democratic partisanship (first) and the two-party system (second) was earnest
and colorful and it is easy to believe that the independent-but-not-neutral
heresy could not have prevailed or even survived in Kansas City if anybody but Bill Nelson had espoused it.

Various experts have tried to estimate the size of the disturbance created by the political crusader and builder from Indiana who founded the
Star. One historian determined that there were two factors accounting
for the phenomenal development of Kansas City—the great bend of the
Missouri at Kawsmouth and Nelson.

Julian Street interviewed Nelson for a national magazine and left with
the impression that he had been in the presence of a volcano. "He is even
shaped like one," Street wrote. The editor tapered upward from a vast
waist to a snow-capped peak and when he opened his mouth a Vesuvian
rumbling came forth. William Allen White, handing down a final opinion in an article for *Collier's* wrote: "Mr. Nelson literally gave color to
the life and thought and aspirations of ten millions of people living between the Missouri River and the Rio Grande."

Nelson's associates and admirers called him Colonel. "Not that he was
ever a colonel of anything," explained White, who worked for Nelson
before he moved to Kansas to make the *Emporia Gazette* famous. "He
was just coloniferous." The Colonel's enemies called him Baron Bill and
the Baron of Brush Creek, titles suggested by his bearing and his real
estate holdings which were on a baronial scale. The accolade of nobility
was intended as a term of derision but didn't have that effect, for everyone thought of Nelson as the Baron even when they called him Colonel.

Nelson was a Hoosier with a good middle-class background based on
several generations of property owning. There was a family legend of

aristocratic English connections and Baron Bill liked to think that Lord
Nelson, the hero of Trafalgar, was one of his ancestors. He occasionally
spoke of "Uncle Horatio" in a joking manner, but no one took the allu-
sion too lightly for the sea lord who made a monkey out of Napoleon
would obviously have been proud to acknowledge kinship with the
booster who put Kawsmouth on the map.

He was thirty-nine years old when he came to Kansas City and already
had managed one successful career as a businessman, amassing a sizable
fortune as a real estate operator, bridge builder and contractor. A large
part of that first pile was lost in a disastrous cotton plantation venture in
the South. Nelson entered the newspaper field as an owner of the Fort
Wayne, Indiana, *Sentinel* a year before he saw his big chance in Kansas
City. He and his partner, Samuel E. Morss, sold out their Fort Wayne
holdings and put their capital in a new Kansas City paper, the *Evening
Star,* which started its long run under Nelson, September 18, 1880, with
a brashness that amused the established newspaper proprietors.

There were two morning and two other evening papers in the Kansas
City field at the time but an evening paper was still a novelty in 1880 and
Nelson's *Evening Star* was greeted with some derision by the morning
newspapermen, who dubbed it the Twilight Twinkler. Eugene Field,
poet, columnist and antic spirit, then working as editor of the morning
Times, suggested the nickname with this verse:

> Twinkle, twinkle, little *Star,*
> Bright and gossipy you are;
> We can daily hear you speak
> For a paltry dime a week.

The *Evening Star* was well on its way to domination of the whole field
before the opposition realized that a new era had dawned. The *Star*
absorbed the *Times* in 1901.

Nelson quickly bought up his partner's interest in order to have a completely free hand. He could never bear the thought of the *Star* having any
other voice than his own.

"The *Star,*" he said repeatedly and firmly, "is the Daily W. R. Nelson."

Readers of the *Star* had the impression that Nelson was speaking to
them personally each afternoon, and twice a day after he added the *Times*

as the morning issue of the *Star*. They could hear the great voice booming and feel the power of his personality even though they never saw him. Few saw him, in fact, after he was well established. He avoided luncheons, clubs and political meetings, partly because he was somewhat self-conscious in the public gaze, but mostly for the reason that he liked to sit in the *Star* office and let people come to him. Although he didn't do any of the writing, Nelson's stamp was on every line in his paper. He outlined what he wanted the *Star* to say, and because he spoke clearly and colorfully, many of his own words got into the copy. He imposed anonymity on all other members of the staff so that nothing might interfere with the communication between the people and the Daily Nelson.

Foundation of the Colonel's success was the cut-rate principle. He offered the *Star* for two cents an issue against the standard price of a nickel a copy. He had to import a large supply of pennies to make change for the customers, and Nelson's kegs filled with shining coppers appeared, to accustom this free-spending community to the idea that the penny was useful for other purposes than buying licorice sticks. Nelson built up volume at two cents a day and a dime a week for regular subscribers. He edited his paper according to the formula that the public didn't want glaring headlines, half-tones, comics and sports news but was hungry for lots of particulars about their neighbors' business. He devised a conservative format, which he considered artistic and which outsiders generally describe as odd or quaint. In this dress the *Star* furnished all the details, from murders, triangles and business operations to the activities of dogs and bluebirds and the antics of babies, presenting these happenings along with tasty literary and educational items clipped from books and magazines.

Mr. Nelson had arrived in Kansas City prepared for a strenuous fight with the politicians and he had picked a place where he could get a maximum amount of action for his money. His quarrel with the party regulars had roots that extended to New York and the early battles against Tammany Hall. The Baron was himself a Democrat but not one of the Jackson County variety. His hero was not Andy Jackson of Tennessee but Sam Tilden of Gramercy Park, New York, nemesis of the Tweed Ring and the Canal Ring. Nelson served as Tilden's campaign manager in Indiana when the New Yorker ran for President in

1876. Tilden won in the actual balloting but was counted out by one electoral vote when Congress was called on to settle a dispute over the returns from four states. Nelson renounced affiliation with the Democratic Party in 1880, the year he started his paper in Kansas City. There is a legend that his bolt was induced by pique over the failure of the Democrats to offer Tilden a second nomination, but the practical consideration was that the independent line gave him a free hand in the task of subduing the bosses of both parties to the Nelson will.

The Tilden influence was important, however, in Nelson's development as a reformer. He found that most of the evils of corrupt politics encountered by Tilden in New York were duplicated in Missouri. The parallel was so exact, in fact, that he used Tilden's biography,* giving his account of his battles with the Tweed Ring and the Canal Ring, as a *Star* campaign textbook in one of Missouri's greatest political battles. That was the campaign of 1904 which brought the Folk reform, and was toward the end of Nelson's career; but long before that, the publisher had discovered that the machine operation was highly developed in this Middle Western region. It included some rackets not adequately described in Tilden's reports, and Publisher Nelson had to devise methods of his own to oppose the Little Louisiana Lottery, the policy gambling gyp, the traction monopoly, the gas gouge, the loan shark steal, the legal fee grab, the bunco game routine, the paving graft and other profitable promotions of a fast-growing community which had an untrammeled sense of freedom.

The politicians immediately discovered that the Baron had the disposition and capacity for the rough-and-tumble style favored by the Kawsmouth partisans. Since the antagonists were about equally matched, these struggles were both long and fierce. A classic example is the battle with the traction interests, which raged through the thirty-five years of Nelson's career in Kansas City. Nelson led off by putting down the Corrigan mule car line monopoly when it attempted to block franchises for the new cable lines and at the same time extend its own exclusive concession. The *Star* routed the mule car reactionaries by promoting a "hanging party" for the aldermen controlled by the Corrigan interests. Fastening the label

---

* *The Life of Samuel J. Tilden*, by John Bigelow, 2 vols., 1895.

of the Shameless Eight on the men who took Corrigan's orders, the paper took the lead in organizing a committee of safety headed by the town's leading citizen, Colonel Kersey Coates, and the vigilante spirit ran high. A mass meeting of citizens "with ropes" was called for the night when the Council was expected to act on the franchise matter and the Shameless Eight lost their nerve. Corrigan's mules lost out and Kansas City got cable cars to speed the wheels of progress, but the cable line interests formed a monopoly and the battle was shortly resumed.

The *Star* used fighting words with such abandon that its editor incurred a definite personal risk. His critics found that he was fearless and well protected. One of the notable exhibitions in this field was given when Joseph J. Davenport, who served a term as mayor in 1889 and tried unsuccessfully to make a comeback in 1892, called at the *Star* office to settle issues with the Baron in the manly way. Editor Nelson was at his desk in his private office on the second floor when Mr. Davenport hove into sight, dark and menacing. Nelson moved with an agility surprising in one of his bulk but, in his haste to square off or get out of range, he got his feet tangled in his chair and was helpless for one awful moment.

Whether the Colonel was actually struck or not remains a question to this day, for there are two versions on that point of the encounter. There is, however, general agreement on what followed. Four men, stout and true, arrived in time to form an adequate reception committee for Mr. Davenport. They included T. W. Johnston, managing editor, Ralph Stout, city editor, William Allen White, reporter and editorial writer, and a telegrapher named Phillips. Between them they ousted the former mayor, or rather they threw him to the landing halfway down the stairs to the first floor. When the ex-official landed he looked up and saw Ralph Stout in a throwing posture, holding a cuspidor and Mr. Davenport is supposed to have cried out:

"Drop that cuspidor, Ralph Stout! Put that spittoon down!"

It was also reported that Mr. Davenport had a pistol and made a gesture of using it but the testimony on that point is not conclusive. One veteran of the *Star,* Charles I. Blood, who joined the staff in 1887, became the paper's best-known city editor and still is in harness, doubts that Davenport tried any gunplay. If he had, says Charlie Blood, he would have been potted by Bill Campbell, stockyards reporter, who was stationed at the top of the stairs in an alcove, drawing a bead with a long-barrelled pearl-handled six-shooter.

"The *Star* never loses," Colonel Nelson informed his staff. That remark had a humorous sound, as it was·usually uttered just after the paper had taken a drubbing at the polls.

Defeat never discouraged the Baron, but it did put him in a rage and filled him with a deep suspicion that he had been cheated at the polls. This made him a remarkably efficient watchdog of the voting places and produced a series of election scandals that early accustomed Kansas Citians to the idea that their political organizations were extraordinarily corrupt. The *Star*'s extremely lurid and elaborate accounts of election thievery and thuggery served the double purpose of intimidating the politicians and discrediting them, building up a reservoir of public wrath which the newspaper exploded at the proper time. Nelson showed the effectiveness of this kind of crusading in memorable fashion in the county campaigns of '92 and '94, when he warred to wrest control of the prosecutor's office from the Combine, which was much too tolerant of gambling and vice conditions to suit the *Star* editor. The newspaper lost the first round but made a tremendous scandal over the conduct of the election, in which Scar-Faced Charley Johnson, the celebrated bunco artist, and his troupe of traveling crooks appear to have taken a conspicuous part. This agitation contributed to the defeat of the Democrats two years later and prepared the ground for a violent public outburst, which occurred when the newspaper trumpeted disclosures of a crude conspiracy to steal the offices of county prosecutor and marshal for the Democrats. Forgeries were committed in the official returns after the unofficial count had shown a clear victory for the Republicans. With Nelson's paper furnishing the thunder and lightning, a committee of safety was organized, mass meetings were held, lynch talk was encouraged and a large prosecution fund raised. A grand jury returned twenty-one indictments for election frauds, twelve politicians fled town and one committed suicide. The Jackson County men played Courthouse politics for keeps.

Baron Bill's battle with the party organizers and demagogues entered a curious phase with his greatest single civic undertaking, which was the building of Kansas City's beautiful parks and extensive boulevards. With the politicians playing a dual role, offering both resistance and assistance to the construction, this program eventually produced 4,025 acres of parks and 119 miles of boulevards in a continuous system. All of it has grown upon the foundations that Nelson and his generation built, and a large part of it was created or projected during his lifetime. In fact, the town had no park property whatever and no boulevards when he arrived on the scene. Citizens were still falling from the mountains and burying themselves in the mud and Mr. Nelson immediately saw that Herculean measures would be required to get the town over the hill and out of the mire. The superhuman spirit for grading, widening and paving was what Bill Nelson had.

"Great as was the greatest of the Caesars, greatest was he as a road builder," said a Nelson editorial. "Civilization treads established thoroughfares. Literature must have circulation or be impotent. Art cannot ennoble or uplift or delight the multitude it cannot reach." The *Star* was civilization, literature and art, and, by God, Mr. Nelson meant to have a large circulation. The Caesar of modern transportation in the Middle West served notice on the taxpayers of what was coming, in an early issue of his paper. "The pinching economy, the picayunish policy, the miserable parsimony, which characterize our city government must be abandoned," he proclaimed. "Kansas City needs good streets, good sidewalks, good sewers, decent public buildings, better street lights, more fire protection, a more efficient police and many other things."

The town got more streets, sidewalks, sewers and other things but it seldom had peace again. Builder Nelson fortunately found a company of tireless park, paving and sewer men ready and anxious to work with him. He discovered an architectural genius when he invited a young engineer and architect by the name of George E. Kessler (later architect of the St. Louis World's Fair) to submit a plan for the improvement of West Bluff. Kessler discarded all conventional ideas of landscaping as inadequate for this project, producing a plan that adapted parks and boulevards to the Kansas City terrain rather than attempting to make nature conform to man's ideas of order and prettiness.

The park-and-boulevard vision moved August R. Meyer, a mine and smelter owner, to devote his life to the Nelson cause. He proved to be a great evangelist and was surrounded by a band of vigorous disciples recruited from various businesses and professions that naturally take a special interest in building contracts. Pure altruism and private interest were combined in a very effective way in this cause, as was illustrated in the case of Nelson himself. The newspaperman engaged in extensive real estate operations at the same time that he used his *Star* to inspire civic improvements. The dramatic size of his ambition was shown when he took twenty acres south of the city to build a massive stone house, called Oak Hall, on a wooded hill above Brush Creek, in a region that was supposed to have no future except for pig farming. No one but Baron Bill expected that the Kansas City enterprise would ever reach that far south. He hurried the movement his way by laying out miles of streets, building miles of decorative stone walls and planting miles of elm trees at his own expense. These activities entailed large investments on which there was no prospect of early profit but Nelson did not expect or seek to make his fortune from real estate. His aim was to create the right setting for more happy *Star* subscribers and advertisers.

Nelson and his associates encountered terrific resistance from loafers and taxpayers who felt that the proper limits of progress had been reached, and the result was a civic disorder that extended over many years. Those of the people who didn't want new paving, sewers and parks were organized by Nelson into Hammer and Padlock clubs (a hammer for every improvement idea, a padlock on every money pocket). They were flailed, scourged and browbeaten by Nelson's reporters, cartoonists and editorial writers as croakers, knockers, mossbacks and men without any redeeming qualities. In the election campaigns and court battles over boulevards and parks, the *Star* gave an awesome exhibition of the spirit of progress and an impressive demonstration of the newspaper's force in urban society, but still this was not quite enough to accomplish the desired purpose.

During this period the party bosses had acquired considerable additional power and prestige, and the battles over civic improvements did much to enhance their importance, as the croakers and knockers turned to them to oppose Nelson's schemes. Fortunately for the parks and boulevards, some of the influential party professionals were boosters, too. Jim Pendergast was a notable public improvements man. More boulevards, parks and public buildings meant more jobs for his followers and the

Alderman was credited with being the author of that great slogan of all up-and-coming societies: "You can't saw wood with a hammer." Another was Mike Ross, ward boss and contractor, who set out many of the elm trees lining the streets. Still another was Hugh J. McGowan, a leading figure in the Combine and an agent for the Barber Asphalt Company whose asphalt was favored by the City Council.

The keystone of the park-and-boulevard system was established with the aid of political bosses who delivered the necessary votes for a price, providing a majority for the charter amendment which made the extensions possible. The story of that deal has been told in the *Star* itself in an article written by H. J. Haskell, the present editor, and published on the fiftieth anniversary of the newspaper. Editor Haskell related the incident as it was told by Mr. Nelson to his associates.

Hugh McGowan called on Nelson at the height of the campaign for the amendment.

"Colonel," he said, "you seem to feel strongly about this amendment."

"It's the biggest thing that has been before Kansas City in years," was the reply.

"Well, if you want it you can have it. But it will take a little money for the workers."

"Nelson became practical for the moment," the *Star* article explained. "The details were arranged and the votes were forthcoming."

This account was published fifteen years after the Colonel's death, and doubtless reminded some Democrats that Nelson should have been more grateful than he seemed to be to the organization boys for their historic service in the cause of Kansas City expansion. It was in that time that he began to preach with increasing vigor the gospel that the party men should be ditched for the nonpartisan system favored by Mr. Nelson.

Out of this agitation grew the wedding of the *Star* and the Republican Party, which eventually became such a solid union that the Democrats ruefully observed that there was no Republican Party in Kansas City, but only the Democratic and the *Star* parties. This fusion was not caused by the fact that the G.O.P. was any less devoted to special interests, bossism and spoils than the Democratic organization. It signified mostly that the Republican bosses had smaller powers of resistance than the Democratic machine men.

Democrats probably will not concede that the *Star*'s interest in non-partisan city government had much to do with its growing favor toward the Republican Party. They like the simpler explanation that Nelson naturally became more Hamiltonian as his moneybags piled higher and he found the Nonpartisan scheme was useful in promoting the Republican cause. It is true, however, that his antipathy for spoils politics was genuine and that there was always a large measure of democratic liberalism mixed with his capitalistic philosophy. He demonstrated his independence on notable occasions in Missouri and Kansas campaigns and in the Bull Moose crusade with Teddy Roosevelt. If the Kansas City Republicans were ever actually less partisan in local affairs than the Democrats, it would seem that a large share of the credit should go to Nelson and the *Star*.

One factor in the development of the long contest between the *Star* and the Pendergast organization was the growth of the saloon power in politics. Jim Pendergast's own financial stake in the liquor business was of modest size but his political following was made up largely of men whose main economic interest was in beer and whisky or who regarded the saloon as an absolutely essential social institution. The brewery and saloon combine had grown into a very rich and powerful vested interest when William Rockhill Nelson decided to declare war on it in 1905.

The autocrat of the *Star* was not a prohibitionist by personal taste or temperament. He did not start out as an agitator for the suppression of the saloon, but turned that way when the liquor interests resisted reasonable restraints and at the same time obstructed other Nelson projects. This happened in 1905, when the Heim Brewery boys, the saloonkeepers and the Democratic boss factions lined up to defeat a new charter, containing provisions for better regulation of saloons along with measures for more businesslike administration in the City Hall, which the *Star* had vigorously championed. The editor read the election returns in one of his blacker moods. He called his business manager and ordered him to accept no more liquor or beer advertising in the *Star*. The business manager, who knew just how much the publisher admired the advertiser's dollar, entered an amazed protest but the painful order stood.

Agitation for the dry cause in Kansas City thereupon took a vigorous upward turn and grew steadily in the succeeding years. The propaganda against saloonkeepers became so derogatory that it alarmed and saddened Alderman Jim Pendergast.

"The saloon business is on the bum now," he commented in a newspaper interview in 1907. "I'm going to be a farmer."

He did try his hand at farming but at the same time he continued successfully to operate his saloon and his political machine. Brewers, distillers, boss men and Democrats flourished for many years thereafter despite the fact that they found it increasingly difficult to ignore the voice that loudly declared: "The *Star* never loses."

2 *Fifty-Fifty*

Stormy Petrel

PENDERGAST politics took on new color and significance in the period when James A. Reed roamed the platform as the Stormy Petrel of Missouri's Democracy, during which time he served successively as prosecuting attorney of Jackson County for one term, mayor of Kansas City for two terms and United States senator for eighteen years (1911-29). This was the period when great battles were fought over the issues of electoral, legislative and municipal reform, Prohibition and American isolation. Jim Reed was in the forefront of some of those struggles, appearing variously on the sides of reform and reaction but giving a consistently spectacular performance. No simple explanation or classification will do for Jim. The complicated character of the politician's role in American life and the intricacy of the political personality were demonstrated to a remarkable degree in his case.

The range of the man is suggested by the numerous cognomens he collected. He was, first and last, Fighting Jim, Missouri's Stormy Petrel. For a while he was known as Woody Dell Jim, a title conferred in recognition of his superlative efforts to capture the votes of poetic Missourians by declaiming on the pastoral beauties of the Show Me State in campaign time. Some of his admirers hailed him as the Greatest Roman of Them All, finding that the conventional Noblest Roman designation did not adequately convey the uniqueness of Jim Reed. The *Star* under Nelson called him the Yankee from Iowa, a label whose appropriateness became more apparent in later years when he publicly consorted with the Republican Old Guard on two notable occasions. His chief Missouri Republican critic, next to Nelson, dubbed him Bridlewise Jim of the Pendergast stable. The national leader of his party in the First World War, Woodrow Wilson, branded him a marplot. Probably fifty per cent of the Missouri Democrats looked upon him as a stranger in their midst in several campaigns. But the Pendergasts believed in him, surrounded him with hero worship, fought for him, boomed him for President and never publicly complained about his party irregularity even when he turned against the Pendergasts themselves in the last days of the machine.

In his old age, when he had mellowed a bit, Reed protested against his popular reputation as a fighter, saying that his fame as a prosecutor tended to obscure the constructive side of his career. His plaint was not considered seriously by the Missourians. They couldn't remember a time when Jim wasn't promoting a knockdown and dragout.

The story of Reed's rise to the United States senatorship was an essential part of the story of the Kansas City machine's genesis through a decade when corrupt city and state political organizations provoked a national revulsion, and figures like Teddy Roosevelt of New York, Tom Johnson of Cleveland, Golden Rule Jones of Toledo, La Follette of Wisconsin and Joseph W. Folk of Missouri arose to give vigorous leadership to the reform movement. Nelson of Kansas City was a large voice in that agitation, but the Kansas City battle did not command national attention because the Kansas City machine was having starter trouble. Its development had been retarded by Baron Bill and several other factors including, particularly, the peculiar factional division created by Joe Shannon and the Rabbits.

Up to this time, Pendergast and Shannon were still only two of several factional leaders in the Jackson County field, although they had been rising steadily in influence for years. Notice that they were advancing to a higher level, where their disputes for dominance overshadowed other party interests, was given in the series of factional battles that revolved around Candidate Reed.

The Pendergasts began to take the lead in the factional competition when they realized that in Reed they had discovered a winner who could confound all their foes. They started their forward march with him by successfully challenging Joe Shannon's power as the county boss. This contest was made in the campaign of 1898, when Reed ran for the office of county prosecutor. He won the nomination over Shannon's man, showed himself to be a good vote getter in the election, and established a record as a brilliant prosecutor. The Democratic factions met in another bitter test of strength in the city campaign of 1900 and Reed again carried the day for the Pendergast faction. After downing Shannon's candidate for mayor in the primary, he led the Democrats to a landslide that broke the Republican victory string in the city.

Political animosities in Kansas City had been greatly intensified by this time, a situation which many regarded as a tribute to Reed's flashing style of attack. The lash of his tongue when he was in the Senate left welts on the hides of Harding, Coolidge and Hoover, but those flailings were routine affairs compared with his vitriolic attacks on the *Star* and the Kansas City Republicans in the days when he was first winning public recognition. The force and effect of the early Reed oratory are illustrated by the case of Jimmie Jones, a Republican mayor for two terms, who retired from politics and left town to seek a living in more peaceful fields after the stormy city campaign of 1900.

In the previous city campaign, Reed and Jones had come to blows as a result of the former's disparaging remarks about the Republican mayor. Jones, who campaigned for re-election as "the best little mayor that Kansas City ever had," was handy with his fists. On one occasion he beat up a barker at Buffalo Bill's Wild West Show who happened to make a remark which Mr. Jones deemed insulting to his wife when the Mayor and his lady were entering the tent. He started looking for Jim Reed after the latter had given a hilarious burlesque of the best little mayor. The talented Democratic mimic concluded his droll performance before an appreciative crowd with the charge that while the Mayor was being eulogized as an exemplary character by a minister on the east side of the city, Jimmie Jones was downtown "dead drunk." Mr. Jones caught up with Mr. Reed in the neighborhood of the stockyards and, according to the *Star*'s gleeful report of the meeting, Jones set upon his adversary and "Reed fell like a log and lay in the gutter unconscious." When he awoke, he was credited with uttering that famous line: "What hit me?"

The bump on the head which Reed suffered at the hands of Mayor Jones served merely to heighten his zeal as a crusader against Republican oppression and *Star* dictation, which he brought to an end two years later. He was, of course, a reformer at this time and there was little in the picture to suggest that he would someday be a figure in one of the country's most notorious boss organizations.

In 1900 the Goats and Rabbits were all filled with cleanup sentiment as a result of six long years of Republican rule in the City Hall, and none had greater passion for a change than Jim Reed. And it did seem that a change was overdue. Perhaps the situation in the City Hall was not so bad as Candidate Reed pictured it, but there was some reason for believing that the Kansas City machine was going to be a Republican rather than a Democratic outfit before the Stormy Petrel came along with his reform. This development of the spoils system in the G.O.P. had escaped the notice of the *Star,* which was preoccupied with its work of calling attention to the growing boss tendency in the Democratic Party. Reed denounced the *Star* as chief among the special interests favored by the Jimmie Jones administration, or rather as the power behind the Jones regime. It was one of his more vigorous prosecutions. Whatever he lacked in evidence was more than offset by the passion and sweep of his indictment, and the Democrats roared in the happy knowledge that at last they had a special pleader who was a match for Baron Bill.

Reed's duel with Nelson's paper was a protracted affair which demonstrated the durability of the Stormy Petrel more than any other single thing. Fighting Jim eventually emerged from the conflict holding a top position on the *Star*'s honor roll. That reversal occurred some time after Nelson died and was a development that is popularly supposed to have spoiled the Colonel's peace in heaven. Such an outcome seemed far outside the realm of remote possibility in the exciting years when Nelson was directing the attack and Reed was pronouncing the Kansas City *Sta-ahr* in insulting accents that left no room for forgiveness. Nelson's editors devoted their best efforts to the task of punishing and suppressing him. They tried to ignore him, giving him a long treatment of the *Star*'s "thunderous silence," but Reed continued to gain. They gave him a fierce lambasting and lampooning and still he showed no signs of suffering great pain. Is it any wonder that the editors were glad to make peace with this rugged individual after Nelson departed?

It became increasingly difficult to ignore Reed after he was elected mayor as he showed himself to be an efficient and forceful executive. His administration listed numerous achievements in the public regulation of utility corporations. Reed prevailed on the streetcar company to relinquish a 25-year franchise that had been rushed through the City Council in the last days of the outgoing Republican regime. He got the company to grant universal transfers, increased its valuation, induced it to rebuild its system and pay the public eight per cent of its gross revenues. He reduced the city lighting bill, introduced a competitive telephone system that improved service and lowered rates, fought the paving monopoly and cut taxes. Still the *Star* was not satisfied with Reed as a champion against the interests and an opponent of the spoils system. It found numerous causes for agitation, including a matter which it called the Gamewell Gouge, involving a contract for a new fire alarm system. It raised a cry over the rise of political influence in the Police Department and the spread of the state machine's power to Kansas City through Democratic channels. Its greatest fire was centered on Reed in the fight over the Metropolitan Street Car Company, the *Star* contending that the corporation had received too generous treatment in the "gentleman's agreement" that was negotiated in the Reed administration. This difference continued for years, extending into the streetcar franchise and fare battles and the fight for a public utility commission in which the *Star* was arrayed against powerful elements in both party organizations.

The attempt to stop Reed in this period was encouraged by certain Democrats, notably members of the faction headed by Joe Shannon, whose interest in reform politics grew steadily while the Goats were growing in power with Reed. Shannon's Rabbits had a vigorous reformer in the person of Frank P. Walsh, an idealistic and optimistic Irishman, who combined radical agitation and practical politics in a most uncommon fashion. His interesting crusade developed to the accompaniment of his conflicts with Mr. Reed, a dispute that enlivened Democratic affairs in Jackson County for many years before they both moved to Washington to follow their divergent lines in the party of Jefferson and Jackson. Reed later held the national stage in his battles with Woodrow Wilson and Franklin D. Roosevelt over the League of Nations and the New Deal. Walsh left Kansas City for Washington to serve as chairman of

Wilson's industrial relations commission and he later was co-chairman of the first War Labor Board. He closed his career as a Roosevelt appointee in the chairmanship of the State Power Authority of New York.

Reed and Walsh had started up the political ladder together as friends and fellow reformers, but parted early in the factional and philosophical debates that disturbed the party. They clashed on the platform, in conventions, in the public prints and in courtrooms, the conflict reaching its dramatic climax in a famous murder trial in 1910. The feud was still going in the twilight of their lives. In the late 1930's, Walsh returned to Kansas City, after a long absence, to represent the International Ladies' Garment Workers Union in court against the Donnelly Garment Company, owned by Reed's wife, and Reed defended the company in its effort to prevent unionization of his wife's employees under the Wagner Act. Kansas Citians were then reminded that there had been no improvement in the feeling between the two old antagonists, who hadn't spoken to each other for years. At one hearing in the case, Reed turned angrily on Walsh when he interrupted a witness and Walsh retorted drily: "Thank you for speaking to me." Reed glowered and explained that the exchange was purely involuntary on his part.

In Jackson County, Walsh is remembered for the long list of progressive causes that he espoused there, a program reflecting the wide unrest and demand for change that had been provoked by the business and political manipulations of the age of Frenzied Finance, the packing trusts, the Standard Oil monopoly, the insurance swindles and the Wall Street rigging. Walsh's interest in reform had its roots in a fierce hatred of poverty and social inequality which he formed when he was a boy in St. Louis. Of thirty boys he remembered in his neighborhood, he later recalled that only three survived to a useful and normal manhood. He early determined that the main issue of the day was "the material one, the economic one." "The rights of man of this time," he declared, "are the right to eat, the right to live decently, the right to work, the right to a comfortable home, the right to have children without wondering whether his children hadn't better die than grow up." It didn't take him long to discover that the chief barrier to the exercise of those rights was maintained by organized wealth's domination of the parties which controlled the machinery of government. In 1900 he severed all his connections as a lawyer with corporation clients and enlarged his field of operations as an agitator against the economic powers.

In the years that followed, Walsh raised the boss issue in his own party on numerous occasions and found himself in the midst of a growing Democratic tempest. He pressed this fight in city, county and state campaigns and his allies were numerous and strong enough to make the antimachine movement a major action. This storm in the party had been developing over a long period during which the Democrats enjoyed too much success. The boss system entrenched itself in whichever party was dominant, and the Democrats had been running things in Missouri for thirty years. Seat of the organization was the State Capitol in Jefferson City, and the boss group was known as the state machine, maintaining its hold through the party committee, the convention system, the legislative power, the lobbies and other devices that had been created to concentrate authority, patronage and other means of control in a few hands. The effort to break up this monopoly, and to arrest extension of the boss system in the city, reached its peak in the first four years of the twentieth century and had an important bearing on the factional conflict that swirled around Jim Reed.

One of the important antimachine endeavors was the Home Rule cause, a point of protracted disagreement between the Kansas City factions. The Home Rule agitators wanted to end state control of the police, which had been established by the Democratic Legislature, placing the appointive power over the police board in the hands of the governor. Since the state administrations were Democratic, and had been regularly for three decades, this system gave the Democrats control of a major function of the city government regardless of changes in local administration. Naturally, the Home Rule reform was popular with Republicans, and very unpopular with many Democrats. However, it was espoused by Frank Walsh, Joe Shannon and other figures in the Rabbit faction with growing fervor as it became increasingly clear that the Pendergast faction was making gains with the state powers. Although it was evident that both sides in this dispute were affected by selfish partisan or factional interests, the main fact was that the state control arrangement was an antidemocratic system which created a strong tie between local and state boss elements. State control of the police, excise and election machinery was one of the principal means by which the machine seized complete control of St. Louis. Kansas City had numerous illustrations of the defects of this system but nothing to compare with the St. Louis scandal, thanks in part to the nearly equal division of the Kansas City parties and to the conflict of the Democratic factions over the Home Rule issue.

It was the Rabbits' crusade for Home Rule that had produced the party split in the county campaign of 1900, when Pendergast's followers voted Republican in order to cut down the antipolice ticket which the Jackson County Democrats had nominated. "This defeat will tend to purge the Democratic Party," was Alderman Jim's happy comment. Joe Shannon, the county chairman, retaliated by publicly branding Jim Reed as a leader in the revolt, returning to him a fifty dollar contribution to campaign funds with "the recommendation that the Mayor at once institute a careful investigation among his appointees and subordinates in the City Hall, and in case one can be found who voted the Democratic ticket at said election, that he present the fifty dollars as a reward for his fidelity to the party which Mayor Reed publicly pretended to favor in the campaign just closed."

Another minor Walsh project in the anti-boss cause was an episode that was known as the Celebrated Cardwell Case, or the Mysterious Mr. Brown, a political comedy that occupied the attention of the voters in 1901-02. One pamphleteer who compiled a history of this remarkable affair declared that the question: Who is Mr. Brown? belonged in the same category with the three classic conundrums of the ages: Who was the Man in the Iron Mask?, Who wrote the Letters of Junius? and Who struck Billy Patterson? It appears that the Missourians in the good old days derived much pleasure from the Who-is-Mr.-Brown mystery and at the same time acquired an advanced lesson in machine politics.

Frank Walsh gave a serious purpose to this farce by directing the investigation for the Honorable W. O. Cardwell, a Kansas City member of the state Legislature, who blew the lid off the party scandal by charging in a speech that the Democratic State Committee solicited and received contributions from corporations. Agitation along this line continued until the Secretary of the State, who was involved in the charges, lost his temper and called the Honorable Mr. Cardwell a liar in a letter published in the *St. Louis Republic*. Cardwell sued the paper for fifty-thousand-dollar libel and Walsh, as attorney for the aggrieved politician, took over the questioning of important party figures.

Depositions collected by Walsh quickly established that the State Committee had sought and accepted large gifts of money from railroad, traction, brewery, race-track and Kansas City stockyard interests. Further startling disclosures were about to be made when the Mysterious Mr. Brown appeared on the scene. He did his work for the party shortly after Colonel James Monroe Seibert, chairman of the committee, had been served a writ of attachment in St. Louis for defying a summons to give a deposition in the case.

Mr. Brown called on Plaintiff Cardwell in Kansas City, paid him seventy-five hundred dollars in settlement of the libel suit while Colonel Seibert was waiting in St. Louis to be rescued, and then disappeared. Mr. Cardwell announced that he had been paid a "dignified sum" that satisfied his honor, and instructed Attorney Walsh to drop the case. All that he could tell about the Mysterious Mr. Brown was that he was "tall, thin and cadaverous." Various experts in the field of deduction figured that Mr. Brown was the law partner of Colonel William H. Phelps, chief of the Missouri Pacific lobby at Jefferson City, but the pundits did not let the matter drop with that simple solution.

The agitation had angry repercussions when Walsh led a fight to break the corporations' control of his party two years before Joseph W. Folk brought a showdown on the issue in his race for governor. The Kansas City disturber, armed with the Cardwell case disclosures, created a storm in the Democratic state convention when he presented a platform resolution denouncing corporation contributions to campaign funds. Party leaders tried to get him to pocket his resolution and let him understand he could have the honor of being the convention chairman if he would be reasonable. They next offered to support his resolution if he would direct it at the Republicans. When he persisted in his course, they told him they would flatten him under the party steamroller. Walsh rented a hall and delivered an inflammatory attack on the bosses and their moneyed friends. They kept their promise to run over him and his following in the convention but then lost their nerve and put his resolution in the platform.

Walsh's stand against the state machine and the corporations brought no immediate change in the organization command, but the Democratic difference over this issue was fought out two years later, in 1904, in a campaign that shattered party lines and produced a reform that had lasting effects. Kansas City staged one of the interesting preliminaries in that Missouri battle when Reed entered the race for governor. The Shannon Democrats, Walsh and other Home Rule advocates lined up solidly against him, raising the antimachine banner and striking their first blow in the 1904 city campaign after Mayor Reed attempted to pick his successor in the City Hall.

For this fracas, Mayor Reed ushered onto the stage, with Pendergast assistance, the Honorable William T. Kemper, who was later to make history as the Uncle Bill of Kansas City finance. Kemper served as police commissioner in the Reed administration and cooked up a fifty-fifty proposition with the Mayor: Reed agreed to help Kemper in his ambition to be mayor in return for support for the Reed gubernatorial aspirations. While negotiations with Alderman Jim Pendergast were still being worked out, Kemper resigned his police commissionership and announced his candidacy for mayor. Such amateurishness appalled the North Side leader and he remarked: "They have buncoed him. They've made him give up his gun, disarmed him out on the prairie." Alderman Jim threatened for a time to throw his support to Kemper's rival, George M. Shelley, a former mayor who was trying to make a comeback with the Rabbit leader, but this was simply a Pendergast deceptive play, and eventually he backed the Reed choice.

In the fight that followed, Joe Shannon had the large assistance of Editor Nelson, who was interested in the Democratic factional dispute not only because it improved Republican chances but because it gave the *Star* an opportunity to arouse public sentiment against the abuse of the police power in politics. That power was used forcefully and effectively for Kemper in the primary election of delegations to the Democratic city convention which eliminated Shannon's candidate George M. Shelley.

The *Star*'s report on the election was filled with charges that police control of the polls and intimidation of voters had produced a fraudulent victory for Pendergast's candidate, and the agitation continued until Shannon and his allies decided to hold a rump convention. They nominated Shelley as the mayoralty candidate of the "antipolice ticket," spreading consternation among the Goats and creating a sensation for the whole town.

This last reaction was provoked by an incident in the noon-hour interval when the rival conventions recessed for lunch. It started when Martin Crowe, sergeant-at-arms of the Kemper convention, took a stroll past the hall at Twelfth and Walnut streets where the Shelley convention was being held. Up to this moment there had been a universal feeling that no harm would ever come to Martin Crowe. He was the champion hammer thrower of Kansas City, a title he won regularly at Irish picnics. Not long before this, he had beaten up several railroaders in Cronin's saloon. At a dance in Casino Hall he had knocked out a half-dozen men. The only individual with enough foolhardiness to tackle Martin alone was a mountainous Swede teamster, who had been thrashed and then picked up bodily and tossed into his wagon. So Mr. Crowe expected no interference when he took his walk past the assembled Rabbits. He was, however, accosted by one Cas Welch, a sturdy Shannon lieutenant with a deputy marshal's badge. Deputy Welch reproached Sergeant Crowe over his conduct in the recent primary, and his protest was heartfelt because Martin was an old friend and until a year or so earlier had been a fellow member of the Rabbit faction. He deserted to the Goat side after Tom Pendergast became county marshal and gave him the contract for supplying bread to prisoners in the county jail. Cas's sorrow over the corruption of his former friend caused him to make his remonstrance more spirited than was healthful and he was immediately knocked down. Welch drew a pistol and fired three times, striking Crowe twice, once in the rump and once in the heel, for the great Martin had turned to run.

"It was just a friendly argument," Cas Welch told the police when they arrived. "I felt friendly again the minute I fired that third shot."

The combined effect of Cas Welch, Shannon, Shelley, Walsh and the *Star* was too much for Kemper, Pendergast and Reed, and the final decision went to the Republicans. It left the Democrats still quarreling, and nursing wounds that were long in healing. The same forces that figured in the Kansas City factional storm entered into the larger Missouri struggle that reached its conclusion in the summer and fall of 1904. In the primary race for governor, Reed encountered some of his stiffest resistance in his own bailiwick and his defeat was conceded long before the last round. Joe Shannon's uprising was not, however, the main factor in sidetracking Candidate Reed. Kansas City's recently retired mayor simply had picked a poor time to run for governor on his reform record.

The spirit of reform was in the air but the spotlight was held by Joseph Wingate Folk of St. Louis as a result of his work in breaking up the St. Louis aldermanic combine and conducting prosecutions against important individuals in the business and political life of Missouri's largest city. Operations of the gang, which Folk uncovered in 1901-02 when he was serving as circuit attorney, made "boodling" the great term of the day. The Disgrace of St. Louis startled even the muckrackers of the period. (See Lincoln Steffens' *Autobiography* and *The Shame of the Cities*.) As the St. Louis grand jury pointed out in its final report, "although there may have been corruption in other cities as great as we have had here, yet in no place in the world and in no time known to history has so much official corruption been uncovered and the evidence shown so that all could see and understand."

Among the interesting exhibits uncovered was a fantastic oath for aldermen in the secret combine serving the transportation, utilities and garbage disposal monopolies. It read:

I do solemnly agree that in case I should reveal the fact that any person in this combine has received money for illegal purposes, I hereby permit and authorize other members of this combine to take the forfeit of my life in such manner as they may deem proper, and that my throat may be cut, my tongue torn out and my body cast in the Missouri River.

The investigation reached high up, trapping several millionaire businessmen-politicians, including one who fled to France, another who fled to Mexico and two who were saved from prison when the Missouri Supreme Court reversed their sentences. Seven boodlers were sent to prison and the St. Louis scandal was combined with an exposure of legislative bribers at the state capital; the attorney general and a grand jury at Jefferson City working with Folk and the St. Louis probers.

Folk was the man of the hour and he signified that he was willing to accept the governor's office to continue his cleanup. His challenge met considerable opposition from party regulars and conservatives, particularly in the cities. Outstate Missouri rallied heavily to Folk's side. His two opponents were overwhelmed in the pre-convention primary and he was nominated on the first ballot at a convention which wrote many of his progressive ideas into the party platform. Reed had withdrawn from the race two months before the convention and his defeat was underscored by the loss of his home county. Shannon and Walsh had climbed on the Folk bandwagon early and were large factors in the Jackson County movement for the St. Louis prosecutor. One of the principal journalistic voices in the Folk revolt was Colonel Nelson's. His *Star* carried on a vigorous fight for the Democratic Scourge of the Rascals in the nominating campaign and supported him against the Republican candidate for governor in the final election, at the same time plugging for the national Republican ticket headed by Teddy Roosevelt, the Trust Buster.

Missouri elected Folk and returned a Democratic majority to the upper house of the Legislature, but otherwise moved into the Republican column, giving its electoral votes to the G.O.P. presidential candidate for the first time since Reconstruction. The Mysterious Stranger, as Missouri was labeled in a famous post-election cartoon by McCutcheon, was starting on a long rampage in politics.

Hope that the progressive movement would prevail over the old corrupt system soared high in the Folk administration. It was in this period that Missouri adopted the direct primary law and the initiative and referendum. A rigid antilobby law, a child labor law, provision for the removal of derelict public officials, a compulsory education law, an eight-hour law for some industries, pure food regulations and a public utility commission for cities were some of the other important reforms introduced under Folk. The Democratic governor was not the only conspicuous figure in the high tide of progressivism in Missouri. Kansas City produced one of the main actors, Herbert S. Hadley, later governor of the state, who was elected attorney general on the Republican ticket in the Mysterious Stranger year of 1904.

Hadley, a Kansan, a Jayhawker by birth and education, started his political rise as an assistant city counselor of Kansas City and prosecutor of Jackson County, exhibiting uncommon zeal in the fight on lawbreakers and political tricksters. As attorney general of Missouri he drew the national spotlight with the antitrust proceedings he instituted against the Standard Oil Company and was credited with paving the way for the

Federal action which broke up the greatest monopoly then existing in America. The oil interests were fined and ousted from the state by the Supreme Court, being permitted to return later, on payment of fines and with pledges to discontinue their illegal business methods. The Attorney General also warred against the harvester trust, the insurance and lumber trusts and the railroads, but these actions were still uncompleted when he ended his term in office.

Elaborate efforts to improve the morals and the social habits of the people in the cities were combined with the action to restrain predatory business interests. Race tracks were closed down under a new law enacted in the Folk administration. Dramshop laws were so rigidly enforced in St. Louis, Kansas City and St. Joseph that many saloons shut their doors permanently and dry Sundays came to the parched city dwellers. This kind of crusading earned Folk the nickname of Holy Joe and eventually created an unfortunate complication in the Missouri reform, with the old quarrel over boozing and gaming overshadowing more important aspects of the uplift. Folk protested that he was not a dry fanatic, and his efforts to restrain the liquor interests could have been defended on practical political grounds, as well as on loftier premises, for the boss organization against which he was contending was entrenched in the saloons. However, the sportive citizens were not yet prepared to sacrifice their loose social customs in order to get rid of corrupt politicians, and Holy Joe found himself identified with repression rather than progress by a large segment of the public in the urban centers.

It appears that Folk may have contributed further to the shortening of his political life by his determined effort to take the police out of politics and reduce election frauds. Police and election commissioners appointed by him were credited with effecting some improvement, but this was not alone enough to change the results in many of the old boss-controlled wards of the city. At the same time, it brought on Folk the enmity of powerful individuals and groups in his own party.

The boss system weathered the storm, and the return to power of the old order was forecast even before the Folk administration ended. While the business interests attacked the new reform laws in the courts, and succeeded in killing some of the measures regulating business, the regulars staged a comeback in the party organization and at the polls.

In 1908, Missouri used for the first time the direct primary law that had been enacted in the Folk administration and was regarded by the insurgents as one of their chief weapons against the bosses, who had so long held power through the convention system. Ironically, the principal architect of this reform was himself eliminated in the 1908 primary by Senator William Joel Stone, who had the backing of the Kansas City and St. Louis organizations. Folk ran for the senatorial nomination that year because Missouri governors constitutionally are prohibited from directly succeeding themselves. While he was going down to defeat, he saw the party regulars score another important triumph in the governorship race with the nomination of a veteran organization man from Kansas City, William S. Cowherd, former mayor and a member of the national House of Representatives who had been unseated in the 1904 upheaval. His Republican opponent in the November election was Kansas City's Herbert S. Hadley, who ran on the Folk-Hadley reform record, was elected and kept the progressive movement alive a little longer.

The organization showed that it had completely recovered two years later when Jim Reed made his successful campaign for a seat in the United States Senate. Reed was favored that year by both fate and the political trend. He got the jump on rivals for the senatorial nomination by stealing the limelight in a murder trial that held national attention for six weeks just before the campaign opened. The rivalry of Reed and Frank Walsh reached a melodramatic high point in this case, which had its origin in Independence, Harry Truman's home town. The trial, which was held in Kansas City, has found a place among the classic American murder cases.

As a trial lawyer, Walsh was destined to win national fame and among his notable later victories was his successful fight to win a pardon for Tom Mooney, the labor agitator who was condemned in the San Francisco Preparedness Parade bombing. But in Jackson County Walsh and Reed were recognized as two equally matched giants of the bar, when they met in 1910. Reed, as county prosecutor, had won all except two of the 287 cases he had tried, and it was remembered that Walsh was his successful opponent in one of those two actions. That earlier trial had attracted wide attention as the defendant was Jesse James, Jr., son of the immortal train robber, who was accused of attempting to carry on the family tradition in the hold-up of a Missouri Pacific train near Kansas City in 1898. Young Jesse was acquitted, later became a lawyer and practised for a time in Kansas City, took a fling in Democratic politics and attracted brief attention as an insurgent agitating for the overthrow of "King Tom" Pendergast. The courtroom drama provided by Walsh and Reed was exciting enough to inspire him in that choice of a career, but their clash in the James trial was a small skirmish beside their engagement of 1910 in the Swope case.

Reed's histrionic talent was given full play in the prosecution of Dr. B. Clark Hyde, charged with the murder of Colonel Thomas H. Swope, millionaire real estate owner and philanthropist who gave Kansas City the 1,323-acre park that bears his name. Hyde, husband of one of Swope's nieces, also was accused of doing away with two of Swope's heirs and attempting to kill several others. A highly theoretical and circumstantial case was built on the contention that the defendant, a reputable and widely known physician before the trial, had turned into a monster in an effort to enhance his wife's share of Swope's four-million-dollar fortune. Jim Reed was hired as the special prosecutor by Dr. Hyde's mother-in-law, who had opposed the doctor's marriage to her daughter, Frances Hunton Swope. For four years she had nursed a morbid fear that her unwanted son-in-law was after the Swope millions which she was guarding for her numerous children, and then a run of death and sickness in the family turned her suspicions into certainty. However, she could not convince her daughter, and Frances Swope Hyde went before the court to brand the whole case against her husband as a fabrication based on prejudice, distortions, unfounded suspicions, malicious gossip and excited imaginations.

The things that Special Prosecutor Reed did with this fantastic complication made the undoing of Clark Hyde a Reed show. Memories of Reed swaying the jury to convict the doctor were still vivid twenty years later, when a veteran *Star* man was inspired to add this tasty bit to the book of journalistic hyperbole:

"Jim Reed reached for the stars in that speech. He found pathways in the clouds never before trodden in criminal cases. He finessed with meteors which dropped headlong into the path along which his feet took him. That golden voice could be as plaintive as a lute or as bold as thunder ringing from mountain peaks."

That reminiscence was in the flamboyant style of Reed himself and scrutiny of the court record shows several passages in which he soared nearly as high as the author quoted above. He was terrific, no doubt about it, and the special prosecution served as a revealing introduction to the Stormy Petrel when he stepped on the national stage to give the Kansas City Goats a loud voice in the American hurly-burly.

Curiously, the question of Clark Hyde's guilt or innocence has never been entirely settled, despite the Reed eloquence. Three juries in all heard the evidence in the case. The first voted eight to four for acquittal on the first ballot, but there was one powerful pleader in the minority who won the eight over to a conviction after three nights and two days of deliberation. That verdict was upset by the Missouri Supreme Court, which remanded the case for a new trial, and the second round ended in a mistrial when one of the jurors suffered a nervous breakdown and escaped from the jury room. The third trial ended in a deadlock, with the jury reported standing nine to three for acquittal, and the state finally dropped the case seven years after the first trial.

There is ample room for doubt that Reed would have obtained even a disputed conviction if the trial judge in the case had not permitted the prosecution to proceed on the broad theoretical course which the state Supreme Court condemned, and erred in several other important respects that were discussed in the stunning reversal. Finally, the Supreme Court declared that it was likely that Colonel Swope died from the effects of senile debility, in his eighty-second year, on the basis of the evidence developed at the trial.

So the story ought to show that Frank Walsh won his most spectacular engagement with Jim Reed, taking the decision on the points of law and evidence, but the course of justice, like the play of fortune in politics, is often confused and sad. Dr. Hyde found that the public did not digest or remember the sober opinion of the Supreme Court, and the legend that was formed in the melodrama and bombast of the six weeks' trial became fixed in the popular mind. He retired to spend the remainder of his life under a cloud. Reed went directly from the courtroom to campaign for the Senate seat and he had won that race before the Supreme Court's decision against the special prosecution was returned.

An impressive demonstration of Democratic harmony was given when Reed was sent to Washington. At that time, the election of United States senators was still held in the Legislature, after nominations in the preferential primary. Not a single dissenting Democratic vote was registered in the legislature when the Kansas City candidate was chosen. The time for revolts in the Democratic Party of Missouri was over, and there would be no great disturbance for another quarter of a century.

Through the storms of the last decade the Pendergast faction had proved its strength and it was resuming the expansion that had been interrupted by the varied interference from Walsh, Shannon, Folk and Nelson. Tom Pendergast had taken over full command of the faction from Alderman Jim in the same year that Reed ran successfully for the Senate. Big Tom and Fighting Jim had become fast friends in the struggles of the last dozen years, and they were to stand together in larger actions in the city, state and national arenas. The trend for the Democrats of Kansas City, and particularly for the Pendergast organization, was up from here on.

A turning point had been marked in 1900 when Reed appeared on the scene as mayor. It ended six straight years of Republican successes. It was followed by four decades in which the Republicans counted only ten years in control of the City Hall, and about the same number in the Courthouse. Joe Shannon, the Rabbit leader, had succeeded in strengthening his position and restoring the balance between the Democratic factions through the disturbances of the reform period, but the road ahead for Shannon was rocky. His ally, Frank Walsh, soon would leave Kansas City and other figures who had assisted him in the political competition were about to pass on. Mr. Shannon wasn't going to have much time for rest despite the fact that peace had been restored to the Jackson County Democracy under Fifty-Fifty, the historic trading agreement between the Goats and Rabbits which had been devised during a lull in the battles of the last decade. It wasn't the poet's kind of peace.

Although Reed in Washington placed himself above the rough-and-tumble in which the city machine grew big and tough, his relationship with Tom Pendergast remained unbroken until near the close of the boss show. The Senator did not control much patronage that was useful to the Kansas City Democrats, but the prestige of his position, the power of his voice in campaigns, his advice on policy and strategy and his influence with state and national party leaders were large assets to the organization out of which the machine grew. It took fifteen more years to complete that development, but the building process began to attract major attention not long after the Missouri reform ended.

REFORM IN OLD TOWN

MURDER, economic injustice and political corruption were much less interesting to the general public as daily propositions than the problem of ordinary vice and it seemed that a large part of the population believed that if men could be induced to give up guzzling, dancing, whoring and card playing all would be well with the Republic and such matters as good government and social right would more or less take care of themselves.

The hard-shell Baptist idea in political endeavor had a very interesting subject to work on in Kansas City's First Ward, which included old Market Square and extended south to Twelfth Street—all of it a notable center of resistance to the puritan philosophy. Twelfth Street, with its new White Way, its hotels, restaurants and theaters, carried the spirit of old Battle Row and Union Avenue into the new metropolitan age.

Holy Joe Folk's crusading against tipplers, horse players and dice experts had a temporarily depressing effect on this lively neighborhood and revived the North Side's fanatical opposition to reform and reformers of all kinds. When Folk passed from the scene at the end of his one term, his Republican successor, the Honorable Herbert S. Hadley, endeavored to carry on the good work of improving the moral tone of the cities, as the Protestant devil chasers were still making a great commotion with their notion that an enormous uplift would be derived from a vast shutdown in public merriment. Moreover, it appeared that the G.O.P. would be strengthened by a little practical reform under the auspices of Republican officials and policemen, at the expense of Democratic saloonkeepers and dive operators. The result was a most earnest application of the clean-up principle in Old Town, producing a reaction which showed that the vice problem required something more than the simple political action favored by the reformers of this period.

For this great work, Governor Hadley selected a Republican lawyer by the name of Tom Marks, a sportsman, social philosopher and swashbuckling fellow with ambitions to displace the Pendergasts as the power in the First Ward. Naturally he centered his improvement project in that district. Much work needed to be done both for the Republican cause and for salvation in the North End, as the North Side then was called. With the city's rapid march southward, the original part of the community in and around Market Square had become a seedy relic of a picturesque past. Sentimentalists called it Old Town and regarded it with affection, but the people in the higher-rent districts to the northeast and south looked upon it with distaste or tried not to see it. They entered it by day only when they had business that took them to the City Hall, the Courthouse or some commercial establishment. They saw it at night when they were making the rounds or going to and from theaters, in the neighborhood, which held out against the decline. They knew it vaguely as the part of town in which Negroes and Italians were crowded with Jews, Irish and native Americans at the bottom of the social and economic heap, the area in which the bawdyhouses operated and the underworld had its roots.

Police Commissioner Marks set about the cleanup task with commendable zeal but before long it appeared that he was too advanced for the town. A reformer of the sophisticated type produced by the new metropolitan age, he felt that the old-fashioned raiding-and-closing tactics of the Folk period were inadequate to deal with the modern pace in larceny, homicide and forbidden joy, but he found that many horse-and-buggy ideas in public morals persisted when he attempted to introduce reforms that had a rather Parisian flavor.

Mr. Marks produced a blast of righteous indignation from holders of various profitable downtown properties by drawing plans for a segregated vice district in the North End. This proposal was based on a foreign doctrine of compromise with Beelzebub which was ever hateful to the native Baptists and Methodists. Furthermore, the plan threatened to jeopardize important real estate values and restrain trade. The North End had a large daytime industrial and commercial importance as well as an interesting nighttime traffic. It had its own way of accommodating itself to the social evil, so that neither the daytime nor the nighttime business suffered, and it did not propose to change.

"There must be some regulation," Mr. Marks declared. "Vice cannot be suppressed and it cannot be scattered like measles along our boulevards. So we must reduce the evil to the minimum."

His radical scheme to achieve this end with a police-sponsored red-light district was shouted down at a meeting of two hundred angry businessmen who were not idealists like Tom Marks and didn't believe there was any such thing as a minimum in sin. It was the consensus of the meeting that Mr. Marks had been absolutely insulting to the respectable property owners with his broad insinuations that they were responsible for the existing social conditions, and they adjourned after adopting a resolution formally changing the name of the North End to the North Side, which was thought to have a less unsavory sound. The problem was left approximately where it was, until it was dealt with a little later in more orthodox American fashion through a tremendous revival directed by the Religion Forward Movement with the earnest co-operation of the businessmen. That was declared to be a wonderful campaign and its good results were summed up by the head of the Movement, who said: "The present social evil is indeed a long-time problem. I have no doubt but what a speedy solution will be arrived at. Just what that is will be hard to prophesy."

The speedy solution was still hard to guess when the Marks cleanup ended after a run that was made brief by the usual complications attending partisan administration of the Police Department.

The chief political result of this Republican concern over Old Town's morals was to increase the North Side's affection for Democrats. Although they were roundly abused as the men most responsible for conditions, the political heroes of the saloonkeepers were models of sobriety and encouraged uplift in their own quiet way. Joe Shannon, the Rabbit boss, for example, had a record as a teetotaler which few wearers of the white ribbon could match.

Joe delighted in telling the story of his success in resisting temptation in any alcoholic form. It began when he was a boy of twelve and had to quit school to help support his widowed mother and her large family.

Joe's first job was in Martin Keck's beer garden atop an eminence later known as Union Station Hill, later the site of Kansas City's imposing First World War Memorial. When Mrs. Shannon learned that her son was working in a beer joint, she gave him a long lecture on the evils of drink.

"Promise me that you will never touch whisky or beer or any of those things with alcohol in them," she said. "The devil's in them."

"I promise, Ma," said little Joe.

"And I never have," concluded the Rabbit chieftain, draining a glass of milk with a show of vast relish.

The Pendergasts, who depended on the saloon for their main income, could not go so far as the Shannons in discouraging interest in liquor, but old Jim did what he could to impress the temperance people. He gave up drinking fairly early in his career after he underestimated his own strength in a friendly brawl with another Irishman, when both he and the other man were artificially stimulated. As befitted a naturally peace-loving man, Jim suffered profound remorse over his friend's abrasions and contusions and thereafter he passed when the drinks were ordered. He began to develop a reformer's zeal, eventually establishing some kind of a record in hoisting the young to the driver's seat of the water wagon. One of the prized documents in the safe in his saloon was a list of the men whom he had forced to take the pledge. The list contained nearly a hundred names of citizens who had been corralled by Jim Pendergast in the company of John Barleycorn and rushed in a hack to a Catholic church, where they were sweated by the saloonkeeper and the priest until they signed the pledge. Pendergast stored these papers in his safe after solemnly warning the signers that if they broke their promise they would lose the frienship of Jim Pendergast. It was no light threat and it worked in a reasonable number of cases. Several men who later became important figures in Democratic affairs owed their start on the straight-and-narrow way to the saloonkeeper of Old Town.

Tom Pendergast had a normal liking for the taste and effect of bourbon but he, too, eventually became one of the abstinence men although he never tried to pose as a temperance model like Shannon or compete with evangelists like Jim.

Alderman Jim carried his temperance ideas into his political work to the extent of refusing to do anything for any member of the police force who was dropped for intoxication while on duty. By personal example and disciplining of his political following, he sought to inculcate the good saloonkeeper's creed that liquor was something to be enjoyed and not abused, and reform was an individual problem. At the same time that he encouraged saloonkeepers and their patrons to conduct themselves with moderation, he used all of his influence to fight their battles. He followed this line in all of his operations on the North Side.

Pendergast's attitude on the liquor question was based on practical business and political considerations, of course, but it also was possible to see in it the honest conviction of a man who accepted things as they were and tried, with the limited means at his disposal, to make them bearable. There is no doubt that he had a great sentimental attachment for the North Side and its people. To him the inhabitants of the slums, the floaters in the flophouses, the shanty dwellers of the East Bottoms, the laboring men in the West Bottoms and the people of Little Italy were not the teeming masses so luridly described in the literature of the period as the flotsam and jetsam of society. They were personal friends of Alderman Jim Pendergast. He liked to listen to their stories and took a genuine interest in their problems. He got them jobs on the city or county payrolls or with business friends of the organization.

The North Side people who lived daily with want and insecurity naturally could make more sense out of Alderman Jim's measures to assist them than they could from the arguments of the agitators who wanted to make over America and change everybody's habits. The North Siders went to Pendergast for more than jobs. They went to him when they were in trouble and needed someone to soften the stern hand of justice. Many of them got fuel and other supplies·from his precinct captains when they were down and out. Others ate his turkey and trimmings at the free Christmas dinners which he gave for the Old Town derelicts, beginning with fifty guests and growing into the hundreds as the number of drifters increased year after year.

These people remembered Alderman Jim as the hero of the 1903 flood that inundated a part of the North Side and made hundreds homeless. Jim lived in his buggy, day and night, traveling over the scene directing rescue work and the temporary housing and feeding of the refugees.

Afterward he took the lead in the movement to rehabilitate the North Side. The agitators and reformers might some day make it possible to remake Old Town but while the millennium was being prepared the first Goat boss served as an efficient sort of practical humanitarian.

Alderman Jim's hold on the North Side reached its high point at the same time that the fights on the saloon and the boss system entered their major phase. Making his ninth and last race for alderman in 1908, Jim rolled up his largest majority, 1,330 to 443, and had the pleasure of seeing a Democratic administration returned to power in the City Hall.

By 1910, Jim Pendergast was failing in health and ready to retire, although he was only fifty-four years old. He looked forward to a serene period in which his brothers would take care of the saloon and political interests of the family while he devoted his attention to chicken raising on his farm. "No mixed breeds for me," he said.

All angles of the prospect were pleasing. The organization was at its peak and Brother Tom, then thirty-seven and fully seasoned for his work as boss, was taking over the Pendergast aldermanic seat from the First Ward.

"Brother Tom will make a fine alderman, and he'll be good to the boys —just as I have been," Jim remarked to a group of cronies in his saloon. "Eighteen years of thankless work for the city; eighteen years of abuse, eighteen years of getting jobs for the push is all the honor I want."

He died a year and a half later.

On the base of Pendergast's statue in Mulkey Square this inscription was placed:

This monument is erected by general contribution as a tribute to the rugged character and splendid achievements of a man whose private and public life was the embodiment of truth and courage.

A more flowery statement was written in a second bronze tablet on the base of the monument but perhaps the sincerest tribute came from Colonel Nelson's paper, which said:

"Alderman Pendergast had a code of ethics all his own. He never failed to take political advantage of an opponent. But he regarded a political promise as binding and never broke his word. He hated an ingrate. Ingratitude in his mind was an unforgivable sin.

"His support of any man or measure never had a price in cash."

Whose Town?

The enemies of Colonel Nelson had to wait until two years before his death before they got a chance to see him humiliated in a way that seemed adequate to their profound sense of grievance. They had almost given up hope that retribution would overtake the Baron when a sensitive Circuit judge turned a divorce case into a *cause célèbre,* declaring that Nelson's *Star* was guilty of contempt in reporting the domestic difficulty and ruling that the judicial dignity would be satisfied only when Baron Bill was behind jail bars.

For years the Colonel had been guilty of a very low opinion of numerous judges and on the subject of lawyers he was generally full of contempt. Lawyers had shaped the laws of the land, packed the courts and conducted their business in a manner that made justice a commodity reserved for the highest bidder, as the Daily W. R. Nelson said often and in various effective ways. Lawyers were the fixers for corporations and manipulators of the political machine. In the *Star's* language the lawyers were, with few exceptions, fee grabbers.

Nelson's reporters and editors usually aimed their shots well, but they fired so many salvos in so many directions at once that it was only natural that they should wound a bear now and then, with the familiar consequences to the luckless gunner. One notable instance was when a Kansas City lawyer who was a former member of the Missouri Legislature collected fifteen thousand dollars for libel on two innocent-looking words. He demanded redress after the *Star* carried a story reviewing his career and reporting that he "did well" in a legislative way. This legal fellow refused to regard doing well as a fair estimate of his efforts, but instead considered the phrase a scandalous imputation of political boodling expressed in a familiar Missouri language, and he found a court that agreed with his interpretation.

A more famous example of reportorial embarrassment was given in the contempt issue raised by Circuit Judge Joseph A. Guthrie early in 1913. The Judge was elected to the Circuit bench of Jackson County in 1910 with the backing of the Pendergasts. He brooded for a long time over the *Star's* attitude toward his profession and it is conceivable that he was unable to get the *Star*'s policy out of his mind when he considered the question of whether Colonel Nelson ought to go to jail.

The case grew out of the divorce action of Clevinger *v.* Clevinger, a quarrelsome couple who set the stage for an incident that drew national attention when they decided not to go through with dissolution of the matrimonial ties. Mrs. Clevinger asked that her suit for divorce be dismissed and her three lawyers requested the Court to order that her husband pay her attorney's fees, the total amount involved being sixty dollars. The Court so ordered, following well-established precedent in the matter. His Honor hit the ceiling of his chamber when he read the *Star*'s account of this routine affair, for the newspaper story was thoroughly garbled and unfavorable to the Judge. In brief, the story and headline created the impression that the Court had subordinated the client's interest to the lawyers', holding that fees must be paid before alimony was allowed, and that he had awarded sixty dollars each to three lawyers in a divorce suit which never came to trial.

The Judge decided on drastic reprisals, and he didn't need the encouragement which he found in Democratic circles, for he was explosive spontaneously. However, some of the leaders of his own party were disturbed by the impetuousness with which he went about the business of humbling the great man on the *Star*. One of his judicial colleagues and a fellow Democrat, Judge Ralph S. Latshaw, criticized him publicly.

"This is the greatest outrage ever perpetrated by a court of justice," said Judge Latshaw. "It's a case of putting away Caesar that Rome might have a holiday."

Goats and Rabbits, nourished for years on *Star* hating, crowded into Judge Guthrie's court to witness the spectacle of Colonel Nelson being clapped in the calaboose. The proceedings before Judge Guthrie were brief and the defense's efforts to introduce certain evidence were brushed aside. Joe Guthrie had made up his mind as to the defendant's guilt and his punishment—one day in jail.

But the sentencing of Colonel Nelson didn't turn out to be the circus that the enemies of the editor expected to see. The *Star*'s official biography of Nelson carries this awed report of his effect on the assembled lawyers, sheriff's deputies, spectators and apparently everyone except Judge Guthrie:

"Those who were in the courtroom that day will never forget the scene; the noble dignity of the white-haired man, while about him shuffled and whispered and leered the crowd of political creatures, and he the only calm, unruffled, unexcited one amid it all. The political rabble that day was given to glimpse the strength of character of a great man, and it awed them, absolutely awed. Then they began to sense the wrong they were doing, and it shamed them. When the proceedings were over, even the judge on the bench saw that his crowd had slunk away from him."

The thing that actually impressed the Judge and disappointed the leering crowd was the quick work of Frank P. Walsh, one of the Democratic lawyers engaged to defend the Colonel. Mr. Walsh noticed the Judge reading from a paper when he began to deliver his decision. He respectfully interrupted the Court, asked if he was reading his opinion. Upon being informed that such was the case, he asked when the decision was written and was advised that it had been prepared the night before the hearing. The official court record contains this colloquy:

Mr. Walsh: I think the record ought to show that your honor had his decision in this case written before the hearing began, if that be a fact.
Judge Guthrie: That is the fact.
Mr. Walsh: Then let the record show that at the conclusion of the arguments the judge of this honorable court read his decision, which was prepared in advance.
Judge Guthrie: The decision was in the breast of this court and it was as easy for this court to prepare its opinion at one time as another.
Mr. Walsh: Then it was prepared before this hearing.
Judge Guthrie: Yes.

The Judge was not only in an excessive hurry to prepare and deliver his opinion against Nelson; he also was impatient to see Colonel Nelson in the hands of the sheriff and on the way to jail. He insisted that the editor be not allowed to loiter in the courtroom while his attorneys hastily prepared application for a writ of habeas corpus to spare him the indignity of being seized by the sheriff and hauled off before the riffraff. Mr. Walsh asked for only ten minutes for his distinguished client but Guthrie said the case was closed and called for the sheriff to do his duty.

The courtroom crowd grew impatient, raising a shout: "What are they waiting for?" But Lawyer Walsh was an expert at stalling and he was killing time with a purpose. He and another Democratic lawyer, James P. Aylward, had prepared for this eventuality. In a room on the floor above Judge Guthrie's court, a judge of the Kansas City Court of Appeals had been posted to go in session the moment that word was flashed. The signal was given when Nelson was sentenced, and while Walsh pleaded for time from Guthrie, his associate obtained from the Appellate Court a temporary writ of habeas corpus. That instrument finally was served in time to permit Nelson's release before he actually suffered formal arrest and imprisonment.

The Court of Appeals quickly decided it did not have jurisdiction in the case and passed the difficult question on to the Supreme Court of Missouri. Meanwhile the newspapers of the nation took up the cudgels for Nelson, raising a great clamor over the manner in which Guthrie was attempting to railroad the Kansas City publisher to jail, and hailing the Colonel as one of the immortals in the ancient battle for freedom of the press.

Three months later the Supreme Court delivered its opinion, a masterpiece of legal logic, philosophical wisdom and political sagacity. In an exhaustive report prepared by Judge Woodson and concurred in by all other members of the bench, the Court found that the *Star* was guilty of contempt, as charged, and freed Mr. Nelson. The opinion pointed out that the editor was only "constructively guilty," the real culprit being a reporter named Murphy. Nelson had no knowledge of the contemptuous item until after it appeared in the paper, but under the law he was responsible for the publication. He was discharged from the sentence of a day in jail because the Supreme Court found he had been deprived of his rights as a citizen under the constitutional provisions for due process of law, and upon this point the Supreme Judge was most eloquent, citing appropriate sections of the Missouri and United States constitutions, quoting from Proverbs and Revelation and listing an impressive array of precedents. Winding up on a patriotic note, the Court slipped in a line that seemed to express its exasperation over the whole business, when it remarked: "This is the best form of government given to man upon earth, but thank God we are promised a better one in the world to come."

The *Star* accepted this draw as a victory and celebrated it with a long and forceful editorial restatement of its case against lawyers and judges in general.

The aging Baron had no intention of retiring or even relaxing before he had to, and his bout with Judge Guthrie simply served to focus more attention on the grand finish he was making. A year earlier he had made his supreme effort in the national political arena when he resigned his post as Republican national committeeman to follow Teddy Roosevelt out of the G.O.P. and stand with him at Armageddon battling for the Lord and Bull Moose progressivism.

"The Republican Party is dead, as it deserves to be," he told an Eastern newspaperman who interviewed him. "The contest will be between Roosevelt and Wilson. The Republican Party has gone as the Whig Party went. It has finished its work and is done."

After Roosevelt's defeat and Wilson's election, Nelson threw the *Star*'s support behind the progressive measures introduced by the Democratic president in the New Freedom phase of his administration. Meanwhile, at home, the Colonel's paper pushed the Nonpartisan movement in municipal affairs with fresh vigor. In 1914, a little more than a year before he died, the *Star* conducted a stunning campaign for Nelson's pet proposition—the commission form of city government. It was in this campaign that the *Star*'s agitation finally broke the will of the local Republican organization.

Nelson's farewell in the long struggle over the City Hall occurred at a time when the Democratic factions were beginning to quarrel again. Tom Pendergast, feeling his oats as the new boss in Alderman Jim's seat, was growing restive over his partnership with Joe Shannon under Fifty-Fifty, but the Goat and Rabbit factions closed ranks to meet the latest threat presented by the *Star* Party. There was a Republican ticket in the race but the Nonpartisan represented the real opposition. The *Star* conducted a long preliminary educational campaign and climaxed it with a mammoth rally.

Three days before the election, the Republican candidate for mayor dramatically withdrew from the race and released his following to the Nonpartisan ticket. It wasn't enough to turn the tide and the election

ʼresulted in another Democratic landslide. Mayor Henry L. Jost, running
for re-election, almost doubled his majority of two years before.

Following the city election campaign, Nelson engaged in another
furious battle which was precipitated by a proposal, backed by the Jost
administration and both Democratic factions, to give the Metropolitan
Street Railway Company a thirty-year franchise. The *Star*'s publisher,
then in his seventy-third year and beginning to fail in health, personally directed the newspaper's attack on the machine's generous plan to
bolster up an inefficient corporation at public expense. The case against
the franchise for the company, which was floundering in the morass of
receivership through mismanagement and long watering of stock, was so
one sided that many party leaders who were known friends of the corporation declined to enter the public debate.

Despite its weakness in argument, the new franchise won approval
at the polls by a majority of 6,788 votes, carrying all but three of the city's
sixteen wards. Labor joined with the corporation and the political bosses
to carry the day, as the street railway employees had been promised better
wages and working conditions if the franchise was adopted. It was not
simply a victory for the Democratic administration but a victory for the
machine that operated in both parties. Republican ward bosses worked
side by side with Democrats for the franchise. The banner majorities
came from the Pendergast river wards, showing that the trend which
crushed the Nonpartisans was still working.

Nelson put his reporters to work developing a postelection scandal,
airing various charges that the franchise majority had been obtained by
fraud through purchased votes and repeaters. This storm blew strong
for several days after the newspaper published the confession of a vote
repeater, a floater from Chicago, who admitted he had earned two bucks
by voting twice. However, the investigation expired suddenly when he
was whisked away on a two-year prison sentence meted out by a Circuit
Court judge who said he was making an example of the prisoner as
a warning to all election cheaters. The two-year term also served as a
warning to squealers, and no further confessions were forthcoming.
This swift disappearance of the vote-fraud informer had the effect of
deflating the *Star*'s agitation for a grand jury investigation to seek out
"higher ups," and the furor ended with the newspaper supporting a

S. J. Ray in The Kansas City Star

The *Only* Issue

The machine issue grew steadily until 1940. This cartoon appeared in the climactic campaign of that year.

movement to get a parole for the poor Chicago citizen who had exposed the system and was the only one seriously affected by this crusade.

Following this run of election setbacks, Nelson opened a campaign for a new law establishing election machinery for Kansas City that would discourage vote frauds, and he was in the midst of that struggle when he fell in his last illness. Exhausted by the franchise fight, he took a vacation in the Colorado mountains but when he returned he didn't move with his old vigor. His employees noticed that he left his desk at five in the evening instead of the customary six. Then his physicians ordered him to stay in his home, Oak Hall, but he did not rest, for he had telephones installed in various rooms so he could keep in hourly communication with the office. He was put to bed and slipped into long periods of unconsciousness, but a month before his death he rallied and called his editors to his home to map out new plans for the election reform bill then pending in the Missouri General Assembly. He followed that by telephoning the office with suggestions for a cartoon and an editorial. His last editorial was a call for reform, and in it he spoke again as the Tilden Democrat, appealing to the Wilson Democrats of Missouri to rise for the progressive cause and force their representatives to approve the election bill. The campaign aroused twelve Democrats and one Republican in the state Senate, far too few to save the election reform. The bill was killed by the simple expedient of keeping it buried so deep on the calendar that it couldn't be considered before adjournment. The machine lobby was working so efficiently that it even seriously threatened to upset the primary law that was adopted in the Folk reform days.

Shortly after this, Nelson dropped into his last sleep. The man who never lost had closed his career with three defeats, and the tide of reaction was rising fast. Apparently his mind was on this, for he roused one night at midnight and sent his farewell to the *Star* through his son-in-law. "Those messages of sympathy and appreciation have been fine," he said. "But remind the men at the office of one thing. The interests that are against Kansas City are still in control. The fight on them mustn't let up, no matter if they do say nice things about me." He died April 13, 1915.

They said an extraordinary number of nice things about him after he was dead. Indeed the praise was so fulsome that it seemed that William R. Nelson was to be canonized in the popular mind as one of the American saints. This undoubtedly would have pleased the old man, for he was vain and loved flattery, but some of it must have bored him profoundly. For William Rockhill Nelson, the public-spirited citizen, the great humanitarian, patron of the arts and education, builder of parks and boulevards, was also Baron Bill, the imperious man of wealth and privilege, the hard-fisted businessman and ruthless fighter.

He left in trust to his heirs—his wife and a daughter—a large estate that was eventually devoted mostly to public benefit through the funds that financed the magnificent William Rockhill Nelson Gallery of Art on the site of old Oak Hall. The Nelson trust had grown in value to some twelve million dollars when his daughter died in 1926. The publisher's widow and daughter left personal fortunes totaling nearly three million dollars which were added to Nelson's memorial in the art gallery.

Nelson knew that his paper would continue for some time under the control of his family and he probably guessed that his old associates would show enough enterprise to purchase the property after his wife and daughter died. At any rate, he expected that his influence would not die with him, and he spoke of the crusade for free and honest elections and for impartial courts as his legacy to the *Star*. "My scheme is to drive the money out of the voting booth and out of the courthouse," he explained in a letter to his great friend, Theodore Roosevelt. "The government must bear the entire expense of all elections and justice must be really—and not merely nominally—free."

His heirs immediately faced a number of fights in carrying on his work but on the day of his funeral there was a general truce in honor of the town's First Citizen. Stores and public schools closed in the afternoon. Post offices were closed during memorial services in Oak Hall. Trolley cars stopped for five minutes in tribute to the streetcar company's greatest opponent. Politicians of Kansas and Missouri came to attend the rites. Courts and public offices in Kansas City, Kansas, closed, but on the Missouri side some of the offices in the Courthouse remained open and none of the offices in the City Hall closed, for there were many Goats and Rabbits who knew that Baron Bill wouldn't stay in his grave.

THE KNIFING

DESPITE its name, the famous Kansas City Fifty-Fifty deal didn't always come out even and it operated only about half of the time. It was, however, a very useful device in the building of the machine. Without it, the Democratic organization might have disrupted itself permanently in factional warfare. When the machine finally developed to the point where Fifty-Fifty was considered no longer necessary by Tom Pendergast, the organization began its spiral out of control. For anyone interested in the mechanics of boss government, a little attention to Fifty-Fifty is time well spent.

Joe Shannon is reputed to be the architect of Fifty-Fifty and it is certain that he expected to be the principal beneficiary from it, as in fact he was. Mike Pendergast felt oppressed by Fifty-Fifty and long agitated for its abolition. Tom Pendergast benefited somewhat from it but never seemed happy with the arrangement. Jim Pendergast, wise founder of the Goats, put it into effect after a private confab with the Rabbit boss in a campaign where the positions of both were being jeopardized by factional strife.

A political organization composed of two approximately equal factions, one serving as a check on the other, would have certain advantages over a single command if a way could be found to establish effective coordination, and Fifty-Fifty offered that way. It provided that the rival bosses get together before a campaign in an effort to agree on a slate of candidates. Where there was a difference on certain offices, each faction offered its favorites in the primary and both sides abided by the result, supporting the nominees in the final election. No matter which faction succeeded in getting more men on the winning ticket, the patronage was to be divided fifty-fifty. That was the hitch in the plan, and the thing that finally wrecked it.

Tom Pendergast eventually changed Fifty-Fifty to Seventy-Thirty, and he started in that direction a year after Nelson died when the Goats and the *Star* worked together to pry Mayor Jost out of the City Hall and give Joe Shannon more time for reading his law and history books. The collaboration did not entail a change of policy on the part of either the newspaper or the North Side Democratic boss. Suppression of the Rabbit leader at this juncture was to the mutual advantage of the newspaper and Pendergast, although for the latter it meant temporary eclipse of his party in local affairs.

Pendergast had been fairly quiet but not idle in the four-year period when Shannonism was reaching its crest through the Rabbit boss's association with the Honorable Henry L. Jost. While Shannon advised, and Jost administered the city government, Tom organized the precincts as they had never been organized before. He went about this prosaic spadework with the diligence and methodical care of a census taker. He studied election returns with the same interest that Joe Shannon displayed when he read a paper by Jefferson. Alderman Jim's efficient former bookkeeper was a businessman and he worked on the theory that politics was not a science, an art or a drama of campaign time but a year-round business. The basis of that business was not candidates or policies but trained precinct workers who served each day in the year, and voters who were registered, pledged, committed, satisfied and ready to deliver.

Pendergast began the work of restoring the Fifty-Fifty balance by raiding in Shannon's old stronghold, the county. Winning a controlling hand in the County Committee along with Shannon, he emerged as a state committeeman. He followed that by electing a majority of the County Committee and naming one of his lieutenants to the chairmanship. Another important gain was the election of one of his chief lieutenants to the post of presiding judge of the County Court, which was an administrative body corresponding to the County Commission in other localities. A series of operations against the Rabbits in the City Hall accompanied these maneuvers in the county.

Politicians were quick to recognize the qualities that made Pendergast a forceful leader, but to the general public he was largely a name— a saloonkeeper and a ward boss who was seldom seen—despite the fact that he had held three offices. He had been street superintendent in Mayor Reed's first term, a county marshal for one term, street superintendent for a second time under Mayor T. T. Crittenden and a councilman for three terms. He retired with a reputation as a public servant who made no speeches, handled patronage matters most efficiently and intimidated opponents with his powerful fists. His pugnacity brought

him into a brush with the law in his second term as street superintendent.
Pendergast's arrest was ordered following an incident in which he interfered with, and frightened off, three police officers in Sullivan's saloon
on the North Side when they attempted to arrest two suspected miscreants. Called to a hearing before the mayor, Tom explained that he
had stopped the police because they were hounding one of the two fugitives, a former convict who was trying to go straight. The Mayor dismissed the case with a light reprimand for his persuasive street
superintendent.

A Pendergast interview acquired a certain fearsome quality as the
result of an incident in his tenure as an alderman. A fellow alderman
who had crossed him was summoned to Pendergast's cubbyhole office
off the lobby of his Jefferson Hotel. The Boss was reported to have locked
the door so the erring public servant could not escape until Mr. Pendergast tired of hitting him.

These stories tended to exaggerate the Pendergast pugilistic prowess,
which was formidable enough, at the expense of his other attributes. The
Boss did much to correct the popular impression of himself in the campaign of 1916, when he exhibited talent as strategist, intriguer, organizer
and long-range planner along with ruthless fighting spirit.

The Shannon-Jost forces won the first round when Pendergast attempted to corral the mayoralty nomination for his personal friend and
business associate, R. Emmet O'Malley, who rode on Tom's coattails
to power and pelf and later followed him to prison. Pendergast made a
bitter fight in the primary campaign but was unable to overcome the
combination of Jost's popular prestige and Rabbit control of the City
Hall and the Police Department. Mayor Jost was nominated for a third
term but the fight did not end there. Pendergast decided the time had
come for a revolt.

At the Democratic city convention which ran roughshod over the
Goat candidates for mayor and aldermen, Pendergast bluntly stated
his intention not to abide by the result. His revolt took the form of a
political knifing, an operation that was accomplished by an order to his
following to vote for the Republican candidate for mayor. At the same
time, Pendergast offered a set of independent candidates for aldermen
in the wards he controlled.

The police power figured spectacularly in this new showdown between the factions with the advantage on the Jost-Shannon side, representing a reversal of the situation that existed in 1904 when Shannon had made his bolt. Pendergast awoke on election day to find that police friendly to his faction had been moved to the woods for the day. The Jost-Shannon guardians of the law exhibited extraordinary concern in preserving order, starting with a roundup of Pendergast workers long before dawn. More than two hundred were jugged before the polls opened, and exciting scenes were staged in courts and police headquarters when Goat politicians obtained writs of habeas corpus to free their friends, and police officials defied them. However, the Rabbit coup failed to save the Jost-Shannon ticket. The North Side boss elected five of his followers to the lower house of the Council and could count the knifing a complete success despite the fact that the Republican-*Star* ticket took everything else.

Joe Shannon was demoralized and "muling in his tent," to use old Jim Pendergast's phrase for a sore factionalist. Fifty-Fifty was dead for the time being and Tom was free to play a solitary hand until he found it profitable to renew the Goat-Rabbit alliance. He followed up the knifing by winning firm control of the County Committee in the August primaries. His ticket for county and state offices was nominated and elected. Jim Reed was returned to the United States Senate. The new governor, Frederick D. Gardner, was a Democrat who was politically indebted to the new leader of Jackson County's Democracy. The Goats moved into the Courthouse and events were forming that would restore them to power in the City Hall at the next election. Boss Tom Pendergast had arrived.

Free and Easy

THE STORMS attending expression of the popular will at the polls created a widespread impression that boss politicians spent most of their time hatching plots and schemes to complicate the lives of normal people. The contrary was the case. The Kansas City politicians as a class were among the most convivial of men, full of the milk of human kindness, and they devoted no more time to the business of mayhem and assassination than the nature of their operations required. Between campaigns they concentrated on the task of restoring peace and cultivating happiness.

The social side of boss politics was particularly conspicuous in the Goat faction, which was so earnest in the endeavor to relax the community that the entertainment went on almost continuously, regardless of changes in administration, factional disturbances, economic and social crises that shook the nation and wars that upset the world. Tom Pendergast gave major encouragement to the Democratic tradition of festivity, and his success in this promotion increased his personal popularity and widened his political following. It also drew upon him the unfavorable attention of an important element who felt that the frivolity on the North Side was sinful competition with more sober lines of business, but the Boss did not let these solemn individuals spoil the fun.

Pendergast had the assistance of numerous sports who were imaginative and industrious in devising ways to break the monotony of living in a money-making society. Prominent among the interesting characters in this company was Booth Baughman, who had been an intimate of Alderman Jim Pendergast and moved in Brother Tom's inner circle. He took the lead in promoting some excitement in the early days of Tom's regime. Booth combined both the practical and romantic sides of recreation. He never took a serious interest in any game unless it was played with money, but he was always a sportsman in business. In recognition of this distinction, the money circulated in games of chance was known as Baughman currency.

Baughman lived at Tom Pendergast's Jefferson Hotel and assisted in its operation, the establishment being conducted in a manner to suggest the extreme liberalism of the founder of the Democratic Party in whose honor the hotel was named. Shortly before participating in the Jefferson venture, Booth staged a determined revival of Missouri River revelry which agitated the *Star* and other guardians of civic decorum for a couple of seasons.

In the river entertainment, Baughman was assisted by two other widely known Goats, Phil McCrory and John J. Pryor, who first attracted political attention as North Side saloonkeepers and later were more celebrated as business associates of Tom Pendergast in wholesale liquor and concrete. With their backing, Baughman brought the river boat *Saturn* to Kansas City, fitted it out as an excursion craft with accommodations for adventurous and sentimental ladies and gentlemen, running on a schedule designed to mock the bluenoses of Missouri and Kansas. The proprietors literally and figuratively thumbed their noses at prosecutors and peace officers of city and state, declaring they operated under the navigation laws of the Federal government, which allowed for wide latitude in excursion pastimes.

The *Saturn*'s 1910 season was highlighted by a mass raid when the boat docked at the foot of Main Street, police rounding up about a hundred and fifty excursionists on charges of frequenting a gambling establishment. That was followed by court action against the proprietors, which ended with the judge ruling that the city's police authority extended to the middle of the river. Mr. Baughman was only temporarily discouraged by this interference, but the river celebration finally ended in 1912, when public agitation over the *Saturn* reached its height after a gambler committed suicide by diving from the deck of the boat into the Big Muddy.

The Jefferson Hotel, which Pendergast purchased the same year that the *Saturn* made its final excursion from Kansas City, carried on the Old Town revival for seven more years. The hotel was a six-story brick affair, a modest establishment in the old part of the city, near Market Square, but it acquired more than local notoriety after the Goat boss made it the headquarters for politicians and convivial citizens who never wanted to go home. The hotel's chief charm was the cabaret in its basement.

There was nothing quite like the Jefferson celebration anywhere else. Some survivors describe it as a revival of the original Free and Easy, which started in the joints of Old Town where first were combined the dramatic and musical arts for frontier society. It was easy to get in, but it cost plenty to get out. These places were called burlesque houses, but developed along quite classical lines and carried such imposing names as The Coliseum, The Theater Comique and The Fountain Theater. They mixed entertainment and refreshment in much the same manner as the Jefferson Cabaret.

In Hank Clark's place, the original Free and Easy, the drinks came with frontier jokes, songs and dances. In Valentine Love's Theater Comique, variety numbers were offered between the acts of famous melodramas like *Mazeppa, The Mountain Meadow Massacre* and *The Flaming Arrow,* the customers being served at the bar or at their seats before the stage. In Martin Regan's Fountain Theater, dizzy blondes served the drinkers at tables while the show went on. Martin was a Democratic ward boss and a character, one of the founders of the showman tradition in politics. Nobody figured out what sort of shows Martin actually put on, and nobody cared. Everybody sang and danced. Nobody paid much attention to the actors on the stage and everybody applauded them loudly and called them back repeatedly for encores. Everything was good. Nothing was rotten.

The show at the Jefferson had these characteristics, and apparently a fine time was had by one and all except, now and then, when some member of the company became too exhilarated or was unexpectedly struck by despondency. A brief but vivid description of the scene has been preserved in an account of one of the unfortunate incidents at the hotel.

A young woman, in Room 508, shot herself at the end of a long evening in the midst of the merriment in the cabaret. Her man had done her wrong and she was trying to drive the blues away in the stimulating company of a traveling man from Fort Worth, Texas. Shortly after she and her companion had ascended the marble stairs from the cabaret and retired to their room, she attempted to end her life.

The story of this unhappy affair was printed in the *Star* at the height of the city campaign of 1914 in which the *Star* was opposing the North Side boss. It was intended to focus scandalized attention on Pendergast's hotel, but the reporter who wrote the piece was more seduced than repelled by the picture he drew. "Cabaret entertainers wandered from table to table, singing sensuous songs," he wrote. "Midnight passed and the crowd of underworld habitués became hilarious. At one o'clock, the hour required by law at which to stop selling liquor, the orgy was at its height. The hours passed and the waiters were busier than ever dispensing drinks, for the Jefferson Hotel has police protection and is free to ignore the closing law, observed by other cabarets. Outside the cabaret, motor cars and taxis were lined against the curb and there was a babble of song and laughter in the grill in the basement."

Each step along the primrose path to the pistol shot in 508 was described in this fascinating style. With so many interesting things going on, the reader was left to wonder how anyone could contemplate suicide.

Pendergast also figured in the Twelfth Street activity, which was more extensive and varied than the night life on Sixth Street. He started with ownership of a saloon on East Twelfth and another on West Twelfth and became the proprietor of the street's best-known saloon when he purchased the Schattner brothers' three-door dispensary of cheer at 5 West Twelfth. This oasis in the heart of the business and theatrical district was celebrated not only for its service but its social standing. For twenty-five years it had been the property of a prominent Republican family under whose direction it negotiated a gentleman's agreement with the ministerial brotherhood to observe Sunday closing—one of the earliest and most notable gains for reform on Twelfth Street. After Pendergast purchased it, the saloon continued to give excellent service and became political headquarters for the society dedicated to the cause of keeping reform away.

The Twelfth Street battle against the change that was coming was led by Pendergast's friend and political ally, Joe Donegan, who managed a theatrical hotel, the Edward. In connection with the hotel, Joe ran the Edward Grill or Cabaret and the Century Burlesque Theater. Joe was a sentimental reactionary who often declared that the three great evils of the twentieth century were Prohibition, Vaudeville and the Movies. He lost a fortune and broke his heart opposing them.

Donegan resorted to various expedients to keep burlesque going as the true dramatic art of the people. He was responsible for that great innovation, smoking in the theater, and he pioneered in staging boxing exhibitions as added attractions. When those novelties failed to revive the popular taste for variety shows, Joe introduced lady wrestling matches with a special riot squad included. One of his backstage assistants for a time was the redoubtable Frank James, reformed train robber and brother of immortal Jesse who once lived in Kansas City under various aliases. The combined Donegan activity has been best described as the Uplift by the late Steve O'Grady, writer and troubadour who made an extensive study of the performance when he was a reporter for the *Star*. Joe Donegan himself was the spirit of the Uplift and his followers called him the

King of Twelfth Street and also the Angel of Twelfth Street in recognition of his free-spending and easy-lending ways.

Joe's work for burlesque and humanity has been forgotten, but his pioneering in the cabaret started something that had long-range political and social consequences. Tom Pendergast's assistants at the Jefferson Hotel copied the cabaret routine and developed it into a political issue for several seasons. This evolution began in the basement of Donegan's Edward Hotel. It started when Joe opened a basement room as a place where the showgirls who lived in his hotel could get a glass of beer with a sandwich, after the theater closed. At that time it was against the law to serve liquor to women in public and the Donegan retreat appealed to many other ladies besides showgirls. They crowded in with their escorts and Joe put in a piano and hired a hunchback, called the Squirrel, to play it. The music, the beer and the food did the rest. He expanded the place, introduced a good floor show and a large orchestra, and the cabaret became the popular resort of the theatrical district.

Politically, the thing about the cabaret that was disturbing was that it provided a popular way to circumvent the old social taboo and law which imposed on women the awful indignity of not being allowed to get tight with their men in public, and it also gave encouragement to the dance craze which alarmed the puritans in the years before the First World War. Pendergast's Jefferson Cabaret became the outstanding exhibit of this trend, provoking agitation that continued until it produced one of the major struggles of his first years as a political boss.

The public scandal which the reformers created over the cabaret has discouraged historians from making an adequate appraisal of the old grill as a social institution. America's habits were altered in several ways in those exciting basement rooms, and not the least consequential result was the grill's effect on the nation's ear for music. To this day, no one has given proper credit to Joe Donegan and Tom Pendergast for their aid in ushering in the crooner and the torch song, without which it is difficult to imagine how Americans could have withstood the strain of Prohibition, two world wars, the collapse of machine government and various other disorders. The old master of crooning, according to some authorities, is Tommy Lyman, who coined the term "torch" and charmed the crowds in the Jefferson Carbaret with his singing before he went on to fame in the cafés of Paris and New York. His theme song is "My Melancholy Baby," a light blues number that received its finishing touches in the Edward Cabaret where its composer, Ernie Burnett, was musical director for several years before the First World War. Another famous song of this period is Euday Bowman's "Twelfth Street Rag," which was composed in a Twelfth Street honky-tonk patronized by gamblers and politicians. The spirit of the buoyant and sentimental time when Donegan and Pendergast ran the Free and Easy is embalmed in those two old numbers.

There were various other fascinating novelties and innovations in the cabaret, along with operations of the kind that aroused newspaper editors, politicians, W.C.T.U. members and professional snoopers. None of this foolishness bothered Tom Pendergast himself for some time. The Jefferson was strictly a business proposition with him. He maintained his political headquarters in the hotel, working in a small office off the lobby, and left the details of the hotel's management to others. He had no ear for music and he wasn't the dancing type. After his marriage in 1907, he settled down fast as a family man. He went home early at night and was sleeping the sound sleep of a solid citizen when the rounders in the cabarets were attempting to attain a new level of befuddlement.

Pendergast met the attacks of the reformers with patience and good humor for several years. In 1916, he found it more difficult to treat the opposition lightly, for in that year the drys staged a mammoth parade under the direction of the W.C.T.U., which was followed by an election in which Jackson County voted for statewide Prohibition for the first time in its history. Thanks to the voting strength of the beer swillers of St. Louis, the Prohibition proposal was defeated in the state but it was obvious that the white ribbon wearers were becoming irresistible.

The Boss's uneasiness over the future of his hotel, cabaret and liquor operations was heightened by the activities of a busybody named Nat Spencer who made a career out of private supervision of the public morals. Spencer conducted his reform work as secretary of the Society for the Suppression of Commercialized Vice. He devoted major attention to the harassment of the Jefferson Hotel and Cabaret, which reached its climax in the final triumphant movement for the dry law.

Spencer was a tireless investigator, persisting in the face of long dis-

couragement from the police, who were unimpressed by his reports of
improper activities at the Jefferson. His campaign was helped along by
occasional disturbances at the hotel, among them the previously mentioned incident of the woman in Room 508 who shot herself, the slugging
of a railroadman who alleged he was attacked when he left the cabaret
after resisting two persistent ladies who were attempting to take his
dough, a fist fight in the hotel washroom and the slaying of a youth by
the Jefferson houseman, who said the unfortunate fellow was a bandit
who had tried to hold up a poker game on the fifth floor of the hotel.
The Jefferson bar license was suspended for a week following the washroom brawl and this was followed by a more determined assault in which
a ministerial and W.C.T.U. delegation joined Spencer, going before the
Police Board to demand action against the Jefferson. This agitation, combined with the clamor raised by the *Star,* brought about a reorganization
in the Police Department in 1918.

In the same year that the anti-Jefferson crusaders disturbed the control
of the Police Department, the drys carried the day in Jackson County
for a second time in the statewide contest over Prohibition. The St. Louis
wets again kept the state from adopting the proposition but the margin
of victory was very discouraging to an observant politician with large
liquor interests.

Perhaps the most irritating thing to Pendergast in all the reform agitation was the action of Joe Shannon, his factional rival, who added his
voice to the chorus against the Jefferson. Joe, as usual, could tell which
way the wind was blowing. He also had a jealous proprietary attitude
toward the name of Jefferson, regarding himself as the spiritual heir of
the Jefferson tradition in these parts and the proper custodian of the
Jefferson legend. He let it be known that he felt that Tom Pendergast,
who was a Jacksonian rather than a Jeffersonian, was bringing dishonor
to the name of our Third President through the notoriety of Pendergast's
hotel and cabaret. Joe's Rabbits made much of the point that they had
their headquarters in a drugstore while the Goats had their seat of command in a saloon. Tom's irritation over these didoes of the Rabbits hadn't
settled when the reformers stirred him to wrath by questioning his patriotism. The drys charged that the breweries and distilleries interfered
with the war effort, using manpower, fuel and supplies that were needed

for military production. Pendergast's enemies elaborated on this argument, declaring he was handling "unpatriotic German beer"—a beer that was brewed in Milwaukee.

The combined effect of these blows opened Pendergast's eyes to the approaching disaster, and he quietly disposed of his liquor interests before the crash came. The wartime Prohibition act was adopted November 21, 1918, when the people still were whooping it up in the saloons over the signing of the Armistice, ten days earlier. It became operative June 30, 1919, to last until the completion of demobilization. Few politicians or saloonkeepers believed the drought would last long and there were confident predictions that a national reaction would immediately set in. Pendergast did not share that view and turned his attention to the commercial prospects in mineral-water sales while the Prohibitionists proceeded to obtain ratification of the Eighteenth Amendment in a whirlwind tour of the states.

Prohibition killed the Jefferson and the Edward and a lot of other gay places. Many saloonkeepers and cabaret operators were ruined financially and never recovered, but Pendergast went through the emergency in excellent condition. He was able to dispose of the Jefferson Hotel with the assistance of the city government, which suddenly got around to ordering an important civic improvement, widening Sixth Street to a point where it took in a corner of the Goat boss's hotel, for which he was awarded $79,550 in 1919. The foreman of the condemnation jury, a Pendergast lieutenant, pointed out that the price allowed was larger than the amount that Tom had asked. He mentioned this as an illustration of Mr. Pendergast's moderation where his own and the public's interests were involved. It also served as a timely example of Pendergast foresight and luck.

The saloons closed "forever," January 16, 1920—actually for thirteen years, eleven months and eleven days. Anyone who soberly watched the spectacle of the final night in the saloons, grills and hotels could tell that this was not the last revel before the age of national sobriety dawned, but the beginning of a time of tremendous unrest and confusion. The sense of foreboding was wide and deep but no one guessed the disturbance would be as bad as it actually was. Tom Pendergast may not have shared these misgivings. It is not known how he spent that long evening when the nation said farewell to booze, but he had more reason than most people to celebrate. His investments were secure, he had made a good start in lines of business that would prove to be more profitable than liquor dealing, and his political organization was intact. The reformers had given him a beating and driven him out of the business which was a part of the family's tradition, but the chief result of their efforts was the creation of conditions that hurried him on the way to wealth and power.

3 *Boom Time*

DEMOCRACY, INC.

MICHAEL J. PENDERGAST contributed belligerency, fanaticism and incorporation to the Goat organization. Although he played second fiddle to his older and younger brothers, Jim and Tom, he was a major factor in building and operating the machine in the two periods dominated by the other members of the family. A monopolist at heart, he was the first ward leader to operate under a charter from the courts with his Tenth Ward Democratic Club, Inc. He pioneered in the development of voting-line tactics at the polls and was forward in corporate enterprise in other businesses besides politics.

Mike made himself the undisputed master of the Bloody Tenth and the pleasure he derived from surveying his domain was spoiled only by the proximity of the Ninth Ward, which was the home and stronghold of his immortal enemy, Joe Shannon, the Rabbit leader. Mike engaged in a long but disappointing effort to convert the Ninth into an adjunct of the Bloody Tenth.

The principle of compromise, particularly compromise with Rabbits, was regarded by Mike as one of the main fallacies of democratic doctrine. Although he went along with his two brothers when at various times they decided that Fifty-Fifty was an advantageous proposition, Mike consistently preached the extermination of all Rabbits. The depth of his feeling in this matter was revealed in a campaign in which the Rabbits joined forces with the Ku Klux Klan to down the Goats. Addressing a group of his Irish followers, Mike uttered a memorable expression of Goat contempt for anti-Catholic yahoos and concluded: "Gentlemen, I'd

sooner believe a Klansman than any Rabbit of the Rabbit faction. They
want everything."

The founder of Democracy, Inc. was in a combative mood all the time
or so it seemed to people who didn't get along with the Goats. When
things were too peaceful and dull, he stirred up the animals—the Rabbits
—just for the exercise. One Saturday afternoon he stepped into a Fifteenth Street saloon that was a Rabbit hangout. Inside were ten robust
trenchermen of the enemy who eyed him suspiciously and squared off
for trouble. Mike advanced to the bar and pleasantly invited the Rabbits
to join him in a drink of beer. The surprised loafers lined up at the bar
and stood with their glasses watching Mike while he raised his glass in a
toast to Fifty-Fifty. When they lifted their glasses to drink, Mike hurled
the contents of his glass in their faces. He didn't have a chance to escape
and took a severe beating. "But it was worth it," he said afterward.

Mike infused the whole Goat organization with his gay spirit, generated much of the wild elation that swept the boys on election day and
made the guarding of polling places a dramatic event. One of his effective
devices was the double line at the polls, a gantlet that sometimes extended for hundreds of feet and was filled with men and women trained
in the ways of persuasion. The chief of the Bloody Tenth was a strategist
who observed the old Confederate admonition to get there "fustest with
the mostest." Pendergast voting lines formed the night before election
in districts where the contest was hot. On occasions when the enemy stole
a march and formed its lines first, the Pendergast flying wedge went into
action and usually managed to recover any lost positions.

When the evangelist and disciplinarian of the Goats wasn't cast down
by grief over a Rabbit victory or some similar trespass, he was lifted up
by the sense of glory in the fellowship of the Goats. No call of distress
from anyone whose name was on the golden roster of the Bloody Tenth's
brotherhood could go ignored. Mike devoted both time and money to
the perpetuation of this legend, and was resourceful in finding ways to
ballyhoo his unique society. He got national publicity for the Tenth
Ward Democratic Club, Inc., in 1923 when it went to the rescue of Oklahoma's Jack Walton, about to be impeached as governor. Walton's enemies in the Legislature cast aspersions on his Democratic standing and
the Governor, a Kansas City product, confounded them by producing a

membership card signed by Mike Pendergast. In honor of this loyal son who was upholding the Pendergast prestige in foreign lands, Mike ordered a special convocation of the boys, at which suitable speeches of confidence were given, resolutions adopted and $250 raised for the Walton defense fund. This did not save Walton but it entertained the Goats and impressed everyone with the wonder of Pendergast fealty.

Along with his many other interests, Mike Pendergast was an inveterate public servant and it was in this capacity that he was most useful to the House. He served variously as clerk of the Circuit Court, license inspector and city clerk, and the duties of these offices gave him a chance to observe closely the way business is operated and enabled him to put a finger in many pies.

All of these activities and interests laid the basis for the Pendergast expansion in other lines of business when the saloon industry failed and the income from public officeholding proved inadequate to satisfy the growing needs and ambitions of the Pendergasts and their associates. Both Tom and Mike were energetic and resourceful in the corporate field and each acquired the dignity and title of "business executive" to go with their growing political importance. Mike became president of the Eureka Petroleum Company, specializing in selling oil supplies to local government agencies and concerns that cultivated Democratic popularity. Tom took a hand in various enterprises, devoting his main attention to the sale of concrete to politically wise contractors.

Mike's service did not end with his work as an organizer, enforcer of loyalty, promoter of monopoly in business and political affairs and innovator of Democracy, Inc. He kept alive the family's dynastic idea that began with Alderman Jim, King of the First, and provided the House of Pendergast with an heir—his son Jim, who was named for the founder.

The permanent chairman of the Tenth Ward Democratic Club, Inc. suffered from only one frustration. He went through life burdened by the knowledge that he was not an orator. Mike finally worked up courage to make his premiere in 1923 as a Democratic Demosthenes before the Ninth Ward Democratic Club, Inc. which he had established in Shannon's preserve. The chairman introduced him in glowing words to an admiring audience, but Mike was overcome by stage fright and unable to rise to his feet. The elocutionary honor of the Pendergasts was saved by his son, Jimmy, who closed the meeting with a few characteristic remarks.

"We are but a minority now," said James, "but we will be an organized minority, and the day will come when the organized minority will become the organized majority."

Young Jim prophesied truly.

DEMOCRATIC AID SOCIETY

THE ADROITNESS of the Pendergast command was demonstrated most impressively in the period when the Goats were turning from the organized minority into the organized majority. Although Boss Tom was in fundamental agreement with Brother Mike's all-for-one ideal, he did not completely or prematurely abandon the methods of compromise, and several of the successful operations of this time were based on the beautiful principle of collaboration. The most remarkable one was the Democratic Aid Society affair, which was carried out in a fashion that should favorably impress current experts in the field of political co-operation.

Democratic Aid Society was the name given by the *Star* Republicans to a rival faction in the G.O.P. which contended for party supremacy in Kansas City for some time, the contest reaching its high point in the first two years of the 1920's. The so-called Aid Society fellows also were designated as the Boss Republicans by the element which the *Star* backed. Whether these Boss Republicans earned the Democratic Aid label chiefly because they worked with or for Tom Pendergast, or mostly because they obstructed and threatened to eclipse the *Star* Republicans, is a question that has never been entirely settled. It is clear, however, that this imbroglio did give great delight and comfort to all classes of Democrats, who could see nothing but right and good in the idea of Republicans serving their Democratic superiors.

Although Tom Pendergast may not have had as much to do with Democratic Aid as the so-called anti-boss Republicans charged, he was in fact a large beneficiary of this movement. The legend that he had a numerous company of Republican politicians in his service grew through the years. It was said that this element in the G.O.P. conspired to offer weak candidates in opposition to Democrats; that it worked to place docile or friendly Republican members on the bi-partisan Police and Election boards and co-operated in other ways in exchange for favors. Throughout the Pendergast reign, there were various incidents and situations which heightened or confirmed suspicions of extensive connivance between politicians of the rival parties. In addition to receiving such direct aid, the Democratic boss profited from the public cynicism, apathy and sense of helplessness over machine politics that were induced by the widespread talk of collaboration behind the scenes. The popular attitude was expressed in the frequently heard comment that Republican politicians differed in no way from machine Democrats, except that they obviously were not so smart.

Republican leaders recognized the harm done their cause by such gossip and were chary about publicly airing charges of collusion with the enemy, so it is possible that this intrigue might have remained for the most part an open secret if the factional rivalry in the G.O.P. had not flared beyond control. This crisis was provoked by the rise of Tom Marks, who originally appeared on the scene as a cleanup police commissioner for Governor Hadley and as the Republican who was going to take the measure of the Pendergasts on the North Side. Mr. Marks retired from the police commissionership with considerable prestige and influence and progressed so fast that he alarmed some members of his own party. But for some time before this schism developed all Republicans seemed pleased over the Marks success in raiding the river ward precincts that traditionally belonged to the Goats. It was the Republican Tom rather than the Democratic Tom who appeared likely to become the top man on the North Side, or so the Republicans said.

Republican happiness over the new turn of events had largely evaporated by 1920, when the faction opposed to Marks staged an uprising. These insurgents had received a rude shock when aldermen loyal to Marks voted with the Democrats to elect a Pendergast lieutenant to fill a Council seat vacated by a Republican before his term expired. They asserted that the Marks men had voted with the Democratic aldermen on every commercial measure coming before the council in four years, obtaining some nice plums for the business interests and making a farce of some of the Council sessions.

Anti-boss Republicans declared that Marks's henchmen conferred nightly with Democratic leaders in a Broadway buffet. On Council night the members of the Society—four out of five of the Republican members of the lower house and several Republicans in the upper house—caucused at a downtown restaurant to get their orders for the evening's performance at the formal meeting of the Council. Then, fortified with liquor, food, good humor and benevolence, they marched to the City Hall to operate the steamroller.

Showdown stage in the G.O.P. factional row was reached in the spring of 1920 when the anti-Marks Republicans seized control of the party's city convention and nominated their ticket, headed by a crusader whom the Democrats denounced with righteous passion as the *Star*'s "silk underwear" candidate. The newspaper had made potent use of the Democratic Aid label in downing the rival party faction in the primary campaign, and it charged that Pendergast tried to save Marks by sending his followers to vote in the Republican primary for Marks delegates to the city convention. However, it appeared that more voters objected to silk underwear than Democratic Aid, for in the final election the Democrats swept the field. Their own factional breach had been closed with the return to the fold of Joe Shannon under Fifty-Fifty.

It soon became evident that in this set-to the ruling cliques were fighting over something more than City Hall peanuts, as the Democratic Aid contest was resumed with greater vigor in the August primary campaign, in which the *Star* again reported that Pendergast meddled for Marks, and again the anti-boss group triumphed, winning control of the Republican County Committee. Pendergast's desire to help Marks at this point was understandable, for the Republican North Side boss was trying to hold the line in Jackson County against the *Star*'s hero, Arthur Mastick Hyde of Trenton, Missouri. He roared on the scene in the 1920 primary to win the Republican nomination for governor, starting a long career that seemed especially designed to irritate Jackson County Democrats.

Art Hyde made Pendergastism one of his chief targets and announced that, if elected governor, he would fire the Kansas City Police Board every thirty days if necessary to make the cleanup thoroughly pleasing to his fellow Republicans and Methodists. Alarm in Kansas City Democratic circles grew apace as the politicians watched Mr. Hyde win in the Republican primary by neatly skinning the favorite fence straddler of the St. Louis G.O.P. machine, who tripped over the dry issue while waving the flag in one hand and the Constitution in the other. Hyde was the kind of prohibitionist who infuriated abstinence men of the Pendergast and Shannon type. The blood of the pioneer Sons of Temperance ran in his veins. He came from Grundy County, the home county of the Spickardsville Crusaders, a band of ladies who introduced the hatchet-and-rake-swinging tactic to dry uplift ten years before Carrie Nation started out to wreck the bars in Kansas. With Mr. Hyde denouncing Kansas City bossism and sin in tones that left no doubts about his intentions, the Democrats called on their hatchet man, Jim Reed, and instructed him to cut the Grundy County flash down to size. The Stormy Petrel entered upon this task with great relish.

"Hyde," snorted Jim, "comes from a hick town. He isn't city broke."

Hyde's home did indeed have an exceptional claim to fame in this regard. Historians have traced the mythical community of Poosey, traditional home of the rubes, to Grundy County. It is located somewhere near Trenton, but no one has ever found it as it always is around the next bend in the road, over the next hill. So Jim Reed was merely touching a point of civic pride when he called Hyde a hick.

"Bridlewise Jim," retorted Art Hyde, "complains because I am not city broke. We of the hick towns call a horse bridlewise when he responds easily, canters, trots or gallops at the slightest touch of the reins. Jim Reed is bridlewise."

Once they got warmed up, their slugging match ran on for years, settling nothing but providing vast merriment for the electorate. Republicans thought that Hyde's sarcasm was immensely superior to Reed's invective and they found that he had a gift for delicate imagery. One delightful example was his likening the golden stream of Reed oratory to a muddy creek in floodtime overflowing into a hog wallow. Democrats thought that Reed had the last word when, after much thought and straining, he described the mellow Hyde bass as "the steam whistle on a fertilizer factory."

Long before this debate died down, Art Hyde was in the governor's chair, keeping his word to put the lid on wicked Kansas City in the long and painful police reform of 1921-22. During this time the Democratic Aid issue remained alive, as Tom Marks was fighting vigorously to make a comeback. The political competition took a sensational turn in the episode of the *Sunday Spotlight,* a clandestine publication which scandalized Republicans and built up circulation by championing the cause of Denny Chester, a police character who was tried for the murder of an heiress, Florence Barton. She was shot in a parked motor car one night while accompanied by her fiancé. Chester's defense contended that he was the victim of a frameup engineered by a private detective agency, and won a speedy acquittal for him at a trial in 1921 that produced many lurid and bizarre incidents. Spectators were searched for weapons before entering the courtroom. Chester baffled medical authorities and the prosecution by losing his voice, saying nary a word throughout this storm. The *Sunday Spotlight* provided more than enough clamor for him, accompanying accounts of his martyrdom with broadsides against the *Star,* the anti-Marks Republicans, the Hyde police and various crusaders in the community until it finally was suppressed by the county authorities as a scandal sheet.

Although by this time Tom Marks was on the way out of the political picture, the family quarrel in the G.O.P. still ran strong, for it had broadened to include many other matters besides the original Democratic Aid. The faction to which Marks belonged had important connections over the state and influence in Washington, and there were others in it besides Marks who hoped to take over direction of Republican affairs in Kansas City. Its outstanding local ornament was Walter S. Dickey, millionaire claypipe manufacturer, who entered the publishing field in opposition to the *Star,* and devoted his best efforts to the work of trying to save the Republican Party from the influence of Governor Hyde.

Dickey turned to politics and publishing for relief from the dull routine of amassing millions, and succeeded only in getting rid of his money. In 1916 he ran for senator and was beaten by Jim Reed. However, he made such a good showing against the Democratic champion that he never got over the notion he was destined to be a statesman. Needing an organ to further his political ambitions, he purchased the *Kansas City Journal,* a pioneer newspaper which had come on bad days and which he picked up in 1921 at a fire sale for one hundred thousand dollars. A friendly banker warned Mr. Dickey that he would lose his shirt in this venture, but the claypipe man went ahead in his stubborn way and was credited with dropping eight million dollars or so in the newspaper hopper before he died.

The *Star* publishes both a morning and an evening paper and Mr. Dickey felt that he, too, needed to be heard twice daily, so in 1922 he purchased the *Kansas City Post* from Bonfils and Tammen, the Katzenjammer Kids of Denver journalism. Bon and Tam had invaded the Kansas City field in 1909 with a silent partner later identified as J. Ogden Armour, directing magnate of the streetcar railway and electric light systems. This swashbuckling team conducted a noisy, colorful, libelous and unsuccessful effort to break the *Star* monopoly and were glad to unload on Dickey for $1,250,000. Mr. Dickey ran the *Post* and the *Journal* as respectable sheets, as was becoming a man of his dignity, social standing and Republican conservatism. Although he was unable to offer the *Star* much competition in advertising and circulation, the new publisher succeeded in making himself a power in the Republican Old Guard in the Harding period.

The Dickey-Marks crowd ran a pipeline to the White House through one of its local worthies, the extraordinary E. Mont Reily. E. Mont made history by climbing on the Harding bandwagon when he was all alone there. He was the original Harding man, distinguished among politicians for his powers of intuition. He started getting flashes of coming presidential events when he was a boy in Texas and was the first person to suggest Harrison for President in 1888, according to his own account. He did the same thing for McKinley. He announced himself as the original Hughes man in 1916. He wanted to be the original Vandenberg man in 1936 but the Michigan Senator, probably recalling E. Mont's part in the Harding business, hastily deflated this boom from Kansas City.

E. Mont saw the Harding handwriting on the wall one night while he was lying in bed. He awakened his wife with the exclamation, "I have found the man," and immediately wrote Harding a letter describing his vision and congratulating the Ohio Senator on his forthcoming elevation.

When Harding came through Kansas City on a swing around the country just before the "smoke-filled room" convention in Chicago, the chances for Normalcy didn't look any better than one to one thousand to anyone except Mr. Reily, who was the only Kansas City politician to meet the Senator at the Union Station. He arranged a party for the lonely Ohioan, introducing him to Dickey and other Old Guard cronies. Harding was grateful and after his election he allowed E. Mont to advise in Missouri patronage matters and rewarded him further by appointing him governor general of Puerto Rico.

Both the Puerto Rican and the Democratic Aid Society episodes were closed at about the same time. Tom Marks's last attempt to recover power in the Republican County Committee was put down in the August primary of 1922. E. Mont Reily found the Puerto Ricans unappreciative of his efforts to bring Kansas City civilization to their backward island, and he stepped out as governor general after the natives had kicked up a storm that was heard in Washington. He returned to Missouri to resume his work with the Republican Old Guard and found various things to do while waiting for another hunch on a presidential boom.

Tom Marks and many other Boss Republican figures passed from the scene, and the reorganized G.O.P. tried to bury the ghost of the Democratic Aid Society but was troubled by Republican involvement in Pendergast politics to the last days of the machine.

Retiring the Little Czar

In those days when he was laying the basis for Goat supremacy, Tom Pendergast cleared the field for himself by greasing the skids for a fractious sub-chieftain, Miles Bulger, and jockeying his principal Democratic rival, Shannon, out of position. In the first of these undertakings the Goat boss had the good wishes of the *Star* for at the time Bulgerism was more distasteful than Pendergastism to the Republican taxpayers.

Miles Bulger brought out the best and the worst in Tom Pendergast. He had that effect on many men, but the reaction was more spectacular in the case of Big Tom. Miles was a little man who made a big splash, a bantam who ran with the large roosters. His bright plumage, his strutting and crowing were both impressive and amusing. For twelve years he enlivened the aldermanic sessions with his quips and antics. His work for machine government has been forgotten, but one of his utterances still is remembered and quoted, more than thirty years after it was first delivered. It was tossed off one day when the Honorable Mr. Bulger refused to attend a ceremony at the Kansas City Art Institute.

"Art," said Alderman Bulger, "is on the bum in Kansas City."

This authoritative appraisal was greeted with hilarious appreciation in all quarters, but particularly on Twelfth Street. For some time the boys in the downtown saloons and poolhalls had looked with misgivings at the progress of things esthetic on the South Side and Bulger's comment served as a timely statement of their opinion.

Pendergast hoped to use Bulger to break the Shannon hold on the Courthouse. He backed Bulger for presiding judge of the County Court and then sat back to enjoy the show.

Tom's pleasure in this maneuver was short lived. Miles had large ideas of his own and his sense of importance was based on a record of considerable achievement. Starting out as a plumber's apprentice, he had forged ahead rapidly in both political life and business. He became a wealthy man through his operations in the construction field as one of the owners of a cement company. His skill as a political organizer brought him recognition as the Little Czar of the Second Ward. With his elevation to the County Court, an office carrying authority over the administrative affairs of the county, he seemed to feel that he was in a strategic position to set himself up as one of the big bosses.

Republican critics of Bulger's regime made "road cinch," "pie-crust" paving and "deficit" familiar terms to the Jackson County voters. The deficit in the road and bridge fund ran beyond a million dollars. Bulger's extravagance didn't upset Pendergast, but the Little Czar and the Rabbits worked together too well to suit some of the Goats. Important members of the Goat faction complained that Bulger monopolized the patronage and business favors in the county and warned the Boss that the Little Czar was double-crossing him, but Pendergast was slow to believe it. Pendergast put down a revolt in his faction to elect Bulger for a second term and went to his assistance to checkmate a grand jury investigation of the handling of road funds. But Bulger continued to build up his monopoly and run with the Rabbits, and the break came when he flopped to the Shannon faction in a dispute over the control of some sixty road overseers, the bulwark of the county machine. He followed that by supporting a candidate for governor in opposition to Pendergast's choice and climaxed his defiance by proclaiming that he was going to take over the Boss's seat at a time when Pendergast was dangerously ill from a mastoid infection.

To carry out the work of ridding the world of Bulgerism, Mike and Tom Pendergast made two of their most celebrated selections of winners. For one of the places on the Jackson County Court in 1922, they picked Henry F. McElroy, who later drew national attention as the despotic city manager of Kansas City, the official spokesman of the machine and the chief engineer of the municipal steamroller. For a second place on the County Court, the Goats backed Harry S. Truman of Independence, later United States Senator and Vice-President and now the President of the United States. They were nominated and elected and gave an efficient and economical administration of the County Court, cutting in half the $1,200,000 deficit which Bulger left.

The business of properly disposing of Miles Bulger remained unfinished, however, during all the time that McElroy and Truman worked together to restore Goat authority and prestige in the Courthouse. After leaving his county post, Bulger succeeded in getting himself elected to the state Legislature, through a beneficial redistricting which he had attended to while he was still presiding judge of the court. In the Legislature he amused himself thinking up measures designed to harass the Goats. Bulger remained annoyingly healthy and well to do. Cut out of big contracts by the political combine, he managed to keep his cement company going with the commercial contacts he had formed. It seemed that nothing less than the full treatment would suppress Miles Bulger, and this thought was impressed on the Goats in painful fashion one day in 1923, when the Little Czar used his fists to settle accounts with Judge Henry F. McElroy. The Judge, who was tall, muscular and alert, was reported by the *Star* to have suffered all the damage in this ruckus. Besides injuring the Goat dignity, this story aroused the Goat sense of injustice, for it explained that McElroy was attacked when his hands were in his pockets and the Little Czar's husky bodyguard stood by prepared to interfere if McElroy resisted.

The Bulger farewell in politics was a bum's rush in which the Pendergast and Bulger factions staged a classic exhibition of the "mob primary," the local institution perfected by the ward bosses to enable them to keep the party organization firmly in their hands. Under this system, delegates to the state convention of the party were nominated at mass meetings held in each ward or township. In some of these party contests packing-house rules prevailed and the voters who mixed in the affray had to be bold and strong.

The Goats had both passion and numbers on their side on the seventh of March, 1924, when their forces moved into the Second Ward stronghold of Miles Bulger. The voting was to take place in the evening at South Side courtroom, annex of the Nineteenth Street police station. Bulger was prepared for trouble, having recruited a strongarm squad headed by Oscar Benson, the Terrible and Unterrified Swede, who considered himself a match for the Terrible Solly Weissman, mastodonic champion of the Goat bruisers. But Miles depended on more than brawn to carry the battle. He had read of the Trojan War and his version of the wooden horse trick was a morning visit to the South Side court by sixty or so men and women from his headquarters. They sat through the morning proceedings and when court adjourned at noon they remained in their seats. They intended to stay until evening, holding the line against the Goats. The police judge ordered them to leave but they refused to budge. He called attendants to oust them and there was a tussle in which a clerk of the court got clipped on the jaw. Then the judge ordered the crowd locked in.

In the afternoon the Pendergast forces gathered outside the building and milled around when they found the doors locked. The Bulgerites inside stood at the windows and hooted at them. The Goats shouted insults and threats in return. Miles Bulger arrived with his bodyguard to survey the situation and found everything going according to plan. He swaggered about, ignoring the hisses from the Goats in the line surrounding the building, waving at his followers inside, who cheered him. He ordered coffee and sandwiches sent in to the gallant band holding the fort, and retired to his headquarters on the West Side Hill to direct the final action.

Bulger's major stroke was delivered at dusk, shortly before the court was to be opened at seven o'clock for the voting. To the relief of his besieged followers he sent an army several hundred strong. Leading the band was a mangy donkey, escorted by the Terrible and Unterrified Swede Benson himself. When the Bulger army approached the court building, the Goat warriors locked arms.

"Hold that line," shouted Aldermen William Flynn and William E. Kehoe, Pendergast lieutenants in charge of the Goat army of men and women.

"Break that line," the Bulgerites shouted.

The Terrible Solly was looking for the Terrible Swede, but before this desirable meeting could take place the police seized the Swede and his donkey. It required the services of forty stout police officers to separate the partisans. One man was shot. Three men were badly cut up. Women fainted. The son of Alderman Flynn suffered a knife wound in the throat which required thirty-nine stitches. He exemplified the political fortitude of the Goats by announcing he would be out of the hospital to vote in the city election five days later.

Solly Weissman was among the fifteen battlers arrested on the scene. He continued the struggle in the police holdover and was testing his weight against four men when officers interfered and sent him to a separate cell.

Fifteen minutes after the fight outside the South Side court started, the Goats were in complete command of the situation and their delegates were named. Five days later they won the Second Ward again in the city primary. The Bulgerites planned to rush the polls to vote for their own delegates to the city convention, but turned back when they found a long double line of Goats waiting for them.

Pendergast had decreed political exile for the Little Czar and the sentence was final but Miles couldn't quit without another gesture. He attended a party of his followers and danced for the first time in twenty-five years to exhibit his lightheartedness. Then he joined Joe Shannon in the climactic struggle between the Rabbit and Goat factions that developed almost immediately after the mob primary and reached a fateful decision in the fall campaign. In this endeavor he was able to extract a moment of delicious revenge—but it was only a moment.

LITTLE TAMMANY

CAS WELCH, the boss of Fifteenth Street, had to do some heavy thinking after Miles Bulger was eliminated for the Little Czar's fall brought up the question of the Welch future in a very pressing fashion. In thirty years of steady advancement as a politician, businessman and dispenser of Rabbit justice, Cas had not faced so weighty a problem as this one: Where would he stand in the final conflict between Joe Shannon and Tom Pendergast? That showdown engagement developed swiftly in the summer of 1924, roaring to a double climax in the August primary and the November general election.

Judge Welch was a personal friend and sometime business associate of Pendergast. He was the protégé and chief lieutenant of Joe Shannon. Joe had picked him when he was eighteen for the role he was to play, showing rare judgment, for Cas became the most useful ally of the Rabbit chieftain, the one who held the line in the city against the encroaching Pendergast faction. The Welch organization by 1924 had grown to a size where Cas could consider the advantages of setting himself up as an independent boss.

Boss Shannon doubtless knew what Boss Welch would do in this situation, and Boss Pendergast surely had a good idea of what to expect. The answer was, of course, that Mr. Welch would do whatever was good for Cas and his boys, regardless of personal, factional or party allegiances. The boss of Fifteenth Street played machine politics more primitively and openly than either Pendergast or Shannon. His headquarters was called Little Tammany in recognition of the fact that it was a perfect model of the New York organization of the days of Tweed and Croker. An old garage building served as the control center for two important wards in a business and residential area bordering the downtown section. The job of serving the political needs of this region required the services of a man of many talents, for the Little Tammany district contained most of the elements that go to make the modern city a bewildering complex. The boss had to work with important commercial interests and at the same time satisfy a large population of native whites mixed with Negro and foreign-born groups who existed on the subsistence level.

Welch rose to power administering justice, after he had won some political recognition through his Irish geniality and pugnacity. His fighting ability when he was a boy impressed Kansas City's First Citizen, William Rockhill Nelson, who looked on appreciatively while young Cas thrashed a rival newsboy who was trying to muscle in on his corner. Colonel Nelson offered the winner a job as office boy at the *Star* but Cas, for some unexplained reason, refused the golden opportunity for journalistic fame and fortune.

The hero of Little Tammany figured so frequently and spectacularly in fist fights that many people got the idea that he owed his success largely, if not entirely, to his athletic prowess. Cas had many engaging qualities besides skill in slugging. He was recognized early as a natural leader of men and a favorite of the ladies. No party of the Little Rosebud Club or the Lady Boilermakers was a success without the presence of this smiling, magnetic, flashily dressed Irishman.

Although his formal schooling ended when he was nine, Cas quickly learned enough to qualify himself as a justice of the peace in a court where the wisdom of Solomon and the patience of Job were needed every day. Judge Welch didn't have a lawyer's degree—fortunately for him none was required by the law—but he had the judicial temperament without the legal solemnity. Justice rather than dignity was his ideal. He made that plain at the start, posting a set of rules that pleased the proletarians in his district and amused members of the Kansas City Bar Association. Cas didn't like lawyers at the moment and his first rule read:

"My idea of a justice mill is a place where people can get justice without a lawyer declaring himself in on it. I'm not going to run this court for the lawyers."

Rule 2: "I don't know what's in the books but I can read a man's face as good as the chief justice of the supreme court."

Rule 3 warned the corporations that they would not be able to deprive the poor man of justice in this court. "A lot of people have been bluffed out of court. No bluffs will go here."

Rule 4: "People won't have to have a lawyer to get justice here. I'll be their lawyer."

Rule 5: "There are too many delays and continuances in the law. They are part of the lawyer's game. Justice quick and cheap is my motto."

The Justice also announced that "no spitting will be tolerated." His regulations for sanitation and decorum in the courtroom were enforced with a tolerant hand, however, for the seekers of justice who came to him included many men whose democratic philosophy was inextricably bound up with spitting tobacco juice where they pleased. Among them, also, were a number whose passion for right demanded fistic expression and Cas's free legal counsel included expert services in separating brawling litigants.

Cas's prejudice against lawyers and his bias against corporations, did not mean that these individuals and interests could not get justice in his court. His sympathies were so broad that citizens of every class and condition received his earnest attention. An illustration of Cas's desire to see everybody happy was given in the case of two litigants, both of them deserving parties and each bearing a promise from the Judge that he would get justice. Cas did not realize the predicament he had placed himself in until the case was called and the two friends of the Court stood before him. Recovering quickly from his lapse, Judge Welch declared that this issue was of such a special nature that a change of venue to another court was required.

The J-P courts, as they were called, in this time were in very low public esteem. The *Star* promoted a constant crusade to abolish them, but made little progress, for the justice-of-peace-court system was deeply rooted in machine politics. Political lawyers, professional bondsmen and fixers operated openly in some of these tribunals which were once called "the poor man's court."

The reform agitators threatened to interrupt Cas Welch's career on the J-P bench when they organized a movement in the state legislature for adoption of a measure that would have required justices of the peace to have law degrees. That effort failed and Cas confounded his critics by introducing a private reform that improved his legal tone. Developing a studious bent, he took a short course in Blackstone and arranged a special examination for admission to the bar, which he passed with flying colors. He was a versatile citizen and he continued his work for practical justice for trouble-laden Fifteenth Street society while expanding his political duties and business interests.

Before he finished Welch had a sand company and interests in other concerns. He looked and dressed like a successful businessman and moved in the company of prominent citizens. He took up golf, gave up hard liquor and courted a genteel lady who had been a teacher of music and arts in the Kansas City schools. This woman supervised Cas's refinement, but her good work was interrupted one night when she committed suicide. Welch's enemies circulated the snide report that his teacher friend took her own life out of discouragement over Cas's backsliding and it was said that the Little Tammany boss grieved over this incident long afterward. It is easy to believe that Welch regretted many things in his life but it's a mistake to assume that he was lacking in a genuine desire to rise in the world's esteem. In fact, it may be said he was an exceptional success considering the environment and the system that produced him. Of those that grew up with Cas Welch in the hazardous society that created Little Tammany, hardly any had done well at all and no other did so well as Cas.

The keenness and ruthlessness of the competition were demonstrated in numerous impressive ways in the 1924 race when Welch found he must choose between Pendergast and Shannon. The break between the major bosses came six years after the old Fifty-Fifty arrangement between the Goats and Rabbits had been restored. Shannon had made a rapid comeback after 1920 and his demands for recognition and spoils indicated that he had not been sufficiently chastened by the knifing he received from Pendergast some years earlier.

The new factional war followed a Democratic defeat in the city election that came less than a month after the sad affair of Miles Bulger. Boss Tom Pendergast felt very bitter about that defeat, for which he blamed Shannon. The losing candidate, Mayor Frank Cromwell, was an amiable butter-and-egg man who suffered a spectacular decline in political popularity in a two-year turn in the City Hall. Shannon had insisted on his renomination in the face of Pendergast's warnings, and protests from even some elements of his own faction. The electorate's quick confirmation of Pendergast's judgment on Mayor Cromwell was accepted by the

North Side boss as final evidence that Shannon had lost his old political acumen as well as the right co-operative spirit. The difference between the bosses grew until it reached the point where Shannon determined on a full-scale assault in an effort to reassert Rabbit dominance over the Goats or at least to stem the onward march of Pendergast. He obviously sensed that this was his last chance to arrest the trend in favor of the North Side organization.

Shannon made his bid for state power with Floyd E. Jacobs of Kansas City as a candidate for the gubernatorial nomination while the Goats backed an outstate man, Dr. Arthur W. Nelson of Bunceton, for the place. Shannon offered a rival slate of candidates for county offices to restore Rabbit influence in the Courthouse, where the Goat prestige was flourishing under the administration of McElroy and Truman. Shannon's alarm over the recent vote trend was fully justified when the Goat county ticket won a complete victory and Dr. Nelson was nominated for governor. There was only one alternative left for Joe Shannon—he must resign himself permanently to a minor place in the machine or use the knife as Tom Pendergast had done eight years earlier.

The November election campaign presented a very confusing picture. Another large complication besides the Democratic factional dispute was the interference provided by the Ku Klux Klan. This hooded organization of religious bigotry, racial hatred and general human cussedness was in the height of its postwar revival. The confusion it created in Jackson County was heightened by the fact that the Klansmen in this region were not the ordinary one-hundred-per-cent Americans who were the Klan ideal. They were two-hundred-per-cent Americans, so aptly described in a popular joke of the period. They didn't hate just Catholics, Jews and Negroes. They hated everybody.

The Pendergasts declared that the Klan in Jackson County combined with the Republicans against the Kansas City Irish. Cas Welch refused to go along with this hated combination, deserting his old leader to stand with Pendergast. His Catholic and party loyalties figured in this decision, along with practical political foresight. Even if Shannon succeeded in his current maneuver, it was evident that he was slipping, for the basis of his power was disappearing with the whole county finding its center in the city. Logically Little Tammany belonged in an alliance with the city machine rather than the old county-boss faction.

In the last stand against this trend, Joe Shannon and Miles Bulger crossed the party line in November, delivering votes that helped to elect the Republican ticket to the county offices and put a Republican in the governor's chair. For Bulger, it was his moment of revenge. For Shannon, it was a brief reprieve. It would be four years before Pendergast would have another chance to promote a man for governor, two years before he could hope to recover control of the Courthouse. By this knifing, it appeared that Shannon was gaining enough time to rebuild his shattered organization for another round with Tom Pendergast. But his time had run out and he had permanently lost the services of Cas Welch, without whose aid he was never again in position to challenge Boss Tom.

The Goats were furious over Shannon's treachery and there was immediate talk of drastic reprisals. The only happy Democrat the morning after election was Miles Bulger. He read the news of the Goat debacle over his morning coffee. The sun was shining and the birds were singing when he left his home to go downtown to celebrate the victory with his few surviving followers. He had waited long for this day and meant to enjoy every minute of it. Waiting for a streetcar, Miles saw a battleship-gray limousine pull up at the curb. The tires screeched to a sudden halt, the car door swung open and there was Tom Pendergast, all two hundred and twenty-five pounds of him.

"Hello," said Tom in a tone that silenced the whistling birds and made Miles Bulger's world stand still. Mr. Pendergast also had waited long for this moment and his joyous anticipation of the next few minutes was obvious as he propelled his bulk toward the one hundred and thirty-five pound Bulger.

Miles had no time to think, but even in this emergency he displayed his characteristic wit and agility, raising hands to nose to thumb a last insult at the same time that he turned to run in the direction that Pendergast was going. Big Tom soon gave up the race and stood watching the former Little Czar disappear, marveling at his speed and the special dispensation that kept him just out of reach of Pendergast fists. Miles was still running several minutes later when a friend hailed him and asked where the fire was.

"Tom Pendergast," puffed Mr. Bulger. "He's got a gun." He didn't pause for further explanation.

The celebration over Tom Pendergast's defeat in 1924 was a very brief affair all around. On or about this day, the Goat boss scrapped Fifty-Fifty, leaving nothing for Shannon. Cas Welch would get whatever fraction Pendergast decided he should have. The day for the next act, which brought Big Tom to the center of the stage as the supreme boss of Kansas City, was much nearer than Joe Shannon or the Republican managers suspected.

THE NONPARTISAN CHARTER

IN THE WINTER of 1924-25, when the Coolidge inflation and Prohibition were beginning to hurry America's millions down the road toward financial and moral disaster, a band of earnest men ushered in what was declared to be a new era for municipal government in Kansas City. As a result of their efforts, the charter under which Kansas City now operates was adopted. This charter was designed as an instrument to toss the old political bosses in the ash can. By an ironic turn of political fortune, it actually introduced the long period of Pendergast boss rule.

The charter proponents were business and professional men, educators, ministers, club women and labor representatives who did not share the prevailing postwar cynicism over the condition of democracy in America. They believed that democracy as an agency of political government could be made to work, and even was working to some extent. Conspicuous among these optimists were R. E. McDonnell, head of the Charter League, and Walter Matscheck, director of the Kansas City Civic Research Institute.

Mr. McDonnell, a practical idealist, was the chief of an engineering firm which specialized in public utility projects for municipalities. He was one of the pioneers of the charter reform movement that grew out of the Nonpartisan agitation led by the *Star* under Nelson. Mr. Matscheck, a solemn academic gentleman, was a strange type on the local political stage. He came to Kansas City in 1918, with a degree from the University of Wisconsin, to head the Civic Research Institute, an organization with

no official standing which was supported financially by a small group of
business and professional men who were sympathetic to modern ideals
and impressed by scientific talk.

Mr. Matscheck's somewhat statistical style of oratory made an impression that alarmed a lot of politicians who were perfectly satisfied with
the state of democracy in the 1920's.

"The point is," Mr. Matscheck argued, "that the real business of government, particularly local government—the unit of the city—is not
governing in any strict sense. It is administering. It is doing work, carrying on operations like street cleaning, building sewers, putting out fires,
and so on. That's not a matter of political science, not of governing in
the older sense. It's administrative science, and that's where democracy
is working. The cities that have adopted the manager form of administration are showing the state and federal governments how democracy can
be made to work freed from the political machinery that has been built
up around them."

In other words, bureaucracy was preparing to save government of the
people, by and for the people. Mr. Matscheck had evidence to support his
case. The city manager system had a record of increasing success extending over a quarter-century. It had been adopted in hundreds of cities,
both large and small, where it created city councils that were thoroughly
representative through nonpartisan redistricting. It stopped graft,
boodling and extravagance by the institution of a budget system to control funds. It brought a vast improvement in technical departments like
engineering, health, street and fire protection and elevated the quality of
personnel by introducing the merit system for selecting, retaining and
promoting employees. It encouraged planning and kept the city expansion on a sound basis with adequate sinking funds. It enlarged the functions of city government to include social welfare, health activities and
public provision for recreation.

"These are really revolutionary processes," said Mr. Matscheck. "They
are triumphs for democracy. The state and national governments are
showing the same tendency that is found in city government."

This was the hope of the charter campaign which reached its climax
in February, 1925, a hope that seemed certain of realization. The charter
election had been well timed by its friends, for it came on the heels of

the factional war between the Democratic Goats and Rabbits, traditional opponents of the nonpartisan scheme. The Democratic internal strife was not the only thing that cheered the Charter hopefuls. They remembered the Republican gains in the city election of 1924, and felt secure in the thought that the G.O.P. still held the upper hand for the Republicans, under the leadership of Mayor Albert I. Beach and backed by the *Star,* were formally committed to the new charter cause.

Under the circumstances, it was not surprising that T. J. Pendergast became a convert of the charter evangelists, following the old axiom that if you can't beat a movement, join it. His faction possibly could have defeated the charter if it had chosen to oppose it but Big Tom had decided that he should be the one to bring nonpartisan government to Kansas City. He and his associates saw some things in the proposed charter that they liked. Joe Shannon saw the same things and was vastly alarmed. He resisted the reform vigorously but was overwhelmed by the strange combination that worked on election day to adopt the charter, 37,504 to 8,827.

Two of the most advertised features of the new nonpartisan charter were things that appealed to the town's greatest exponent of partisan organization schemes.

Concerning the provision substituting a single nine-man City Council for the old aldermanic Council of two houses with thirty-two members, Pendergast remarked to a reporter who respected his confidence:

"It ought to be as easy to get along with nine men as thirty-two."

The new electoral system established by the charter was equally appealing to the organization leader. The charter set up a primary for nomination of two candidates for each office, to be followed by a run-off or final election a few weeks later. All candidates were to be entered in the primary as "Independents," appearing on the ballot without party label or designation. There was no limit on the number of candidates filing for the primary and the nominations went to the two candidates polling the largest number of votes—the winner and the runner-up. As the system actually worked out, it strengthened the control of the bosses and the party organizations over the selection of officeholders. The idea that independent citizens would run for office without the encouragement of an organization was a fantasy that never provoked anything except mirth among practical politicians. Under the nonpartisan system, Kansas City's history has been a continuation of the old struggle between the two major parties behind the independent façade.

Under the old charter, the city's two-house Council had a lower house with one seat from each of the sixteen wards, an upper house of sixteen aldermen elected at large, and a mayor elected at large who sat in neither house.

The new charter divided the city into four districts, replacing the sixteen wards, and they were expected to be more difficult to control than wards. Each district elected one councilman to the one-house Council and four councilmen were elected from the city at large. The mayor, also elected at large, was stripped of most of his old powers and reduced to the status of president pro tempore of the Council. He was given one vote in the Council but of his old powers he retained only the control of the Park Department while the authority over directors of the various other departments was invested in a city manager who was elected by the Council. The city manager, who was supposed to be a professional administrator rather than a politician, was of course responsible to the Council and could be removed by a vote of a majority of the Council. He was, in effect, the city's "hired man" and was so called in the innocent early days of the reform, but it was apparent that he would wield enormous authority and that he might become a greater power than any mayor had been if, by some mischance, he controlled five of the nine Council votes in carrying out measures that were not consistent with the spirit or letter of the nonpartisan charter.

The charter promoters were not unduly alarmed over such a prospect for they were men of good faith who took seriously the pledges of the party leaders and, moreover, they expected the Republicans to win. Mayor Beach, the man who upset the Democratic machine in the spring of 1924, had a smile that had been good for five thousand votes then, and there was no reason to suppose that a year in the City Hall had seriously tarnished his toothsome charm. The Election and Police boards, which were not affected by the charter change, were filled with men appointed by a Republican governor, so it was certain that the Democratic vote getters on the North Side would not be encouraged to run wild in the first nonpartisan election.

S. J. Ray in The Kansas City Star

"Ah, a Loophole!"

Final machine trick under the 1925 charter occurred in the 1939 Recall contest, which inspired this cartoon.

The dominant Republican and Democratic organizations went through the motions of observing the nonpartisan charter conventions, each offering tickets that ran without the old party labels but none the less were recognizable to all true partisans. The Beach group of candidates, selected by a city-wide committee of sixty-five and headed by Mayor Beach, was obviously the choice of the Republican Party and the *Star*. The group selected by the Democratic statesmen at a meeting in a downtown club was called the Jaudon group in honor of Ben Jaudon, the popular city treasurer who was picked for the mayoralty spot in honor of his outstanding work for the Democratic Party, he being the only representative of that party who had survived in the Republican city landslide in the previous year.

The light vote cast in the election which established the new charter had indicated the nonpartisan manager idea wasn't very exciting to the citizens as a whole, but the primary campaign that followed produced a record city primary vote. The sudden surge of interest was not caused by the eloquence of the candidates in presenting the nonpartisan idea but by a renewal of the old struggle for power behind the nonpartisan pretense. The complacency which the citizens later revealed in the face of glaring violations of the nonpolitical principle of the new charter was not surprising in view of the manner in which the campaign of '25 was conducted. The *Star* maintained its historic association with the movement that had been fathered by Nelson by indorsing two of the Council candidates in the Jaudon group. This handsome gesture from the Republican newspaper did not make much of an impression on the cynical Democratic politicians, however, for the two men approved by the *Star* were two of the Democrats most likely to be elected, and otherwise the paper was working for the election of a Republican mayor and a Republican majority in the Council.

The turning point in the contest was reached one day when T. J. Pendergast and Joe Shannon came face to face in one of their rare meetings on a downtown street. This chance meeting of the bosses occurred October 15, 1925. That was two days after the primary in which the Jaudon group, the ticket backed by Pendergast and Welch, triumphed over the Shannon candidates for the right to meet the Republicans in the city election, November 3. Tom and Joe had a large curbstone audience, which included George K. Wallace, a *Star* reporter who had grown prematurely gray covering the shenanigans of politicians. Another witness, and one who had a closer view than he relished at the time, was George Hamilton Combs, Jr. Mr. Combs is now a news analyst and commentator for radio station WHN, New York. In 1925 he was a rising young lawyer in Kansas City with an ambition to sit in Congress. He served a term in the Seventieth Congress, 1927-29, but on October 15, 1925, it appeared that he had put an end to his political career when he attempted to serve as a peacemaker between the Goats and Rabbits.

The city primary contest had left more bad blood and neither Tom nor Joe would make the first move toward patching up the new dispute. "They avoided each other with studied Celtic blandness and it looked as if the party would be split wide open again," said Mr. Combs, recalling the incident some twenty years later. His memory of that occasion was made doubly vivid by the explosiveness of Tom Pendergast.

"During this period," Mr. Combs related, "I was informed that Mr. Pendergast was incensed over what he regarded as my personal attacks on him during the campaign. Aside from the reference to him as not big enough to dominate the party, I had made no such assault and felt badly about the misunderstanding because both of these Irishmen were the sort to command a good deal of affection (as well as respect!) and Tom had been generous to me in the past."

So Mr. Combs attempted to clear up the matter when he encountered Mr. Pendergast on Walnut Street, and Mr. Pendergast immediately launched into a tirade. It was going full blast when Joe Shannon strolled along and horned in on the argument, which attained greater velocity when Shannon justified the Rabbit criticism of Pendergast with the explanation: "You were trying to grab all the jobs."

"There the issue was joined," Mr. Combs continued, "with Joe hardly looking at either of us and Tom shaking an angry finger at both of us indiscriminately."

Time passed, the crowd grew in size, Mr. Shannon and Mr. Combs grew unhappier and unhappier, and a *Star* cameraman appeared and focused his camera without interrupting the Pendergast lecture. Finally the camera snapped and the *Star* got a picture of Tom brandishing his index finger under Mr. Combs's nose as he declared he didn't know whether his people would ever again be for any of the Rabbit people. Or the phrase was, as Reporter Wallace reported it, "I don't give a damn what you do."

However, the outburst resulted in Tom and Joe's getting together, "either the next day, or the day after," according to George Combs. He should know, for their reconciliation after this highly satisfactory blow-off resulted, for one thing, in their handing him the nomination for Congress in 1926.

Pendergast's browbeating of his old rival figured decisively in his rise to power for the Rabbit votes were needed to save the day for the Democrats in the city election that followed less than three weeks after the exciting scene on Walnut Street.

Political control of Kansas City for the next thirteen years was decided November 3, 1925, by fewer than two hundred votes. The all-important margin was registered in the case of George L. Goldman, whose election in the most closely contested Council race gave the Democrats a five-to-four majority in the new governing body. His majority was 304, so a shift of 153 votes would have given the majority to the group headed by Beach, who was re-elected mayor by a majority of only 534 votes.

As the full implications of five-to-four dawned on Pendergast's opponents, they attempted to forestall disaster by contesting the Goldman election, making the usual election theft charges. The Democrats checkmated them by going to the Supreme Court with a mandamus action compelling the Election Board to certify the returns showing that Goldman had been duly and properly elected.

A few days after the election, Pendergast and the other Democratic leaders met in Banker Kemper's office to decide on the man for city manager. Their choice was Henry F. McElroy, the businessman who had done such good work in eliminating Bulgerism from the County Court.

When the new city government was inaugurated in April of the following year, City Manager McElroy bluntly put an end to the non-partisan nonsense. His would be a Democratic administration, he announced. No one would be in doubt where the responsibility rested, he said. And no one would fail to know who held the power.

The scientific administration that began on this April day in 1926 showed Walter Matscheck and his college-trained experts many things that weren't taught in schools.

COUNTRY BOOKKEEPER

HENRY F. McELROY represented the final flowering of the idea that what government needed was a businessman to run it. In selecting him for city manager under the new nonpartisan charter for the unicameral form of municipal government. Boss Tom Pendergast impressed the Real Estate Board and the Chamber of Commerce with his fundamental soundness for Mr. McElroy was the practical man par excellence, a self-made successful citizen and the one-hundred-per-cent type of common-sense American. The only real dissent came from the circle represented by Walter Matscheck and the Kansas City Civic Research Institute, who felt that the Council should go outside the city and import an administrator who had some academic background and professional standing in the new science of government. Their suggestions were not well received for they irritated local pride and violated the long-cultivated notion that success in running a store, a poultry house or a real estate office uniquely qualified a man to manage the public's affairs.

Kansas City had elected numerous businessmen mayors in the past without producing startling confirmation for the theory that they were handier at this trade than politicians or bureaucrats. However, it was felt that this did not constitute a fair test, for the mayors were so hedged in by politicians that they had little chance to introduce the efficiency, discipline and economy that prevailed in their own private enterprises. Conditions established by the new charter were believed to be ideal for a full-scale demonstration of the businessman's genius for government. And Henry McElroy seemed to be the ideal man for the task from both the commercial and political points of view. Bankers, real estate men and merchants knew him as a shrewd and hard-headed operator, a man who had started from scratch, understood the value of a dollar and made a pile. Boss Pendergast knew him as a thoroughly dependable disciple of Tom Pendergast.

The new administration began with the introduction of the celebrated

McElroy Country Bookkeeping system, which had been developed by
the City Manager in the days when he was a storekeeper in Iowa and a
real estate dealer in Kansas City, and which gave the taxpayers the giddy
feeling that they belonged to a solvent concern while at the same time
they supported the machine politicians in unaccustomed style. With a
few swings of his pencil, McElroy cut in half a five-million-dollar deficit left over from the previous administration and announced he would
order a slight tax increase to wipe out the remainder of the deficit.

"By this plan the city will get out of its embarrassing position without
the necessity of a $5,000,000 bond issue," the Judge explained. (McElroy
was fond of his former County Court title of Judge and retained it.) And
it was done, or at least nobody had the courage to dispute the Judge's
statement that the city was at last out of the red.

"It's just a little country bookkeeping," the Judge remarked. He had
started his business life in Dunlap, Iowa, and his proudest achievement
was the accounting method he devised when he was a youth of seventeen,
clerking in the store there. He worked out a hog-feeding scheme on the
side and by the time he was twenty his books showed a surplus of four
thousand dollars, with which he set up a store of his own.

City Manager McElroy clowned his budget-balancing act a little for
the benefit of the boys who knew and admired him as a wit as well as an
executive, but no one made the mistake of taking the Judge too lightly.
The bankers and other businessmen were not disturbed by his corny
humor or by the touch of magic in his computations when it was combined with the simple arithmetic of honest old Dunlap. The crossroads-
store high-finance hokum perpetuated the legend of McElroy efficiency
for more than a decade. It established Judge McElroy as the businessman's politician. He played the role vigorously at all times, in big
matters like the deficit and in little affairs like the case of the whelping
dog.

A woman who was a breeder of fine dogs had a problem in biology
and finances which she took to the City Manager. She explained that she
faced the prospect of a deficit in connection with a female who was supposed to have a litter. The woman had contracted to sell four of the pups
before they arrived, accepting twenty-five dollars down on each pup.

"Oh, you anticipated," McElroy interrupted.

"I've done worse than that," the woman replied. "I have absconded or something. Last Friday my little dog had just one pup—a son. I've collected twenty-five dollars of the purchase price of three nonexistent pups and I've spent the money. You see what a fix I'm in. What shall I do?"

The City Hall's financial wizard thought hard.

"I'll tell you what," he said at length. "Issue anticipation notes for each pup you owe. Later your little mother will have other sons, maybe. Good day, Madame."

The Country Bookkeeper did considerable anticipating on his own account but he was very good at it and no one questioned his financial wisdom for a long time except Walter Matscheck, the Civic Research Institute director. Several months after McElroy took office the Institute reported in one of its weekly bulletins that the new administration was spending the people's money at an unbudgetlike rate. The City Manager pooh-poohed the analyst's report and wanted to know where the hell the Civic Research Institute got the right to butt in on government. Mr. Matscheck's answer was a series of bulletins showing a mounting deficit. It was then that Judge McElroy showed some of the other conspicuous political talents besides budget-balancing skill. He silenced the deficit talk temporarily by forcing the Council to order a tax reduction in the face of rising expenses, and that satisfied the businessmen that the city had a surplus or high anticipations of one.

Walter Matscheck issued more disconcerting statistics and the Republicans took up the issue for campaign purposes. The Country Bookkeeper stole their thunder by announcing that he was putting up a one-thousand-dollar personal check, payable to Mercy Children's Hospital if and when anyone could prove the existence of a deficit created in his administration. Since no one could audit the books without his consent, he didn't worry about his thousand dollars and continued to get a balance in his own way. When the deficit eventually was established beyond all question it was a figure high in the millions but by that time the one-thousand-dollar McElroy check wasn't available for cashing.

Mr. Matscheck became the most consistent and effective critic of the McElroy administration in the first part of its tenure. Although he was usually able to figure up some way of distracting the public's attention from the Matscheck findings, McElroy was nettled at his inability to silence or rattle the Civic Research Institute man. Walter Matscheck was a shining exception among critics. Others who got in the way of the lean, turkey-necked, frostbitten man from Iowa found him both ruthless and irresistible.

The first important individual to feel the weight of McElroy disfavor was Dr. E. W. Cavaness, the city health director. The good doctor carried his control of municipal health to the point of decreeing what color paint should be used on the new nurses' quarters. McElroy favored a different color. It was a small issue but enough to get the McElroy dander up and he demanded the health director's resignation. Dr. Cavaness held out for a while with the support of the medical fraternity but the City Manager had made up his mind. In addition to having a poor eye for color, Dr. Cavaness neglected to follow McElroy suggestions in filling certain hospital jobs and spending money on contracts.

Dr. Cavaness and the nonpartisan dream went out together. Under the new charter the health director was not answerable to the city manager but to the Council. With its margin of one vote, the Democratic majority made the Council a rubber stamp for its Hired Man. "Five to four" became a monotonous refrain at roll call.

McElroy worked up hardly more than a sweat in eliminating the non-partisan health director who had defied him. His main attention was reserved for the Republican police and the Republican mayor. The Council's Hired Man spent four happy years pre-empting the social and ceremonial prerogatives of the mayor, which were about all that was left of that executive's authority and dignity under the new charter. Although he was immediately eclipsed by the City Manager at the City Hall, the Mayor supposedly retained his rights to open the baseball season, shake hands, smile and formally open conventions and hand the keys to the city to visiting notables. He kept his high silk hat shined and his swallow-tail coat pressed but didn't realize how few opportunities he would have to wear them until Queen Marie came to town on her barnstorming tour in 1926. Then Mayor Beach learned that Judge McElroy had made his own arrangements for the official welcome and had to scuffle to win a place in the Queen's carriage for the parade downtown. His Honor was the victim of an even more grievous slight when Amos 'n Andy came to town for their first visit. The Mayor waited at the City

Hall to greet the radio blackface team, whose personal appearance was a much greater event than the visit of third-rate European royalty. When the parade arrived at the City Hall there was the City Manager in the first limousine with Amos 'n' Andy. He had gone to the station to meet the comedians and taken all the bows on the long ride to the Hall where the forlorn mayor waited.

As Andy eloquently expressed it, Mayor Beach was "regusted"—so much so that he abandoned political ambition and pined for the day of his return to private life. Goaded by the Republican City Central Committee to assert himself, the Mayor got a running start on the City Manager at the opening game of the American Association baseball season in 1927, racing to the mound with the pitcher's mitt. McElroy glared at Mayor Beach but restrained himself and accepted the situation. Donning catcher's mask and glove, he squared off to catch the first ball and signalled for a fast one right over the plate. Mayor Beach threw a nasty curve, the ball bouncing and cracking the Judge on the shin. The crowd roared and Catcher McElroy grinned ferociously at Pitcher Beach as he rubbed his shin.

The City Manager appropriated the Mayor's office, assigning Beach to an office behind that of the city clerk. He took away the Mayor's motor car, which was embarrassing but not as humiliating as it might have been if the Mayor had not been able to get another car from the Park Board, the one department which he still controlled. Judge McElroy elbowed Mayor Beach away from his exclusive position at the head table at Chamber of Commerce luncheons. If the Mayor was called on to speak, Judge McElroy also had to be invited to say a few well-chosen words. At a bridge dedication, the City Manager took the choice spot, cutting the pretty blue ribbons at the mythical boundary line between North Kansas City and Kansas City proper, while the Mayor rode in the rear seat of a motor car far back in the parade. When the new passenger station at the municipal airport was dedicated, Judge McElroy crowded out the Council as well as the Mayor, staging the whole show for the city, himself. There was, perhaps, a certain appropriateness in his monopolizing of the various dedication ceremonies since he represented the guiding spirit in the expansive projects requiring the presence of an official dignitary. Kansas City was a-booming at this time and there was no greater booster in the movement than the big man to whom Judge McElroy reported each Sunday at his mansion on Ward Parkway. McElroy saw to it that credit due Uncle Tom was not appropriated by Republican stuffed shirts.

When the time for another election rolled around, after four years of undiluted partisanship, Judge McElroy was just getting warmed up. There was some grumbling against him in the ranks of his own party and much loud Republican talk about McElroyism but absolutely no prospect that the Country Bookkeeper from Dunlap would be retired. Tom Pendergast was completely satisfied, as he should have been. McElroy was hiding a deficit, as Walter Matscheck reported, but the city's credit rated high with bankers and the government managed to meet current obligations each month. Contracts for public works and supplies went to politically favored concerns. Pendergast's Ready-Mixed Concrete had a monopoly and the prices paid were those fixed by the paving combine, but McElroy diverted public attention from this gouge with his ballyhoo about the good quality of the materials purchased under the political system. The merit system provided for in the charter was ignored in the employment of personnel but Judge McElroy was able to persuade the big taxpayers that the partisan jobholders were giving satisfaction on a low wage basis.

The administration exhibited rare skill in promoting and ballyhooing services that made the maximum impression on the public. It concentrated its effort on making a showing in garbage collection, fire protection, street maintenance, band concerts and budget balancing, and combined these with a few spectacular expansion projects. These last included the building of a municipal airport and the purchase of two toll-free bridges over the Missouri, which unquestionably were profitable undertakings for the general public as well as the private interests concerned. The political effectiveness of this course was demonstrated in the McElroy efficiency reputation. Among other things, it drew the praise of the *Star,* which said editorially in 1930:

"For the last four years, with all its faults and failures, Kansas City probably has had the most efficient city government in its history."

The Judge's greatest achievement probably was the winning of that indorsement from the old champion of the nonpartisan movement and the G.O.P. The *Star* was disturbed by the "intrusion of politics," as the editorial phrased it, but not unduly alarmed, for the extent of the city government's deterioration was not yet apparent.

The *Star* at this time was just getting well started on a new phase of its life, with the Nelson ownership finally at an end. For the last four years the new managers of the paper had been somewhat preoccupied with reorganization problems of their own and with litigation growing out of purchase of the paper from the Nelson estate. Following the death of Nelson's daughter, Laura Nelson Kirkwood, in 1926, the paper was put up for sale under the terms of the Nelson trust which provided that the *Star* be disposed of through competitive bidding, with three trustees being given fairly wide latitude in selecting the best bid. They accepted the bid of eleven million dollars, submitted by a stock company that was formed by a group of *Star* editors and advertising executives and limited to officers and employees of the paper. Walter S. Dickey, publisher of the *Journal* and *Post,* challenged the sale in the courts, contending he had submitted a higher bid, but the United States Supreme Court upheld the sale to the *Star* group.

Although all the figures in the new *Star* command were Nelson men, collectively they lacked the fire and domineering force of old Baron Bill. There had been steady moderation in the fighting tone of the paper since the death of Nelson. After the sale in 1926, there was a marked increase in emphasis on objective reporting in contrast to the angling and coloring which had been so conspicuous in the Nelson news coverage. There was, moreover, an obvious effort to give approximately equal space to the arguments of both sides in a political campaign, which was something that would have been unbearably painful to Colonel Nelson. However, despite these changes, the *Star* still was generally recognizable as a Nelson product and any suspicion that its crusading spirit had died was set at rest in this period by the paper's vigorous campaign against the Doherty interests in an effort to get a reduction in gas rates, and by its fight on Dr. J. R. Brinkley, the Milford, Kansas, medical wonder who specialized in rejuvenation and compound operations for prostate trouble.

The *Star*'s position in the McElroy matter remained a subject of debate for many years, with many Democrats eventually seeking to give the *Star* the chief credit for the City Manager's popular success. John G.

Madden, a Democratic lawyer who was Pendergast's attorney in his days
of trouble, gave a forceful presentation of this point of view in the 1940
campaign, when he said:

"The *Star* denies that it supported McElroy and put him into office.
However, I want to be fair, even to the *Kansas City Star*. The plain fact
is that in McElroy and certain of his appointees the *Star* was deceived.
The citizens of Kansas City were deceived. I do not challenge the good
faith of the *Star* in believing in McElroy, but the *Star* cannot challenge
the good faith of the Democratic Party in believing in McElroy. Let us
confess, which is the fact, that however bitterly we opposed McElroy, we
were mesmerized into believing that he was a financial genius, and that
political hypnosis from which we suffered was the product of the praise
of the *Kansas City Star*."

It is apparent from this plaint that Mr. Madden and his fellow Democrats neglected to read the *Star* during the last six years of the McElroy
regime but it is true that the early McElroy appeal kept the *Star* from
giving the G.O.P. in 1930 the special assistance which the Republicans
traditionally had received from the Nelson paper.

Although the *Star*'s neutrality in 1930 constituted a rare example of
nonpartisanship in Kansas City, the editors could have had no illusions
about the future of the nonpartisan cause. There was no Nonpartisan
ticket in the field in 1930 and very little evidence of interest in the nonpolitical principle. It looked as if the movement fostered by Nelson to
eliminate the party bosses was in the grave with the Baron.

1908 MAIN

THE UNOFFICIAL SEAT of government in Kansas City was the Jackson
Democratic Club at 1908 Main Street, some fifteen blocks south of the
old red-brick building in Market Square where City Manager McElroy
held court daily. Since the downtown had moved away from the anti-
quated City Hall, the new center of municipal authority was more con-
veniently located to carry on the business of the town.

The neighborhood in which Tom Pendergast established his last political headquarters was a southern extension of the business district, a

region of small hotels and restaurants, taverns and stores, wholesale houses, machine shops, motor car sales-and-accessory plants and freight offices. It was picked for a larger development when the central railroad terminal was moved from the West Bottoms to the valley of old O.K. Creek in 1914. Colonel Nelson moved his *Star* Building down this way a couple of years before the Union Station was built on the new site. Pendergast came along in the mid-twenties, locating his Democratic Club on Main Street two blocks from the railroad terminals yards. His offices were two blocks south and two blocks west of the *Star* Building. Close to his political club was the plant of his Ready-Mixed Concrete Company and his wholesale liquor company, revived after Prohibition's repeal, had quarters a few blocks away. The working public rode past his club every morning and evening from the South Side to the downtown and North Side. Strangers arriving in Kansas City passed 1908 Main Street without noticing it, riding streetcars and busses from the station to the down-town center.

The Jackson Democratic Club occupied three rooms on the second floor of a two-story yellow-brick building, flanked on the north by a small hotel which Pendergast owned. On the first floor were a wholesale linen shop and an eatery. You climbed stairs to reach the club, entering a large room, arranged like a lodge hall, which was bare of decoration except for three pictures on the walls—pictures of Woodrow Wilson and James A. Reed in unnatural companionship, and a painting of T. J. Pendergast. On the left was an anteroom occupied by a line of people patiently waiting their turn to go through the doorway of the adjoining office. The visitors were interviewed briefly by a tall, gray, weatherbeaten man, Captain Elijah Matheus, former steamboat pilot and Pendergast's secretary, who escorted each caller into the presence of the club's founder.

The line moved fast for Pendergast was quick with his answers to his public.

"All right, who's next," he called out when the door opened to let one caller out and another in.

A framed cartoon of Alderman Jim Pendergast carrying a ballot box, an old caricature from the *Star,* looked down on Pendergast as he sat at his desk handling the business of the town. The cartoon was the one political touch in the office. The whole aspect of the place and the big man at the desk suggested that this was a business operation rather than a political activity. It was, in fact, big business. From this unpretentious headquarters Pendergast directed a large, smoothly functioning organization of precinct captains, block workers, party leaders and officials, a company that worked 365 days of the year. The thoroughness of the system was explained once in a few words to a visiting British woman member of Parliament, who was curious to see a real American boss in the flesh and arranged an interview. She was received by the Goat leader in his Ready-Mixed Concrete office and found herself facing a brisk businessman.

"Tell me something of the system of your organization," she said. "Is it by the bloc or how?"

"Yes," replied Tom, with no attempt at humor. "The block system. We're organized in every block in the city."

This visiting member of Parliament, Miss Marjorie Graves, would have learned, if she had pressed the Boss for further details, that the system combined features of a corporation and a military organization. There was one worker for every five voters and the command or inner circle included ward leaders, township leaders and a group of business and professional men. The organization had an espionage service that included thousands of volunteer reporters.

Mr. Pendergast conducted affairs at 1908 Main in such a manner that it only occasionally occurred to the people that this was a very odd way to run a democracy. The thing that was mostly said about the Jackson Democratic Club manager was that he got things done. A piece of paper from him, marked with his distinctive red pencil and containing the brief request to add the bearer's name to the payroll "and oblige," cut through all red tape. Businessmen saw him there as an important executive who understood all the practical details of his own enterprises and got to the heart of their problems with a few direct questions. Small fry saw him as the influential citizen who was interested in their affairs—the big man who had a use for them, the head of an organization that operated on a mutual benefit basis.

Pendergast's influence in placing deserving workers was not limited to public employment. There were numerous companies and individuals who acted promptly on a Pendergast recommendation. During periods when the Democrats did not control political patronage or when the pickings were slim for other reasons, the Goat leader had found his connections with private employers of extreme importance in sustaining his organization. After the Democrats returned to power and his voice became the dominant one in deciding who should get the jobs and the favors, T.J. did not abandon his interest in commercial operators who were anxious to cultivate good relations with the organization by helping out the boys.

In campaign time the opposition operators drew a lurid picture of the Boss as a sinister figure pulling the strings of hidden government, but the fact of the matter was that the machine rule wasn't hidden and the legend of Pendergast that grew up at 1908 Main Street was quite unlike anything in the stock of the old political melodrama. In this time the people had become so accustomed to the inadequacy of the official government machinery which they had established that they accepted the Pendergast kind of administration as a normal and even indispensable service. The Boss was able to operate openly, without apology, and he busied himself making a reputation as a substantial citizen—the man of property, the good family man, the friend of the masses, the Jacksonian of large simplicities who hadn't been spoiled by wealth.

He arose each morning at five o'clock, went direct to 1908 Main or to his Ready-Mixed Concrete office, and was occupied until six o'clock in the evening. Three mornings each week he sat at his desk at 1908 Main, meeting the public. He didn't leave his office for lunch, for he belonged to no clubs except his own political society and looked with disdain on "resolutin' bodies," as he called the clubs in the businessmen's luncheon circuit. A tray containing plain food was sent up to the Boss from the little restaurant below his office. In the afternoon Pendergast moved to his Ready-Mixed office. As the pressure of political callers became heavier, the Goat leader had one of his lieutenants sit in for him at 1908 Main three days a week. One of his frequent substitutes was Jim Pendergast, son of brother Mike, who was being trained to take over the Goat scepter.

Pendergast seldom left his home at night, except to go to a movie with his children, and usually was in bed by nine o'clock. His main recreation was an occasional motor car ride into the country with a friend or a member of his family. His favorite ride wound over the highways through the Clay County hills north of Kansas City, a picturesque region in which he purchased a large country estate with ample stables and pastures for his race horses.

Pendergast made so many friends through his interviews and services at 1908 Main Street that the picture of him in his headquarters was spread widely by word of mouth and became familiar to thousands of citizens who never saw him outside the newspaper photographs. He gave a good account of himself in newspaper interviews. Newspapermen found him both formidable and attractive. His brusqueness was a part of his restless energy. He was seldom relaxed. He sat forward on the edge of his chair when he talked, emphasizing his remarks with forceful gestures. He was all business—dynamic, plain spoken, impatient. This was the impression he made on George K. Wallace, the *Star*'s Missouri correspondent, who covered the Pendergast assignment over a long period, including the years when the paper was doing its heaviest fighting against the organization. Wallace called often at 1908 Main, went with Pendergast to state and national conventions, talked to him long distance in various cities and even aboard a liner at sea, traveled to New York, Chicago and other places for interviews in times when things were popping in the Democratic leader's absence.

To the reporter from the Republican anti-boss newspaper the gruff Democratic boss was always accessible and courteous. Newspaper opposition was a part of the political game and he didn't mix personalities with his business. His attitude was summed up in one of his informal remarks to the reporter.

"Mr. Wallace," he said, "there are three sides to every question in politics—your side, my side and the right side."

Which isn't the statement of an altogether simple man.

With the growth of his wealth and power, Big Tom was forced to deviate somewhat from his simple routine. His wife and children wanted to spend some of the new money and the good family man indulged them. He was intensely proud of his family, his wife, their son and two daughters, and was gratified at the quiet way in which they conducted themselves. They sought no exotic adventures and engaged in none of the escapades that were popular with people of their privileged position.

Outside of exhibiting a delight in display of luxurious possessions, they conducted themselves about as modestly as Big Tom himself. He spent $175,000 to purchase and furnish an ornate home on Kansas City's fashionable Ward Parkway. He bought flashy sports roadsters for his older daughter and son, and lavished silks, furs and diamonds on his wife. He also dressed himself more smartly, for he always had a strong taste for style. He favored blue and gray tailor-made ensembles, picked nobby hats and was fond of wearing spats.

Tom's sartorial improvement drew statewide attention when he blossomed forth in top hat and cutaway at his older daughter's wedding in 1929. Miss Marceline Pendergast was spliced to a prominent local butcher's son, W. E. Burnett, Jr., with all the proper trimmings and with T. J. holding the spotlight. He posed jauntily beside the bride in the wedding picture, which was a political mistake. The Republicans made five thousand prints of the photograph of Tom in his elegant getup and scattered them over the state in the following election campaign. It was more effective than a cartoon, for Tom's resemblance to a figure from a Nast cartoon of a political tycoon was remarkable. The Goat leader quietly swallowed his chagrin and thereafter restrained his fashionable inclinations.

The wedding incident was preceded by an equally spectacular exhibition of the Pendergasts' pleasure in rich adornment. Several weeks earlier robbers had broken into the home and made off with jewels, furs and other articles of personal attire valued at $150,000. The loot included numerous baubles ranging in value from $1,100 to $13,750 and 480 pairs of silk stockings that had been assembled for the trousseau of the bride-to-be.

The family used their surplus for other of the customary pleasures of the leisured class. One of their favorite pastimes was travel, and their greatest adventure was a trip abroad with Tom in the summer of 1927. They made the Grand Tour. The Kansas City boss enjoyed all of the journey except the passage from London to Paris, which was made by plane. "Flying is not what it is cracked up to be," he remarked upon his return. Pendergast kept his followers informed of his progress abroad by postcards. One of his missives which has been preserved sheds interesting light on the sentimental quality of this famous tourist and his relationship to the boys back home. Dated *Hotel de l'Univers, Tours, France,* and addressed to "all members" at 1908 Main, it read:

As it is impossible to write to all members, I am taking this means of letting you all know that I think of all at some time or other on my trip, and I can truthfully subscribe to the old adage, "Distance makes the heart grow fonder."

My family and I are having a wonderful time. We have all enjoyed the best of health and have toured through England, Ireland, Scotland and Wales, and found the rural parts very lovely; the cities not so good, with the exception of London, which is very large and very busy; traffic about as congested as New York, but not as well regulated.

We flew to Paris from London. I do not think I would do it again. The noise from the engines was deafening and our ears rang for twenty-four hours afterward.

Paris is truly a wonder city. We spent eight days there and were treated with every consideration by all. I found no evidence of bitterness or price gouging.

When he returned to Kansas City after an absence of about three months, Pendergast was received in the manner of an oriental potentate coming back to his realm. Crowds gathered at the Union Station to greet him and followed him to 1908 Main Street. His office was stacked with baskets of cut flowers and the boss spent several hours meeting well-wishers, shaking hands, answering questions, until he grew weary and went home to rest only to return in the evening for more flattering treatment. Touched by the demonstration of devotion and cheered by first reports on the situation at home in his absence, he remarked:

"A reporter met me on the ship in New York and told me of the awful state of affairs out here. He did not scare me one bit. I told him I would bet any odds he liked to name it was just the outs trying to put ignominy upon the ins, and that I had played that game myself many a time. I get home and find things fine."

Mr. Pendergast thereupon delivered one of his longest public statements, and one that contained his most cogent expression of his political and business philosophy.

"The New York reporters told me there was a paving combine here in Kansas City," he said. "I told them if there was it was twenty-five years old and no Democratic invention. They know that as well as we do.

"Another bunch howled because I have my name on Ready-Mixed

Concrete wagons. So I have. I live here, am in business here, own property here, pay all my taxes here. Does any man say I have not a right to try to make a living here? My business right now is selling Ready-Mixed Concrete. I am selling all of it I can to anybody I can induce to buy it, and in that particular I am exactly like the maker of sewer pipe, or vitrified brick, or tiling or any other material. They all hustle for business.

"Let me say something: If everybody would hustle for business like I do and others who compete with me do, this would be a livelier town than it is. I am for more and better and bigger business, from Ready-Mixed Concrete to ice cream cones.

"Everything honest and legitimate goes with business or politics," he concluded.

Pendergast's capacities as a businessman had been shown from the beginning but for a long time were not widely recognized outside his intimate circle because of his inclination to run things from a quiet nook in the background and because his renown as a politician diverted public attention from his other activities. As a young man, he was marked as a comer in business as well as politics when he and Cas Welch, his personal friend and factional rival, joined forces to form a messenger-boy monopoly, merging the Hasty, Hurry and Speedy services into an enterprise that eliminated rivals through the combined brawn of Tom and Cas. In his days as a saloonkeeper, Tom had three saloons on Twelfth Street at various times and quickly branched into the wholesale liquor line, becoming president of the company which he operated until shortly before Prohibition. When he sold out he had the foresight to make a large investment in warehouse receipts and was in position to cash in with bonded stuff after repeal. After selling his liquor interests he organized a distributing company that handled nonalcoholic beverages. He had a hand in the insurance business and teamed up with his friend and political shadow, Emmet O'Malley, in a cigar company, serving as vice-president.

After Mr. Pendergast took over the Ready-Mixed Concrete operation, the Kansas City paving combine faced only one serious challenge from an outsider. A Tulsa, Oklahoma, contractor by the name of Carl Pleasant tried to horn in, with unpleasant results for himself. The Tulsa contractor was a Jayhawker by birth, a former football star at the University

of Kansas, and apparently was fired with the traditional Kansas spirit of
rivalry in all matters involving Missourians, for he must have known
his Kansas City venture was more of a sporting proposition than a smart
business deal.

Mr. Pleasant violated the local business code by bidding twenty-
five per cent below the Kansas City contractors on several paving
jobs, interrupting a rising trend that had carried the cost of concrete in
Kansas City as high as $3.75 a yard compared to $1.75 a yard paid on
some contracts in the county. The Tulsa man was awarded seven contracts by the Park Board, which was under Republican control. So the
daring effort to break the Pendergast monopoly began. It provided political excitement for several months of one otherwise tedious summer
and fall.

The situation was made to order for that master of harassment, Judge
McElroy, who ordered his Department of Public Works to give the Park
Board's new contractor the full inspection. Such concern over an honest
measure in paving material has never been displayed before or since in
Kansas City and before the army of inspectors had completed their work
the Pleasant paving was thickly spotted with patches marking places
where test borings were made. The organization's inspectors knew what
they were doing, for Mr. Pleasant had innocently neglected to supervise
each job personally to make certain that the materials he had ordered
in were actually used. Finally, with an air of great surprise and mortification, he admitted that the tests showed his paving skimped on specifications in spots. He announced that he would make refunds to the city
to cover the discrepancy, and returned to Tulsa to stay.

The city administration's zeal in protecting native enterprise in this
period was illustrated forcefully when the Thiokol Corporation, then
a small concern backed by Eastern capital, was forced to move out of the
city to get relief from government supervision. It seems that the company
neglected to lease or rent a site for its plant from Joe Overly, a hustling
Goat politician, and Mr. Overly was offended by the odor produced by
chemicals used in manufacturing Thiokol, a synthetic rubber.

The substance called Thiokol was discovered by two young Kansas
City research chemists who accidentally produced a form of synthetic
rubber while searching for an antifreeze agent. Local pride in their

achievement was somewhat chilled by the fact that they got outside financial interests to exploit their product. And then Mr. Overly's sensitive nostrils brought complaints which compelled the city health director to hold hearings. Finally the company announced it was moving its plant to Trenton, New Jersey, so it could do business without expensive litigation. The incident provoked a brief flurry of interest and was forgotten until it was recalled by the vast wartime expansion in the synthetic rubber industry, when it was found that Thiokol was booming on government contracts.

The Republicans, of course, attempted to make some political capital of the Pleasant and Thiokol incidents and Pendergast's Ready-Mixed was one of their principal talking points in the campaigns of 1930. Their efforts, alas, did not make a great impression on the public, which could see that Tom Pendergast was not alone in the monopoly game and was made cynical by the Democratic propaganda that the Republicans were sore only because they were on the outside looking in. The citizens talked and thought less about the ruthlessness of Pendergast's methods than they did about the size of his take. His profits from his part in the concrete monopoly were estimated at five hundred thousand dollars in a good year, two hundred thousand dollars in a lean one. That kind of money demanded and got respect for a man, in the society of hustlers.

Mayor Beach injected Pendergast's business interests into the 1930 campaign by propounding six questions to the City Manager, asking him to reveal the amount of business done with Pendergast concerns and suggesting that he comment on the propriety of such traffic with the leader of the party controlling the city government.

The humorist who occupied the city manager's office replied that all the work had been done according to plans and specifications. The Mayor continued his agitation until he irritated the county attorney, James R. Page, a member of the Pendergast faction, who demanded that Beach put up the evidence for his charges and insinuations, or shut up.

A county grand jury, which was meeting at this time, decided that it ought to take some notice of the paving issue. It took a quick look and dropped the matter with the announcement that neither the Mayor nor the Prosecutor offered any evidence which warranted further investigation. Moreover, the report said, the jury felt that the inquiry into Mr. Pendergast's affairs had "a distinct political aspect and as such would jeopardize the dignity of this court."

The Goat rhetoricians could always be counted on for a laugh.

Home Rule

Home Rule had a good democratic sound but after a few years' experience with the new Democratic administration it suggested only Mc-Elroy-Pendergast oppression to Republicans and Nonpartisans. Home Rule actually meant substitution of local control for state authority over the Police Board. Republicans and Nonpartisans had taken the lead in agitation for this measure of autonomy in earlier days when the state administrations were consistently dominated by the Democratic Party. The Pendergast Democrats were satisfied with the arrangement that placed the appointive power over the board in the governor's hands until the Republicans began electing Missouri governors and legislatures. Then the positions of the rival politicians on the Home Rule question naturally were reversed.

The new city charter did not change the status of the Police and Election boards. Republican direction of the Police Department remained the one missing link in the machine chain and so long as there was a Republican governor in Jefferson City there appeared to be no prospect of a change in the Kansas City police power. However, the Republicans had no feeling of security in this situation, and City Manager McElroy added immeasurably to their alarm with his measures in reviving the Home Rule agitation. His offensive was a double-barrelled affair, consisting of elaborate harassment of the Republican police together with defiance of the law under which the department operated, combined with a movement in the Legislature to substitute a McElroy-written law for the old police statute.

In an effort to hold their last line against Pendergast in the city, the G.O.P. leaders wrestled desperately with the dual problem of increasing crime and police inefficiency. A series of reform police chiefs were introduced, each being rapidly eliminated by political interference and new explosions from the underworld. The contest reached its height with the coming of Major John L. Miles, the crusading peace officer from old Independence. His appointment grew out of agitation led by the *Star,* which temporarily impressed the G.O.P. politicians that they must relax partisan management of the police in order to meet the emergency created by the crime situation and the Democratic attack on the department.

Major Miles served in the First World War as commanding officer of Battery A of the One Hundred and Twenty-ninth Field Artillery. One of his brother officers was Harry S. Truman, captain of Battery D in the same regiment. They were old friends. When they returned from the war both entered politics at about the same time, Miles as a Republican and Truman as a Democrat, with the backing of American Legion members, veterans of the One Hundred and Twenty-ninth who went through the fire in France with Miles and Truman. That group of Jackson County men formed loyalties while they were in uniform that transcended party interest and had important consequences for both Jackson County and the nation. Harry Truman scratched the Democratic ticket for the only known time in his career in order to vote for Miles when he first ran for office.

Major Miles, like Truman, came from solid Jackson County stock. A son of the soil, product of a long line of Fundamentalists, he manifested a reformist zeal that was perhaps stronger than his political ambitions. He was elected county marshal in 1920 when he was the rural champion in the crusade headed by Governor Arthur M. Hyde and the *Star.* Four years later, when the office of county marshal was abolished, Miles was elected sheriff in the same campaign that brought Truman his first and only political reversal. That was the election in which Shannon and Bulger bolted the party and the future President, who was running for re-election to the County Court, went down with the rest of the Democratic ticket.

As marshal and sheriff, Miles did as much as one man possibly could do to keep the automobile from bringing the city's vices to the country.

The magnitude of the Miles undertaking in Kansas City was observed and neatly summarized by a neutral reporter, a young English-

man who came to town in the summer of 1929 to make a polite survey
of the state of civilization in the Heart of America. The visitor was
Alfred P. Perry of London, a guest on the staff of the *Star*. He was a
junior fellow of the Walter Hines Page Fellowship in journalism, a
hopeful enterprise designed to promote Anglo-American understanding and world peace. Mr. Perry composed a couple of pieces on the
hopelessly complicated international problem and thereafter devoted
his attention to more interesting subjects, such as the races at Pendergast's Riverside Park, the new skyscrapers, motor cars, luxurious hotel
accommodations, the Kansas wheat crop and the shows on Twelfth
Street. The two aspects of the Kansas City picture that impressed him
most were the beauty of the newer residential districts and the crime
situation.

After a tour of the Country Club district on the South Side, the
man from London concluded he was in one of the world's garden
spots. Then he turned to the North Side, passing block after block of
dingy business buildings and slum dwellings on the way to the City
Hall and police headquarters, where he interviewed Chief Miles, ex-
amined records and took notes for a well-mannered little essay on crime.

"Last year eighty-nine persons were murdered in this city," he wrote.
"During those twelve months three murderers were sentenced to be
hanged, four were sentenced to life imprisonment and six were given
terms which averaged fourteen years each. In England, with a population more than eighty times as great, seventeen persons were murdered in the same length of time. Of the murderers, thirteen were
hanged and four were sent to penal servitude for life; two cases remained
unsolved at the end of the year.

"In 1927 Kansas City outdid Chicago with a murder rate of sixteen
for each 100,000 population, compared with 13.3 for the latter city; and
last year holdups totaled 1,178 and burglaries 1,142, or an average of
more than seven crimes a day.

"Such a record scarcely can be described as flattering. Although it
would be unjust to attribute this condition of affairs solely to police
inefficiency, I gained the impression a disproportionate amount of time
and energy was being expended on the pursuit of petty misdemeanors
to the detriment of the more serious duties of public safety.

"It is an error to which all police are liable," the British reporter tactfully concluded, "and one from which the London department is by no means exempt."

Mr. Perry of London unwittingly picked up one of the main arguments of the new Home Rule advocates with his statement that "a disproportionate amount of time and energy was being expended on the pursuit of petty misdemeanors." The "petty misdemeanors" were liquor and gambling violations and Chief Miles's concentration on these infractions violated the major premise of the machine government's theory of crime control. The Home Rule utopians had a beautifully simple theory designed to solve the whole crime problem. They envisaged an orderly and happy society in which gamblers flourished, speakeasies and night clubs thrived, bootleggers and rumrunners kept their appointments without fear of interruption, while bandits, hi-jackers, burglars, thieves and murderers were suppressed. The reasoning behind this philosophy was that the liquor and gambling industries would operate under any circumstances, and it was better to have them regulated by responsible people under the eye of government than to have them conducted by enemies of constituted authority. Further, it was felt that if these petty misdemeanors were overlooked, the vice traffic would absorb the principal energies of the people who customarily get into trouble and thus would reduce the opportunity and incentive for the rough stuff like bank holdups. In return for the co-operation from government, the gambling and syndicate owners would work to discourage and discipline the more rambunctious spirits of the night and the police would thus have full time to concentrate on traffic, robbery and homicide regulation.

Some critics of the Home Rule theory could see the merit of the argument that means must be found to make the law square with the prevailing social habits of the city but didn't think that nullification of the law was the way to go about it. Only a change in the form of the law and progress in social education could bring about sane regulation of the liquor and gambling traffic. The notion that divekeepers could be induced to co-operate in discouraging major crime, or that they would be able to do anything in that direction even if they were so minded, seemed childish to anyone who looked at the daily report of bank failures and bank lootings, car thefts, filling station and theater robberies, hi-jackings, stink bomb throwings, dynamitings, window breakings and arson racket operations. None the less, this theory was seriously entertained by a considerable number of individuals in places of political power and by a much larger number of simple citizens, most of whom honestly wanted to see a more sensible and decent order of affairs.

Even if he had been inclined to look tolerantly on gambling and boozing, Chief Miles could not have classed these misdemeanors as petty, for any honest police officer could see that the gambling and liquor rackets were the main supports of the crime industry, and the whole underworld gravitated around the speakeasy and the gambling dive. The pay-off from the games and joints was the main source of political corruption for official protection.

Chief Miles was not dismayed by the size of his task and indeed he was so successful in his efforts to enforce respect for Prohibition and antigambling laws that he produced a revolt on Twelfth Street and in other centers of liberal sentiment. The Chief did not give all of his time to suppressing petty misdemeanors, although at times it seemed that he was devoting twenty-four hours a day to this uplift. He was an intelligent and capable police officer, who brought both military discipline and a stern moral code to the department. He set about modernizing his organization, following some of the suggestions made by a police expert who was imported to make a survey of the Kansas City system. Many technical improvements in the department were introduced and some civil service standards were set up for the employment and training of officers.

It was true, however, that the Chief took more pleasure in raiding than in his other work, and his actions in personally leading the raiding squad marked him as a grandstander, exposing him to popular derision and making him vulnerable to the charge that he spent too much time on small-time outlawry. His sad experience in this field of endeavor was illustrated by his marathon contest with the East Side Musicians Club, a Twelfth Street institution maintained by a company of distinctive Negro boogie-woogie and jazz artists. Miles, who had no appreciation for true Jackson County rhythm, insisted that the bandmen's clubhouse was a gambling establishment rather than a musical hall and nightly sent out his raiding squad to break up the entertainment. His men made hundreds of arrests but failed to obtain evidence that resulted in one conviction. After the ninety-seventh raid the musicians' president, Doc Fojo, announced plans to serenade the police on their one hundredth raid, offering to play for the Chief a special arrangement of "I Can't Give You Anything but Love, Baby."

By this time Chief Miles had had a number of other experiences that convinced him the Kansas Citians would never attain his Independence standard of virtue. Among other things he found that a petition was being circulated, under the direction of the Democratic opposition, asking for his removal as an oppressive official.

City Manager McElroy put his heart into the business of baiting Miles, and he found that the flexible nonpartisan charter gave him considerable power to interfere with and embarrass the police while he was waiting for the turn of events that would bring complete Democratic control. He began by objecting to the size of the police budget, arbitrarily refusing to pay certain expense bills of Chief Miles and other items. He held up the wages of policemen for months at a time, upset the police benefit fund and otherwise demoralized the department. He made an issue over a bill for fifteen dollars for flowers for a slain officer and staged a hammy comedy act over a clothes cleaning bill for the police. To one touching plea for money needed to pay the police wages, he replied with a letter advising that the officers be fed castor oil.

The Police Board went to the courts in a mandamus action to compel the city to accept their budget estimates and release the needed funds. McElroy forced the litigation into a long series of hearings before a commissioner of the court. These hearings were carried to four different cities to collect testimony showing how towns of like size handled the budget matter. This became known as the See America First Tour, cost the city about fifty thousand dollars, and produced nothing much of importance except some wry entertainment for the taxpayers. High point of the hearings was a debate over the question of whether the court could consider population figures taken from the *Encyclopaedia Britannica,* counsel for the police objecting because the *Encyclopaedia* was a British work dedicated to King George V and the authors could not be produced in court to verify their statements. After this frivolous performance had been carried to the point where everybody was bored with the whole business, the Commissioner found against the Police Board but he was overruled by the State Supreme Court, which held that the board had the right to fix its own budget. However, the City Manager was not long depressed by that reversal.

McElroy and the police commissioners were in the midst of this fight over the budget when the underworld undertook an operation which called national attention to the fact that the Kansas City situation was out of hand and impressed everyone that neither the Miles system nor the Home Rule theory was adequate to deal with it. This crime was a kidnaping, which marked the inception of the extortion racket as a national menace and which had a significant relationship to the so-called minor lawbreaking which Chief Miles so earnestly tried to break up. The kidnapers and torture bandits were a by-product of the illicit liquor and gambling traffic, trained for their work in the hi-jacking and gangland ride of the beer and alcohol wars under Prohibition. The booze and gambling industries produced such rich profits that the bolder adventurers of the underworld began to prey on the successful traffickers. The syndicate operators were particularly vulnerable to this attack because of their position outside the law and their adherence to the underworld code of silence.

The ransom gangsters of the Prohibition nightmare were at first called tape bandits because of their habit of taping the eyes and mouths of their victims. They seized a man, taped and bound him, tortured and threatened him with death until he or his friends paid the amount demanded for his release. Or they killed him. The tape bandits began by kidnaping bootleggers and gamblers. The people who survived these ordeals were too frightened or too smart to talk above whispers. Emboldened by their success, the tape bandits turned their attention to larger game—to wealthy businessmen and their wives and children—until they were finally suppressed by the G-men of the F.B.I.

The rise of this sinister business was traced in a series of unsolved murders and rumored kidnapings of underworld figures that occurred over a period of two years in Kansas City.

Then came the most ambitious raid of the terrorists, which shattered what little was left of the city's peace. Political bickering over the police question and McElroyism had reached fever point in the city election campaign of March, 1930, which the tape bandits chose as a propitious time for their big show. It began with an alarm at the home and the office of the Kansas City boss.

T. J. Pendergast was in his office at 1908 Main Street the morning of March 18, 1930, when he received a frantic telephone message from his wife reporting that their son, Tom, Jr., had been kidnaped. The Democratic boss reacted to this stunning announcement with an explosiveness that alarmed his associates and paralyzed normal activity at 1908 Main. Two men from the North Side were summoned to Pendergast's office and arrived in a rush. They were tough and resourceful individuals who knew the characters and the customs of the underworld. Showing the strain under which he labored, the Goat leader told them of his son's disappearance and gave them just two hours in which to return him safely to his family. When these men attempted to explain that they knew nothing of the case and that they needed more than two hours for their search, Pendergast lost his temper and struck out furiously with his fists, knocking down one of the men and slugging the other one so hard that he reeled into a door, breaking the glass.

Well within the two-hour limit, eighteen-year-old Tom, Jr., was found, for he had not been kidnaped. He was discovered sitting in his classroom at Rockhurst College in Kansas City, unaware of the incident that had caused the excitement over him.

The false alarm had its origin in a mysterious happening at about nine-thirty o'clock in the morning, on Ward Parkway, almost in front of the Pendergast home. Roy T. Collins, a building contractor, was alone in his car approaching Ward Parkway from an intersecting street when he observed what plainly was a holdup and kidnaping. A Packard sports roadster, occupied by one man and driving north toward the downtown section, was forced to the curb and stopped by two men in a Chrysler coupé. One of the bandits leaped to the running board of the Packard, struck the driver over the head with a revolver butt or a blackjack, climbed in and took over the wheel, forcing his victim to the floor. Then the two cars roared away.

Two patrolmen—A. E. Perrine and Charles Connell—were standing at the patrol box on the corner near where the kidnaping occurred. They were calling their police station and did not see the crime that was committed less than half a block away. The one witness, Collins, notified the officers of the incident and the police made some quick deductions that produced pain and embarrassment for all concerned. Because the Pendergast home was so close to the scene of the abduction, and because young Tom drove a Packard of the same model (but a different color) as the one Mr. Collins had seen, the officers figured the youth was the victim of either a kidnaping or a college hazing stunt. They called on Mrs. Pendergast, produced the scare that upset 1908 Main Street and retired from the case in confusion while Boss Tom expressed relief over his son's safety in colorful language describing Republican police inefficiency.

For five days the hold-up on Ward Parkway remained a mystery to the police and the general public. Then the *Star* obtained the details, scooping both the newspaper opposition and the authorities.

This kidnaping was obviously the work of an outside gang although there was at least one Kansas City hand in the operation. Some one who knew a great deal about Kansas City and Twelfth Street planned the crime. All the big-time kidnapings of the 1930's were sensational, combining equal parts of horror and tragedy, but few were quite as original in conception or as expert in direction as the Katz case. The victim was the younger of two regionally famous brothers, Ike and Mike Katz, owners of a chain of drugstores that grew from a confectionary store on old Union Avenue. Their offices were in a building less than a block away from the place on Twelfth Street where ransom negotiations for the release of Mike Katz were conducted.

The setting for the opening scene and the timing were remarkable enough, but what followed was even more of a departure from the routine crime and it was all carried out with the precision and suspense of a well-rehearsed stage play. Michael Katz was seized in his car four blocks from his Ward Parkway home shortly before nine-thirty in the morning, while driving on the east side of a well-traveled two-lane boulevard lined with the large homes of the best-protected people in the town. An hour or so later, two Twelfth Street figures were drafted to play unwilling parts as go-betweens, and the drama shifted to a room in a small Twelfth Street hotel in the heart of the business section.

Benny Portman, gambler and bootlegger, received a telephone call to go to Republican First District headquarters on West Twelfth. There he was met by an armed stranger who gave him an envelope addressed to Louis (Kid) Rose, manager of the Sexton Hotel between Main Street and Baltimore Avenue on Twelfth Street. Inside the envelope was a note of instructions to Rose and a letter addressed to Ike Katz, which contained the ransom demand in Mike Katz's handwriting. Rose, a former pugilist, at first refused to let himself become involved in the case but changed his mind after listening twice to a threatening voice on the telephone. Ike Katz and two associates hurried to the hotel late in the afternoon and soon afterward the telephone rang in a fourth-floor room of the Sexton, opening the bidding for the life of Mike Katz. It began at twenty-five thousand dollars and continued until three o'clock the next afternoon, when the weary negotiators accepted the kidnapers' term—one hundred thousand dollars or nothing. The gang's agent on the telephone lost patience at one stage of the negotiations when forty thousand dollars was offered. "Say, keep your forty," the muffled voice said. "We'll bring him home for nothing."

After the final terms were arranged, Portman and Rose left the hotel with one hundred thousand dollars in bills wrapped in a newspaper. They were shadowed to their rendezvous with the kidnapers and directed by telephone along the way. Following orders, they stopped at another hotel, the Coates House on Broadway, where they waited in the lobby until Rose was paged for a telephone call at a booth in the hotel lobby. That call directed them to old Reservoir Hill, a rugged eminence rising above Cliff Drive on the Missouri River bluffs in the northeast part of the city. They parked their car on the top of the lonely hill and walked away from it, as instructed. They didn't look back when they heard a motor car roar up to their parked machine, pause and dash away. When they returned the bundle of bills they had left in the front seat of the car was gone.

Returning to the hotel, Rose and Portman resumed their vigil with two representatives of the Katz family. Three hours passed. The telephone rang five times in that interval, each time with a report from the kidnapers that there had been a delay. At seven-fifteen, when the cover of night had descended and the watchers in the hotel had about abandoned hope, the final call came in. "All right," said the muffled voice. "Go to the Concourse. Your man is waiting there for you now."

At that moment Mike Katz was sitting on a bench in the colonnade of the Concourse, a small park above Cliff Drive in a northeast residential district which once had been a fashionable center. His head and face were covered by a hood and he sat quietly. He had been instructed not to remove his hood for five minutes and he patiently counted off the time. No one disturbed him. A street car clattered by and a few motor cars rolled past on the boulevard near the colonnade but their drivers did not notice the dark figure on the bench. After several minutes Mr. Katz lifted the hood from his head but did not stir from his seat in the recess of the colonnade. This was his first view in nearly thirty-four hours, during which his eyes had been either taped or covered by a hood while he was held a prisoner in two different houses. He still was dazed when a motor car roared up with his rescuers and he took his first steps as a free man again.

The people read the details of the Katz experience along with reports of the Democratic organization's victory in the election of mayor and Council. The election was a spirited affair—two G.O.P. workers were kidnaped and Republican police officers made off with a Democrat and beat him over the head with blackjacks—but the election disorders were comparatively petty matters. The Democrats made a clean sweep of the city offices by a majority of twenty-five thousand, winning every Council seat. Boss Pendergast took two thirds of the patronage and Boss Shannon, who had returned to the fold, got one third. Even the most optimistic Democrats were surprised at the results but the rejoicing of the Goats and the Rabbits was cut short in the crisis provoked by the Katz kidnaping. For a week or so it appeared that the underworld had at last forced a showdown, arousing the leading citizens to a revolt against politicians in an effort to correct the system which encouraged criminals.

The businessmen's answer to the challenge of the ransom terrorists was delivered at a mass meeting directed by the Chamber of Commerce, at which the leading politicians and law enforcement officials sat down with the bankers and merchants to frame a rousing declaration of war on the underworld. The vigilante spirit of the old committee-of-safety days ran high and a rope party might easily have been organized if the businessmen had known just who ought to be hanged first.

Chief speaker at the meeting was James R. Page, the county prosecutor, who rose to oratorical heights. "These are dark days of crime and brigandage in Kansas City," said the Prosecutor. "Let public sentiment be aroused."

Then Mr. Page said a curious thing. "I'd rather have the vote of the humblest Republican on earth than all the Democratic bandits out of hell," he exclaimed with heat. His remark was greeted with a roar for it was plain that he was aiming at a North Side element in the Democratic organization with which he had clashed previously.

"Who is the ally of this organized criminal element in Kansas City?" Mr. Page asked. "Who is the Big Shot?" The crowd grew tense, wondering if the prosecutor was going to name names.

"I say the ally is the politician, the crooked lawyer and the professional bondsman," he shouted. "And that goes for both political parties."

The speech thus ended as an indictment of the whole system, and while no one could question the accuracy and justice of the charge that fixers in both parties were guilty of dealing with the criminal, this conclusion had a somewhat anticlimactic and chilling effect. It left the citizens with a depressing realization of the magnitude of the task they faced, and no particular idea of where to begin.

The Katz case remains to this day a mystery in the files of the Kansas City authorities. Chance played a strange part in the brief investigation that followed Mr. Katz's release. Two St. Louis criminals were arrested when the car in which they were riding was wrecked on a Missouri highway and it was learned the car had been purchased in Kansas City with some of the marked ransom bills. The St. Louis characters had an alibi, of course, and were dismissed after Mr. Katz, who said he had been blindfolded throughout his imprisonment, was unable to identify them. The investigation suffered a further setback through the abrupt removal of the stool pigeon on whom the police were depending for information. His death apparently was not induced by a gangster's bullet but by a heart attack resulting from overindulgence in narcotics. To satisfy public indignation over this untimely intrusion of fate, the chief of detectives was reduced to a patrolman's beat and that unfortunate scapegoat soon thereafter died, also of a heart attack.

Last repercussion of the kidnaping was the resignation of Police Chief Miles. Bert S. Kimbrell, the member of the Police Board who had backed Miles in his unpopular crusading, stepped out with him. The Republicans kept control of the police for two more years, but this ended the experiment in nonpolitical administration of the department and set the stage for the terrors of Home Rule.

The Party Men

WITH A FRESH mandate from the people and its Council majority upped from five to four to nine to nothing, the Democratic machine was ready to roll in high gear, and roll it did. The new mayor, Bryce B. Smith, millionaire bakerman, sounded the keynote—more business efficiency. The first order of business was the unanimous election of Henry F. McElroy for another turn as city manager and Mayor Smith thereafter sat back to let the Council's hired man run the show.

The Council contained several interesting personalities of political weight, and the makeup of this body rather accurately reflected the composition of the entire machine. Contrary to the notion fostered by association of ideas, the political machine was not a thing of well-synchronized gears but a combination of dissident elements, frequently quarreling, often in danger of falling apart and seldom in a state of complete harmony. Tom Pendergast got the blame, responsibility or credit for everything that happened although many conflicting voices and interests went into the shaping of the policy that finally prevailed. The man at 1908 Main Street consistently figured in the role of compromiser between hostile forces in the Democratic organization. Without his skill as a co-ordinator or governor, he could never have established himself as a true machine boss. Only five of the members of the new

Council belonged to Pendergast's faction, the others being followers of Welch and Shannon. The way they all fell into line at Council meetings was a beautiful example of team play, and the boss of the dominant faction had to use other talents besides whip-cracking to produce that result.

Pendergast's skill in picking outstanding men in the community for public office was almost as famed as his genius for inspiring devotion among those he supported. His following included individuals who previously had distinguished themselves in other factions or in independent activities. Mayor Smith, for example, first appeared on the political scene with the Rabbits and was identified by the *Star* as a neutral between the factions for some time after he took the mayor's office. Councilman Ruby D. Garrett was another who was labeled a neutral at the outset of his tenure in 1930. He had tried to crash into the political picture as something of an independent in 1920, when he announced as a candidate for governor, and again in 1922, when he defied the bosses to run the steamroller over his boom for mayor. Both campaigns were notable for their brevity and after that Mr. Garrett settled down to the routine of law and politics, making himself useful to the organization as a campaign orator for other candidates, building up his fences in the American Legion, the Chamber of Commerce and other circles. The habit of regularity grew on him through the years when he was winning Pendergast recognition and during his ten years in the Council he developed into one of the organization champions, closing his career with a spectacular effort to hold the line against the reform which swept on the City Hall in 1939 and 1940.

The consistency with which Judge McElroy got his way with the Council eventually produced a general impression that this body was made up entirely of rubber stamps. However, the Republicans were rather slow in selling this idea to a majority of the voters. One of the reasons for that delay was the fact that the party in power included a few conspicuous figures who on occasion made a show of resisting the dynamic Country Bookkeeper. In fact, their combined protest attained a considerable volume and weight over the years, although it did not stop McElroy and his minions. The dean of this unusual company of

Democratic critics was Councilman A. N. Gossett, described by the *Star* as "the most substantial member of the Council."

Councilman Gossett, the popular Farmer Al, had a mind and a conscience that were alternately useful and disturbing to the machine. He was a great vote getter and an indispensable man whenever there was an occasion requiring a speech or a resolution that needed classical adornment and homespun treatment. Mr. Gossett was a lawyer with a high-pay practice and a farmer with rural property that entitled him to classification as an agriculturalist. He detested the word and insisted on being called a farmer. He was the farmer of the First Ward and the farmer of the Kansas City Club, the town's most exclusive retreat for self-made men of means, which, in deference to Farmer Al's democratic simplicity, was always referred to as his humble boardinghouse. Farmer Al impressed his rustic informality on his luxurious surroundings, snapped his galluses, rumpled his hair and wore an old hat. He objected to the formidable array of knives, forks and spoons which he found at his table and dispensed with all the eating gadgets except two or three simple items. "It's my belief," he said, "that all a man needs is one knife, one fork, one teaspoon, one book, one wife or sweetheart and one million dollars."

Puffing on his corncob pipe, made from cobs on his own Jackson County farm and filled with natural leaf from Kentucky, Farmer Al discoursed on beaten biscuits, Greek literature, the solar system and the correct way to age Missouri corn liquor. His special brand was aged in the wind, in a keg lashed to a tall tree, the wind rocking it for several months and blowing in "a sweetness and substance that Nature alone is able to impart."

When he was a boy of ten, Al Gossett had been given a telescope which stimulated a lifelong interest in astronomy and his conversation was interlarded with observations on the eccentricities of the planets, along with Greek and Latin phrases, all combined with Jackson County truisms and expressed in pungent Missouri language. He frequently was seized by the poetic mood and restrained with difficulty. The Council unsuccessfully tried to stop him from delivering an original "Ode to An Aerolite" at one of its duller sessions which he sought to enliven. The ode was inspired by a twelve-pound chunk from a meteorite which he

S. J. Ray in The Kansas City Star

Sympathy, Just Sympathy

The politician's stellar performance as a front man drew this tribute from the cartoonist in 1940.

had seen fall on a farm sixty years earlier, and today it is preserved in the minutes of a Council meeting.

> O shooting Star! Of old,
> A coruscating flame,
> Now spent and cold.
> An air-stone that blazed
> A fiery path across the skies,
> Darkly dull and glazed, marked by fire,
> Shaped in no design
> Close to my eyes, you lie,
> Heavily within my hands.
> Fragment from distant space,
> Cast-off, expelled, from stranger sphere
> How come? What violative burst
> Of Nature sent you here?
> Was it that some devil, cursed
> With Time and Death,
> Made you thus drear,
> If I had been where you have been,
> What would I be?
> Or, were you by some angel thrown,
> Battling with Michael, or against him,
> In that fight,
> And missing, came twisting, sizzling,
> Down to this light?
> Short was your freedom,
> Brief was your glory,
> Pleased to meet you, hunky dory.*

Besides serving as the country-cured philosopher, poet and humorist of the city administration, Farmer Al performed useful work as policy maker and restrainer of the Country Bookkeeper. He strenuously resisted McElroy when the City Manager went to the Legislature to lobby for his own measure to set up Home Rule in Kansas City. Farmer Al publicly declared that turning over control of the police to the home people would give the administration dictatorial power that would be abused. His objection was based further on the sound point that Republican responsibility for the police actually was an asset for the Demo-

* Reprinted by kind permission of Mr. Roy K. Dietrich.

crats with the crime problem in its current stage of development. If his advice had been heeded, the machine might have missed some of the worst storms that struck it.

Councilman Gossett criticized the City Manager for his defense of the slot-machine racket in Kansas City. After Home Rule was established, and an ouster movement developed against McElroy over his charter violations in handling the police, Gossett joined with the Mayor in insisting that the leader of this uprising be granted a hearing by the Council.

He spoke out against the administration on other occasions and once or twice it appeared that he might kick over the traces. The conflict within him continued to the final showdown on the machine question, but then he was too old and too sick to take a hand in the excitement. The opposition honored him by not including him among the members of the City Council against whom recall petitions were circulated.

Mayor Bryce B. Smith teamed with Farmer Al in the liberal or uneasy wing of the Goat faction. Mayor Smith was the popularity man of the organization, the little man loved by the masses, the rich citizen with democratic manners and a heart of gold. He also lent South Side tone to the Goats, being socially well placed and a high figure in Rotary. A pint-sized man with a boyish smile, he wore big hats and puffed on big cigars, thought he had the heart of a lion and was always about to assert his rights against McElroy and the bad boys of the organization. Judge McElroy called him Boss and let him pitch the first ball at the opening of the baseball season.

Garrett, Gossett and Smith illustrated the range of the Goat faction in the upper levels of the city's business, social and political life. Contrasts were equally well marked among other representatives of the organization in government. One of the more important and interesting members of the Council was Charlie Clark, who upheld the honor of the North Side, which was included in the district from which he was elected. Clark belonged to the old order with Alderman Jim Pendergast and carried its early tradition into the final period under Big Tom. He outshone all the other councilmen in devotion to the machine principle, the heroic quality of his service being illustrated by the incident when he was carried to a Council meeting on a stretcher, a pneumonia victim, to cast the deciding vote on a measure of importance to City Manager

McElroy. Clark spread the Goat gospel among the rank and file in many other ways. He was the expert politician whose accomplishments popularized the theory that the organization could perform special favors for large interests and small individuals, and serve the general public at the same time it inflated the power and glory of the Goat boss. He dispensed favors, justice and charity during a long career as legislator, county assessor, clerk of the criminal court, justice of the peace and councilman. The only full-time working member of the City Council, he set up a desk in an anteroom of the city clerk's office and kept himself always on call. He knew his business, for he was a student of government and humanity, and an authority on the statutes and ordinances governing the city.

Councilman Clark was exceedingly useful to the Goats in promoting the legend of Pendergast good will and good works among the numerous lower order of voters. He was manager and host of the Christmas dinners that were given annually by the ruling family for the derelicts of the North Side. These affairs, which were introduced by Alderman Jim when the guests numbered less than a hundred or so, were continued by Tom in the depression days when thousands were served in a large building near Market Square on Main Street. Charlie Clark was at home with the drifters and gandies who crowded in to sit at the rows of tables. His tousled hair, rumpled clothes and weatherbeaten face would have made it easy for a stranger to mistake him for one of the crowd. He knew the names of most of the men in the dining hall. "Don't call it a charity meal," he told them. "We are guests here today of Tom Pendergast."

Blind loyalty like Charlie Clark's was, of course, the outstanding characteristic of the Pendergast following. This myopic condition was combined in many cases with the deafness and dumbness which partisanship and sycophancy customarily produce. In fact, that devastating complication was so widespread that many observers were slow to appreciate the fact that the Democratic organization's representatives in government included one of the town's most vigorous dissenters, who was not intimidated by Judge McElroy and could not be restrained by the desire for harmony at 1908 Main Street.

This disturber in the machine was James R. Page, who was elected county attorney the same year that McElroy became city manager and whose rebelliousness grew at about the same rate as the McElroy despotism. Page was a product of rural Missouri. Possessing some of the tough qualities of the hickory trees on his native Sullivan County acres, he proved that he was as good a hand in rough-and-tumble as the former Iowa farm boy who ruled the City Hall. Determined to win a reputation as a law enforcer and an independent public servant, he established a record as a hanging prosecutor and a man who wore nobody's collar except during campaign time, when he consistently had the support of Tom Pendergast.

The criminal cases handled by Page's office included many of the most sensational crimes in the city's history and constituted glaring proof that the growing slum areas in the industrial community were the breeding grounds of an outlaw generation, which found banditry and murder the quickest way out of poverty and segregation. Page was not concerned with the primary causes of crime but concentrated on its suppression. Leniency of the courts in sentencing prisoners, granting continuances and approving paroles was regarded by him as a major factor in the breakdown of public order and he incensed judges by denouncing their parole board as "a crime-forgiving society." He clashed with City Manager McElroy over police protection of the gambling syndicates and publicly branded the City Manager as a tool of racketeers. He collided head on with one of the principal powers of the Democratic organization, John Lazia, the Big Shot of the North Side.

Lazia was an Italian-American, a son of immigrants. As a youth he had a brief career in banditry, which ended when he was sentenced to the Missouri penitentiary for highway robbery. Paroled long before he had served out his term, he returned to Kansas City, engaged in the bootleg traffic for a while before he emerged as a figure of consequence in politics and business. His political organization was the North Side Democratic Club, and at the peak of his power he was credited with being able to deliver as many as seventy-five hundred votes. His nominal business was a soft-drink manufacturing establishment, selling a line of beverages that were favored by the city administration and concerns that wanted to keep in the organization's good graces. Lazia was reputed to have other extensive interests and was recognized as the head of the gang that played the dominant part in the liquor and gambling rackets and in the night clubs.

Although Lazia was a personal friend and political ally of Pendergast, Prosecutor Page attacked him boldly and with increasing vigor. In one campaign he publicly repudiated Lazia's support and got Pendergast to back him up on the issue. Page's campaign against the North Side leader grew in intensity through six years when he served as prosecutor and afterward when he was elected circuit judge with the Boss's assistance. He was living proof that a man in the organization could talk up to Pendergast or go against the machine's political interests and not be destroyed for his show of independence.

Some opposition orators explained Jim Page as a sham reformer inside the organization, whose function was to provide a distraction that would discourage a more thorough reform from the outside. If that was a correct analysis, then Pendergast permitted Page to go too far with his exciting performance. The Prosecutor's quarrels with Lazia and McElroy at the end of the 1920's and opening the 1930's were the first rumblings within the machine itself of the revolt that was coming.

Gambler's Revival

THE STORY of Solly Weissman's effort to win recognition as a gambler is the longest and perhaps the saddest legend of Twelfth Street. The society in the neighborhood of Twelfth Street and Baltimore Avenue, center of the gambling community, tried for a long time to ignore Mr. Weissman but that was difficult to do, for Solly weighed three hundred pounds and was light on his feet. He was Slicey Solly, sometimes called Cutcher-Head-Off, the Captain Kidd of Thirteenth Street and the Bully of Twelfth Street. He was a bootlegger, an underworld fronter, a strong-arm man for politicians. Police also listed him as a hi-jacker, a gem robber, and an innovator of the gang ride, among other things, but these distinctions he always dismissed with a shrug and a pained expression. "Not me, chief," he said. "Not me. My racket's whisky and gambling."

Solly's faith and persistence were sufficiently large to make him the representative figure of the age which believed that America offered endless opportunity to every man willing to put some dough on the name of a nag or the turn of a card. Neither financial panic, social ostracism nor legislative prohibition could suppress or discourage the gamblers. For half a century the effort had been made to banish the games by outlawing them but throughout that time the habit had grown, producing serious social and economic disturbance along with evidence that the repressive measures that were tried actually had stimulated the growth of the gambling mania.

The growing economic importance of this industry manifested itself in various curious ways in the rise of Solly Weissman until 1930. That was the year when the Coolidge-Hoover Prosperity finally reached its dismal end in the debris left by Wall Street's Black Thursday of 1929. It also brought forth Slicey Solly's most ambitious, and his last, undertaking, but it did not end the gambling boom. By ironic coincidence, Prosperity and Mr. Weissman went out together at the same time that the games in Kansas City were entering their big play. Almost another decade passed before the real depression struck Twelfth Street.

In the beginning of this revival in the early 1920's, Solly set up a stand at Thirteenth and Baltimore as a base of operations and found many things to do while looking for gambling opportunities. Police closed his dive after three men were shot there, one fatally, but they found no one to testify against Weissman or challenge his alibi. A product of the First World War period, when all factors combined to bring the underworld type of citizen to full flower, Solly's progress was traced in police records listing his arrests for everything from vagrancy to investigation for murder. One of his earliest exploits was the rolling of a Kansas farmer for a few hundred dollars by administering knockout drops. Before long he had advanced beyond petty operations and drew wide attention in gambling circles when he was reported to have held up a dice game, taking nine thousand dollars. His elephantine proportions, his airy manner, his daring, luck and political connections combined to make him a very interesting figure in nighttime circles. His reputation as a fronter had firm support in his own record, showing twenty-nine arrests and one conviction. The one rap against him, involving a five-hundred-dollar-fine, resulted from a sentimental lapse when he went to the rescue of an icebox thief. The pilferer had been captured by his intended victims and was being menaced by a street crowd when Solly happened along and spirited him away by impersonating a plainclothes officer.

Solly's soft side was revealed on another occasion when he figured in a daytime New Year's duel on a residential street with his erstwhile friend, Joe Wagner, the bank bandit. A neighbor woman in the apartment where Wagner lived, observing the maneuvering from her front porch, pleaded with Solly to abandon the field on humanitarian grounds and he solemnly considered her advice, then retreated ponderously down an alley. Police were less impressed by the woman's moral power than the fact that Solly's tactical position was bad.

A little later the Captain Kidd of Thirteenth Street took the spotlight in the battle attending the mob primary when Miles Bulger was eliminated from the political arena. Solly's arrest in that riot upset his plan to settle his personal feud with Bulger's strongarm department, Swede Benson, but the feud was revived later when the Terrible and Unterrified Swede and the Terrible Solly led their playmates to wreck and shoot up each other's establishments. Alas, police interrupted that exchange before Solly and Swede got a chance to shoot it out.

With his continued success, Slicey Solly began to polish off the rough edges. He dressed in expensively tailored clothes, wore Harold Lloyd horn-rimmed glasses that emphasized both the comical and ferocious qualities of his fat face, and developed a jolly line of side talk that was both amusing and vastly disquieting. He was a man about town, a familiar figure in the night spots. He prowled the streets in a sports car that was recognized everywhere by its rubber-tired windshield.

Weissman operated a dive near Convention Hall on Thirteenth Street so he could be close at hand for the wrestling shows and other sports circuses that were held in the hall. The sports craze of the record-breaking twenties found perhaps its most vigorous expression in Slicey Solly. The wrestling shows provided both a source of income for the gamblers and a rare entertainment. The clowning of the mat heroes was so good that a vast excitement seized the entire crowd in the hall although everyone knew that the matches were fixed. Solly also had a large interest in that other great popular attraction of the day—the dance marathon— but his attendance at these grotesque exhibitions was prompted less by his delight in art than his pecuniary concern in the outcome. He and his boys stopped a marathon in Convention Hall in 1928 when a couple they were backing to win was eliminated by the judges. The show didn't go on until their favorites returned to the floor. A little later the promoters of the marathon disappeared, along with the prize money, and it was rumored that Solly had taken them for a ride.

The rumrunning, beer and liquor-making enterprises that flourished during Prohibition provided many opportunities for an enterprising operator like Weissman. He formed connections with gangsters in St. Paul, Chicago, St. Louis and New York. At one stage of his operations he was host in Kansas City to George Remus, the Cincinnati booze king, who was credited with making twenty million dollars from whisky piped from government warehouses. Remus came to Kansas City shortly after he had been released from an insane asylum, where he was committed after escaping the penalty for murdering his wife on a Cincinnati street. Twelfth Street buzzed with speculation over the import of his visits with Weissman, but there was no known sequel to the meeting of this fantastic individual and the equally fantastic Solly Weissman.

The Weissman ambition to win renown in gambling circles grew apace and he was reported to have a hand in a large casino in St. Paul. He began to figure in the Kansas City big-time sports when he participated in the financial backing of the dog races that were conducted near North Kansas City, a venture in which he was associated with John Lazia, the North Side politician.

But Mr. Weissman was not yet satisfied with the progress he was making. He was still regarded as socially undesirable in the exclusive inner circle at Twelfth and Baltimore and he wasn't in the big money. He brooded over this until one day late in the third decade of the twentieth century, when he got the idea for his greatest promotion in the gambling racket. His plan was to tap a race wire from one of the national syndicates which carried racing results to the horse book offices where bets were placed. If he could establish a leak whereby he learned the race results thirty seconds or so before they were posted, Weissman would make some large money. In order to establish this private service, Solly called on a quiet and mild-appearing individual named Charley Haughton, who handled the wire for a national syndicate serving horse books on Twelfth Street. An older and much smaller man than Weissman,

Haughton bluntly rejected the gangster's suggestion and was unmoved when the three-hundred-pound bully tried to intimidate him with threats of a beating up and a gang ride.

Not long after this, Weissman hurriedly left town and it was rumored that he wouldn't come back. The police under the direction of Chief Miles were making Kansas City uncomfortable for him and so were the Federal authorities, who were prosecuting Solly in a liquor conspiracy case. Whether his departure had anything to do with his effort to muscle in on the gambling operation was never established, but the affair between him and Haughton had an explosive sequel when Solly recovered from his alarm and decided it was safe to return to Kansas City.

The conflict between the massive Thirteenth Street bully and the little Twelfth Street gambler moved Twelfth Street society to its emotional depths. To the sentimental horse players and dice rollers, it was the David-and-Goliath classic of the century. Charley Haughton was the popular hero for he was not only the little man pitted against a giant, he was also the defender of the old order, the mystical fraternity of sports who regarded gambling as an honorable and vitally essential occupation and labored earnestly to restore the prestige it had enjoyed in Old Town in the heyday of Bob Potee.

Haughton carried the nickname of Hard Luck Charley, a title that he earned in his early days after a run of losses resulting from his refusal to take a hand in crooked games and sports shows. His fortunes improved after he became a figure in the Kansas City horse book business. Hard Luck Charley was one of numerous engaging characters who acquired affluence and added something to the new legend of noble sportsmanship on the street of long hours and short odds. Other substantial citizens in this society were Harry Brewer, the blind bookie of Twelfth Street, who earned a fortune by never making a mathematical mistake or violating the code of fair play; Gold Tooth Maxie, the ethical and indestructible crap shooter; Johnnie Johnston, the friendly fat man who liked to stand on a Twelfth Street corner, smiling at the crowds; Jake Feinberg, who was always sweet to the suckers and respected his obligations; and, of course, Tom Finnigan, the unofficial mayor of Twelfth Street, who impressed on everyone that there was nothing higher than a sportsman's honor and nothing more picturesque than a turf follower's conversation.

Tom Pendergast was both the political and spiritual father of this adventurous company. He proved the depth of his devotion to the gambler's ideal by the size of his bets and the extent of his personal losses while supervising developments that brought a vast expansion in chance-taking opportunities. He stimulated interest in racing by establishing the habit of attending race meets in the East and leading a delegation to the Kentucky Derby each year, and by acquiring a stable of his own. His friends praised his horses and his judgment but learned to beware of his enthusiasms. Only one of his horses was a first-rate animal but Tom regarded all of them with enormous pride and affection, and formed the habit of honoring local or regional celebrities by naming his steeds after them. He named one of his favorites Bo McMillin in honor of the old football star who was then coaching at Kansas State College. Pendergast was so eloquent on the subject of Bo's merits that he induced the Twelfth Street boys to bet everything from the family piano to the washtub on him at the Kentucky Derby. The Bo McMillin fiasco was painful and mortifying to all concerned, but did not dampen the enthusiasm of the Goat boss and his followers.

Pendergast brought horse racing back to Kansas City, ending the banishment that had occurred two decades earlier in the administration of Holy Joe Folk. The prohibition was lifted, or tilted, by a liberal-minded Supreme Court, which reinterpreted the law to declare that the certificate form of betting was legal. Under this construction, a man could go to a window at a race track and contribute a certain amount of money "to improve the breed of horses." Sometimes the breed improved unexpectedly fast, in which case he could collect a refund and stay within the law. A New Orleans group of sportsmen came to Missouri to test this new system, operating a track at Smithville, twenty-three miles north of Kansas City. A year later, in 1928, a Kansas City group organized the Riverside Park Jockey Club and took over the grounds used by a dog track, five miles north of Kansas City. The park was popularly known as Pendergast's Track. The Boss's name did not appear among the organizers but the names of his business associates and close friends were prominent in the list. The plant grew into a large establishment with many windows for contributions and refunds. It drew crowds which at their peak numbered more than seventeen thousand for a single day, operating until another reform struck the state in 1937.

Riverside was the showpiece of the gambling boom that excited the avarice of Solly Weissman and led him to undertake the promotion that highlighted the hi-jacking and muscling-in movement of this period. The gambling operators found that they faced as much interference from crooks trying to horn in as they did from reformers who demanded their business be suppressed. This double trouble manifested itself when Jake Feinberg gave Kansas City its first little Monte Carlo the same year that Pendergast's Riverside Track opened. Jake convinced a group of backers that the very best people would be glad to lose their money if dignified surroundings were provided in a sylvan retreat off one of the new highways running out from Kansas City. The result was the Green Hills Club. It was closed after a short run owing to the agitation of the Presbyterians in Platte County and the overhead costs for "protection."

The Green Hills project was followed by a more elaborate endeavor, Cuban Gardens, a night club and gambling casino on private grounds near the Riverside Race Track. Johnny Lazia was the chief figure in this operation at the outset. Phil McCrory, long-time business associate of Pendergast, advanced him twelve thousand dollars as a first payment in assembling funds to build the Gardens. The Ministerial Alliance of Liberty, county seat of Clay County, started a campaign against the enterprise and the sheriff asserted he was doing his best to suppress the casino. After five raids, he confessed his discouragement. Each time he found no evidence of gambling but was charmed by the sight of fashionably gowned women and men in evening clothes, dancing to the strains of "The Chant of the Jungle" and other current hits played by a large band garbed in Spanish costumes.

It was difficult for an officer or any other intruder to break in on the Gardens without warning. Armed guards sat in a small building at the motor car entrance, sizing up the customers and admitting only those they recognized. Once inside the club, a stranger would not have known he was in a gambling establishment. Well-armed men in evening clothes admitted the knowing ones to the anteroom where the play in roulette, dice and black jack went on under the eyes of more armed attendants.

The many diversions for sportive citizens provided daily and nightly evidence that gambling was big business and was organized on an efficient basis, with the operators making the necessary arrangements to protect their interests. It was an enterprise that required devices to obtain official toleration or to discourage crusading representatives of the law, along with more forceful measures against raids by crooked gamblers, bandits, rival promoters and extortionists. The obvious inferences were drawn by a large number of citizens and there were disturbances among ministerial groups and other guardians of civic order, but the protest was scattered and ineffectual for some time. The troublemakers in the underworld were not so well under control. Individualists like Solly Weissman remained a constant threat, and this fact was rudely forced on the public's attention by the events of October 28, 1930, when Mr. Weissman lumbered off the train from Chicago.

Solly had returned to settle a couple of matters. First on the list was a conspiracy indictment involving him and several others in the operation of a beer and alcohol depot in Kansas City. Solly was in high good humor when he went to the Federal court to attend the final proceedings on this violation of the Prohibition law, for his position had improved sensationally in the interval while he was waiting to be called to trial. This change had been brought about chiefly by the disappearance of the government's star witness, Elmer Hoard. One rumor was that Mr. Hoard was under wraps in Chicago, enticed there by a Weissman offer of profitable employment. Another was that he was well encased in concrete on the bed of the Missouri River.

When the case was dismissed for want of evidence, Weissman swaggered from the judicial chambers, bowing, smiling, waving to old acquaintances and admirers, shaking hands with lawyers, bondsmen and other characters who crowed up to congratulate him. Then he went to a hotel to confer with a few of his confederates.

Within a few hours after his return from his exile up North, Slicey Solly gave every indication of an intention to remain in town for a long period. He picked up where he had left off and set out immediately to see little Charley Haughton. He found his man in a second-floor office above Rayen's Turf Betting Agency at 1211 Baltimore Avenue. Mr. Haughton had served a turn as a peace officer and he was ready when the Terrible Solly marched jauntily into the room. It was all over in a minute. Arley Rayen ducked for safety as Solly made a lunge toward Haughton, who shot once across Rayen's desk. The big hoodlum sank to the floor with a bullet in this throat. He was found there alone a little later by persons attracted by the shot.

Charley Haughton voluntarily surrendered and gave a statement to the prosecutor before Solly died early in the night. The authorities exonerated the gray-haired race wire manager and he was showered with congratulations from all sides. In the bars, hotels and poolhalls, men talked of little Charley Haughton, the giant killer. Twelfth Street celebrated the slaying of Solly Weissman as a victory of the Good Joe's and Honest Andrew's over the criminals, but this actually was only a prelude to the final underworld invasion. The incident was quickly forgotten and the play went on as before while the public agitation over the gambling revival was submerged in the excitement of another political campaign which carried Tom Pendergast forward to new power.

OF THE PEOPLE

IN THE FALL of 1930, when the first political shocks of the depression reverberated across the land, notice was served of the larger roles that Tom Pendergast and Jackson County Jeffersonianism were going to play in national affairs for the next decade. The phenomenal increase in the voting power of the Kansas City organization and the election of the Honorable Joseph B. Shannon to Congress were important features of a campaign which produced a pronounced Republican decline throughout the nation and established Governor Franklin D. Roosevelt of New York as the leading contender for the Democratic presidential nomination in 1932.

"Shannon in Congress will put Kansas City on the map," declared Henry L. Jost, former mayor of Kansas City and a member of Congress for one term in the twenties.

Boss Pendergast sent out the word that everything was to be done to elect his old rival as the representative from the Fifth Congressional District of Missouri, which then embraced Jackson County. Cas Welch, Shannon's errant protégé, forgot recent differences and ordered his faction to "vote 'em and count 'em straight" for the Jeffersonian of the Rabbits.

Not the least interesting phase of the campaign was this demonstration of party harmony, signifying that Pendergast at last had been able to control the factionalism that had dogged the boss organization for nearly a half-century. The most important point in Mr. Shannon's elevation to Congress was, of course, that he was going on the shelf, leaving Tom Pendergast to run the home front pretty much as he pleased.

Although the Pendergast matter dominated the picture, the sending of Joe Shannon to Washington was an event that deserved more attention than it received at the time, for it was of greater moment than the fact that it removed the Rabbit leader from the Kansas City scene and placed him personally under political obligation to the Goat chieftain. As the loyal Mr. Henry L. Jost reminded the voters, Shannon was the right man to put Kansas City on the map, in the *Congressional Record* at least. For a decade he worked diligently to show that Jackson County was the new fountain-head of the old-time Jeffersonian movement. Through his speeches and the measures he espoused as congressman, he gave illuminating expression to a Democratic philosophy that assumed increasing importance in the conflicts attending the New Deal uprising, and which today still affects the national destiny through another Jackson County man in the White House.

The Jeffersonian revival that Shannon staged was one of the most instructive and entertaining of the political shows offered in the off-year elections that brought the first rumblings of the unorthodox New Deal. The Rabbit boss was perhaps as well qualified for this work as any man who ever went from Jackson County to Washington. He had been preparing himself for the role of statesman in all the years that he was mastering the intricacies of practical politics.

In the periods when his faction was out of power and the Goats or the Republicans took over the task of serving the special interests and manipulating the spoils system, Joe Shannon retired to his Jeffersonian library. Law books and books on, by and about his national hero were scattered helter-skelter in his office in the old Scarritt Building. They were stacked on tables and chairs, piled on the floor, stuffed on shelves. He never had time to arrange them but he read most of them. He had been educating himself since he quit school at the age of twelve, in the year that the Widow Shannon moved to Kansas City with her large family. Beginning with a secondhand copy of Blackstone, Joe read law until he qualified himself to pass the bar examination.

This Rabbit student added a course in the liberal arts by combining two of his favorite pursuits—travel and reading. He carried a book on every trip he took, and sometimes made trips simply to have privacy for reading. He took a unique college course when he sent his son, Frank, to California and Missouri universities. When Frank finished with his textbooks he sent them to his father. Shannon studied them and carried on a voluminous correspondence with his son regarding those texts. When Frank finished university, so had Joe.

Shannon didn't learn all of his Jeffersonianism from books and politicians. He got a large measure of his education by mixing with the crowds, keeping his ear to the ground, listening to the argument around the cracker barrel and the hot stove. The interest with which he studied the common people, and the ease with which he communicated with them, was illustrated by the manner in which he conducted his first race for office.

While other candidates centered their appeals on the Kansas City masses and placed increasing dependence on the blaring radio to carry their messages in the fall of 1930, Shannon mounted the stump in towns and villages, addressing friendly and earnest groups that seldom numbered more than four hundred. He started his race early with a show in the nineteenth century style. Somewhere he found an ancient tent, intact with bunting, flags and hardwood benches, that had served in the political wars of the past. He set it up and organized a troupe to travel from town to town. Crowds turned out to see the circus, for memories of the days it recalled were long and vivid. Except for the substitution of electric lights for torches, the show was a scene out of the Forty-Years-Ago column. And the speaker on the platform was a figure out of that earlier day. Mr. Shannon was a handsome man, somewhat in the Great Roman style of Jim Reed but with more of a Bryanesque air. His silvery thatched head, wide-set eyes, bold nose and firm chin were the features of the dignified statesman but his face was perpetually cast in the amiable expression of the countryman and courthouse politician.

Joe's circus got under way with a brass band giving a concert until the tent filled. Before the speaking began three loyal and talented Democrats—Harry Kessel, Dick Okane and Jerry McGee, song-and-dance men from Twelfth Street—entertained the audience with popular songs, gags and wisecracks. Then the future congressman stepped on the platform and for an hour or more held the crowd's fascinated attention with an authoritative exposition of Jeffersonian philosophy, interlarded with colorful references to local history and ending with a stirring call to rally in the never-ending fight of the people for Human Rights against Property.

Shannon's campaign tour in the rural townships brought into the picture a part of the county whose character and real importance were overshadowed by the big city on the Kaw which had taken over the whole direction of affairs. The names of the towns told the character of the country and the people in the fifth district—Independence, Blue Springs, Lake City, Grain Valley, Oak Grove, Buckner, Sibley, Courtney, Hickman Mills, New Santa Fe, Lee's Summit, Grandview, Lone Jack, and others saying that the lay of this land was good and men had made great history here.

Politics was not a practical matter of power and spoils or a theory of government to these people. Politics was in their blood. It was the old time faith. The speaker knew all the key words and organ phrases that moved these people for he was one of them, a true Jackson County Democrat who spoke the language of Benton, Blair, Vest, Champ Clark, Show Me, I'm From Missouri, and You've Got to Quit Kicking My Dog Around.

The Rabbit champion belonged to what might be described as the left of Jackson County Democracy. The Goats inclined to the right, as represented by Jim Reed. Harry Truman, a Goat, later developed into the most conspicuous liberal Democrat from Jackson County, but he was a shining exception. At the time he stood for Congress, Joe Shannon represented the extreme of Jeffersonian radicalism in the Democratic organization.

An interesting expression of the Jackson County Democratic philosophy, suggesting its remoteness from the Jeffersonian ideas of New York's Franklin D. Roosevelt, was given in the campaign of 1930. Joe's main planks for the nation at this grave moment called for elimination of government competition with private business and observance of Jefferson's birthday as a national holiday. He succeeded in getting Mississippi and one less benighted Southern state to adopt the holiday idea and after he arrived in Washington he got himself appointed chairman of a House committee to investigate Federal intrusion in the commercial field.

Mr. Shannon's Jeffersonian fundamentalism was expressed by him in the statement that the "function of our government is political and not economic," a principle he advanced with such vigor that he interested the National Association of Manufacturers and other large business representatives in his reform. His scheme to check bureaucratic competition with private industry was a bill calling for the introduction of a cost accounting system in governmental expenditures, setting up cost standards which, if adopted, probably would have made even Harry Hopkins think that the New Deal experiment was a financially impossible undertaking. His bill died in 1934, in the midst of the Rooseveltian shotgun wedding of government, business and labor.

Jim Reed was to go further than Shannon in upholding the states' rights theory that the Constitution prohibited the use of the Federal authority for any economic and social relief of the people outside of building highways and encouraging education. He not only looked on all New Deal efforts to establish a system of economic justice as interference with American liberties, he also believed that the Republicans had been leading the country down the road toward socialism with such radical experiments as Hoover's R.F.C. for big business and his farm board. Jim's indignation over the way Hoover had run things was heightened by the fact that Reed's old Missouri enemy, former Governor Arthur M. Hyde, assisted the Republican Socialistic coup as Hoover's Secretary of Agriculture.

In 1930, Reed, two years out of the Senate and preparing to run again for the Presidency, was selected to deliver the principal blast from Jackson County against the Great Engineer in the White House who kept on seeing Prosperity Just Around the Corner while he fumbled with measures to arrest the downward spiral. The Stormy Petrel's contribution to public enlightenment was a vivid recapitulation of all of Hoover's mistakes and a dramatic statement of the size of the calamity. "There have been more bank failures in the last few months than have occurred since the days of wildcat banking. Six million people walk the streets. . . . All due to the Republicans." The wealthy ex-Senator from Missouri aligned himself with the oppressed and assailed Senator Capper of Kansas as the tool of big business. He warmed up as he turned to the subject of Farmer Hyde and his futile efforts to conjure away the farm surplus. "He has two remedies, sovereign, complete and pleasing," said Reed. "His remedy for the surplus is that we must eat it up. Women must quit reducing and men must enlarge the capacity of their bellies. It's a wonderful solution and the other day I heard of a farmer who had solved his problems under this system. He took a load of hogs to market but the price was so low that it wouldn't pay him for the cost of transportation and he refused to sell. As he was starting back home, the buyer argued with him and told him, 'No use of you trying to sell these hogs some place else, you won't get a better price.' 'I am not going to sell these hogs,' said the farmer. 'I am going to take them home and sit up nights to eat 'em.'"

Hyde replied with a pleasant irony. "Yes, Reed went after me," he said. "I would have been hurt if he hadn't. The thing that worried me, though, was that he didn't say anything about the Radio Corporation he is suing, and said nothing about the radio trust he represents. I was worried, too, because he spoke kindly of Woodrow Wilson and Thomas Jefferson and I can't understand that unless he figured that they had been dead too long to be registered."

Joe Shannon also was eloquent on the subjects of Hoover, Hyde and the farm surplus, playing on the same refrain as Reed except that he was somewhat more specific than Reed with respect to a remedy for the farm surplus problem. Asked by a heckler to explain what he would do to get rid of the surplus, Joe replied: "I would abolish Arthur M. Hyde." That was about as far as the leaders went in defining the real issues of the campaign.

On election day the people went to the polls in a mass. The experts explained that they went in such numbers to register a protest against the party in power, blaming it for the depression. Although the campaigning hadn't made much sense it was clear that free enterprise for monopoly had made a hash of things and the traditional party of big business didn't have the least idea of how to deal with the breakdown. However, it is doubtful if the Democrats convinced many people that they knew what to do for recovery, either. In Jackson County, for instance, few of the thousands who voted for the Democratic ticket picked by the machine could have been under the illusion that they were balloting for a new order. The facts seem to be that the people turned out, as usual, for many reasons, among which was the desire for a change based on the sound theory that they couldn't get anything worse than what they had, and there was always a chance for a miracle.

It was a relatively quiet election in Jackson County. Kansas City was on its good behavior. The excitement was confined to the county seat town of Independence where there were rumors that two high-powered Democrats were to be kidnaped and Harry S. Truman, presiding judge of the County Court, was alarmed by a reported attempt to kidnap his six-year-old daughter, Margaret. As it turned out, the only person kidnaped was a Republican, Rex V. Hedrick, then chairman of the Jackson County Election Board, who was seized while driving to the Election Board offices with evidence of Democratic vote padding. His abductors gave him a beating, taped his eyes and held him prisoner all day, releasing him in Kansas City on the West Bluffs just after the polls closed.

Democrats swept up everything in Jackson County. Missouri and national politicians paid special attention to the returns from this county, for Pendergast delivered the largest Democratic vote and the largest majority in history up to that time. Leading the ticket were two county men, both from Independence and both of them to have an important bearing on the future of the Kansas City machine, one of them to bring it great prestige and the other to have a very depressing effect. They were Harry Truman, re-elected presiding judge of the County Court by 57,859 majority, and Judge Allen C. Southern, returned to the Circuit Court bench by 58,061.

Joe Shannon was sent to Congress by a margin of more than forty-five thousand votes. The discrepancy between him and the Independence men was not accounted for by friction in the new order of the machine but was directly attributable to the Republican opposition in the person of Rep. E. C. Ellis, running for re-election. Mr. Ellis was a rock-ribbed Hamiltonian who by contrast made a nineteenth century liberal of the

Shannon type seem very radical indeed, and he raised a great alarm over the Jeffersonian revival conducted by the Rabbit champion. He wasn't able to prevail against the Pendergast trend, but he had the satisfaction of leading his ticket in the county, which may have been a tribute to the power of the Ellis oratory and personality but also may be taken as an indication that the old-fashioned Jeffersonian of Kansas City was too advanced to suit a certain element of his party even in 1930.

4 *The Heart of America*

UP AND COMING

KANSAS CITY's "monument to the Depression," so described by Editor Bill White of Emporia in a laudatory editorial, was the Ten-Year Plan that was adopted in 1931. That ambitious undertaking exemplified the native zip which the Real Estate Board still endeavors to cultivate with its Up and Coming slogan for Kansas City. It was also a notable demonstration of the Heart of America spirit, which was peculiarly identified with the Pendergast Goats. The Goats had much to do with the Ten-Year Plan and one Goat was responsible for naming Kansas City the Heart of America.

This story, which has more charm than most yarns with a political flavor, begins back in 1911, when the town was trying somewhat indifferently to publicize itself as the City on the Kaw. That was the year when Edwin J. Shannahan came to town to identify himself politically with the Pendergast faction and win local distinction as a patriot, Commercial Club booster and fraternal leader. He was the local head of the Fraternal Order of Eagles when that order held its national convention in Kansas City in 1914. It was then that Ed was struck with his happiest inspiration. Convinced that his new home had a special significance and destiny in the national picture, he coined The Heart of America for the literature ballyhooing the convention city of the Eagles. The Commercial Club then adopted it as a permanent designation and Arthur Pryor, whose band played here for the Eagles' convention, later composed a "Heart of America March," dedicated to Ed Shannahan. Another bandman, Sousa, chose that march as the official song for Camp Funston in the

First World War and thousands of Middle Western boys marched away to its lively strains.

The location of Kansas City near the geographical center of the United States was not to Ed Shannahan the most important factor in determining the appropriateness of his symbolic label. "It is the spirit the name suggests that is even more significant," he said. "The word 'America' gives it a patriotic flavor and the word 'Heart' stands for all that is noble in life—affection, sympathy, enthusiasm, hospitality, generosity and other warm attributes which Kansas City possesses."

Ed Shannahan himself expressed those qualities in many individual ways despite his involvement in the political rivalries that placed such a heavy strain on the Heart of America before Ed's death in 1944. Mr. Shannahan held political office by grace of Pendergast, serving as city director of personnel from 1926 to 1930, retiring from public life to devote himself to charitable work at a time when the civic harmony and building movement was having its last grand flourish.

The original Heart of America man took only a very mild hope in the future of his movement in the political field. He and other patriots concentrated on hardware conventions, livestock shows, fraternal societies, parades and such to spread their gospel. Ed's own particular prescription for the activity that would bring out the true Kansas City qualities was sociability combined with exercise. His instrument for this work was the Heart of America Walking Club, which set the standard for hiking for a decade or so. "Make your daily walk your most important secular duty," was Ed's advice to businessmen. "A walk will cure you of worries, frets and office fatigue." Each spring he sounded the call to the lanes and bypaths and hundreds of walkers responded. To provide special inspiration, Ed walked a race from the Coates House to Swope Park, a jaunt of eight miles, with Kirby McRill, the Unkissed Farmer and Walking Marvel from Tonganoxie, Kansas. Kirby won easily, of course, but Ed got more converts and drew international attention to his project. One letter of praise came from Marshal Foch of France. President Coolidge interrupted his budget slashing long enough to send congratulations on the promotion of this "most inexpensive" mode of exercise.

The most enduring product of the Heart of America walking venture was Kirby McRill, who dedicated himself to the causes of private enterprise, civic boosting and hiking. He commanded the affection and esteem of all social classes in a community that admires positive individualism but does not look kindly on forms of exhibitionism that are inspired merely by a desire to achieve notoriety. Kirby was the genuine article in native eccentricity. He entered the movement to put Kansas City on the map with as much civic enthusiasm as his backers, and his performance was only moderately tainted with the commercialism that was manifested in the circus stunts of the period.

When other cities, like Baltimore, Chicago and San Francisco, were attempting to enhance their prestige with flagpole sitters and other endurance freaks, Kirby quietly went about his business of providing public entertainment on a year-round basis, with or without special encouragement. He drew attention wherever he went with his long red hair and his fierce red mustache, his magnificent stride and the pushcart he trundled before him. He came to Kansas City from Leavenworth County, Kansas, looking for romance. Here he met Daisy Bell Hicks, a coed at the Timpe Barber College. Their courtship continued through three happy years until Daisy Bell jilted Kirby. He sued her for two hundred and fifty thousand dollars for breach of promise and found solace walking far and wide with his pushcart. He let his whiskers and beard grow into a thick brick-hued bush, devised a distinctive costume consisting of a baseball suit, golf socks and sneakers and wended his way through crowds with the solemnity of a fugitive first baseman from the House of David.

Kirby lost both his unkissed status and some of his walking prestige in 1922 when vaudeville and civic boosters entered him in a contest with George N. Brown, the World Walk King, over a three-mile course through the downtown streets. Two mayors—the mayor-elect and the retiring city executive—stood at the starting line to give the match official dignity. The throngs cheered and Kirby crossed the finish line first but was disqualified on a technicality. He cantered while the World Champion walked. The crowd booed the decision and Kirby was kissed twice, once for publicity by a Twelfth Street showgirl and once for the hell of it by a local lady patriot.

It was decided that Mr. McRill had been improperly matched in this competition for he was an endurance rather than a sprint walker. Conrad H. Mann, sparkplug of the Chamber of Commerce, and several progressive spirits in the Heart of America Walking Club promoted another demonstration to show the nation what the Kansas City champion could do, arranging a walk to Chicago, a distance of more than four hundred and fifty miles. Kirby rolled into Chicago a day ahead of schedule, traveling on track rights granted by the Santa Fe and averaging sixty-three miles a day, but he was dissatisfied with this feat. He was welcomed in Chicago by Con Mann and Ed Shannahan, who sent a telegram advising Kansas City why Kirby didn't do better: "Shoes tight, blisters causing him to lose half a day. Slippery track part way. Snow near Carrollton. Stopped to buy a shirt at Galesburg. Interference at Chillicothe. An hour's delay in railroad yards here waiting for orders."

Kirby hoped to set a transcontinental record for the Heart of America and he announced that in 1926 he would swim the English Channel and break all previous records, after which he would call on King George, but these ambitious plans did not work out. Kirby returned to Kansas City and his pushcart, keeping himself in hiking form as an industrious collector of paper and odd trash. Con Mann found less time for play. Fashions in civic enterprise, private endeavor, exercise and other things changed but Kirby remained true to the old ways and made no concessions to time except that his pace grew slower and his red hair and whiskers grayed while he looked more and more like a minor prophet escaped from the Bible.

Conrad H. Mann's association with the Heart of America hiking and the Kirby McRill diversions illustrated the range of his interests as a citizen and a booster. Con was the Get It Done Man in Kansas City for two decades. Towering of frame, dynamic, indefatigable, filled with boundless personal ambition and civic spirit, he was the personification of the American promoter who shines in private enterprise and public life. A German from "up north" with a mystery in his background, he was long accepted among the native sons as one of the citizens who conspicuously exhibited the qualities that made America great. He came down from Milwaukee and supposedly was a native of Iowa.

Mann's principal work was done in the period between 1928 and 1933, when he directed the Chamber of Commerce along lines that brought it closer to the political organization headed by Pendergast. His monument was the Ten-Year Bond campaign which reached a successful climax in the summer of 1931, midway between the political campaigns of 1930 and 1932 that established Pendergast's position as the boss of Kansas City and the political power in the state. Mann was listed as a Republican but he was a practical nonpartisan who operated among the big men of both parties.

In the twenty years preceding his rise to command of the Chamber of Commerce, Mann impressed his personality on the town in ways that brought profit to both himself and the community. He arrived in the city to work as secretary of the Fraternal Order of Eagles, which in 1907 moved its national offices to Kansas City. Con's promotional zeal made him so valuable to the Eagles that he became the permanent international secretary of that large enterprise in sociability and insurance. He expanded in other lines, stepped up as general manager, secretary and treasurer of a brewery combine and took a hand in downtown real estate and financial operations. Joining the old Commercial Club, later the Chamber of Commerce, he forged to the front and was soon made chairman of the Convention Bureau.

From that time on Con Mann was in the center and usually at the head of every activity designed to elevate and advertise his home town, whether it was arrangements for a convention party that the undertakers or chiropodists would never forget, a scheme to force opera or symphony on the people, a plan to discourage crime, or a charity drive. In 1928 he was elected president of the Chamber of Commerce, a post he held for six years, breaking precedent for length of tenure and retiring with the status of permanent honorary president.

By fortuitous circumstance, Mann's administration was well timed for the city in general and the Pendergast organization in particular. His was the expansive spirit that gave Kansas City a lift at a time when most of the country was going into a prolonged economic recession. And his was the function that enabled all interests to work with the political machine in the most ambitious building venture undertaken since the days when the city's park-and-boulevard system was designed and built under the direction of Kessler, Meyer and Nelson.

Mann was made general chairman of the Civic Improvement Committee that was selected by the new mayor, Bryce B. Smith. His Committee started the ball rolling shortly after the city election that gave complete control to the Democratic organization for four years. Out of it grew the Committee of 1,000 which Mann headed and which planned the Ten-Year Bond Program, conducted the successful campaign and attempted to supervise the execution of the program.

Colonel Nelson had found it necessary at times to make a deal with the machine politicians to get parks and boulevards. It was necessary to do the same thing for the Ten-Year Plan. The deal was nothing like a direct pay-off or a back-room arrangement. The inducement to the machine was the knowledge that it would have direct control of the spending of the millions under the program. Elaborate precautions were taken to insure that the money was spent properly but the building trade was set up in a fashion that made it certain a large share of the business would fall to interests in good standing with the organization, and profits would be large even if there were no boodling. And, of course, the political prestige that went with responsibility for the program was a large item.

The Pendergast organization publicly indorsed the bond plan and the Welch and Shannon factions followed suit. Republican leaders approved the program and participated in its promotion, hoping earnestly that this would turn out to be a Nonpartisan venture, as planned, rather than a Democratic project, as happened. The *Star,* carrying on the Nelson tradition, was in the forefront of the movement. The Committee of 1,000 took in all elements of the population and enlisted the best engineering, business and political minds to work out the details. Projects were approved on the basis of need and a showing of popular preference, determined at a series of public hearings before the various committees. When the plans were finally assembled, the program was presented to the public in a campaign that was notable for its effort to inform rather than excite the voters. It was, in all, a rare and stirring example of democracy in action.

The people went to the polls with the slogan, Make Kansas City the Greatest Inland City, and voted for the bonds four to one, casting more than eighty-nine thousand ballots. It was the largest vote ever registered at a special election. The town celebrated the event with a Jubilee of

Progress, taking five days to express its elation in every form of entertainment from a rodeo to an airplane and autogyro show.

The plan called for expenditure over a ten-year period of thirty-two million dollars for city projects and with it were combined seven million nine hundred and fifty thousand dollars for county projects, making a total of $39,950,000. With the Federal aid money that was later added, it was estimated that about fifty million dollars actually was spent under the program. Out of it came a thirty-two-story City Hall, a skyscraper Courthouse in Kansas City, a new police building, a Municipal Auditorium that covered a block, paved roads that completed one of the most extensive county highway systems in the country, trafficways and boulevards, hospital extensions, a new water works system, parks, playgrounds, sewer extensions and flood protection, a public market and other important installations. The program was providential for Kansas City. The depression was late in manifesting itself in this inland center and it never struck with full force, thanks in large measure to the employment provided by the public construction.

Conrad H. Mann was presented a silver watch at a ceremony honoring him for his effective work. He and his Committee were counted on to restrain the politicians in the spending of the Ten-Year-Bond funds. The Country Bookkeeper had figured in a controversy over employment policy in public construction work several months before the Ten-Year-Plan election. In the first winter of the depression the city found itself facing an unemployment emergency. With his customary resourcefulness, Judge McElroy proposed that the city raise a million dollars by the sale of Water Department notes, the funds to be used to put the jobless men immediately to work building water main extensions. That admirable proposal was approved by Mr. Mann and the Bond Committee, and the City Manager worked out a plan to create a maximum number of jobs by dispensing with tractors and excavating machinery wherever possible, substituting picks, shovels and wheelbarrows. McElroy's pick-and-shovel army created wide interest when it first appeared, and the City Manager was not slow to exploit the political credit. The idea, he said, was exclusively his, and he insisted that his plan suggested the CWA, predecessor of the WPA, to Harry Hopkins and the New Dealers. The favorable impression lasted until the Republicans and the *Star* complained that the city administration had established a system of giving the jobs only to loyal Democrats, ignoring a gentleman's agreement with Mr. Mann to let the Chamber of Commerce employment bureau place the applicants.

Mr. Mann intervened in the relief matter to restore peace, after it was reported that one thousand of the first fifteen hundred jobs were filled through the Democratic precinct captains' employment system, but the agitation over discrimination was revived after the Bond election, and steadily grew louder. It reached its height in the Brush Creek sewer project. South Side taxpayers were horrified at the size of the pick-and-shovel army engaged in clearing the channel of this once picturesque stream, along which Daniel Morgan Boone, son of the great Dan'l, trapped beaver more than a century before it became a sanitary and political problem for the Country Club district. The pain of the South Siders grew more acute when they saw their creek being given a solid concrete bed. The long country-wide howl over boon-doggling probably started in Kansas City. It was provoked by the waste of manpower in the Brush Creek project, and magnified by the combination of Pendergast's concrete monopoly with relief jobs. If it was a fact that the Judge gave Harry Hopkins the idea for his emergency made-work program, he got the CWA off to a very bad start.

It had been hoped that the city administration could be prevailed on to follow the example of the county government under the direction of Harry Truman, presiding judge of the County Court. Truman's work with the citizens' advisory group and the record of his administration were potent factors in the campaign for the Ten-Year bonds. Under a seven-million-dollar-bond program that was authorized in 1928, Truman introduced planning, expert direction and bipartisan control in a manner that was new to Jackson County politics. He engaged two consulting engineers, Colonel E. M. Stayton and N. T. Veatch, Jr., one a Democrat and the other a Republican, gave them a free hand in laying out a new road system and saw to it that their recommendations were carried out in building the highways and a new county hospital. Judge Truman followed the same standards in the additional county building authorized by the Ten-Year Program. Two hundred and forty-four miles of paved roadways were built—twenty more than originally estimated—and the type of pavement constructed bore little resemblance to the pie-crust roads built in the past. When the projects were completed there was a tidy balance in the fund, giving the County Court a chance to wind up its frugal custodianship of the public purse with a characteristic Truman flourish. The Judge used part of the surplus for an equestrian statue of Andy Jackson in front of the new County Courthouse and there was more than enough left over to finance a special bond celebration for the people of Jackson County, a mammoth barbecue at Sni-a-Bar Farms. That affair was historically interesting on two counts. It was the first exhibition of the future President's exceptional talent for mixing serious public business and pleasure, and it produced the damnedest traffic jam ever seen in rural Jackson County.

The bond planners had made provision for a nine-man advisory committee to watch over the politicians in the City Hall and the Council agreed to that supervision, adopting a resolution pledging adherence to the spirit and letter of the bond program, agreeing to follow the committee's recommendations where they did not conflict with official duties and obligations, etc., etc. Mr. Mann appointed a committee of five Democrats and four Republicans. He left himself off the list but the City Council and its Hired Man did not like the idea of not having Con Mann watching over them, too. So the Council appointed him to the committee, increasing the membership to ten, and he was elected chairman. "That makes it completely bipartisan," Judge McElroy remarked with satisfaction.

Early in the Ten-Year-Bond building program, in the winter of 1932-33, the public was startled to read a report from Walter Matscheck of the Civic Research Institute, showing that the city was renting machinery at excessive rates from favored concerns, letting contracts without competitive bidding and otherwise ignoring proper regulations for the program. The matter became a political issue when a group of Republican lawyers filed an equity suit to recover more than $400,000 from city officials, alleging that that amount of the bond funds had been misspent.

Con Mann's advisory committee held a meeting and ordered an audit and City Manager McElroy interpreted the auditor's report as an exoneration of the administration. In fact, he insisted that the audit showed the city had rented the equipment at an actual saving rather than the overcharge of more than $200,000 discovered by Mr. Matscheck. The research man analyzed the audit and declared that the figures confirmed his finding, and even indicated that the excessive payments were greater than he had originally reported. The McElroy view prevailed on the advisory committee and the City Council and the incident closed with a light reprimand to the administration, which was advised to improve its bookkeeping system and supervise the letting of contracts more closely. McElroy thereafter ran the bond program with little interference from any source except the Federal government, which entered into some of the supervision through the extension of Federal aid in public building. Walter Matscheck left Kansas City in 1936 to take a post with the Social Science Research Council in Washington. There were no more audits of the Bond Program until after McElroy retired in 1939, when it was found that more than eleven million dollars of the funds had been spent in a manner that violated charter provisions covering the letting of contracts.

Con Mann and the Committee of 1,000 were no match for the Country Bookkeeper. Mann's real work for his town was done when he stage-managed the Ten-Year-Plan campaign. Not long after this he had troubles of his own with the Federal government which permanently depressed his promoter spirit.

McELROY'S COFFEE GROUNDS

IN LOOKING for a date to mark the beginning of the Pendergast decline, historians may find it in the year 1932, which was some time before the deterioration was visible to the general public. Many politicians and observers say that the downward trend set in with the establishment of Home Rule, giving control of the Police Department to City Manager McElroy and the organization, an event that occurred early in 1932. However, it is possible to discern the turning point in another episode that made a more lasting impression on the popular mind than the Home Rule decision.

As so often happens in a community that is hardened to trouble and has a rugged sense of humor that disposes it to see the light side of practically anything, this break in the peace began as something of a comedy and continued in that fashion, providing some entertainment along with vast irritation. It also produced the first opposition since the beginning of the boom that Judge McElroy was unable to overwhelm, and the portentous significance of this uprising was only slightly obscured by the outlandish nature of the whole affair, which began early in 1932.

Cause of the excitement was a spectacle known as a walkathon, a refinement of the dance marathon, which became both a political event and a popular entertainment when City Manager McElroy decided to suppress it for reasons that had nothing to do with the walkathon's curious psychological effect on the masses. People rode vast distances to sit on their rumps and watch miserable couples who staggered around the floor of El Torreon Ballroom, where the show was staged. Although there was no political emotion in this sports exhibition outside that provided by the Country Bookkeeper, it managed to be a thoroughly grotesque performance bearing a certain resemblance to the obscene party rallies promoted by Hitler's Nazis in Germany. The sweating, rude, shoving, cheering crowd in El Torreon gave itself up joyously to pure animal emotion. It could have been turned into a mob on short notice and, on one or two occasions, it almost was.

The City Manager interfered with the show after it had operated three weeks. He appeared one night accompanied by officials of the Building Inspection and Fire departments and ordered the walkathon stopped within five minutes. His cause of complaint was that the crowd was seated on wooden benches, violating a fire protection regulation. His action followed a dispute between the promoters and Johnny Lazia, the North Side politician. The managers tried to mollify the City Manager, offering to remove any fire hazards they had created, but the Judge insisted that the walkathon close immediately and finally. Asked by a newspaper reporter to state his grounds for closing the show if the fire hazard was eliminated, Judge McElroy replied loftily: "Coffee grounds."

His statement was acclaimed as a masterpiece of cracker-barrel wit and machine arrogance at the supreme moment of McElroy's power, and figured in later political campaigns. Opposition orators asserted

that "coffee grounds" suggested to Lazia the idea of setting up a monopoly in coffee sold to restaurants and hamburger bungalows.

Despite McElroy, the walkathon reopened when the promoters obtained a restraining order against the city from the Federal Court, but
official harassment continued for two more weeks while North Side
hoodlums devised some other methods to discourage the artistic enterprise in El Torreon. Police were called to break up an attack made by a
group of rowdies. A Lazia lieutenant was arrested for setting off a stench
bomb in the ballroom. The city filed complaints compelling the police
to arrest the proprietors, and the police judge rebuked the city administration for imposing an impossible set of requirements. A tear gas
attack and another stink bomb distracted the walkers and their partisans,
but nothing could stop the walkathon, for a large part of the public had
found that it offered a rare form of escape. The excitement spread over
the city and a group of Negroes announced they would have a walkathon
of their own and would go the white folks one better by having a sitting
marathon as a sideshow.

The Torreon circus was a sitting marathon for thousands, who came
early and stayed late. Some of the fans lived on the benches in order to
stay close to their adored champions. An intense rivalry developed between the partisans of young love and the defenders of marital felicity.
Almost all of the contestants were romantic figures. There were brother-
and-sister teams and sister teams in the race, along with several lone
wolves, but the crowd lost sight of them in cheering for the youthful
sweethearts planning to get married on the prize money, and the wedded
couples who were trying to collect something for the grocery bill. Youth
was the popular choice and the outcome was predicted by one of the
promoters, who sagely observed: "I've never seen a married couple win
a walkathon."

One of the romances had national repercussions, for it started Red
Skelton on his way to fame as a wow of the radio and screen. Red entered
the scene when one of the walkathon masters of ceremony wandered
away. The managers hurriedly drafted Skelton to fill the place. Red was
then appearing in the Gayety Burlesque Theater, a Hoosier comic earning fifteen dollars a week in an act called "The Three Bananas." (He was
the Third Banana, the others being Bozo Nelson and Joe Yule, Mickey

Rooney's father.) At El Torreon, Red's attention was drawn to a pretty Kansas City girl, Edna Stilwell, and his admiration for her grew as he watched her outwalk several partners, perambulate through a high fever and finish with the winning couple. She was disqualified from a part in the one-thousand-dollar prize money because she had no partner. She did not despair but married Red immediately after the contest ended and set about changing his act and writing skits and gags for him. Thus El Torreon in its lunatic-days made its major contribution to the happiness of a nation which can't get enough of Red, Junior and "I dood it."

So tough is the human constitution and so wonderful the human spirit that by the time the walkathon ended, 117 days after it began, the crowds were behaving almost rationally, everyone was refreshed, sentiment overflowed in all hearts and the contestants had put on weight, some gaining up to fifteen pounds. They were also intellectually improved, the management said. "The walkathon gives them opportunities to develop their minds," declared Leo Seltzer, one of the promoters. "Many of them read good books while walking around out there."

The great event ended the night of May 30, 1932, to the accompaniment of the sweetest story ever told, the winning couple being married at a public ceremony in El Torreon. They were dressed to represent George and Martha Washington, and attended by couples garbed in Colonial costumes in an elaborate setting designed to carry out the Washington Bi-Centennial theme of the year. The Reverend Earl Blackman, an unattached parson who ran around with sportsmen and intellectuals, spliced the winners and everyone went away uplifted.

One possible explanation of the medical phenomenon presented by the good health of the walkathon participants is that they ate more regularly than they had since the depression set in. They also missed entirely several hundred calamities marking the world's plunge into fascism and war. In addition to hearing nothing about the Japanese bombardment of Shanghai, the failure of the League of Nations, the crisis in France, the Mannerheim Fascist coup in Finland, the Japanese-American diplomatic crisis in China and Hoover's fumbling with the American unemployment crisis, they were not aware that while they slept on their feet Home Rule had come to Kansas City.

When they left El Torreon the night of May 30, they stepped back into a world that was a very disorderly place measured by the walkathon standard. For several days Kansas City had been in the midst of one of its greatest disturbances, which grew out of Home Rule and Rabbi Mayerberg's objection to that reform.

THE CHALLENGE

In the month of May, 1932, City Manager McElroy was out of the city enjoying a well-earned vacation, Tom Pendergast was preoccupied with state and national political affairs, the next city election was two years away and the Republicans hadn't even begun to think about what they would do then. It would have been difficult to select a less likely time to start a full-scale offensive against the city administration, which was the moment that Samuel S. Mayerberg chose for his campaign to drive McElroy from the City Hall. The attack failed of its main purpose, but it was the beginning of the revolt which overwhelmed the boss organization seven long years later. And it was no small beginning, despite the irregularity or inappropriateness of the Mayerberg approach.

Mr. Mayerberg was the rabbi of Temple B'Nai Jehudah, one of the leading congregations of the town's substantial Jewish community, and he had been a citizen of Kansas City less than four years when he issued his surprising challenge to Pendergast, McElroy, Lazia & Co. Naturally it took the public some time to get adjusted to the idea that this was a serious political movement against the machine. With a few minor exceptions, the clergy in the past had rigorously observed the tradition that government was a monopoly of the businessman and their political stooges. Some elements of the body politic never got over the feeling that Rabbi Mayerberg was embarking on a radical and dangerous course in ignoring this old precedent. The Rabbi could not at one blow knock out the deep-rooted convention that the preacher's place was in the pulpit, far above the mundane concerns of men, but he did succeed in demolishing the popular notion that ministers have no talent for the political life.

The Rabbi was a slender, intense figure who radiated friendliness, forebearance and positive convictions, combining a brisk modern manner with an Old Testament look. A Reform rabbi, he had served his church eleven years in Detroit, Michigan, and Dayton, Ohio, before he came to Kansas City, where he immediately served notice of his intention to take a full part in the life of the community. His fight on McElroy was not the result of an impetuous decision and the Rabbi was not the political tyro that he appeared to be to many people who had not closely followed his work. The contest against the machine was, in fact, the climax of a three-year one-man crusade in which Mayerberg had learned his way around in Kansas City and Missouri politics and found that the local disturbance was but one aspect of a rather broad disorder in the Heart of America region.

The Rabbi's first important exchange with the politicians occurred in the sex-questionnaire episode which rocked the University of Missouri and brought a change in administration at that conservative institution of higher learning. Mayerberg teamed with Kansas City's liberal Protestant churchmen, Burris Jenkins and L. M. Birkhead, in that fight. With the assistance of Kansas City and St. Louis newspapers, and a few other bold spirits, they made a spirited stand against the bigots who gave a performance that was only slightly less comical than the famous Scopes Monkey Trial at Dayton, Tennessee, and one that was almost as sad.

The M. U. issue, which started in 1929 and ran on for many months, grew out of a harmless research project in Sociology. A graduate student instructor in Psychology, one O. H. Mowrer, prepared a questionnaire that was circulated among the students of Dr. Harmon O. DeGraff, assistant professor of Sociology, the students being asked to give honest answers to several intimate questions covering their attitudes and experiences in sex relations, if any. The idea that boys and girls of college age should be required to consider such indelicate questions enraged many of the rural editors, most of the preachers and a large proportion of the politicians. E. M. Watson's *Columbia Daily Tribune,* published in the Athens of Missouri, as the university town was called by its Chamber of Commerce, did a thorough job of alarming the home guard with its disclosure of the research project. North Todd Gentry, a Republican saint and a former attorney general of the state, roused the Columbia merchants to sign petitions demanding the removal of Mowrer and Professor DeGraff along with the head of the Sociology Department, Dr.

Max Meyer, one of the school's most eminent scholars. Dr. Meyer's responsibility for the sex inquiry consisted merely of failing to interfere with it, but the Fundamentalists were not disposed to let him off on a technicality for they knew him as a confirmed freethinker.

The politicians in the Missouri General Assembly leaped eagerly into the ruckus, defending the old hayloft moral code against the whole kit and caboodle of modern agitators and debunkers, and threatening to reduce the legislative appropriation for the University unless the school administration got back on the old-fashioned basis. While the legislators ranted and the curators sweated, the M. U. students expressed their disgust in various derisive ways. When the Board of Curators reported its findings, firing Mowrer and DeGraff and dismissing Meyer for one year, the students were restrained with difficulty from going on a strike. The American Association of University Professors entered the controversy, censuring the board and criticizing the administration of the school under a president who was more of a politician than an educator. Agitation continued until the Curators finally admitted that the University was under an oppressive regime and called for the resignation of the president. However, the order against DeGraff and Meyer was allowed to stand and the incident ended with Rabbi Mayerberg still in a crusading mood.

The furor created by the M. U. business had hardly settled when he was drawn into a couple of other episodes that broadened his knowledge of Missouri social prejudices and political customs, and strengthened his fighting spirit. In January, 1931, Mr. Mayerberg was traveling in Northwest Missouri, returning to Kansas City from a speaking engagement, when his train stopped at Maryville and a stranger in the seat next to him remarked: "If you want to see a first-class lynching come back here a week from today." Investigating further, the Rabbi learned that the promised lynching was in the case of Raymond Gunn, a Negro, who had been arrested for the rape-murder of a young white woman who was the teacher in a rural school near Maryville.

Mr. Mayerberg called the Missouri governor by long distance telephone and succeeded in convincing that official that an emergency existed in peaceful Nodaway County. A unit of the National Guard was sent to Maryville for the day when the Negro, who confessed the crime, was to be arraigned. The guardsmen remained idly in the Maryville Armory while the savage play ran its course. Raymond Gunn was chained to the roof of the little school where the tragedy began and burned to death before fifteen thousand watchers. The exhibition of official indifference in submitting to mob rule was followed by a round of buck-passing which did nothing to improve Rabbi Mayerberg's opinion of politicians.

A more intimate experience with politicians and the American system of justice came in this period when the Rabbi attempted to save the life of a Jewish youth. The victim was Joe Hershon, son of immigrants and a product of the slums, who was involved in the murder of a policeman late in 1929 and paid the supreme penalty some two years later on the gallows in the Jackson County jail. Mr. Mayerberg realized he was inviting criticism when he intervened in this case and took that course in the face of his own expressed conviction that a Jew, if found guilty of a crime, "should be doubly punished, once as an individual guilty of an anti-social act and once because he brought disgrace upon the Jewish community." There was no question of Joe Hershon's guilt but Rabbi Mayerberg went to his assistance because justice in this instance was unequal.

The bullets that killed the policeman were fired by one of Hershon's accomplices, who committed suicide in jail after making a confession. Charles M. Curtis, leader of the gang, got off with a life sentence after Hershon was condemned to death. The jury was reported deadlocked by one juror's opposition to the death penalty, and the dispute composed by agreement on a life sentence for Curtis. The inconsistency between the two verdicts added to his opposition to capital punishment, led Mr. Mayerberg to make a vigorous fight to have Hershon's sentence commuted to life imprisonment. His campaign ended in the governor's office, where the chief executive listened sympathetically to the Mayerberg plea and explained the things that made it politically inexpedient for the governor to intervene.

Mayerberg's effort to save the Jewish slum boy was overshadowed in public interest by another of Jim Reed's sensational performances in a court of justice, which occurred in this period. Reed appeared as the de-

FIGHTING JIM

James A. Reed came on the scene with Pendergast backing, served eighteen years in the Senate, made two bids for Democratic presidential nomination, broke with Wilson and Roosevelt and finally turned against Pendergast.

JACKSON COUNTY JEFFERSONIAN

The Honorable Joseph B. Shannon was a member of the National House of Representatives for six terms (1931-1943) and head of the Democratic faction which alternately warred against and worked with the Pendergast organization in Jackson County. Mr. Shannon reputedly was the author of Fifty-Fifty, the trading agreement designed to bring peace between the rival factions, the Shannon Rabbits and the Pendergast Goats. The story is that the pact was negotiated in 1902 and one of the first beneficiaries of it was Tom Pendergast, who went on the ticket that year as county marshal. The Rabbits eventually were subordinated to the Goats and Joe Shannon went to Congress to draw attention as an apostle of the old-time Jeffersonian philosophy. He died in 1943 and the Rabbit faction now is directed by his son, Frank P. Shannon.

JUST BEFORE THE FIREWORKS STARTED

This pleasant exchange occurred between the mayor of Kansas City, Bryce B. Smith (at the left), and the chief critic of the city administration, Rabbi Samuel S. Mayerberg, in May, 1932. A few minutes later, Rabbi Mayerberg was speaking before the Council, demanding that it remove from office City Manager H. F. McElroy.

COUNTRY BOOKKEEPER

The title that H. F. McElroy liked was Judge, which he acquired when he was a member of the Jackson County Court, but he is remembered chiefly for the Country Bookkeeping system he introduced in the City Hall when he was city manager. This photograph was made near the end of his thirteen-year regime, which ended in 1939.

BIG TOM

A rare picture of T. J. Pendergast in the days when he was beginning to throw his weight around in politics. It dates back to the period when the future Democratic boss of Kansas City made his first race for office—in 1902, when he was 30 years old—and was elected marshal of Jackson County, Missouri.

THE BRIDE'S FATHER STOLE THE SCENE

Perhaps the most familiar picture of T. J. Pendergast, posing with his daughter's wedding party. Unfeeling Republicans, more interested in partisan advantage than romance, made thousands of prints of Boss Tom's figure in top hat and cutaway and circulated them over the state in the campaign of 1930. In this section of the wedding picture, Mr. Pendergast is shown with his wife and their daughter, Marceline, who was married to W. E. Burnett, Jr., in 1929.

THE HEART OF AMERICA

The Kansas City panel of the mural by Thomas Hart Benton which adorns the walls of the House of Representatives' lounge in the Missouri Capitol at Jefferson City. Placing of Boss Pendergast's figure in the foreground (seated on platform) was one of the details that aroused critics of the mural, who stormed at both Benton and his Social History of Missouri in 1936-1937.

WHERE "KING TOM" HELD COURT

This modest building at 1908 Main Street was the seat of political power in Kansas City during the thirteen years when the organization headed by Pendergast was on top. The Boss met his public in an office on the second floor where his Jackson Democratic Club occupied three rooms. The 1908 Main address still is headquarters for the town's dominant Democratic faction, now headed by James M. Pendergast, nephew of T. J.

POLITICIAN'S DAUGHTER

City Manager McElroy's daughter, Mary McElroy, sought the limelight. Excited by the drama of politics, she planned to write a book entitled "A Politician's Daughter." Her own life turned into melodrama and tragedy, and left her no time for writing.

GETTING THINGS DONE

Progress in the construction of Kansas City's new six-million dollar Municipal Auditorium was being observed by T. J. Pendergast and City Manager H. F. McElroy when this photograph was made in 1935. The Auditorium was a large item in the Ten-Year Bond improvement program, an undertaking that had many political complications.

CRUSADING EDITOR

William Rockhill Nelson was publisher and editor of *The Kansas City Star* from 1880 to his death in 1915. His imprint still is large on the town and on the *Star*, which now is employee-owned. His domineering personality earned him the sobriquet of "Baron Bill"; his work in building his paper from a four-page daily to a large-scale enterprise, and his battles for civic improvements and political reforms made him a national figure.

CAPTAIN HARRY

Harry S. Truman was captain and commanding officer of Battery D, 129th Field Artillery, Thirty-fifth Division, in the First World War. This overseas picture is a prized item in the albums of the Battery D boys, a unit composed of Jackson County men, who became Captain Harry's original and warmest political supporters after the war.

THE SENATOR ──────▶

FROM MISSOURI

Harry S. Truman was fifty years old in 1934 when he first ran for a seat in the United States Senate. This picture from that period shows a dapper Truman who won handily in a campaign which he described as "just a lot of fun." It was in that campaign that T. J. Pendergast gave a show of vote-delivering power which caused political observers to hail him as the undisputed Missouri boss.

ON WAY TO THE WHITE HOUSE

The scene is a room in the Jackson County Courthouse, the time is 1933 and the men are Harry S. Truman, presiding judge of the County Court, and Battle McCardle. Mr. Truman established a record in the Court that started him up the political ladder.

NECKTIES AND POLITICS

It was a dull day, commercially speaking, in the Truman and Jacobson haberdashery, at Twelfth Street and Baltimore Avenue, Kansas City, when this photograph was made, but the political prospect was interesting. Harry Truman (in the foreground) opened this store in partnership with his war buddy, Eddie Jacobson, soon after he returned from war service. The store failed in 1921.

JUDGMENT DAY

One of the last pictures of Tom Pendergast is this photograph showing him at a table in the United States Federal District Court in Kansas City, where he waited while his counsel and the prosecutor discussed details of his case. In May, 1939, he was sentenced to fifteen months in prison for income tax evasion.

FOUNDER OF A POLITICAL DYNASTY

The Democratic organization which produced Tom Pendergast's machine of the 1930's was established in the late nineteenth century by Big Tom's brother, James Pendergast. This statue of Alderman Jim stands in Mulkey Square, above the West Bottoms.

CAMPAIGN TIME IN INDEPENDENCE

The Goat faction of the Jackson County Democracy staged a vigorous revival in the August primary of 1946. President Truman contributed to the rally when he flew from the White House to his home in Independence, Mo., to vote. In this scene, on the lawn of the summer White House, the President gives ear to remarks from his friend, Jim Pendergast. Near the President is Mayor Roger T. Sermon of Independence, who is talking to Mrs. Truman. At the extreme left is Nat T. Jackson, Independence businessman. This welcome to the Chief Executive was an incident in a campaign which drew national attention through the Pendergast group's successful effort to "purge" Congressman Roger C. Slaughter, at Truman's request.

PLANNING THE COMEBACK

Once it was Alderman Jim, then it was Big Tom and now it is Jimmy Pendergast in the order
of things for the Goat faction of Kansas City Democrats. The nephew of T. J. Pendergast,
who has directed affairs for the Jackson Democratic Club since the retirement of his uncle,
poses on a corner of a desk in his political headquarters. On the wall is a portrait of President
Truman and below it a framed check for $6, signed by Harry S. Truman, in payment of his
1946 dues.

"REACH FOR ALL!"

The foregoing words are quoted from Judge Albert L. Reeves' charge to the Federal grand jury in December, 1936, which started the long vote-fraud investigations that resulted in more than 250 convictions. Judge Reeves also instructed the Federal grand jury which indicted T. J. Pendergast in 1939 for income tax evasion.

fense champion in an affair that made the headlines from coast to coast. This was the celebrated so-called Bridge Murder trial of the era of bathtub gin and sophistication. The principal was an attractive young matron, Mrs. Myrtle A. Bennett, who was charged with shooting and killing her husband, John G. Bennett, in September, 1929, a few months before Joe Hershon participated in the holdup and murder that ended his brief career. The fatal bridge game was played in the Bennett apartment in the fashionable Country Club district, at the end of a gay weekend which the Bennetts spent with their friends, Charles and Mayme Hofman. Bennett was set two tricks doubled in spades on a contract which his wife hiked to four after he had opened with one spade and Charles Hofman bid two diamonds. The inevitable husband-and-wife quarrel followed. Bennett slapped his wife's face. She went to the bedroom and returned with a revolver which exploded four times before her husband died with two bullets in his body.

Former Senator Reed's appearance as chief of the Bennett defense at the trial in 1931 stirred recollection of his dramatic conduct as special prosecutor of Dr. Clark Hyde in the Swope murder case twenty-one years earlier. (Judge Ralph S. Latshaw, who presided at the Clark Hyde trial, was also the trial judge in the Bennett case.) Asserting that this was his farewell as a criminal lawyer, Jim Reed demonstrated that age had not rusted his histrionic and legal abilities. The jury sat fascinated through a trial that was highlighted by a weeping act by Reed, by sharp exchanges between the trial judge and Prosecutor James R. Page, and by the Prosecutor's angry comments in court over deviations in Charles Hofman's testimony between the preliminary hearing and the trial, and Mayme Hofman's lapses in memory on the stand. Reed gave a highly emotional recital as he described how Mrs. Bennett got the revolver for her husband to put in his traveling bag, as he was leaving on a business trip in the morning, after the bridge game; the slap; how she stumbled and accidentally fired the weapon twice; how her husband then mistook her intention, struggled to seize the revolver and shot himself in the arm pit. Climax was reached when the court ruled the prosecution could not introduce its star witness, a relative of the dead man, because the Prosecutor had waited to present this individual as a rebuttal witness when he should have been offered in direct testimony. The jury brought in a verdict of not guilty and some anonymous versifier closed the episode with these lines, which were printed in the *Star*:

> One spade he bid,
> Poor dud, he is dead,
> She sits in widow's weeds;
> He went down one,
> She got her gun—
> One spade is all he needs.

The futile effort to arouse the interest of politicians and the public in the fate of Joe Hershon went on until January, 1932, when Rabbi Mayerberg went to the county jail to spend the last night in the cell with the condemned man. From midnight to five-thirty o'clock in the morning, the Jewish teacher and the prisoner prayed together, played card games, exchanged jokes with the jailer and ate the lordly meal that the state provides just before it takes a life. The Rabbi walked to the gallows with Hershon and the two men recited the Sh'ma together in Hebrew and English just before the trap was sprung.

There is a memorial to Joe Hershon in the form of a little paper written by Rabbi Mayerberg the day after the execution. It may be found in the files of the *Star,* which published it, and it has been preserved in a book of Mayerberg lectures that was issued in 1944 under the title, *Chronicle of an American Crusader.* The document is of interest today to anyone who appreciates forceful rhetoric, lucid thinking and humanitarian sentiments: It is illuminating to anyone who desires to understand why America produces Joe Hershons and why its system of law is so ineffective in restraining evildoers. It should have made more of an impression than it did some fifteen years ago, for it contained a call to a political battle which soon followed.

"Before judging the enemy of society," the Rabbi wrote, "the state must judge its own imperfections. But even in an imperfect social order I believe that crime can be held in check, not by severity of the penalty, but by the speed and certainty with which justice is rendered. Let society rid itself of corrupt police departments, public officials and conniving politicians; let men of courage and ability be elected to our benches; let the legal procedure be rid of all the technicalities by which testimony is hidden or perverted or delays are manufactured; in brief, establish a

swiftly moving machinery of justice in America and the criminal will
surrender to society." *

Rabbi Mayerberg decided to take the reform initiative in the political
arena shortly after Home Rule came to Kansas City in mid-March, 1932,
in a surprise package from the Missouri Supreme Court, which threw
out the law under which the Kansas City Police Department operated.
The ruling climaxed the second mandamus action which the Police
Board had instituted to force the city government to accept its estimate
of funds required by the department. Reversing its previous ruling, the
court held, five to two, that the old statute covering the Kansas City
police was unconstitutional because it delegated to the Police Board the
legislative power to tax, "in violation of the organic law." McElroy declared he was equal to the emergency and had the Council rush through
a measure authorizing the appointment of a police director. He named
as director E. C. Reppert, who opened his regime with the announcement that he would concentrate on the suppression of major crimes and
the cultivation of polite manners among traffic cops.

The need for more efficiency in dealing with big-time criminals was
clear to all citizens and was doubly emphasized at this time by a case
that created a sensation extending over more than six months. The crime
was a kidnaping that occurred a few months before the inception of
Home Rule and was followed by a dramatic manhunt and a prosecution
that were carried to a successful conclusion by Democratic law enforcers.
Victim of the abduction was Mrs. Nell Donnelly, wealthy dress manufacturer, who was seized in front of her South Side home at dusk on
December 16, 1931. She was in her Lincoln sedan, which was driven by
her Negro chauffeur, when the car was stopped in the driveway. Both
Mrs. Donnelly and the chauffeur were spirited away. Former Senator
Reed, a neighbor of the Donnellys, hurried to their home and took charge
of the rescue effort. Mrs. Donnelly was both financially and politically
important, and very important to Jim Reed—he married her two years
later, following Mrs. Donnelly's divorce from her husband and the
death of Reed's first wife.

* From *Chronicle of an American Crusader* by Samuel S. Mayerberg, copyright 1944 by
Samuel S. Mayerberg, published by the Bloch Publishing Company. By permission of
the author.

Police ran in circles without a clue to the kidnapers. They were so desperate for a lead that detectives and Senator Reed finally decided to listen to a clairvoyant who offered her services. The crystal ball indicated that Mrs. Donnelly was "down a slope" somewhere and the detectives rode around town looking vainly for a likely slope.

Johnny Lazia, the North Side regulator, called out his scouts to look for the missing lady and her abductors. Evidently the shadow of the Goat power fell across the kidnap hideaway with telling effect for the kidnapers freed Mrs. Donnelly and her chauffeur after thirty-four hours without collecting the seventy-five thousand dollars ransom they had demanded. The prisoners, who had been held in a place about an hour's drive from the city, were released at four o'clock in the morning near an all-night café on the Kansas side. The bandits left Mrs. Donnelly with a towel over her head and the laundry mark on that towel served as an important clue in the investigation that followed. One member of the outlaw gang was pursued to Johannesburg, South Africa, and returned to Kansas City. He was given a life term in prison along with one of his accomplices. Jim Reed closed his career as a criminal lawyer with a flourish by serving as special prosecutor in the trial of a third member of the gang, who drew a long prison term.

This example of swift justice was too exceptional to allay widespread concern over the Home Rule policy on crime control. Rabbi Mayerberg's dismay over the new order grew until it forced him into explosive action late in May, 1932. The immediate background of his blast included two speeches by public officials. One came from McElroy, who declared before a meeting in a church that he regarded the last election results as a mandate to carry on a partisan administration, which was his way of warning ministers to stop their complaints about violations of nonpartisan provisions of the charter. The second incident was an address by County Attorney Page, who called attention to the alarming crime conditions and fixed the blame on the political system. Mayerberg's reaction to those two speeches, combined with the agitation over the extensive changes which the Democratic administration was making in the personnel of the Police Department, set off the crusade of 1932.

It began without advance warning or fanfare of any kind when the Rabbi went before the Government Study Club, a woman's organization, for a noonday address in a downtown hotel. Much of its effect might have been lost if a new reporter for the *Star* had not chanced to observe Mr. Mayerberg going to the meeting. Ordinarily a session of the club was not something a newspaperman made a point of attending, but the cub took a chance because he had heard the Rabbi speak on cultural matters and was impressed by his erudition and eloquence. What he heard this time was a flaming assault on the machine. Reporter Alvin S. McCoy, later a political writer and war correspondent for the *Star,* got the details right and his story made a smash in the afternoon edition.

"You've turned your city over to a gang and given it into hands of crooks and racketeers because you are asleep," Mr. Mayerberg informed the Government Study ladies. "The time has come for action. The time for study has passed."

One of the Rabbi's main points was that the City Manager had violated Section 124 of the city charter, which made it illegal to solicit a member of a political party for campaign funds or to discharge city employees because of their political affiliations. Repeated violations of that section had been made in the "lug" openly placed on city employees for campaign funds and in the wholesale firing of Republicans from the Police Department. Penalty for the violation was a fine of fifty dollars to five hundred dollars and a sentence up to six months in jail. The idea that any such action would be taken was, of course, ridiculous. That was what Mayor Smith and members of the Council said. With their boss away on vacation, the councilmen tried to suppress the Rabbi with ridicule. Mr. Mayerberg developed heat and elaborated his charges as he went along.

A few days later he met with the Ministerial Alliance, representing 104 Protestant churches, set the preachers cheering with his oratory and drew them into the fight.

"If the churches of this city have not developed a laity that will rise up and correct conditions, they have no right to exist," the Rabbi declared. "I am not discounting the wide ramifications of political racketeering and am fully aware of the difficulties that will be found right in the congregations of the various churches."

A day later the Rabbi's own board had a serious talk with him and the president made it plain that Mr. Mayerberg was representing himself privately and not B'Nai Jehudah. He didn't slow down, however.

As the revolt grew, the City Council, heeding the advice of Mayor Smith and Councilman Gossett, decided that it would be a good idea to go through the face-saving motion of granting the Rabbi a hearing. It allowed him ten minutes; and responded with a resolution affirming its complete faith in the City Manager and declared the Rabbi's charges were not worthy of further attention.

Leaving the Council chamber, Mr. Mayerberg was stopped by John Lazia, whom he had been calling a gangster, a racketeer and an ex-convict. Mr. Lazia was then a poised, well-groomed man of thirty-five and at first glance he suggested the conservative businessman more than anything else. He deliberately affected an air of mildness that was heightened by his rimless eyeglasses, an amiable smile and his gum-chewing habit.

The North Side leader seemed more amused than angry when he accosted Mayerberg. His first remark was that he wanted to meet the "second Moses" and he shook hands with the churchman. "You didn't get very far, did you, Rabbi?" he added.

Rabbi Mayerberg hurried away and if he was disturbed by the encounter it was not evident from his subsequent activities. The battle gathered momentum as Mayerberg turned in every direction to find allies. He went to confer with the attorney general of Missouri in an effort to have the state institute ouster proceedings against McElroy and his police director. Increasingly bold charges were made against McElroy, Pendergast and Lazia when he went before various clubs and churches to speak. He spoke of "the noble gentleman at Nineteenth and Main streets, the big shot who cracks the whip," and made a thinly veiled reference to a powerful banker who was allied with the Boss. Widening the range of his attack, he even called for the ouster of County Attorney Page after Page refused to consider instituting ouster proceedings against the City Manager.

A bodyguard was formed for the Rabbi by Colonel Charles Edwards, former police chief, together with one of the police officers who had been let out in the Home Rule shake-up. The Mayerberg car was equipped with bulletproof glass and was fired on once. His telephone rang often with whispered threats of character assassination, physical mutilation and death. He lived in a daily and nightly melodrama. For a time he was aroused at three o'clock each morning by a call from a man who identified himself as a gangster, called himself Pal, and offered the Rabbi information and tips in his investigation.

Ministers organized a Charter League, with Mayerberg at its head, to direct a recall movement. They started to raise funds and the Rabbi went to the City Hall to examine records. He asked to see the last city audit that had been made in the McElroy administration and was told that none existed. He demanded to see the city payrolls, which he wanted for evidence of payroll padding, and asked for the personnel records to check on the new police officers being employed by the city. He was given the run-around and openly defied by the city officials until he sought a writ of mandamus from Judge Darius A. Brown, a Republican member of the Circuit Court bench. After taking that action, Rabbi Mayerberg called on the man he was fighting in the City Hall. When their interview ended, he offered his hand to the City Manager.

"I don't care to shake your hand," said McElroy.

"My hand is clean while you have violated every provision of the charter except that providing for the drawing of your salary," Mayerberg retorted.

"That's all," Judge McElroy barked. "We're through."

"But we're not through. We've just begun."

"All right," concluded the City Manager, waving his visitor to the door of his office. "On your way."

The Charter League took the last line of the interview for its slogan, "On Your Way, McElroy."

Rabbi Mayerberg charged that as many as seventy-five ex-convicts were in the Police Department. When he finally was permitted to see the books he could not verify his charges and declared that the records were incomplete. The Charter League found itself shy of full documentary proof needed to convict.

Agitation continued through the summer and the preachers created most of the uproar from their pulpits. It began to subside late in June when Mr. Mayerberg went to the West Coast to a Rotary convention and followed that with a trip to Alaska on the advice of his physicians.

Rumors that he had abandoned the fight under the combined pressure of his board and personal intimidation were widely circulated. The Rabbi issued a public statement denying that he was leaving the city permanently or was on an extended leave of absence. When he returned in July he sought to revive the Charter League movement but it expired not long thereafter. Many influential citizens applauded his efforts but no important leaders outside the church and women's club circles stepped forward publicly to battle for him. The ministers were virtually isolated, for all practical purposes, in the fight against the machine, and the political organization was too strong, and the details of its operations were too well buried, for a successful assault against it at this time. The *Star* sympathetically reported the ministerial revolt, and its news coverage was a large factor in making the furor, but the newspaper did not do any crusading on its own account and made editorial reservations on the Mayerberg impeachment of McElroy's personal integrity and efficiency.

Fear of reprisals kept many sympathizers of the churchmen from joining the parade, but another factor was a strong anticrusade sentiment in the business community. Businessmen and the regular politicians didn't relish the idea of working with ministers—the parsons were too difficult to control, too full of spirit, too unrealistic. The prudent practical men stood back and let the amateurs run the show. They took the common-sense Chamber of Commerce view, which was aptly expressed by its official representative at a meeting of the Round Table of Club Presidents on the Mayerberg challenge.

"It is all right for the churches to go on preaching the old-fashioned gospel and building up a moral laity," said the Chamber man, "but when it comes to ministers fighting politics, I just can't follow them."

WINNER'S LUCK

POLITICIANS, like professional gamblers, are among the least superstitious of men. True, they carry rabbit's feet and other tribal charms, read signs, study portents, make prophecies, feel the finger of destiny constantly upon them and appear to be congenitally optimistic, but on the whole they place small dependence on the hocus-pocus of their trade. While others are planting potatoes in the dark of the moon, the politicians and gamblers are diligently studying the form sheets, watching straws in the wind, listening for rumbles of ground swells, observing the condition of the grass roots and otherwise basing their calculations on observable and predictable factors in any given situation. They are, in a word, the scientists of our age and all of them have a system. The one point where they share the common reverence for Lady Luck is in their sublime confidence in their various systems, unfortunately an attitude that contains a large element of superstition. They get in the habit of thinking that their special knowledge of trends, percentages and averages makes them the favorites of fortune, and they often end by believing that they know all the angles and have a sure thing. The sad result is that the system players, the smart operators and wise citizens, are frequently the victims of the deadliest of all maladies known to sportsmen—overconfidence—and occasionally they become the greatest suckers in the lot.

Tom Pendergast had ample reason to believe that he was the darling of fortune but he worked hard for most of the breaks that came his way and for a long time kept his feet on the ground, soberly sizing up the circumstances that combined to produce fortuitous events and not pressing his luck too hard. In his horse racing and betting he early exhibited a tendency to plunge, and this adventurousness became manifest in his political activities when the growing size of the stakes and the nature of the competition required him to move with increasing daring. Boldness was one of his characteristics even in the days when he was feeling his way. His gambler's instinct naturally became stronger as repeated success increased his confidence in his system.

Events moved with a steadily quickening pace when Pendergast entered on his largest operations in the 1930's. In 1932, while McElroy, Lazia and the Council were putting down the Mayerberg revolt in Kansas City, the Boss made his largest gains in the Missouri arena. In fact, he made such a splash as the supreme Missouri boss and as a figure of national consequence that sight was lost of several unfavorable portents for the Goat overlord.

Chance conspired with the Democratic politicians to give Pendergast unprecedented influence over the Missouri delegation in the national

House of Representatives in 1932. This was an unexpected by-product of the 1930 census, which revealed a growth and a shift in the Missouri population from farm to city and called for a redistricting of the state. Pendergast had been a potent factor in producing a Democratic majority in the state Legislature in 1930, and that majority approved a redistricting bill which the Republican governor vetoed, denouncing the measure as a plain gerrymander. The parties then fell into a protracted quarrel over the problem and the deadlock continued until it was seen that the redistricting could not be made in time for the congressional elections of 1932. The result was that the congressional candidates were voted on by the state at large instead of by districts. Thus every Democratic candidate for Congress who hoped to be nominated had to have the big Jackson County majority and Pendergast's indorsement. They all called hopefully at 1908 Main Street.

Fate or chance was very busy in that campaign of 1932. Death intervened to place the selection of the governor directly in Pendergast's hands. Leading candidate in the campaign was Francis M. Wilson of Platte City, who won the Democratic nomination with Pendergast's indorsement. Although he was a machine politician and a personal friend of Pendergast, he had built up wide popular prestige as a representative of the original Missouri Democracy, a true son of the Kingdom of the Platte. Missourians were delighted with his high-flown oratory and his poetical effusions on the natural beauties of their state. They liked the way he looked and talked. They called him the Red Headed Peckerwood of the Platte—he had red hair and freckles—and found he combined democratic informality, dignity, humor, sentiment and statesmanly qualities in about equal proportions. Facing the certain prospect of election to the governorship he died a few weeks before the final balloting.

Selection of Wilson's successor on the ticket was made by the Democratic State Committee, which Pendergast dominated, and the choice was unanimous. The call went to Guy Brasfield Park of Platte City, a little-known country lawyer and Circuit judge. Park's chief points as a politician were his party regularity and his devotion to the memory of Francis Wilson. It was obvious that he would be a faithful organization man during his term as governor and that his feeling about Wilson would make him doubly grateful to the Kansas City boss for the honor he received. During his four years in Jefferson City the State Capitol was popularly known as Uncle Tom's Cabin.

Signs that Pendergast was beginning to overreach himself and that his phenomenal good luck was running out were given in this same campaign, in which he backed an unsuccessful candidate for the United States Senate. Tom's choice was Charles M. Howell, a Kansas City lawyer.

Candidate Howell was defeated for the nomination by Bennett Champ Clark of Bowling Green, son of the famous Champ Clark, who had represented Missouri in Congress as speaker of the House and was a leading contender for the Democratic presidential nomination in 1912.

The crosscurrents of machine politics manifested themselves in this competition when the Kansas City organization's elder statesman, Jim Reed, a former law partner of Howell, gave his support to Clark. His commitment to the Bowling Green man antedated the 1932 contest for he was a friend of Bennett Clark's father. Reed had placed Champ Clark in nomination at the Baltimore Convention where the Missourian was the favorite until Bryan stampeded the delegates for the dark horse, Woodrow Wilson. Bennett Clark later was to work alternately with and against the Kansas City organization, but his principal effect on Pendergast was depressing. His successful race against Pendergast's senatorial candidate classed as an upset, and the Howell-Clark episode served in every way to illustrate the hazards and uncertain elements lying in the path of the city Boss when he stepped beyond his home grounds and began to spread himself.

The cooling of relations between Pendergast and Reed, which eventually led to a break, started with the Bennett Clark raid. This was one of the strange turns in the operation in which the Kansas City boss tried to keep a Reed-for-President movement alive at the same time that he attempted to send Howell to the Senate. He stood with Reed when his political judgment must have told him that he wasn't doing himself any good, and then found the Stormy Petrel opposing his Senate candidate after the Reed-for-President boom flopped.

Reed's presidential hope was a long shot which the Pendergast family backed heavily. If they won, they would be kingmakers and national figures for all time. If they lost, it did not for long appear that they would be out anything but the time and money that they could well afford.

Pendergast's promotion for Reed in '32 was the climax of an eight-year presidential build-up. Or rather it was the anticlimax of 1928, when the Missourian was believed to have some chance as a compromise choice if anything happened to discourage Al Smith from making a second bid for the nomination. The Kansas Citians put on a colorful show for their hero at the Houston Convention, but when the shouting was over all they had to show for their efforts was an unused campaign song.

Bound by ironclad instructions to stay with Reed until he released them, the Missourians held out for Jim until they missed a chance to get seats on the Al Smith bandwagon and Pendergast expressed the general mood of the delegation when he threatened to knock the blocks off of a couple of Smith men who tried to wrest the Missouri standard from Big Tom's nephew, Jimmy Pendergast.

As the time for the national convention of 1932 approached, it was seen that the Kansas City boss was following a lost cause with Reed and missing the chance to put himself high in favor with the winner. The backing of a favorite son candidate did not ordinarily jeopardize a party leader's position with the successful candidate, but the opposition to Franklin D. Roosevelt that came from Kansas City went deeper than the usual pre-convention rivalry. Reed did not conceal his hostility toward Woodrow Wilson's old assistant secretary of the Navy. The difference had its origins in the conflicts of the Wilson period and in a basic philosophical difference. Reed saw the New Deal trend in Roosevelt's administration as governor long before it was recognized by the general public, and he talked darkly of Socialistic and Communistic heresies that were spreading over the country. He was in the vanguard of the Stop Roosevelt movement, and also served as the rearguard. Reed went to Texas to confer with the Lone Star State's favorite son, John N. Garner, but Garner kept himself in a position to trade with either Roosevelt or the hated McAdoo of California, and Reed faced the prospect of standing alone in the convention with a divided Missouri delegation.

To keep Missouri in the Reed column, Tom Pendergast staged the most spectacular state convention show in Missouri's political history. An army of five thousand Jackson County Goats and Rabbits descended on St. Louis. Behind the scenes, Pendergast broke the hearts of a couple of important individuals entertaining gubernatorial and senatorial ambitions, shaped the party platform and dictated the selection of delegates to the National Convention. He named the Big Eight—the delegates at large—but for all his intimidating force, was not able to get a full delegation pledged to Reed in a satisfactory manner. Outstate Democrats and some St. Louis Democrats remembered how Reed had refused to release the Missouri delegation at the Houston Convention in time to make any hay with the Al Smith contingent, and they balked at an ironclad instruction for Reed at Chicago in 1932. The best that the Missouri boss could do was to obtain an agreement for the entire delegation to vote for Reed in the early balloting. Even then there were rumblings of protest, and it was evident that Pendergast could not keep the delegation together long, after the Roosevelt stampede started.

There were signs of tension and jumpy nerves in the Pendergast party during the preliminaries in Jim Reed's last stand. Pendergast's temper flared at St. Louis in an argument with a delegate from Greene County, a dispute that was said to have ended with one swing of the Kansas City man's mighty right arm.

George Wallace, the *Star*'s veteran Missouri political correspondent, heard a report of the encounter and hurried to Pendergast's hotel room to verify the account. Pendergast had retired to bed when Wallace aroused him. Big Tom stood in the doorway and eyed the reporter inquiringly.

"So you slugged a guy," said Wallace.

"No, I didn't, George."

"They tell me there's a delegate from Greene County out cold and that you slugged him."

"You've got it wrong, George."

"Let's see your knuckles."

Pendergast held out his fists and there were no marks on the knuckles. It seems that Big Tom was technically correct in his denial. He hadn't slugged the Greene County guy with his fist but knocked him out with the palm of his hand, and one blow settled the matter. As pieced together from gossip, the story was that the quarrel started in a hotel elevator. The complete details were never obtained as there was no official investigation. It is said that the police were called but beat a hasty retreat back to headquarters when they learned the identity of the winner.

No one was disposed to bring charges or willing to be quoted, and the story remained one of the little-known tales of King Tom's biggest convention show.

BATTALION OF DEATH

A SPECIAL TRAIN carrying some four hundred Kansas City Goats and Rabbits arrived in Chicago the night of June 26, 1932. The travel-stained Missourians were weary from a day-long effort to make a loud noise over the more than four hundred and fifty miles from the Heart of America to the Windy City, but they immediately started capering and shouting to let the world know that the Jim Reed party was in town. They arrived at a moment when the Reed cause looked hopeless, but were determined to show at least that the Jackson County spirit was awesome and indomitable.

In the succeeding days the Jackson County politicians continued to whoop it up while their great Roman grimly but vainly tried to hold back the Roosevelt tide in the hotel rooms and on the Convention floor.

Pendergast beat down all arguments that Missouri, by refusing to reach an understanding with Roosevelt, was missing a golden chance to cast the deciding vote on a presidential nomination. Tom based his stand entirely on personal loyalty.

"I am here for my friend, Senator Reed," he said. "For forty years we have been friends."

At one stage of the controversy in the Missouri delegation, Big Tom took exception to some things that were said by L. J. Gauldoni of St. Louis. He moved menacingly toward Gauldoni but the St. Louis man was too nimble for the aging Kansas City boss, removing himself from harm's way.

Sam Fordyce, who nominated Reed, perspired under the Chicago Stadium lights acclaiming the man from the Heart of America as the Apostle of Americanism. It was the familiar convention oration except for some adroit references to Reed's record as an isolationist and his ultra-conservative ideas of the correct way to handle the depression.

"If you want the Democratic Party to be suspected of radicalism, communism, socialism, do not nominate him," Sam needlessly advised the delegates.

Missouri's thirty-six votes were cast for Reed on the first ballot, but twelve of the thirty-six shifted to Roosevelt before the totals were announced. Reed picked up eleven Oklahoma votes from Alfalfa Bill Murray's delegation on the third ballot, reaching his top figure of thirty-three. Tom Pendergast still stood fast with his friend and waited for the signal that would release the entire Missouri delegation to the winner.

Reed sat in the Missouri section, surrounded by his faithful followers, glumly watching a Roosevelt demonstration that roared and swirled around him. A cigar was clenched in his teeth, his face was set in stubborn lines and the old eagle look was in his eyes. Few persons noticed the silvery haired, commanding figure in the Missouri group. This was the last convention in which he would appear, the end of his political career, the beginning of the political exile in which he would spend his last days. Ten years earlier he had fought back from a decree of exile which Wodrow Wilson sought to impose on him. The shadow of Wilson was present in the Chicago Stadium when Reed was humbled and defeated.

Breckenridge Long, the Missourian who carried the banner for Woodrow Wilson against Jim Reed in the struggle over the League of Nations, was in the Chicago Convention acting in behalf of Roosevelt. The friends of Wilson, Long and Roosevelt sat in stony silence when the nomination speech for Reed was given, and their emotions must have been strong indeed when the speaker declared: "One great battle in Senator Reed's career entitles him to an everlasting place in the Hall of Fame—his relentless, his successful fight to keep this country from ignoring Washington's warning to avoid all foreign entanglements."

The tableau in the Chicago Stadium recalled the dramatic scene at the Democratic National Convention in San Francisco in 1920, when Reed was read out of his own party for his fight on Wilson and the League of Nations. Before going to San Francisco, he had been tried for disloyalty and found guilty by the Democrats of Missouri at their state convention, which voted 1070 to 490 to refuse him a seat in San Francisco as a delegate from his home county. The Kansas City organization gave him a set of credentials and sent along special pleaders like Francis M.

Wilson to press his cause with the national party leaders. The National Committee denied him a seat on the temporary roll call of the convention and the Credentials Committee voted overwhelmingly to bar him. An outcast, branded by the President of his party as a "marplot," Reed faced political oblivion. It was widely expected that he would retire when his term in the Senate expired in 1922, but such expectations were based on a lack of knowledge of Reed and the Pendergasts.

Tom Pendergast's participation in the League struggle, like his stand for Reed in 1932, was based on personal rather than political grounds.

"I don't know anything about the League of Nations," he had told George Wallace of the *Star* in 1919. "But if Jim Reed says it is wrong, it's wrong."

In the years between Reed's vindication battle in Missouri and the Chicago Convention most men had forgotten the struggle that rocked Missouri in the 1922 campaign and little was said of its bearing on the '32 conflict and the events that followed. It is a story that places the city machine in the center of a world tragedy and illuminates the operations of the reactionary forces that combined to kill the Wilson dream of brotherhood and peace.

The Battalion of Death was the name given to the band of Senate irreconcilables by one of its members who thrilled to the political melodrama. Reed of Missouri was its flashing sword and he reached the high point of his oratorical effort in September, 1919, two months before the first vote test in the Senate, when he spoke three hours before packed galleries. His argument, and the whole argument of the Battalion of Death, was summed up when he declared:

"Washington fought to establish the right of this nation as a sovereign to control its own affairs. Woodrow Wilson counsels with the representatives of kings to transfer the sovereignty Washington gained to a league they will dominate. The man who is willing to give any nation or assemblage of nations the right to mind the business of the American people ought to disclaim American citizenship and emigrate to the country he is willing to have mind America's business.

"I decline to help set up any government greater than that established by the fathers, baptised in the blood of patriots from the lane of Lexington to the forest of the Argonne, sanctified by the tears of all the mothers whose heroic sons went down to death to sustain its glory and independence—the government of the United States."

Bedlam swept the Chamber. Women screamed, a group of doughboys recruited for the occasion took off their steel helmets and clanked them together and Vice-President Marshall gave up attempts to enforce the Senate rule against applause. It was a well-staged show.

In this way the people were persuaded that the interests of their national state prohibited their meddling with novel measures intended to secure world peace and equality of opportunity.

Strategist Lodge produced a steady flow of ideas for ways to delay action and talk the League to death. The issue of the Monroe Doctrine was raised, together with the Irish Question, the Vatican Issue and the Yellow Peril. One of Reed's contributions to the false alarm was the bogey of dominance by the world's colored people. The resolution for ratification of the League Covenant was killed with a basketful of reservations and the great mischief was done a year and eight days after the first anniversary of the Armistice.

In the campaigns that followed, Wilson's friends set out to punish the Democrats in the Senate who had opposed the League, and Reed became their chief target.

Wilson had brought the fight to Missouri in the tragically interrupted speaking tour of the country which he undertook while the Battalion of Death was holding the stage in Washington. He delivered one of his most memorable utterances in St. Louis in the same September, 1919, when Reed was making his gaudy America First speech in the Senate. Wilson's St. Louis speech contained his prophecy of the Second World War and was given in the city where the Missouri conflict over the League issue was decided against Wilson. For Reed's own people the ailing War President had reserved his direct warning, declaring:

If it [the Covenant of the League of Nations] should ever in any important respect be impaired, I would feel like asking the Secretary of War to get the boys who went across the water to fight, together on some field where I could go and see them, and I would stand up before them and say:

"Boys, I told you before you went across the seas that this was a war against wars, and I did my best to fulfill the promise; but I am obliged to come to you in mortification and shame and say I have not been able to fulfill the promise. You are betrayed. You fought for something that you did not get."

And the glory of the armies and navies of the United States is gone like a dream in the night, and there ensues upon it, in the suitable darkness of the night, the nightmare of dread which lay upon the nations before this war came; and there will come some time, in the vengeful Providence of God, another struggle in which, not a few hundred thousand fine men from America will have to die, but as many millions as are necessary to accomplish the final freedom of the peoples of the world.

Although St. Louis was the center of anti-League sentiment in Missouri, it produced the champion in the Show Me State fight on Reed. Breckenridge Long, who had been an assistant secretary of State in the Wilson administration, entered the senatorial race in 1922 on the one issue of Reed's disloyalty to the wartime President and the wrecking of the League. Former President Wilson personally intervened in the Missouri contest, asking that Reed be defeated. "I hope and confidently expect to see him repudiated by the Democrats at the primaries," he wrote in a letter to Lon V. Stephens, a former Missouri governor.

The prevailing notion is that the Middle Western farm and small town are the strongholds of isolationist sentiment. That was not the story in Missouri when Reed sought vindication for destroying the League. The Democrats of rural Missouri caught the Wilson dream and held it. Wilson still is their hero. They rolled up majorities against Reed in 1922 and they struck another blow for Wilson two years later when they killed the Reed boom for President.

The city machines of Missouri's two metropolitan centers, Kansas City and St. Louis, worked to save Reed, and the isolationist idea inspired them to employ the technique of collaboration on a scale never before witnessed, for Republicans in large numbers crossed the party line to vote with the urban Democrats, who supported Reed.

Senator Reed went into the race with the advantage of the popular fame, the personal allegiances and the organizational ties he had built up through more than twenty years of campaigning, facing a candidate who was not nearly so well known to the voters and the party men. Reed had a tremendous advantage in oratorical skill and he gave his greatest performance on the stump in this campaign. Regardless of their convictions, Missourians thrilled to a fighter who struck with daring and ferocity, and the Stormy Petrel was spectacular in his defiance before hostile audiences in communities dominated by Rid Us of Reed Clubs. "The man who is incapable of thinking for himself is too great a fool to send to Congress," he thundered. "The man who would take the office of congressman upon condition that he should vote according to the dictates of some other man is too contemptible to send to Congress." Listening to him, anyone who did not have a clear idea of the true issue involved would have been persuaded that Reed was being persecuted simply for his heroic refusal to serve as a "rubber stamp." Bridle Wise Jim succeeded in so convincing many voters. Observers declared that he was one hundred thousand votes behind Breckenridge Long when the campaign opened but on election eve all agreed that the outcome was a tossup.

The Missouri senator's opposition to Prohibition and his stand against the Klan also worked in his favor in the more populous centers, for these issues were agitating the state at the time and the cities were more disturbed over interference with their liberties by Kluxers and drys than they were over the peace of the world.

Finally, Reed received substantial assistance from Nelson's old paper, the *Star,* which performed yeoman service in the crusade to save the country from "entangling alliances." The *Star's* role in the fight on the League stands in notable contrast to its part in the isolationist struggle before the Second World War, when it was one of the potent Republican voices raised in support of Franklin D. Roosevelt's foreign policy. One of the large factors in this change in position is the newspaper's present editor, H. J. Haskell, twice winner of Pulitzer awards for editorial work.

Early in the League fight in the Senate, Reed called aside the *Star's* Washington correspondent, Roy A. Roberts, now its managing editor, and extended the Goat hand in fighting fellowship. Co-operation between the Republican newspaper and the Democratic Senator was limited to the League question alone, and did not extend to the support of Reed in the final contest with the Republican nominee, but their teamwork before the nomination of 1922 marked the end of the long feud between Reed and the *Star.*

Without the city machine and without the help he received from the Republicans, Jim Reed could not have survived the attack by friends of Wilson and the League. He won the nomination by a margin of five thousand votes, and what saved him was a majority of nearly twenty-five thousand from Jackson County. In the final election, Reed lost his home county by almost one thousand votes but won in the state by more than thirty thousand. The Republicans of St. Louis overcame the large out-state majorities against Reed, turning a normal sixty thousand Republican majority into a forty-three thousand majority for the Democratic "marplot."

Thus Wilson was cheated of a victory in his last political battle for the League cause. Jim Reed went back to the Senate and the politicians took up their normal business of building fences and strengthening the party organization. By the time the situation was right for Reed's final bid for the Presidency, Wilson was dead, Wilson's men were scattered and the lightnings of the Second World War were flashing over Asia and Europe.

It was certain that there would be no League issue at the Democratic National Convention and there was none, but the world disorder could not be stopped at the doors of the Chicago Stadium and the cause that Wilson represented could not end with the failure of his imperfect scheme for a concert of nations. The same conditions, ideas and hopes that produced the Fourteen Points created a large collection of problems for the politicians and the demand that their government undertake drastic measures to correct social and economic wrongs beat insistently on the delegates. The Stop Roosevelt men—Reed of Missouri, Garner of Texas, Alfalfa Bill Murray of Oklahoma, McAdoo of California and the Tammany holdouts supporting Al Smith—came to the meeting with their routine schemes to save the Ship of State, preserve the status quo and not rock the boat. But they couldn't get together and by some miraculous chance the nomination went to the great humanitarian among them, the one who believed that the people could create an order of security and peace.

The climax was reached on the floor of the Chicago Convention the night of July 1. Jim Reed sat in the Missouri section, chewing his cigar and glowering at Roosevelt delegates who left their seats to join in a tumultuous parade for the candidate from New York. Near him was Mrs. Nell Donnelly. She jealously guarded the Missouri standard for the man who was her hero and whose bride she became eighteen months after the Chicago Convention. At an earlier session of the convention she had engaged in a spirited exchange with a St. Louis woman, Mrs. Nat Brown, who wanted to put the Missouri standard in a Roosevelt demonstration.

"You go and sit down and think it over," Mrs. Donnelly said to Mrs. Brown.

"You go and sit down and think it over yourself," was the tart reply.

"Well," said Mrs. Donnelly with an air of great finality, "this standard is not going to be moved. It would be accepted as a slight to Senator Reed."

The standard was not moved then or for some time afterward.

The Donnelly vigil at the Missouri standard for Reed ended shortly after McAdoo released the California delegation to Roosevelt on the fourth ballot. Tom Pendergast retired to the Convention corridors to confer with leaders of the delegation. The Roosevelt men in the Missouri delegation were impatient as Garner was about to release the Texas delegation to Roosevelt and this was the last chance to get on the bandwagon.

When the Missourians returned to the floor the entire Missouri vote was cast for Roosevelt, but Reed declined the honor of making the announcement. He later accepted an invitation to address the Convention, and confined his remarks to his favorite topic—the misdeeds of Herbert Hoover.

This was the first conspicuous manifestation of the incompatibility between the Roosevelt administration and the Kansas City Democratic organization, which became pronounced in later years, when Goats with troubles found their influence in Washington was decidedly limited, and eventually saw the national administration take a leading part in investigations and prosecutions that wrecked the Pendergast machine. No one has seriously contended that Washington's intervention was motivated by personal or political differences between the national head of the party and the local organization, but the record plainly raises the question whether the anti-Roosevelt sentiment among important figures in the Goat company predisposed the administration to take a large and critical interest in Kansas City affairs at the very time when Pendergast was embarking on some highly dubious undertakings.

The Boss came home from Chicago and delivered a record Jackson

County majority for the ticket in the November, 1932, election, impressing everyone that he had everything under control and apparently Mr. Pendergast himself wasn't entirely prepared for the crisis that developed swiftly after the campaign that buried the Reed presidential hope.

SUCKERS, PURE AND SIMPLE

IF TOM PENDERGAST had not been a gambling man it is possible that he might never have developed into a successful political boss. On the other hand, his political machine might never have smashed up if he hadn't been a gambling man. Gambling had been a matter of prime interest to Pendergast from the beginning, but it may be doubted that he had ever seriously considered that there were two sides to the question for him as well as for the public, before 1932. Up to that moment he had found pleasure in his association with gamblers, together with enough profit to convince him that the odds in this enterprise were in his favor. Starting then, there was a series of incidents that compelled him to consider the other side of the question.

The Kansas City agitation over the gambling issue included an effort to impress the tolerant Goat view on the new man in the White House and a large part of the nation, and that ambitious undertaking began December 5, 1932. It started with a demonstration in Kansas City's massive Union Station. Travelers had difficulty getting to their trains during one hour of that winter night because of the crowd that filled the lobby. Banners were raised over the heads of the throng. One sign read: "Welcome back to Kansas City." Another announced: "Kansas City Has Faith in You." A third proclaimed: "Our Own Conrad H. Mann."

Con Mann was coming home from New York, where the day before a Federal jury had convicted him of violating the Federal lottery laws. He was sentenced to five months in jail and fined twelve thousand dollars, the sentence growing out of a charity frolic, dance and lottery conducted through the Fraternal Order of Eagles. It was a $1,759,373.60 party in which International Secretary Mann and the manager of the lottery shared $460,000 of the proceeds.

Mr. Mann was visibly affected by the demonstration in his honor at the station. City Manager H. F. McElroy, who had been with him on the painful visit in New York, walked beside him. They were welcomed by Ruby D. Garrett, city councilman and an official of the Chamber of Commerce, who had worked hard to organize this spontaneous tribute. "There are not more persons because the station lobby will not hold them," Mr. Mann was informed by J. E. Woodmansee, vice president of the Chamber, armed with a resolution from the Chamber stating its unshaken faith in its president.

It might have been added that there also would have been a brass band if the Ministerial Alliance hadn't adopted a resolution protesting against the reception when plans for it were announced. The Chamber men then decided to dispense with music as a concession to puritan sentiment.

Kansas City was telling the world that it didn't consider gambling a crime. It was telling Uncle in Washington where to get off. The show at the station was the beginning of one of the greatest pressure campaigns in American history to spring a violator of the law. It was also part of the long and earnest educational campaign conducted by Pendergast and his associates to acquaint backward citizens with the ways of the world and the futility of attempting to suppress gambling, a crusade that was just entering its final phase when the Chamber's president got caught with a fat lottery rake-off.

Great progress had been made in the movement to make the world safe for poker enthusiasts, horse book players and crap shooters, but the Goat statement of the Kansas City attitude still lacked a certain finality despite the commercial weight and official dignity of the demonstration for Con Mann and other activities of the right faction. The Kansas City boss encountered some of the most troublesome opposition to gambling in his own party and one die-hard in particular was that old disturber of the Goat peace—Jim Page. In 1932, in the closing months of his six-year tenure as county attorney, he conducted what was popularly known as Jim Page's one-man war against the slot machines, or "one-arm bandits," as they were more accurately and effectionately described. This campaign was undertaken at a time when Page was running for election as Circuit judge with Pendergast's support. Since the Prosecutor succeeded in delivering a body blow to the Goat organization and at the

same time managed to retain the Goat boss's backing, his performance
was both impressive and bewildering to the onlookers. The fact that he
was able to go ahead without more effective interference from 1908
Main Street may have signified that Pendergast was open minded on the
gambling issue, but most observers liked the simpler explanation that
Old Hickory Page had Big Tom buffaloed.

Mr. Page was indeed an intimidating figure when aroused, but he
did not have Pendergast's man, Hank McElroy, bluffed. The City
Manager happily responded to the call to battle for his master, making
great sport in putting down the Page uprising. When the Prosecutor led
sheriff's deputies on a series of raids, McElroy's police confiscated slot
machines and smashed the evidence to the dismay of the Prosecutor.
Page promoted a grand jury investigation and asked the jury to return
fifty-seven true bills in slot-machine cases he had developed. McElroy
appeared before the jury and argued so well against this kind of law enforcement that the jury returned only two indictments, neither of them
involving slot machines.

After he became a Circuit judge, Page attempted to revive the slot-
machine prosecution and succeeded in getting his successor in the county
attorney's office to press the charges in a justice of the peace court. His
Honor's humiliation was made complete when the J.P., a veteran Pendergast henchman, dismissed all of the cases for "lack of evidence" immediately after Judge Page himself had testified.

This exhibition provoked wide amusement in the town along with
protests from numerous ministers, club ladies, P.T.A. leaders and an
editorial writer on the *Kansas City Star*. Judge McElroy saw the need
for further public instruction and, with the enthusiasm of all crusaders
and zealots, overreached himself. The opportunity for this performance
presented itself when the *Star* carried an article on the growth of the
slot-machine industry in the town, emphasizing its effect on school children, who happily squandered their milk and chocolate money to watch
the pretty cherries and lemons go around. This story was accompanied
by a statement from the City Manager, a statement of policy combined
with a lecture to suckers, parents and reformers which must rank as a
major contribution to the downfall of Pendergast for it goaded the opposition to force a showdown on the gambling question.

"I'm glad to see the slot machine come out in the open," Judge McElroy said. "As city manager, I am looking the situation squarely in the face. I won't dodge. I am willing to accept responsibility.

"The man who plays a slot machine is a sucker, pure and simple. He gets the thrill and the slot machine gets the money. There you are."

The remainder of the brief statement had the same bluntness and candor of this stimulating opening. Coming quickly to the point, the Judge announced:

"If there is an agitation in this city against slot machines, I will order their removal from the larger stores that can afford to pay for morality. But I will not remove them from small, independent stores. Why? Because they are keeping small, independent stores in business.

"Furthermore," added the City Hall's man of business, "I do not believe slot machines corrupt children. Their parents corrupt them. Any child who must be reared by the police probably will turn out to be a police character."

It seemed that everybody except the suckers resented having the truth stated about this business. Reason, logic, ridicule, disgrace and impoverishment could not discourage the sportive citizens who were certain they would hit the jackpot on the next pull of the slot-machine levers, and they continued their moronic pastime while the responsible people denounced McElroy for officially admitting that the government's morals were no better than those of businessmen and parents.

The City Council found it expedient to do something to restore appearances and Countilman Gossett took the floor to proclaim that the government's attachment to the ideal of civic virtue was what it was before the Council's Hired Man spoke out of turn. He sat down to a light round of applause after giving McElroy a tap on the wrist, asserting that the City Manager should at least have consulted the Council before issuing a statement of policy that amounted to nullification of a city ordinance and a statute of the Grand Old State of Missouri. Councilman Gossett explained that he did not make his reprimand more severe because Judge McElroy was not present at the meeting to defend himself. Mayor Smith arose, expressed his full agreement with the Gossett sentiments, and complimented Farmer Al on his restraint in view of the City Manager's absence. The Council then adjourned with a feeling that the moral crisis had been met and mastered.

Then, suddenly, the Pendergast organization found itself in the midst of a major emergency provoked by the gambling operation.

The explosion was set off by two good Democrats, Judge Page and Judge Allen C. Southern, who inspired the grand jury investigations that made the summer and fall of 1933 an exciting time in Kansas City. Judge Southern made Jim Page's war on the gamblers a two-man affair when he issued a ringing call for an inquiry that should go to the bottom and the top of the racket industry.

The jury went immediately to work hunting slot machines, which vanished with phantomlike speed and were stored in safe places for the duration. Undiscouraged, the jury broadened the scope of its probe to include the monopoly in beer and beverage distribution, and the city buzzed with excited speculation when Johnny Lazia, the North Side kingpin, and Big Charley Carollo were called before the jury.

Excitement was heightened by a move in the United States District Court to revive the Federal government's prosecution of Lazia for income tax evasion. Tom Pendergast had exerted all of his influence to have this prosecution dropped but heavy pressure for action developed after new public attention was directed to the case by a member of the Federal grand jury, who arose in open court to ask the judge what disposition had been made of the matter. The judge turned the question to the United States district attorney, and he explained that action in the case had been deferred on "orders from Washington." This interesting exchange was followed by a message from the attorney general in Washington which reopened the Lazia case in the late summer of 1933.

Meanwhile, the courts of Circuit Judges Southern and Page provided fresh sensations.

Pendergast himself started the Goat counteroffensive with one of his infrequent interviews. This was a command performance, staged in Chicago, where the Democratic leader was visiting on political and private business. A reporter from the *Star* was summoned for an important pronouncement, and was ushered before the Boss with unusual solemnity. Mr. Pendergast had put on an air of remoteness and gravity to suit his new consequence and the nature of the occasion. With a very earnest manner, he announced that he had become a convert of the antislot machine cause. The slots must go, he asserted, and at the moment they were being whisked out of sight by his loyal subjects.

Kansas City's First Citizen also wanted to let his people know that he was thinking ahead for their moral welfare, and he took this opportunity to state that he was against the return of the old-time saloon and in favor of stringent liquor regulations upon the imminent repeal of the Eighteenth Amendment. In passing, he let his competitors know just what to expect, asserting he would revive his wholesale liquor company when Prohibition ended.

Mr. Pendergast then suggested gently that the agitation over gambling and racketeering in Kansas City was exaggerated. He plainly felt that he was a misunderstood man, and that his organization was being misrepresented.

"I have been around quite a bit," the Boss remarked with engaging modesty. "I know the ins and outs of life, know lots of people. Many know me and I do not want to leave any impression that does not reflect me as I am.

"There are all kinds of people in a political organization, just as there are in the world. Among them are the best and others who take advantage.

"In recent months I have been in New York, Philadelphia, Chicago and other places, resorts and otherwise. I say there is more gambling in these cities in comparison than there is in Kansas City, except as may have existed there thirty years or more ago down on the state line in the Bottoms. It is the same throughout the country in every large center.

"So far as rackets are concerned, I can say advisedly that Kansas City is freer from racketeering than any city its size in the country. Outside of the gambling and slot-machine complaints, I say that Kansas City is the standout city of the country so far as the protection of its city by the police is concerned."

While the Boss in Chicago was complimenting Kansas City on the safety of its people, terror struck behind the scenes. Grand jury witnesses were threatened with reprisals in business and even with bodily injury. Members of the grand jury received missives and telephone calls telling them that they were jeopardizing their own lives and the safety of members of their families. The jury was forced to meet in secret places in order to escape surveillance and intimidating whispers.

The gangster tactic that made its appearance in the fight on Rabbi Mayerberg had now developed into a permanent feature of machine rule, and would be used in the future on an increasingly larger scale. It was effective to a degree in the Southern jury investigation. It silenced some people, forced many reputable citizens into perjuring themselves before the jury and succeeded in concealing the evidence that was needed for the prosecution of the important gamblers and slot-machine managers.

Southern's grand jury returned a final report that should have provoked a wave of mass meetings, the ringing of fire bells and at least one riot in a liberty-loving community. Nothing quite like that happened. Fear, incomprehension, bewilderment and the habit of being ruled by political machines seemed to have paralyzed the democratic will.

There were still a few individuals who had not lost their powers of indignation and initiative, and the most vigorous one of this select company at the moment was the fractious Goat, Judge Jim Page. While the Southern jury was preparing its devastating answer to Pendergast's pretty description of the Kansas City situation, Judge Page had been busy calling the public's attention to the larger implications of the businessman's philosophy of tolerance for gambling, beer joints and easy government. He seized an opportunity to slug the City Manager and his system one September day when three young Italian bandits were brought before him for sentencing. The Judge had prepared a rather lengthy address for this occasion, for there was something about this case that distinguished it from the long list of crimes involving products of Little Italy on the North Side.

"The Court is of the opinion that these three boys do not belong to the organized criminal gang of Italians in this city," Judge Page began. "If they did, they would be represented here at this time by lawyers who make their living off the proceeds of crime. If they didn't have the money to pay for that kind of lawyer, the gang would furnish it for them. The good Italian people of this city, and there are thousands of them, are fortunate in having in their community a lawyer of the character of Judge Benanti [the defense counsel].

"I do not believe," the Court continued, "that these boys ought to receive the same punishment as the boys that are known members of the criminal gang in Kansas City, and protected, in my judgment, by the Police Department of this city.

"The purpose of punishment is not for retribution but for the purpose of preventing others from committing crimes if it can be done. We have a condition in this city, which these three boys, as bad as they are, are not responsible for, entirely. We have at the head of our city government a man who openly permitted violation of the law and made a public statement to the newspapers he was going to continue to do it and what could the people do about it? Now, so long as we have at the head of our government a man of this kind, and a man at the head of our Police Department of the kind we have, how can we expect boys like these to have the respect for the law that they ought to have? I do not believe that the Court ought to impose the highest penalty on boys of this kind on account of the condition which has been brought about by some of the law enforcement agencies of our city and our county."

Old Hickory had much more to say in the same vein on the government's immorality, the North Side rule of terror and the public's apathy before he let the young desperadoes off with twenty years each in prison.

McElroy's only reply to this blast was a typical McElroyism. "I refuse to get into an endurance contest with a skunk," said the pride of Dunlap, Iowa.

"All law-abiding citizens would rather smell the odor of a skunk than that of his coffee grounds and rotten police administration," Page retorted.

The Judge was profoundly dismayed by the public's attitude in this struggle. "The community generally gets the kind of law enforcement that it wants and earns," he remarked to the Prosecutor. "The people can't sit still and delegate this to the public agents. The people themselves are responsible. When they are going to wake up to the situation, I do not know, but it is time they ought to begin to help us. If they don't begin pretty soon it is going to be too late."

When the Southern jury returned its challenging report, Page observed the slight agitation that it caused and struck again with a call for another grand jury to complete the work of the first investigation. His charge to that jury was his supreme effort to put some spunk in a demoralized people.

Instructing the jury to "go after crime" in all of its phases, the Judge observed with broad emphasis: "He who violates the law is neither Democrat nor Republican. He is a criminal."

Page's deepest scorn was reserved for the "substantial businessmen" who appeared before the Southern grand jury and gave false testimony on slot-machine operations.

"I hope," the Judge said, "that you will be able to return indictments for perjury against some of these so-called businessmen and good citizens of this city. They are not good citizens. They are not businessmen. They are racketeers just the same as the organization or other members of the organization who are engaged in other rackets."

Warning the jury that they could expect no assistance from the Police Department but that they could count on threats of violence against them and their families, Judge Page closed with this challenge:

"If something should happen to one of us, we would only be making the supreme sacrifice that thousands of American boys made a few years ago in order that this might be a country fit for you to bring up your families, and fit for your homes, and that you might sit around your fireside without fear of anyone."

The jury took elaborate measures to cloak its operations and shield witnesses, but the organization's espionage system was very effective and the terror came out again. While the fear spread, the slot machines were trundled off once more by the syndicate's spooks and many gambling places closed. At the same time the principal game operators made a bold demonstration of contempt for the investigation and thirty-eight of the gambling spots ran full blast at the height of the probe.

Nothing untoward happened to the grand jurors for daring to do their duty and as the investigation progressed the citizens called as witnesses began to show more courage. The jury had been carefully selected and it included men prominent in the business and professional life of the city. Its work, together with that of the Southern grand jury, was the beginning of the belated revolt against Pendergastism in the business community.

Sixty-one indictments were returned by the jury, which adjourned after meeting for thirty days. Those indictments made hardly more than a dent in the rackets but the jury's final report became a key text in the furious city campaign that came a few months later. The approaching political uprising was signalled in many ways in the grand jury work. Foreman of the Page jury was an important Democrat, Russell F. Greiner, who became a leader in the 1934 campaign against Pendergast. Another member of the jury, D. S. Adams, figured in that battle as a successful Council candidate. Alex S. Rankin, a Democratic stalwart with prestige in both business and political life, joined the antimachine leadership and ran for a seat in the Council. While the Page grand jury was meeting the Republican Party showed new signs of life. Although the next election was months distant, crowds turned out for a party rally with campaign-time fervor, and were not chilled when their leaders offered to join any group irrespective of party label to fight the machine. The significance of this co-operative gesture was underscored by the activities of a strange outfit known as N.Y.M., or the National Youth Movement, which had just come into the open after a long underground campaign. For months the Goats had been disturbed by the work of this secret organization, which dropped the disguise with the announcement that it would enter a ticket in the next city campaign.

While the forces of opposition were coalescing and beginning to develop a leadership, Boss Tom was busy with both local and national affairs. In his travels he discovered that the Kansas City struggle was attracting wide attention and that the unfavorable reaction to the gambling and racket development had spread from Kansas City to Washington. He was jolted by this rude trend when he was in the national capital on business, and incidentally to intervene personally on behalf of Con Mann in the Eagles lottery case. Mr. Pendergast seemed to have been unprepared for this humiliating experience, as he had every right to be, for the campaign to get a presidential pardon for Mr. Mann was a marvelous example of the machine process's efficiency on the higher levels. Appeals in behalf of the Kansas City Chamber of Commerce leader were signed by the governors of eight states, senators from ten states, eighty-one congressmen, four national labor leaders, seventeen judges in five states, thirty lawyers in six states, and fifteen bankers in four states. Boss Pendergast sent some of his ablest pleaders to confer

with the national party leaders and the Justice Department. They argued
that Mr. Mann was entitled to special consideration not only because of
his previous record and his standing in the Eagles and in society, to say
nothing of his relations with the Goat organization, but also because a
Federal jury had acquitted former Senator James J. (Puddler Jim)
Davis on similar charges growing out of a lottery in the Loyal Order of
Moose.

After these emissaries returned with unsatisfactory reports, and the
United States Supreme Court refused to review the evidence in the
Mann conviction, Mr. Pendergast decided to show his formidable presence in Washington. Accompanied by Senator Bennett C. Clark of
Missouri, his sometime rival and ally from St. Louis, the Kansas City
boss sought an interview with President Roosevelt and received a quick
rebuff. The Chief Executive sent word through a secretary that he was
unable to see the Missouri overlord, adding that it was a Roosevelt rule
never to take up personally questions of presidential pardons. T. J. left
hurriedly for New York to confer with Jim Farley.

Five days before Mann was scheduled to surrender himself in New
York to begin his term in jail, the Page grand jury returned its sensational report, declaring that "gambling and racketeering permeate the
entire community and could not exist without paying for protection and
consequently going unpunished." The public was allowed to lose interest
temporarily in the approaching martyrdom of its business and civic leader
while it considered fresh evidence that it lived under a reign of terror,
created to perpetuate illicit enterprises which, the jury report said,
"will continue to flourish so long as they are cultivated by that potent
trio, the predatory businessman, the predatory politician and purchasable
gangster hired by the first two."

The furor caused by the jury's report hadn't quite spent itself when
Con Mann departed by plane for New York. Machine leaders in the City
Hall and the Chamber of Commerce appeared to be more depressed over
the loss of their Get It Done man than they were by the grand jury's
indictments and denunciations.

Mr. Mann surrendered to the United States marshal in New York City
November 15. He wept when the judge signed his commitment papers
and waited in the Federal Building nearly four hours before going to

the House of Correction. He had been checked in as a prisoner when he received word that he was a free man again.

The pressure to make justice for the Eagle equal that for the Moose moved President Roosevelt to grant a pardon on the jail sentence but the Chief Executive waited until Mann was actually in custody before announcing this action, and left him under a fine, which was reduced from twelve to ten thousand dollars. Leaving the House of Correction, Mr. Mann joyfully made preparations to set out for home, sending word ahead that he was returning by plane.

This pathetic vindication was good enough for the boys in the City Hall and the Chamber, putting them in a mood of high elation. The City Manager hailed Roosevelt's action as one of the great decisions of the ages, and there was happy talk of a reception for Con that would make the earlier one at the Union Station a colorless affair by comparison. Plans for a rousing homecoming demonstration were abruptly abandoned when the home newspapers carried a brief item announcing that Mrs. J. Howard Hunt, corresponding secretary of the Parent-Teacher Council of Kansas City, had sent the Chamber a letter asking that there be no public ceremony for the returning chief. The Council members unanimously adopted the request, which explained that no personal feelings were involved but "as a child welfare organization, we feel that all good citizens should observe and respect the law. It is impossible for parents to instil in their children right principles of citizenship when prominent citizens who have disregarded the law are received with public acclaim."

The weather caused Mr. Mann's plane to be grounded on the way home. He returned several days later, without fanfare. The games were reviving when he came home, and everything seemed to be going on as before, but the words of the P.T.A. ladies echoed loud through the turbulent months that followed.

The New Youth

THE CAMPAIGN which brought the first full-scale political assault on the Pendergast machine reached its climax in February and March of 1934.

Although it failed of its immediate purpose, it plunged the community
into a state of continuous uproar for the next six years, during which
the principal aims of the challengers were realized. The turmoil has not
entirely settled even to this day.

Among the many interesting factors in this uprising, there were two
that shared the principal attention and produced the major damage to
the Democratic organization. One was the *Kansas City Star's* return to
all-out war on the Pendergasts, crusading in the old Nelson spirit. The
other was the N.Y.M., the National Youth Movement. The *Star's* participation, which had the most depressing long-range effect on the Boss,
will be detailed at some length later in the story. This section is reserved
for the N.Y.M., which was the newest and most spectacular element of
the Pendergast opposition.

The battle began with young Joe Fennelly and a few contemporaries,
whose N.Y.M. was a national phenomenon that started and ended in
Kansas City. The "national movement" legend was designed to give
some false prestige and mystery to the maiden venture in politics of the
youthful South Side amateurs. Their movement got under way nearly
two years before the test at the voting booths in '34.

N.Y.M. started with a membership of five young persons, meeting in
a home in May of 1932, the month when Rabbi Mayerberg entered his
fight on the machine. The number grew to twenty-five and then to eighty
men and women, when the group elected officers and incorporated the
N.Y.M. under the laws of Missouri. Progress at first was slow, for a good
reason. From the Mayerberg experience, Joe Fennelly's youthful rebels
had ample warning to proceed cautiously. They soon discovered that the
underground approach had other advantages. It appealed to the native
taste for melodrama and preyed on the Goats' superstitious fear of the
unknown.

Fennelly and his fellow conspirators spread the impression that they
had the multitudes by giving members metal disks beginning with the
number 2,301. They encouraged the notion that this was a national movement by circulating the rumor that General John J. Pershing was the
head of it. Some Fu Manchu tactics were employed effectively in recruit-
ing members. One of the young master's lieutenants would softshoe up to
a young local banker, broker, advertising or real estate man, and fur-

tively hand him ten cards to be filled out with applications of new members. A week later another "stranger" tapped the young banker or other prospect on the arm, saying: "I have called for the cards." The young banker nervously handed them over, glancing around to be certain that no Goats were watching or listening. "They're all filled out, too," said the y. b., his forehead glistening with honest sweat of fear and desperation. Or maybe the sweat just indicated normal perspiration, for this was a time of drought, heat and dust in Kansas City.

Finally, after more than a year, the N.Y.M. had four hundred members and their exercise had so toned them up that they came boldly into the open, talked of thousands of members and announced they would enter a nonpartisan ticket in the spring election of 1934.

The perambulating and card-passing of the New Youth went on at a furious rate in the next two months and the spectacular progress of the revolt on the South Side was indicated in September, 1933, when more than a thousand men and women crowded into the ballroom of the Hotel Kansas Citian to hear the N.Y.M. officers explain their aims and plans.

With the mystery removed, the machine opened a vigorous propaganda campaign of its own to discredit the N.Y.M. as a South Side silk-stocking and collegiate boy scout endeavor. For years the Democratic politicians had profitably exploited the difference between the North Side and South Side but this was to be the most illuminating exhibition of the complication in municipal politics that was created by the old cleavage between the haves and the have-nots.

The class character and ideological content of N.Y.M. were, in fact, pronounced. It was primarily a movement of the conservative people of property and it did represent a national agitation to some extent. It was animated not only by indignation over Pendergast corruption and oppression, but also by fear of revolution growing out of the universal social, economic and political crisis then known as the Depression.

Joe Fennelly expressed the basic concern of the N.Y.M. reformers, showing that it transcended the issue of bossism in local government, when he discussed the movement in an interview published in the *American Magazine*.*

* "Youth Goes Into Action," by Hubert Kelley, *American Magazine*, 1934.

"Communism isn't a way out," he said. "It's a way into more difficulty. Why not begin changing things at home?"

The magazine writer who interviewed Fennelly was Hubert Kelley, a former reporter on the *Star,* who hailed the activity in his old home town as "a new youth movement, concerned with things and action, not with words and dreams." He was impressed with its social and financial rating. Joe Fennelly (University of Virginia) was then a paint salesman headed for bigger things in business. ". . . He and his friends lived in the better part of their city, played golf on fashionable courses, attended country club dances with their young wives, motored into the countryside in their sport models. All had jobs, even for depression times. . . ."

It was the national crisis that started the junior executives thinking about local government. The boys home from Princeton, Harvard and other good colleges began with a discussion of the Hoover policies and the Roosevelt revolution. Then the debate naturally grew to include banks and banking men, liquor, women, marriage, love and finally municipal government. The argufiers learned that none of them had read the city charter, so they got a copy and made some interesting discoveries. One of the chief points that engaged their attention was the bonded indebtedness set-up, particularly the provisions covering the Ten-Year bonds. They were amazed to learn how many millions of dollars they were going to have to pay off during their lifetime, and their agitation over the way this money was being spent naturally became intense.

This concentration on the dollars-and-cents costs of machine government inevitably made N.Y.M. more appealing to businessmen and large taxpayers than to any other class, so the movement was dominated by the people who fear economic change and don't do much crusading with organized labor.

Not all of the N.Y.M. people were collegians, however, and not all of the college men had the conventional South Side viewpoint. At least two or three of the latter were contrary individuals who didn't labor under the illusion that they were opposing Pendergast and Karl Marx. They knew very well that they were fighting American bossism and fascism, or a reasonable facsimile thereof. This kind of understanding was found in the N.Y.M. ward organization rather than in the higher

ELECTION
APRIL
2

North Side, South Side, All Around the Town

The movement that brought the cleanup victory in 1940 started with the N.Y.M. campaign of 1934.

branches of the South Side movement. The ward workers had a better chance than most to get around and meet the people in all parts of town. They found the people on the North Side living in a bondage to the machine that was older and more subtle than the oppression which the organization recently had extended to the people of the South Side. They found that the machine was rooted in a society that operated on the basis of social and economic inequality. The machine came into being because it was effective in serving special interests above the common good, and grew until the machine itself was about to become the largest special interest—the supreme monopoly of the system that produced it. When and if the South Side people could be subdued, the revolution of the machine would be complete.

Unfortunately, this simple lesson had not been learned by many Kansas Citians in 1934, and N.Y.M. neglected to make its crusade as interesting to the jobless man, the union man and the Negro as it was to the good businessman. Quickly noting this defect in the opposition movement, the boss politicians once more staged their grotesque farce of fighting the battle for the masses and they were uncommonly adroit in playing on all the old class antagonisms and confusions.

The significant fact was, of course, the N.Y.M. could not have promoted a broad democratic revival even if it had had more of a will to do so. The N.Y.M. was very young, and the political thinkers haven't yet devised an effective program to unite the lower economic orders with their superiors in enthusiastic citizenship. There is even a question whether such an idea is practical under the American competitive system. It wasn't practical at all in the Heart of America some twelve years ago.

In addition to this handicap, the N.Y.M. had to get along with the Republicans. One of the most important consequences of the Fennelly enterprise was this affair with the G.O.P., for the N.Y.M. either saved or buried the Republican Party in Kansas City. The debate over the correct interpretation of what happened goes on to this day.

The Republicans joined up after the movement had progressed to the point where the South Side elders felt it was safe to take over the show. A Citizens' Committee of 375 men and women was formed, the committee including both Republicans and antimachine Democrats. The

organization officially named itself the Citizens Party and later became
the Citizens-Fusion ticket after the Republican County Committee
voted to join forces with the N.Y.M. and the dissident Democrats. Some
of the Republican politicians did not make this sacrifice for nonpartisanship without a struggle. Under the prodding of the *Star* they finally
agreed to sink their historic political identity in the uncertain Citizens-
Fusion hope. They complained bitterly that five of the nine places on
the ticket went to the irregular Democrats and a deadlock developed
until cooler heads prevailed and it was seen that under this five and four
arrangement the Republicans had a chance to get four more seats than
they probably would get under any other system. Even so, many of the
G.O.P. elders were not happy, for this was a fateful step. It might mean
the official death of the Republican Party in municipal affairs, a tragic
event if you were a Republican and didn't accept the widely held opinion
that the G.O.P. in Kansas City was in fact defunct before N.Y.M. appeared to revive the fight on Pendergast.

There was a minority of die-hard Republicans who didn't believe the
Citizens-Fusion thing had enough future to justify the exchange or
who seemed to prefer Democratic oppression to fusionism. They entered
a separate Republican ticket to make the '34 primary a three-way race.

While the old heads took over the authority and direction of the campaign, N.Y.M. remained in force as the spearhead of the attack, providing the enthusiasm, the shock troops, the fund raising, the publicity and
much of the oratory. Speakers were trained in an N.Y.M. school and
delivered an average of fifty speeches each week over a period of four
or five months. They carried the Citizens' message to churches, civic
and cultural groups and pepped up the businessmen with food and
oratory at luncheons in downtown hotels. When the final drive for votes
began, N.Y.M. had recruited and trained three thousand ward workers.

In short, the amateurs from the South Side gave an excellent account
of themselves. To N.Y.M. goes the credit for providing the spark, together with much of the sinew and intelligence, for the combination that
held out against boss rule. It brought into the arena a class that traditionally had held aloof from the rough-and-tumble over public offices, and it
impressed a new sense of civic responsibility on a considerable number
of businessmen. It frightened a lot of others with the consequences of

machine rule. It proved that collegians can learn the political game rapidly and make good fighters. Finally, it served as an effective instrument for many citizens who were fighting for a better order in Kansas City and for democratic rights, and not for narrow class, party or business interests. In fact, N.Y.M. was developing along such broad lines in the heat of battle that it is too bad that the antimachine politicians lost interest in this movement after the new youth carried the Citizens-Fusion Party through the terrors of February and March, 1934.

The ticket supported by N.Y.M. represented not so much the youth of the movement as it did the older business interests. Head of the ticket was a youth well up in his sixties, Dr. A. Ross Hill, former president of the University of Missouri and a realtor who belonged to the foremost circle of socially acceptable wealth in Kansas City.

A nice old gentleman like Dr. Hill had no business in a brawl with a bunch of political pool-hall boys. He was, none the less, the logical candidate to raise the banner of the South Side and the businessmen against the machine monopoly. He was a former president of the Real Estate Board and a forceful spokesman for that element which long had been accustomed to the pursuit of profitable enterprise without much interference from politicians and expected to have their requests for tax relief treated respectfully.

Dr. Hill was a recognized expert in real estate tax matters and in this work had clashed with the Country Bookkeeper before he entered the Citizens-Fusion campaign. He backed a bill in the Legislature to break up one part of the city's tax system which was particularly attractive to spoils politicians. This measure called for abolition of the office of delinquent tax attorney, an agency that collected about seventy-five thousand dollars a year in fees. Dr. Hill argued that the office discouraged payment of back taxes because of the high penalty on delinquency and carried powers that were subject to abuse. The bill was on its way toward passage when the City Manager intervened with a roar to obstruct it.

Naturally Dr. Hill was the object of the full McElroy wrath when he entered the fray with the New Youth, and the Judge set out at once to make the campaign his particular show. He gave perhaps his outstanding exhibition of mudslinging, Dogpatch style. His first act was to label the Fusion champion "squaw man," apparently a reference to the fact that Dr. Hill had married the wealthy widow of a prominent real estate developer.

Dr. Hill denounced the City Manager as "arbitrary, petty and vindictive." McElroy answered that he had had one affair with Dr. Hill and "so far as that deal is concerned, I will plead guilty now to being arbitrary and vindictive but not petty." He went on to explain that he had thwarted Dr. Hill and his stepson in an effort to exact an exorbitant price for a piece of land involved in condemnation proceedings for a new highway entrance to the city. "Yes," said this righteous guardian of the public treasury, "I was arbitrary, perhaps a little petty and admittedly vindictive with these high-toned, respectable gentlemen who were trying to get their hands in the taxpayers' pockets." He told the story before various meetings which he addressed in the campaign. It involved complicated details of property value representations, which he made interesting with his pious show of indignation over the Hill morality. The surplus profit which the vigilant City Manager said he kept from Hill's stepson amounted to a few thousand dollars.

The Citizens debated the question whether they should conduct an old-fashioned slambang campaign to match the colorful tactics of the opposition, or a dignified campaign more in keeping with the character of their candidate for mayor, Dr. Hill. They finally decided to have both, with the huffing and puffing to be provided by Colonel Frederick E. Whitten, the Citizens' personality boy, called the LaGuardia of Kansas City.

Colonel Whitten, a young lawyer, reserve officer and veteran of the First World War, concentrated his full attention on McElroy, or Snagboat Hank. His appellation for the City Manager had its origin in the fact that McElroy used city funds to build a boat, the *Mayflower,* which the Citizens described as a pleasure craft for McElroy and friends and which McElroy said was a snagboat on the Blue River restoration project under the Ten-Year-Bond Program.

Whitten was assigned the agreeable task of showing that a snagboat owner belonged to a much lower order than a squaw man in the catalog of political name calling; and what he lacked in imagination he made up in enthusiasm. "Every time Snagboat Hank opens his big mouth he gets both feet in it," he shouted, and the crowds roared approval.

The Colonel, a Democrat who had campaigned for the Pendergast ticket four years earlier, got some of the nonpartisan stuffing knocked out of him when he went blustering into the City Manager's office to demand that he be allowed to examine the city's garbage contracts and the audit.

"I am here not as a candidate but as a citizen, a taxpayer . . ." the Colonel began.

"Let's stick to the truth," the Judge flared. "You are here as a candidate. You probably are an honorable man as a citizen, a taxpayer and a lawyer, but as a candidate you don't tell the truth."

The City Manager brusquely dismissed his visitor and would not let the local LaGuardia examine the city books but, he added, he might permit some one else to see them if he liked his looks. The embarrassed pride of the Citizens retired and the N.Y.M. selected one of its most personable youths, Harold R. Jones, twenty-five years old, to call on the City Manager for the controversial data. Mr. Jones, a Harvard man and one of the original N.Y.M. boys, was received with great courtesy by McElroy and Mayor Smith, and given an eloquent lecture on the beauties of the garbage contract, the budget and the audit, but shown no records.

All this was for the benefit of the crowds, a part of the general action in which the cagey Judge consistently confounded the amateurs. The main struggle, which went on both out front and behind the scenes, was centered in the business community. It was a fight that began long before the climax of March, 1934. Two years earlier the administration had clashed with large business interests when McElroy defied the Real Estate Board, successfully resisting a determined demand for a tax reduction to keep municipal affairs synchronized with the downward spiral that was then whirling toward the bottom of the bank crisis preceding the inauguration of Roosevelt. Instead of a tax cut, McElroy responded with a small increase in the general property levy. This was the first time that McElroy had resisted the Real Estate Board, but he was showing an attitude that grew until he became very difficult for business interests that weren't in the good graces of the organization.

The Real Estate Board picked a poor time for a showdown on tax relief. There were, of course, extravagance and boodle in the city's operation, but they were still so well concealed that the Board could not make a convincing showing that economies were in order, and its demand for a tax cut was interpreted as a demand for wage cutting and reduction of essential city services. Organized labor stepped into the contest to back the City Manager on the tax matter, the Real Estate Board took itself back to its councils to ponder the city administration's new line, and the N.Y.M. soon thereafter took form to channelize growing discontent.

The defeat suffered by the Real Estate Board in its tax-relief plan was not alone enough to provoke the uprising that followed. Signs multiplied on every side that the machine had embarked on a vast scheme to use every resource at its disposal to purchase the favor of cheaply bought voters on one hand and to enrich large politically favored individuals on the other hand. By 1934, it was clear to every sober person who knew the main facts of the situation that the Pendergast monopoly was an economic monstrosity.

In order to sustain itself both politically and economically, the boss organization invaded private business on an increasingly widening scale. Commercial, financial and manufacturing concerns that called on the administration for special services, like getting an ordinance passed, or a building permit expedited or a tax assessment adjusted, found themselves called on in turn to give jobs and contracts to people in good standing with the organization. In the 1934 campaign, N.Y.M. speakers declared that their opponents produced fifty thousand to sixty thousand votes through the merger of business and government, estimating that the organization controlled between five and six thousand jobs in private business and a like number in city and county administrations, each job being required to deliver five votes.

As the campaign wore on, it became apparent that only a part of the business community was joining the crusade. Fear of reprisals and the conventional aloofness of business to direct political action represented only a part of the reason for the failure of the propertied people to close ranks. The machine faction had been allowed to become so entrenched that it had permanently split the business community.

The Citizens played their trump card when Ewing Y. Mitchell, assistant Secretary of Commerce, came from Washington to denounce Pendergast and read the entire list of charges against machine rule. The Fusion-Citizens attempted to don the Roosevelt New Deal mantle for the moment, but it fitted awkwardly, not to say grotesquely. There were few genuine liberals among the N.Y.M. or the Citizens, and Mitchell himself found the Rooseveltian philosophy so unpalatable that he bolted the Democratic Party in 1936 and ran for political office as a Republican in 1940. He was booted out of Roosevelt's Little Cabinet in 1935. An attempt was made to represent this action as reprisal for his intervention in the Kansas City campaign in 1934, but the primary cause of his removal was his private quarrel with Secretary Roper and his disagreement with New Dealers.

When the Assistant Secretary entered the '34 campaign, he came with the prestige of one who was high in the administration and who had served as Roosevelt's pre-convention manager in Missouri in 1932. His differences with Roper and the President had not yet come to public attention. Pendergast was so disturbed by the impression which the Mitchell visit created that he prevailed on his good friend, Jim Farley, to issue a statement that Mitchell spoke for himself alone, and a White House spokesman announced that the administration still adhered to the old rule against interference in local political fights. However, the impression of Washington disfavor for Pendergast lingered, to be revived and strengthened by later events.

Assistant Secretary Mitchell, a Springfield, Missouri, Democrat, used the evidence developed by two grand juries to make the point that crime and boodling found here made the Tammany machine in New York, the Vare machine in Philadelphia, the Mellon machine in Pittsburgh and the St. Louis machine smalltime outfits compared with the Pendergast contraption. The men at 1908 Main Street replied with a statement to the press.

"Kansas City under the Democratic Party has better police protection and there is less crime committed here than in any city of its size or larger in the United States," said Boss Pendergast, who was beginning to repeat himself.

To show his followers his complete confidence, he concluded:

"My final answer to this gentleman is for him to read the Kansas City papers the day after our city election."

City Manager McElroy took his cue from the Boss. To Dr. Hill's charges of payroll padding, enrichment of favored contractors, using the taxing and licensing powers to compel political subservience, juggling of funds, illegal use of the gasoline tax fund and other funds, failure to pay more than six million sinking fund charges, misuse of bond funds, profitable trading in building permits, failure to make a proper audit, etc., etc., Snagboat Hank responded by advising Dr. Hill to read the election returns in the newspapers.

ELECTION DAY

THE TWENTY-SEVENTH of March, 1934, brought good election weather, with sun and a snap in the air. When the first voters went to the polls the mercury stood at ten degrees below freezing. It rose slowly through the day to stop at forty-four.

Weeks of campaigning had produced a feeling of vast tension throughout the city, and the sense of alarm was heightened by numerous and widespread signs and portents of the universal crisis attending the advance of the Kansas City factions toward the day of decision.

Physical force had entered the contest after N.Y.M. undertook extraordinary measures to supervise the registration of voters, arming many of their members with cameras, which they used to photograph repeaters. They continued their detective work to gather other evidence of false registration, producing a formidable list of alleged ghost voters. There were numerous reports that N.Y.M. workers had been threatened and assaulted and the excitement mounted when N.Y.M. leaders charged that police and North Side bullies intimidated many individuals into repudiating affidavits of false registration. Despite the interference, N.Y.M. routed many ghosts and the registration ended with a strike-off of 88,107 names, the largest in Kansas City history. However, all this was insufficient to arrest the rising vote trend produced by the machine and the registration finally totaled approximately 244,000, a new record for the city and a figure that represented well over half the entire population.

The independent Republican organization in the contest gave some comfort to the opposition by challenging the credentials of the N.Y.M.-Citizens election workers and seeking an injunction to prevent the

Election Board from issuing election supplies to Citizens judges and clerks. The injunction was denied but the proceeding gave some Democrats an idea for a new form of harassment. On primary day, many Citizens Party workers arrived at the polls to find their places preempted by strangers with faked credentials. This provoked numerous arguments and fights, including a brawl involving twelve battlers when Citizens went to a voting booth on East Eighteenth Street to investigate the ejection of their challengers.

When the primary ballots were counted, the Democrats were more than 38,000 ahead of the Citizens, Mayor Smith having 103,616 against 65,363 for his rival, Dr. Hill. Clark E. Jacoby, the third candidate for mayor, polled 4,373.

Under the Kansas City election system for municipal contests, the primary served to nominate the candidates winning first and second places in the voting. Although the 1934 primary results forecast an easy victory for the Democratic ticket as a whole in the runoff or final election, there was no slackening in the campaigning for the outcome in a few Council races remained in doubt.

Following the primary the Citizens filed hundreds of affidavits covering sluggings and various other acts of terrorism at the polls. A Servicemen's League then appeared on the scene as the N.Y.M. and Citizens answer to the bullies from the North Side. The League recruited war veterans for service as election workers and watchers. It issued a questionnaire asking these men to list any firearms they possessed. The Democrats exploited this slip, former Senator Reed and other party orators declaring that the Citizens were organizing a Young Civil Army patterned after the Blackshirts and the Brownshirts of Europe. Leaders of the Citizens disavowed any connection with the League and Senator Reed accepted publicly the disclaimer of Alex S. Rankin, a Democrat in the Citizens command, but the damage was done. The opposition had its own army of toughs but didn't talk about it, and the Citizens were stuck with blame for provocation. The Servicemen's League withdrew from the picture after offering its assistance to the police and receiving a curt rejection.

Tension continued to grow, and the Citizens addressed fervent appeals to the governor to send the National Guard to Kansas City for election day. He turned down their request after conferring with the Election Board, saying he was satisfied there was no cause for alarm.

The oratorical battle reached its peak on a Saturday night, three days before the election, when more than twelve thousand party workers received final instructions. Halls in all parts of the city were crowded with excited citizens listening to inflamed speakers. To the people in their homes, radios blared the call to march and vote.

By chance several of the leaders of the opposing groups met in the studios of the *Star's* radio station, WDAF, on election eve. They bowed, smiled, spoke and shook hands after giving their final radio appeals to the voters. That was about twelve hours before the shooting started.

In the editorial room of the *Star*, the first reports of election progress were assembled for the noon edition of Tuesday, March 27, scheduled to reach the streets shortly before eleven o'clock. Calls to various key precincts revealed an exceedingly heavy vote, for the morning hours. Reports from N.Y.M. and Citizens leaders who visited or telephoned the *Star* office disclosed uncommon activity in the machine-dominated downtown precincts. Scores of motor cars, some occupied by Citizens' workers and more filled with their opponents, cruised over these areas. They gave the streets the aspect of a battleground with the opposing armies maneuvering for position. But the unnatural peace with which the day began remained unbroken when the *Star's* political reporter sat down to write his lead for the noon.

The noon was going to press when Justin D. Bowersock, a reporter assigned to the downtown precincts-run for the day, dashed into the city room. His face was blanched, his hair tousled and there was blood on his forehead.

"They're after me," Bowersock shouted. "They're trying to kill me!"

It seemed that everybody in the large room ducked, but in a moment Bowersock was surrounded by editors, rewrite men and copyreaders. He was so nervous and breathless that for a minute he could give no coherent explanation of what was wrong. Sox was a reporter of fertile imagination and dramatic tendencies, but this was no act. The blood on his forehead was real.

Two figures appeared running through the door through which

Bowersock had just entered. Editors, rewrite men and copyreaders looked for a place to hide. A shout went up when the newcomers were recognized as copyboys and a nervous laugh swept through the office, breaking the tension.

Bowersock told his story in short takes and a bulletin on his experience appeared in the first edition. Edition followed edition with accounts of fresh disturbances, growing in violence as the day advanced, and the turmoil in the city room didn't slacken until the following morning. The *Star* posted notice of a five-thousand-dollar reward for the assailants of its reporter along with the news of the attack on him and two companions.

Sox spilled first blood for the Citizens when he went to the near North Side to check the polling places for reports of vote repeating. He made the tactical error of joining the company of young Dr. Arthur Wells, Citizens' candidate for councilman from the First District, who was a marked man that day. They were accompanied by Lloyd Cole, a former policeman and a Citizens' worker, and rode in Bowersock's car to a voting booth at Ninth Street and Troost Avenue, where Dr. Wells intended to investigate rumors of repeating. The reporter was on a newspaper assignment, not electioneering, but a group of Democratic muscle boys didn't wait to ask questions when they observed him with Wells and Cole. Even if they had recognized him as a *Star*man it is doubtful if they would have been more restrained, for the paper's vigorous work for the reform had made it very unpopular with the gangsters. The newspaperman's car was trailed from the booth by two carloads of hoodlums, who riddled it with bullets and ran it down after a block's chase. All three of the fleeing men were slugged, Dr. Wells being injured so severely that he was taken to a hospital. Bowersock escaped by leaping into the car of another Citizens' worker who was passing the scene. Then began a flight of more than a mile, with two gunmen in one car racing to overtake the retreating journalist. He was followed all the way to the *Star* Building, where Sox leaped from his rescuer's car and dashed inside with one of the gunmen at his heels to the entrance of the building.

Excitement over the Bowersock incident had not begun to settle when the *Star*'s editor, H. J. Haskell, loped into the office in a state of great agitation. He had just received word that his Negro chauffeur, James Washington, had been beaten and shot at while driving the Haskell car to the polls with a load of Citizens' voters. The Haskell automobile was run down in an alley near Thirty-first Street and Linwood Boulevard, a business and apartment center. Washington was seized and beaten and escaped by running through yards of homes in the neighborhood.

A Citizens' delegation called on Police Director Reppert to demand better police supervision but he refused to see them.

The hotshot telephone on the *Star's* city desk rang with a report of murder. The presses stopped and there was a makeover flashing the news that William Finley had been killed at 1901 East Twenty-fourth Street by an Italian gang that invaded the voting place there. Finley, a Democratic precinct captain and a Negro, lost his life trying to defend a Negro election judge singled out for a beating by the gang. Finley drew a revolver but the gangsters shot first.

Citizens' leaders sent telegrams to Governor Park demanding that National Guardsmen be called out. He refused to intervene.

Hundreds of armed men rode in black cars, roving the North Side, West, Northeast and Southeast sections. Many of their cars carried no license plates, passing traffic officers and police stations without molestation.

The police made fourteen arrests, twelve of them on the South Side. Those arrested were working for the Citizens and were suspected by the zealous officers of contemplating intimidation. All were released.

The 7 P.M. edition of the *Star* went to press shortly after six o'clock, carrying a late round-up of the voting progress. All records were being smashed and the total would go beyond the previous high figure of 219,000 in November, 1932. (It went to 222,866.) An interesting detail of this late story was a report that C. R. Benton, Democratic candidate for councilman in the Second District, was being knifed in a row between minor Democratic factional leaders. When newsboys on Twelfth Street were calling the headlines of the 7 P. M. edition, the quarrel over Benton reached its climax in the murder of three persons near a voting booth five miles southeast of the downtown section.

The story of what happened was told in extras. John Gadwood, a lieutenant in the Kelly group of the Shannon Rabbit faction, rode with terrorists filling three cars to a polling place on Swope Parkway, in a residential neighborhood, to punish Deputy Sheriff Lee Flacy for defying orders to work against Candidate Benton. Benton was marked for knifing because he belonged to the Johnson group of the Shannon faction, and the Kelly boys were warring against that group because L. C. Johnson, director of the Fire Department, had displaced Kelly in Shannon's favor.

Gadwood's party found Deputy Sheriff Flacy eating a sandwich in a restaurant near the voting booth. They called him to the rear of the restaurant, quarreled with him and shot him. They ran from the place and Flacy limped afted them. At the doorway he stood firing his pistol at the fleeing cars. The gunmen returned the fire and Flacy fell. He died several hours later in a hospital, leaving his bride of seventeen days. Revolver and shotgun fire from the gunmen struck P. W. Oldham, a neighborhood hardware store owner, who was closing his store for the evening. He was killed instantly. One of the cars of the gangsters overturned in front of a Catholic school when its driver attempted to turn it sharply at high speed. In the rear seat was Larry Cappo, a member of the Joe Lusco mob, aligned with the Cas Welch Democratic faction. He was dying from one of the bullets Flacy had fired.

Morning editions carried the score: Four slain, eleven severely injured, bruises, black eyes and cracked heads too numerous to be estimated. The Pendergast ticket had been returned to office by a margin of 59,000 votes for its candidate for mayor, retaining seven places in the nine-man Council. The Citizens won two Council places, for D. S. Adams and Frank H. Backstrom, the margin of victory in the second place being provided by the Democratic factional row which led to the deaths of three persons.

There was one other gain for the Citizens, a victory of slight political significance but one which gave intense satisfaction to a certain element of N.Y.M. Miss Sidney May Smith, Junior Leaguer, had outfoxed T. J. Pendergast himself in a race to be Voter No. 1 in the Eighth Precinct of the Eighth Ward, a decorous South Side neighborhood. When Boss Pendergast arrived at the booth at six o'clock in the morning he found a group of N.Y.M. girls, headed by Miss Smith, lined up before him. A Democratic judge explained the situation to the young ladies. It was sentiment and tradition with the Boss, who had been Voter No. 1 in this precinct for the last several elections, and would they like to stand aside so he could keep his record clean? They wouldn't and they didn't. Big Tom voted No. 5 and Miss Smith got her picture in the paper.

THE SHOWDOWN

THE HUE and cry that arose over the conduct of the election was sufficiently intense and loud to have produced a revolution, which it failed to do. Fire was directed principally against Police Director Reppert and Judge McElroy, who met the situation with his usual poise and resourcefulness. The City Manager was disturbed by neither the local nor national commotion provoked by the Kansas City disorders. In Washington, Senator Royal S. Copeland of New York announced that his Senate Crime Investigation Committee would come to Kansas City and the Judge advised the Senator to take castor oil. On second thought, he welcomed the Senator's Committee to town and urged Copeland, in a manner that was not lost upon those familiar with City Hall ways, to reveal the names of persons who had informed him of local conditions.

N.Y.M. held a post-election mass meeting and proclaimed its intention to march on to the next battle. The crowd that filled Ivanhoe Temple roared itself hoarse for Joe Fennelly, Dr. Hill, Colonel Whitten, Alex Rankin, Louis G. Lower, Webster Townley, Councilmen-elect Adams and Backstrom. William E. Kemp (who became Kansas City's mayor on the Citizens' ticket twelve years later) spoke for a permanent registration law and Fennelly announced that N.Y.M. would immediately open a campaign for its adoption. There was talk of plans for a recall election in six months and the rally ended with a demonstration provoked by a speech demanding the election of a Legislature that would impeach Governor Park, the figurehead in Uncle Tom's Cabin. It was the last important show of force by N.Y.M.

Speakers at the N.Y.M. rally listed several important gains made by the Pendergast opposition in this campaign. They dwelt upon the election of two Fusion men to the Council and the events which had aroused the public to the need for a permanent registration law to eliminate the

frauds that helped the machine to perpetuate itself in power. (Estimates
of the number of ghost votes in the recent balloting ran as high as fifty
thousand.) They reviewed the disclosures and incidents which ripped
the last cover from boss rule. They paid insufficient attention, however, to the most important development of the campaign, which was the
entry of the *Star* for a showdown battle with Pendergast.

On election day the period of half-truce and indecision finally ended.
There would be no more temporizing or compromises, and no more promotions of Judge McElroy. The *Star* had entered the campaign supporting the Citizens-Fusion ticket in a moderate, dignified fashion, and
ended it prepared for a long and bitter struggle whose outcome could
not be foreseen in 1934. On election day the Pendergast challenge for a
slugging match to the finish was given and accepted. The N.Y.M. and
many of the figures in the 1934 fracas would be forgotten, but the newspaper would spearhead the opposition for the battles of '36, '38, '40 and
later. It went into that contest with the fighting spirit of old Baron
Nelson, and with perhaps more generalship than the Old Man had exhibited.

The *Star* was now directed not by one powerful individual but by a
quartet who had come up under Nelson—Longan, Haskell, McCollum
and Roberts. They were men of strong opinions, self-assertive, and full of
vinegar.

First round in the new struggle between the newspaper and the political machine was well under way by the time that the N.Y.M. staged
the post-election rally which was in effect its farewell. During the two
weeks between the election and the day when the new Council was
sworn in, the newspaper editors and the strategists at 1908 Main engaged
in a battle of wits that was distinguished by the skill displayed on both
sides. The general public could see only the surface manifestations or results of the planning and intrigue that went on behind the scenes, but
even from the outside it was apparent that this was a contest of equals
in the art of political maneuvering.

The *Star* opened with an editorial blast demanding that the police
department be reorganized to clean up the city. This was Pendergast's
most vulnerable point not only because of the public agitation over the
election murders and crime conditions generally, but also because a fac-

tional dispute within the Democratic organization revolved around Police Director Reppert. Cas Welch, the Fifteen Street boss, who controlled two councilmen in the new administration, objected to Reppert.

Playing up the factional row, the *Star* pointed out that Big Tom was sure of only three votes in the new Council—A. N. Gossett, Charlie Clark and Ruby D. Garrett. Mayor Smith was also a Pendergast man but it was fondly believed he might be inclined to throw his one vote to the opposition if a revolt looked promising. The Citizens, with two votes, could deprive McElroy of a working majority in the Council if they could promote a coalition including Mayor Smith, Cas Welch's two councilmen and the one councilman controlled by Shannon.

Speculative stories covering this situation, designed to spread suspicion and dismay among the machine factions, were given conspicuous position, and for a few days it was made to appear that a permanent breach in the machine might develop. Attention was centered on Mayor Smith in an effort to stampede him into rebellious action. The *Star* interviewed the diminutive mayor whom McElroy called "Boss," presenting him flatteringly in the role of an independent and forceful executive. It followed that with a long story announcing that the Honorable Bryce Smith had at last seized control of the City Hall from McElroy after being "sidetracked, ignored and humiliated for four years." The stratagem was successful to the point that Mr. Smith kept up the independent pose for four days during which he was publicly committed to a permanent registration law.

At the same time public indignation against the machine was kept alive by a series of news stories that were more eloquent and much more provocative than any fire-eating editorial could have been. There were stories recounting the activities of Sheriff Tom Bash, a member of the Rabbit faction, in his effort to track down the election-day slayers and hoodlums, drawing a glaring contrast to the dereliction of the police. There were stories of the neighborhood mourning for the election-murder victims and more stories along the same line when funeral services were held for them. On Good Friday, Dr. Harry Clayton Rogers, pastor of the Linwood Presbyterian Church, preached a "Black Friday" sermon on the crimes of Kansas City. His sermon, featured on page one, was a signal for the pulpit battery of the Protestant brotherhood to go into action.

The next day Police Director Reppert resigned with a sigh of relief.

It appeared to the spectators that the revolt was beginning to roll, although in fact the dropping of Reppert meant that a deal had been made patching up the rift in the machine rather than that the boys were running for cover. The *Star,* the Republicans and the Citizens whooped for more blood, turning their full fire directly on McElroy, and the ministerial contingent responded with a broadside from the Sunday morning pulpits. The next day, the Ministerial Alliance, representing one hundred and four Protestant churches, met and demanded the ouster of McElroy.

The administration was then ready to make its stand. It led off with a show of shame and remorse over the election day murders when Councilman Gossett went before the last meeting of the old City Council with an impassioned declaration for a purified police force and a permanent registration law. That was the extent of the organization's concession to the public clamor directed by the *Star.*

Farmer Al obviously was deeply moved by his recital of the evils brought to light in the campaign. "I feel like resigning my position, Mr. Mayor," he said, "and am only deterred from doing so by my conviction that it would be a sign of weakness, and I shall, therefore, continue my endeavors to serve the people of Kansas City as best I may."

Reformation of the Police Department was immediately manifested by the dropping of numerous officers in the lower brackets, a series of liquor raids, tightening of regulations on pool halls and the setting of police traps for motorists who had failed to purchase license tags—all of them measures well calculated to make reform unpopular with a large element of the population. Police contributed further to the cooling of the public mood when they manhandled John Gadwood, following his arrest for the election-day murder of Deputy Lee Flacy. Two detectives were fired for beating up Gadwood, and McElroy and the police heads publicly deplored the resort to third-degree tactics. Although it was difficult to imagine that the two detectives acted without orders from above, it was possible that they were two Pendergast loyalists who decided to sacrifice themselves in order to strike a double blow for their side. In maltreating

Gadwood, they were paying off a petty figure in a minor Democratic faction who had got the Goat boss into deep trouble and at the same time provoking a reaction to the demand for greater zeal on the part of the police.

A curious incident served to deflect some of the public anger from Judge McElroy himself. At the height of the clamor against him someone fired a bullet through the front window of his home while he and his daughter were in an adjoining room. The following night Mary McElroy answered the telephone and a man's voice said: "We never miss a second time." Everyone was reminded, of course, of the McElroys' troubles the year before, when Mary McElroy was kidnaped from her home and held a prisoner overnight until thirty thousand dollars ransom was paid. After the shooting, the *Star* printed an editorial suggesting that the harassment of the Judge was an effort to defame the city, and a relaxing of the pressure on the City Manager immediately was noticed.

All of these incidents had a sobering effect on the citizens, suggesting in various ways that the cleanup agitation was producing extreme reactions that were neither intended nor desired.

Four days before the new Council was to meet, it was announced that all differences within the machine had been ironed out with the retirement of Reppert and that McElroy would be retained for his third four-year term as city manager. The *Star* shifted its line of attack to concentrate on control of the Police Department, starting agitation for importation of an Army officer as police director. Mr. McElroy cut that hope short and for the moment confounded his critics on the *Star* by picking a former reporter on the *Star*'s staff, one Otto P. Higgins, for the police director's post.

Mr. Higgins carried no great weight with the *Star* management, but he was personally popular with the staff and his *Star* background made it embarrassing for the newspaper to attack him or even express regret over his appointment.

All of which explains why the great reform of 1934 ended with the selection of the man who soon became a target of the clean-up people and who eventually produced the biggest scandal in the Police Department.

DEATH AND BROTHER JOHN

SOME DAY, perhaps a hundred years hence when the Hollywood influence has begun to decline, praise the Lord, it may be possible to write an adequate account of that significant American type known as the gangster. The wish for more intelligent treatment than is now possible comes up in connection with this all-too-brief chapter on Johnny Lazia, whose remarkable career reached its inevitable conclusion in the months immediately following the reform efforts and election massacre of 1934.

The change in police command was not the thing that adversely affected the fortunes of Lazia at this time. He continued to call at the City Hall and police headquarters and the new police director followed the established policy of consulting the North Side chieftain on the appointment of officers and the regulation of crime. However, the serious trouble that soon developed for the Italian boss did have some connection with the recently suppressed political revolt against the administration, for it was intimately related to the complicated functioning of Home Rule as directed by Pendergast, McElroy and Lazia. The Lazia affair also served as the first large illustration of the personal disaster that was in the making for the principal figures in the machine.

In the fateful month of July, 1934, Johnny Lazia was thirty-seven years old, one of the most successful and probably the most discussed citizen of Kansas City. He drew even more popular attention than either Boss Pendergast or Judge McElroy. His criminal background and racketeer reputation were not the only things that made him fascinating to the curious public. Johnny also had personality. In fact, he had charm. He looked amiable and modest. He spoke good English, told humorous stories, smiled often behind his rimless eyeglasses and chewed gum constantly. There was little about his appearance and manners to stamp him as a gang leader, a man of immigrant stock who had risen from the underworld to a commanding position in political and business circles in a mid-American city.

Unlike the underworld hero of movies and books, Lazia did not go in for mystery and aloofness. True, he rode in a bulletproof motor car and was constantly attended by his portly, solemn bodyguard, Big Charley Carollo. But these were minimum concessions to the dramatic requirements of his role, for purposes of safety. Despite this handicap, Lazia managed to make himself seen in public, for he wanted to be known as a man about town. He went to the night spots, the sports shows and gambling places, and on week ends he went with some of his boys to his cottage on Lake Lotawana, where he raced his high-powered speedboat and splashed waves on the best people from Kansas City who maintained summer homes in this resort. He lived in an apartment on Armour Boulevard with his pretty wife, who made a large splash with the dough that Johnny generously provided.

The doings of Johnny Lazia at the height of his career and the sensational events of his last days so excited the popular imagination that little or no attention was paid to the equally interesting story of his beginning and his rise to power. As a result, a host of questions about him, his organization, his friendship with Pendergast, his political and business connections with the Boss and other leaders in the town, his influence and his meaning in American life have been incompletely answered or not answered at all. The general impression that has been left is that this son of immigrants was an exceptional individual who rose through exceptional circumstances to the place he occupied. However, enough facts about him are known to make it clear that Johnny Lazia was no accident. Somewhat exceptional he may have been in his own small circle, but there was nothing very strange about the circumstances. Some of the incidents of his rise were odd or melodramatic, but the conditions that produced the North Side boss had been familiar features of American life for many years and haven't been greatly modified since 1934.

Kansas City's Little Italy was a trouble spot that entered its darkest period when Lazia was a boy. Toil, poverty and crime were the daily story of the congested district east of Market Square on the North Side. By 1920 the number of first and second generation Italians in Kansas City had been reduced to 6,116, but before the First World War it was estimated that between 12,000 and 15,000 persons lived in the narrow confines of Little Italy. Not all of them were Italians. Negroes encroached on the neighborhood. Segregated themselves and treated daily to discrimination in work and social life, the Italians turned with fury on their colored neighbors. Homes of Negroes were dynamited in an effort to frighten them off and murders grew out of this racial antagonism between the two groups that were the chief victims of discrimination imposed by the white Americans.

The Italians made a large stir in politics and crime for their numbers, but not simply because they had a special talent for these pursuits. Opportunities and rewards for common laborers and hucksters were decidedly limited while the field in vice and banditry was booming. The Mafia appeared to regulate the community with dagger, pistol and bomb. In the decade ending in 1916, the year that Johnny Lazia first figured in the crime news, there had been forty unsolved murders on the North Side. There were sporadic efforts to break up the Black Hand and suppress other kinds of criminals, but for the most part the busy citizens living outside the North Side paid little attention to the newcomers so long as the violence and misery were confined to Little Italy.

In his youth, Johnny Lazia, son of a laborer, a boy whose education did not extend beyond the eighth grade, attracted the favorable attention of influential men with his brightness, friendliness and political precocity. He obtained a clerk's job in the office of a reputable law firm, studied law and seemed destined for a legal career until caught in the act of banditry. He staged a holdup in which he collected two hundred and fifty dollars, a diamond stickpin and a watch, and was captured in a revolver battle with Captain John Ennis. When he was eighteen years old he was sentenced to fifteen years in the Missouri penitentiary. He was even then a figure of consequence in political and gang circles, a fact that was impressed on the public by incidents attending his prosecution and imprisonment. Police reported the discovery of a plot to shoot up the justice of peace court where Lazia was to be arraigned and another plot to deliver him from jail. The jury that convicted him was given a special guard after receiving death threats. The presiding judge remitted three years of Lazia's sentence, reducing it to twelve years, and he served only eight months and seven days. His prison record was distinguished by his good behavior and efficiency as a bookkeeper. His parole was recommended by the county attorney of Jackson County and two other party leaders, and was granted by another good Democrat, the lieutenant governor, acting as the chief executive in the governor's absence from the state. The acting governor justified his haste in this case as "a war measure."

Lazia returned to Kansas City two months before the war ended, re-entering civil life at the moment when the general disturbance provoked by the military conflict, Prohibition and the capitalist inflation-deflation cycle was just getting under way. He announced that "the wild boy" of the recent holdup had died in prison. Having been such a conspicuous beneficiary of political influence, he concentrated on the task of political organization, doing favors, lending money, keeping boys out of jail. He dabbled in real estate and also took an interest in gambling and boot-legging but managed to keep beyond the clutches of the law. In one case he was indicted with a group of men in a liquor conspiracy but was freed when Carollo, his bodyguard, took the rap—a not-very-heavy one.

Lazia's political leadership of the North Side was established in 1928 in an election called to vote on a proposed twenty-eight-and-one-half-million-dollar bond issue. The city rejected most of the bonds and Lazia provided most of the excitement. His fight was made on a Home Rule issue for the Italian community, Lazia's faction challenging the absentee overlordship of Mike Ross, a Goat leader who long had controlled Little Italy before he moved from the North to the South Side. His place was usurped by Lazia through the use of strongarm tactics. Several of Ross's old lieutenants were kidnaped, one was struck on the head with a re-volver and another barely missed a bullet. When the polls closed, it was found that Lazia's boys had delivered more votes and the defeated group attended a mass meeting in Ringside Hall to hail the new leader. A band played, "Here Comes the King," while the loyal followers shouted "Our Johnny" and "You tell 'em, Johnny."

Boss Pendergast gave an interview to the press in which he indicated his displeasure over the riotous events on the North Side and let it be known he would stand by the deposed Mike Ross, with whom he had long enjoyed profitable relations in the concrete business. But Johnny used his charm as well as his power, and he and Boss Tom soon were fast friends. In later years it was rumored that they had quarreled, and that Johnny had stabbed Tom, but there was never any evidence of such a fight and their relationship remained unbroken to the end.

Force was the instrument by which Lazia ruled, but force alone did not account for his success. He had real organizing and executive ability in undertakings calling for something more than the application of fists' and bullets. He mapped out projects for enterprises that would give profitable employment to his following. He was resourceful in working out schemes to take care of his men when they got into trouble. He built up his organization to the point where it was both a political force and a large economic factor in the life of the community. To those who opposed him and stood in his way, he was cruel and ruthless, but to those who acknowledged his leadership and served his purposes he was both wise arbiter and able protector. His henchmen formed a cult of admirers, called him Brother John in recognition of various services of a generous and benevolent nature that were hidden from people outside his circle. Brother John supported the cause of charity for citizens of his realm, who were considered deserving by the North Side Democratic Club. Brother John always had a coin for a panhandler and was large handed with his friends. Brother John was an amusing and considerate companion. Women, particularly women of the South Side who met him or saw him on occasions when their husbands were discussing business or political affairs with the North Side leader, thought him fascinating. Brother John, it was said, objected to "rough stuff" and wanted peace and order. He wanted to lift himself and some of his people to a higher place in the economic and social scale. Grinning, speaking softly, exchanging wisecracks, chewing his gum, Brother John ingratiated himself with many persons in high places while not relaxing the rule of force that operated through the North Side Democratic Club. He advanced to power with the same catlike tread that distinguished the gait of his trim one-hundred-and-forty-pound figure.

McElroy's Home Rule greatly increased Lazia's responsibilities. It was said at the City Hall and police headquarters that the new policy of winking at "minor infractions" and concentrating on major crime had brought a reduction in "rough stuff." Lazia was entitled to some credit for that alleged improvement, for he was one of three who had a voice in naming men to the Police Department, and the turnover was large and rapid. The figures on crime reduction were not very reassuring to the public, however, for there were still a large number of major crimes and the new crime control commission was having obvious difficulty in getting co-operation from some important elements of the underworld. Competition for the gambling and liquor concessions showed signs of increasing rather than decreasing under the combined effect of toleration of petty violations of the law and the monopoly organization of vice syndicates. The underworld regulators faced a constant threat from three sides— from out-of-town criminals who showed a growing disposition to move in and take advantage of Home Rule hospitality, from amateurs or punks who were stimulated to emulate the big shots, and from local rivals like the Lusco gang, allied with the Welch Democratic faction, who complained that Lazia's followers got too may concessions.

An interesting commentary on the conditions under which the Home Rule administrators labored was given by Federal Judge Merrill E. Otis of Kansas City, a distinguished advocate of speedy and stern punishment for lawbreakers. Judge Otis, in an interview published in Lazia's last year, tried to be as reassuring about the situation as he could, saying:

"I believe there are no more criminals today, in proportion to the whole population, than there have ever been. I believe that ninety-five per cent, at least, of the people of this country, both in city and country, are law abiding. The enemies of society constitute a very small minority. . . . I am convinced that humanity is not becoming worse. There has always been a criminal fringe, maybe five per cent, maybe less, that is causing the trouble now. There is an alarming increase in one class of crimes only. There is a startling increase in what we might call the big money kind of banditry."

A ninety-five-per-cent law-abiding nation sounded better than saying that more than six million Americans made a business of thievery and murder. Five per cent of Kansas City's population meant that around twenty thousand citizens were busy with schemes to rook their neighbors. But if, as the Judge said, the total number engaged in this traffic was not alarming, the "increase in what we might call the big money kind of banditry" was. Both Home Rule and John Lazia were ruined by this rush for the big money, a trend that was not entirely confined to the underworld.

In looking for a date and an incident opening the last chapter of the Lazia story, the eye falls on a day early in July, 1932, less than four months after the Home Rule experiment had been inaugurated. In the second week of July a strange event that occurred at a golf club called attention to the fact that criminals of the big time were centering their activities in this city, moving about with a large sense of freedom and living in style. A public golf course that was then popular with police officials and prominent gamblers was patronized one day by four strangers who wore smart sports clothes and played a smart brand of golf. When the round ended, three of the four were arrested by special agents of the division of investigation, Department of Justice, waiting at the clubhouse. The fourth, who got away, was Frank Nash, bank and mail-train robber and killer. The other three were widely known criminals. Among them was Harvey Bailey, one of the chief desperadoes of the period, who was then living quietly but luxuriously in a Kansas City apartment under an alias, posing as a businessman by the name of John Brown.

Bailey was removed to Kansas to answer for a bank holdup and sent to the state prison at Lansing. The golf club incident was forgotten until it was recalled a year later as the opening round in a series of events that tossed Kansas City into deepening turmoil, startled the nation and spelled doom for Johnny Lazia.

Frank Nash and Harvey Bailey belonged to that weird company of public enemies that included Fred (Killer) Burke, Machine Gun Kelly, Wilbur Underhill, Charles (Pretty Boy) Floyd, Adam Richetti and Verne C. Miller. They were boys from the farms, small towns and cities of the Middle West, adventurous spirits of an unsettled time. Floyd, Nash and Richetti came from Oklahoma, Underhill from Missouri. Miller had been a sheriff at Huron, South Dakota. Bailey was a farm boy from Sullivan County, Missouri. He hid Killer Burke on his mother's farm after the St. Valentine's Day massacre in Chicago in 1929, in which Burke was one of the machine gunners. Burke was captured on the Bailey farm after he was identified by a filling station operator from a picture of the killer in a detective magazine.

These dangerous men were not identified with a city gang but moved over a large section of the country, demanding and receiving protection from the underworld wherever they operated. At the time of his arrest in Kansas City, Bailey was working in a large band that roved between St. Paul, Chicago, Kansas City and Hot Springs, Arkansas. Individually the gunmen, bandits, kidnapers and killers of the road dwarfed the city type of gangster, and their collective operations were beginning to make the fratricidal wars of the city gangs look like a minor disturbance. They worked individually, in teams and in family groups, as with Ma Barker and her fearful brood. They robbed and killed with their women. Clyde Barrow and his cigar-smoking, pistol-packing mama, Bonnie Parker, fought their way out of a trap near Kansas City not long before they were killed together in 1934 in a crime tour that took them over several states of the Middle West and South. The gun moll was a familiar figure in the police showup (as Kansas City calls the line-up). These men and women of old American stock made it all too clear that the lawless revival was not confined to the congested centers where the foreign-born were segregated. They also made it clear that crime had passed beyond the stage of local or state problem and had become a national peril.

Three days before Harvey Bailey broke out again, the Kansas City Home Rule order was overturned by four native Americans who had seen too many B pictures and heard about too many racketeers getting ahead in the world. These ambitious beginners exhibited both daring and imagination in their first and last big operation. They kidnaped Mary McElroy, twenty-five-year-old daughter of the City Manager, taking her from her bath to a dungeon where she was chained and held prisoner for thirty-four hours. Their choice of setting for the crime, the home of the City Manager, was in a quiet but populous section of the South Side, and the time was a Saturday morning late in May, 1933, shortly after Judge McElroy had gone to the City Hall.

Two of the four kidnapers called at the house, posing as deliverymen with a package for Judge McElroy's daughter. When the housekeeper opened the door, they forced their way in, and ordered Miss McElroy to dress and accompany them. The City Manager's daughter, who had some of her father's sturdiness and self-composure, finished her bath, donned a becoming summer dress, powdered her nose, adjusted her hair and tossed a gay remark to the kidnapers when she joined them. She left the house to be gone a day, all of one night and part of the next day.

Because the kidnapers were unknown in the underworld, the usual channels of investigation were closed to the police and the girl's father sweated in agony while detectives stumbled over each other seeking vainly for a lead. The gang established contact with the Judge, bargained with him by telephone and demanded sixty thousand dollars. He argued them down to thirty thousand dollars, and Johnny Lazia took over the task of collecting the ransom from his friends and followers among the gamblers.

Reporters who visited the home found the place crowded with detectives, politicians and personal friends. They also found a McElroy they had never seen before, a gentle, pathetic old man. He was surrounded by a large group of his political cronies who attempted to distract him with campaign stories and jokes. The Judge held his head in his hands, staring at the floor.

"You know, gentlemen," he said, "this is the first time in my life that I have been unable to even put forth an effort. My Mary! I can't help her." He began to weep.

There was a stir in the home when T. J. Pendergast arrived in person to express his sympathy to the Judge.

When the final call came from the kidnapers, the Judge and his son left in a car to deliver the money at the appointed place. They dashed out together again when a telephone call informed them that Miss McElroy had been released on a highway near a golf club in Kansas, about four miles west of the Missouri state line. They returned her to her home Sunday afternoon. She was weary, begrimed and breathless with excitement but otherwise apparently unharmed.

Faced with this challenge to Home Rule, the police went to work to make an example of the punks. The pursuit of the four amateurs was efficient, but one got away. The prosecution of the three in hand was swift and ruthless. Sentence of death was meted out to the leader of the band, one of his accomplices was given a life term and the other got a term of eight years behind bars.

Three days after the McElroy kidnaping, the roving big-time criminals entered upon their last major offensive in the Middle West, a reign of terror that continued more than a year until Pretty Boy Floyd and Public Enemy No. 1 John Dillinger were run to earth and slain. It began some forty miles from Kansas City in the Kansas state prison at Lansing where eleven convicts broke up a Memorial Day baseball game, picking a tense moment when the score stood two to two between the Topeka and Leavenworth Legion teams in the fourth inning. They kidnaped Warden Kirk Prather and two guards as hostages, commandeered motor cars and roared away with a flourish of rifles and shotguns. Harvey Bailey and Wilbur Underhill were the ringleaders of the desperate band that staged this sensational break. The fugitives headed southward toward Oklahoma's Cookson Hills, refuge of the outlaws of the period. Underhill wanted to kill the hostages but Bailey calmed him down. Five of the convicts were recaptured in the manhunt that followed, the warden and the two guards were rescued. The rest of the crew, including Bailey and Underhill, disappeared to join up with other desperadoes in the wave of depredations that mounted steadily in subsequent months.

High point in the crime tide was reached in Kansas City with the Union Station Massacre the morning of June 17, 1933, when five persons were slain.

The stage was set the night before when two of the Middle West's most notorious killers, Pretty Boy Floyd and Adam Richetti, drove into town under very peculiar circumstances. They had spent the day riding across a large part of Missouri with Sheriff Jack Killingsworth of Polk County, whom they had captured early in the morning at Bolivar. The Sheriff just happened to drop into the garage of Richetti's brother in Bolivar, and found the bandits waiting there while their car was being repaired. They took another car, put the Sheriff in as hostage and fled. At Clinton, Missouri, they stopped to pick up another citizen, one Mr. Walter Griffith, who was impressed into service as chauffeur. While a wild hunt formed in their rear, they traveled in leisure and caution toward Kansas City. While Richetti filled himself with liquor, cursed, roared threats and occasionally napped, Pretty Boy Floyd solemnly lectured Sheriff Killingsworth on the meanness of peace officers who hounded outlaws into crime and kept them separated from their families, and Sheriff Killingsworth tried not to look bored or disapproving at this old number. The lecture and trip ended at 10 P.M. Sheriff Killingsworth and Citizen Griffith were released in the West Bottoms while Floyd and Richetti retired to a Kansas City hideout for the night.

They did not get much rest, for they were summoned to an interview with another killer, Verne C. Miller, at a meeting which, according to Federal government investigators, was arranged by Johnny Lazia. The government's story of this fantastic enterprise relates that Miller on that same night approached Lazia with the request for a couple of alert and reliable trigger men for an important assignment. It was said that Lazia hastily declined to furnish any of his men for the adventure but referred Miller to the two highly recommended gunmen who had just arrived in the Home Rule city.

Miller had been living quietly in Kansas City for several weeks before this day, putting up in style in a Dutch Colonial house at 6612 Edgevale Road and not attracting much attention in this highly respectable neighborhood. The only thing about him that caused comment was Rex, a large and unfriendly yellow cur, which served as his bodyguard. Miller's vacation at this spot ended when the telephone lines between Hot Springs, Arkansas, Joplin, Missouri, Chicago and Kansas City began to buzz with the news in gangland code that Federal agents had captured Frank Nash, the bank and train robber who escaped from the golf course a year earlier when Harvey Bailey was captured. On these wires, the plot was hatched to deliver Nash when he arrived in Kansas City the morning of June 17, 1933, from Hot Springs, on the way to the Federal prison at Leavenworth, Kansas, under a heavy guard of officers. The phone calls informed Miller that he would need strong assistance in making the delivery, hence the interview with Floyd and Richetti.

The massacre occurred in the parking lot in front of the Union Station a few minutes after Nash, in manacles, and attended by seven officers, walked out of the station. Miller and Floyd were armed with sub-machine guns, and Richetti had an automatic pistol. They had stationed themselves to command the Special Agent's car in which Nash was to be loaded for the scheduled dash to Leavenworth. Miller, it is said, started to approach the machine with a demand that the prisoner be freed but one of the officers fired, wounding Floyd in the shoulder, and immediately the outlaws opened fire, killing four officers and Nash, and wounding two special agents. Two Kansas City police officers were among the dead; the others were Special Agent R. J. Caffrey of the F.B.I. and an Oklahoma police chief.

The three killers vanished swiftly in their automobile but did not leave the city immediately. Their departure was as remarkable as their entrance, and a detailed account of their movements may be found in the government's files. Chief witness for the government on this point was Michael James LaCapra, alias Jimmy Needles, a figure in the Kansas City underworld, who quarreled with Lazia not long after the massacre occurred. He stated that Lazia arranged an escort for Floyd and Richetti the second night after the murders. This service, he said, was arranged by Verne Miller, who walked boldly downtown the night of the crime looking for Lazia and finally found him with some of his cronies in the Union Station restaurant. They had a private interview within a few hundred feet of the scene of the massacre of the June morning, and then Miller vamoosed, leaving the city alone the next day. A physician was called to treat Floyd, who had lost considerable blood from his wounded shoulder, and then a conference was held to determine whether he was able to undertake a flight. LaCapra said this question was settled to the satisfaction of all present when Pretty Boy asked for a machine gun, swung it into a firing position and declared he was able to operate it efficiently. Then, said LaCapra, a party of North Side gangsters was named by Lazia to see that Floyd and Richetti got safely out of the city.

LaCapra's version was not made public until more than a year after the Union Station affair, but the murders provoked an immediate reaction against Lazia and the Home Rule order. The agitation that revived the income tax evasion case against the North Side chief, developed in this period. Federal authorities instituted a vigorous investigation of charges of police laxity in this case while rounding up a large group of conspirators in the attempted delivery of Frank Nash.

Meanwhile, the roving bandits kept things stirred up round about, the furor extending over five states. Harvey Bailey and Machine Gun Kelly took over the main show a month later, in July, 1933, with the kidnaping of Charles F. Urschel, Oklahoma City oil man, for two hundred thousand dollars. That crime entailed no killings but had many extraordinary angles, extending from a hideout in Texas to a pay-off in Kansas City. Part of the ransom money, seven hundred dollars, was traced to Ferris Anthon, a member of the Lusco mob of Kansas City. Although this was a small part of the loot, it drew wide attention, for Ferris Anthon was a central figure in the next violent explosion that brought a crisis for the Police Department and the North Side Democratic Club.

City gang rivalry produced this failure in crime control, and a dispute over alcohol rights apparently was the issue. The difference reached a blazing peak on one of the city's residential boulevards at one fifteen o'clock the morning of August 12, 1933, at a moment when Sheriff Tom Bash of Jackson County arrived on the scene, gossiping with some friends in a car but ready for action.

A few minutes earlier, Sheriff Bash had left an ice-cream social given by the Co-Operettes, ladies auxiliary of the Co-Operative Club. The Sheriff attended this function both as a friend of the Co-Operettes and in his official capacity to provide protection for the receipts from the lawn party. Following a pleasant and successful evening, the Bash party headed north in a car containing the Sheriff's wife and a fourteen-year-old girl, as well as the Sheriff and a deputy, who was driving. They were taking the receipts to the Bash home near Armour Boulevard but stopped when they heard shots on entering the boulevard from Forest Avenue.

The shots came from a sub-machine gun a block away where Ferris Anthon was slain in front of an apartment hotel. The assassins fled in a car, east on Armour. Sheriff Bash seized his riot gun from the floor of his car and dashed out to intercept the killers. They fired on him and he returned the fire, killing two gangsters in the car. Their automobile careened into the Bash automobile while a man on foot ran toward the Sheriff, firing a revolver as he approached. He exhausted his bullets and cringed in terror, pleading for his life. Sheriff Bash spared his assailant who, upon arrest, was found to be Charles Gargotta, a Lazia lieutenant, interrupted in the midst of an assignment to maintain underworld discipline.

Police produced a witness to save Gargotta, for some time at least. The rescuer was an officer who perjured himself when the gunman was first tried for attempting to kill the Sheriff. This officer, who later was given a four-year term for perjury, testified that he found the weapon which Gargotta was accused of firing, a hundred feet from the scene of the shooting, so the jury was encouraged to believe that the gangster was unarmed when he faced the Sheriff. Gargotta remained at liberty until changed conditions moved him to plead guilty to assault with intent to kill Tom Bash.

Sheriff Bash, a Democrat of the Rabbit faction in rural Jackson County, had little time in the following months to spend with his famous Missouri foxhounds and the long-eared mules he loved. He took a large hand in the investigation of the Union Station massacre and other crimes that followed, and joined the cross-country hunt for Pretty Boy Floyd. He was a few miles away in one of the pursuit parties when Floyd was cornered and slain on a farm in Ohio in October, 1934.

Johnny missed the excitement of Pretty Boy's last stand owing to the run of events which distracted the North Side chieftain in Kansas City in the first half of 1934. In the first two months of the year, Lazia was preoccupied with efforts to defend himself against the income tax evasion charges that had been revived by the Federal government, and this ended when Judge Merrill E. Otis sentenced Lazia to the Christian County jail for one year on the first count, repeated the sentence on the second count, but granted probation in that case, and fined him a total of five thousand dollars.

Lazia remained at liberty, on appeal from the jail sentence, but not at peace. His trial was followed quickly by the disturbances of the city election campaign, and this turmoil extended well into spring. The new arrangement under the Otto Higgins police administration had hardly been well established when July brought the final turn for Johnny Lazia.

Curiously, this roaring climax came at a moment of calm when it appeared that the crisis for Home Rule and the public peace of the Middle West had passed its zenith. Under the energetic efforts of the F.B.I., the highway patrol and county peace officers, the threat from the desperadoes of the road was rapidly dissipated. All of the outlaws who escaped in the Lansing prison Memorial Day break were dead or captured. The Barrows were dead. Harvey Bailey and Machine Gun Kelly were in prison for life. Wilbur Underhill's brief life ended in the electric chair in Oklahoma. Verne Miller had been rubbed out by an Ohio gang. And Pretty Boy Floyd's days were numbered. It looked as if the Home Rule operators could count on having nothing more troublesome to deal with than local disturbers of the underworld order.

Lazia stayed downtown late the night of July 9, visiting various haunts and finding everything running smoothly. When he finally turned for home he took a roundabout ride. He wasn't expecting trouble, for he was accompanied only by his wife, Marie, and his faithful bodyguard, Carollo, who sat together in the front seat.

The Lazia car turned into the driveway of the Park Central Hotel, a new apartment building at 300 East Armour Boulevard, and came to a stop under the hotel canopy at approximately three o'clock the morning of July 10. Lazia alighted from the rear seat and had just opened the front door to assist his wife out when the night peace of this South Side neighborhood was shattered by the drilling blast of a sub-machine gun. One bullet almost struck Mrs. Lazia but the stream was accurately centered on Johnny. It was discovered later that the gun was one of the weapons used in the Union Station massacre.

Before he fell, Lazia shouted a warning to his bodyguard.

"Get Marie out of here," he screamed. "Step on it, Charley."

Charley stepped on it, racing the sedan out of the driveway and almost colliding with the car carrying the fleeing assassins at the intersection of Armour and Robert Gillham Road.

Lazia was eleven hours dying in the hospital to which he was rushed. Boss Pendergast ordered that everything possible be done to save him, but three blood transfusions and nine physicians were not enough. While his life ebbed, Brother John's boys, impassive and grim-visaged youths of indeterminable age, gathered in clusters in front of the hospital and watched the line of politicians, businessmen, public officials, relatives and friends of their leader moving in and out.

One of the stricken man's last statements before he lost consciousness was addressed to Dr. D. M. Nigro, a friend and a figure in the Democratic organization.

"Doc," he said, "what I can't understand is why anybody would do this to me. Why to me, to Johnny Lazia, who has been the friend of everybody?"

Dr. Nigro hurried to the telephone with a message to Pendergast that was heard by a *Star* reporter.

"He is very low, Boss," the physician said. "He has spoken of you, Mr. Pendergast, and says he loves you as always."

Seven thousand persons stood in line to attend the wake for Johnny Lazia. Thousands overflowed the grounds of his sister's modest home and rode in the funeral procession. T. J. Pendergast, Judge McElroy, Police

Director Higgins and Mike Ross were conspicuous among the prominent citizens who rubbed shoulders with the obscure friends of Brother John. Miss Mary McElroy rode gravely in the funeral procession. Pedestrians and motorists stopped and gawked.

The police gave perhaps their most strenuous performance in an effort to solve the crime and apprehend the killers. Members of the Lusco gang were rounded up and put through the showup on the theory that the assassination had been in reprisal for the spot murder of Anthon or marked a new stage in the rivalry between the Kansas City gangs. Lusco's men yielded no leads and police turned to the theory that the crime was the work of a local bandit gang which suspected that Lazia had turned up some of its members to the police in the effort to suppress the "rough stuff." Then they theorized that it was the work of an out of town gang which could get no concessions in Kansas City. The police made no progress.

The murder of Lazia was never officially solved but police, Federal men and newspapermen pieced together bits of information and underworld gossip to form the legend that four men carried out the assassination and that Lazia had drawn their wrath by obstructing their racket operations in Kansas City. All four disappeared and at least three of them are not expected to be seen again. If it is true, as some authorities believe, that they were overtaken by gang vengeance, the hand of underworld justice had an unusually wide spread. One of the alleged assassins was Michael James LaCapra, alias Jimmy Needles, who gave the information that involved Lazia in the Union Station massacre negotiations. His body was found in August, 1935, near Platekill, Long Island, where it had been dumped in typical gang fashion. Another one of the four came to the attention of the Kansas City police when he was wounded in a gun battle on a downtown street and later found refuge in the General Hospital. Before the investigation in his case had proceeded far, he was spirited away from his hospital bed by an individual dressed as a police officer and the last heard of him is the rumor that he was turned over to two men who took him for a ride. Details concerning the third man are less complete. He simply vanished. It appears that the fourth man got away and he may still be living in a West Coast city. On the way west, he was credited with shooting his way out of an ambush in Colorado, killing a Kansas City gangster in a party that was trying to capture him. There have been no further developments since that gunman's body was found.

While the story of Johnny Lazia trailed off in whispers of sudden death, his followers rallied under a new leader. Long before the whispers died it was clear that the North Side organization was still a power in Kansas City.

5 *Old Missouri*

HARRY S. TRUMAN is accustomed to having political offices he didn't seek thrust upon him, and Tom Pendergast has been given perhaps more credit than he deserves for bringing up a future President of the United States. Mr. Truman was Uncle Tom's second or third choice for the job of United States senator in 1934, and he wore the boss collar more lightly than any important figure ever identified with the machine. The collar didn't chafe very often for the two good reasons that the Independence man had a strong mind of his own together with a highly developed sense of party regularity, and Tom Pendergast was able to see and appreciate the rare quality of this combination. The result was that Truman made his faithfulness to Pendergast a political legend and the Boss exercised his control in such a way that Truman was able to say in 1939, after the Pendergast crash: "Tom Pendergast never asked me to do a dishonest deed. He knew I wouldn't do it if he asked it. He was always my friend. He was always honest with me, and when he made a promise he kept it."

It is possible that Pendergast was thinking of Truman when he made his statement in the 1933 contention over the gambling issue, explaining the nature of his organization, which, like the world, contained both the good and bad of life—"among them are the best and others who take advantage."

For twelve years Truman had been performing important services for his party with a modesty that made him almost self-effacing among politicians. In fact he was so slow about pushing himself forward for special consideration that Uncle Tom took rather more time than he should have, in recognizing Truman's particular merits.

The Pendergasts needed Harry Truman quite as much as he needed a job when in 1922 they supported him for his first elective office—judge of the County Court from the Eastern District of Jackson County. He was picked for that place not by Boss Tom but by Jimmy Pendergast, nephew of old Alderman Jim, and the indorsement was given by Mike Pendergast, father of Jimmy and Tom's older brother, who had charge of Goat affairs in the county precincts outside Kansas City.

Their political association grew out of the soldiers' friendship of Jim Pendergast and Harry Truman when they were fellow officers in the First World War. With the customary Goat foresight, Mike Pendergast sized up the future candidate from Independence when he visited his son in Camp Doniphan when the Jackson County men were training in an Officer's School. He heard more favorable reports on Truman when the Jackson Countians went overseas with the Thirty-fifth Division, in which Truman served as commanding officer of Battery D of the One Hundred and Twenty-ninth Field Artillery. Jim was a lieutenant under Truman before he became captain of Battery A of the One Hundred and Thirtieth, which fought along side the One Hundred and Twenty-ninth. When the boys came home, one of the men who figured oftenest in their stories was Captain Harry of Battery D, the Baptist farmer from the Grandview neighborhood who established a complete fellowship with a rugged outfit of Kansas City Irishmen on the muddy roads of the Vosges, St. Mihiel and the Meuse-Argonne.

In the first years after the war, Harry Truman was not forgotten by the Pendergasts while he turned to business enterprise with his Jewish friend and war buddy, Eddie Jacobson, in a haberdashery store on Twelfth Street. Truman, spruce, smiling and efficient, made his store a headquarters for his old comrades of Battery D, many of them Legion members who were beginning to take an important interest in political affairs. The store failed after two years, a casualty of the depression of 1921, leaving Truman with a debt of about twenty thousand dollars which he refused to dodge through bankruptcy proceedings and finally paid off many years later.

Captain Harry went back to Independence to consider what to do with his future.

Boss Pendergast looked him over and quickly approved the selection

made by Mike and son Jimmy. The Pendergast family friendship was not
the only large factor in this decision, since a strong movement for Truman had developed in Legion circles in Independence. So the Boss was
impressed at the outset that this countryman did not need to feel that he
owed his whole existence to the head of the organization. Even if he
had been minded to instruct the fledgling candidate in his duties to the
Chief, Uncle Tom was in no strong position to do much dictating to
Truman in 1922. The Ku Klux Klan was then riding high over Jackson
County, raising the flaming cross against the Kansas City Catholics who
dominated the native Democracy. To meet that threat in the county
precincts, stronghold of the two-hundred-per-cent Americans, the organization needed a man who was a Protestant, a high Mason and a war
veteran. Harry Truman, captain of Battery D, Baptist, Mason and a member of a pioneer county family, met the qualifications almost to a unique
degree.

In addition to the Klan matter, the Goats at this time were having
Rabbit trouble in an acute form. Under the aggressive direction of Mike
Pendergast, the Kansas City faction was making a determined effort to
break Joe Shannon's grip on the county property outside Kansas City.
That invasion by the Goats had been complicated by the defection of
Miles Bulger, presiding judge of the County Court, to the Rabbit side.
Under these circumstances, the addition of Truman to the Goat ticket
was doubly advantageous to the Pendergasts, for it brought high into
their circle a man whose Jackson County relatives and background out-
numbered and antedated those of most of Shannon's crowd among the
Rabbits.

Truman's first race for public office was one of the closest of his career
and he was almost eliminated in the Democratic primary by his opponent, E. E. Montgomery of Blue Springs. His rival challenged the
unofficial count, asserting he had won by forty or fifty votes, but the
official count gave Truman a margin of 282. Despite his slight plurality,
Truman was credited with having shown exceptional vote-getting appeal as his victory was won in a Rabbit stronghold. It gave the Goats
control of the County Court, as both Truman and Henry F. McElroy,
his colleague on the court from the western district of the county, were
swept into office in the November election.

The County Court, an administrative rather than a judicial body of three members, exercised an authority over patronage that made it a prize of the spoils system. Its record during the administration when Truman and McElroy represented the majority stands as one of the brighter chapters of Courthouse politics. Both of these men were new personalities on the political scene, eager to win larger public recognition and destined for larger things—McElroy to become city manager of Kansas City in 1926, Truman to go on to the United States Senate and the White House. Their reputations were established in their two years together on the County Court, when they reduced the deficit left by the Bulger regime and otherwise conducted the county's business in a fashion that won for them the most ringing indorsement ever given up to that time by the *Star* to a couple of Democrats. They were put up for renomination in 1924 and won in the primary over the bitter opposition of the Shannon and Bulger factions. Their prospects for re-election were bright until Shannon and Bulger decided on the bolt which defeated the Democratic county ticket and elected a Republican governor in the fall of 1924.

The Klan vote was also credited with being a large factor in the opposition that gave Harry Truman his first and only defeat in an election race. Charges that Truman was once a member of the Klan were raised by the opposition to Roosevelt and aired in the Hearst press twenty years later when Truman was running for vice president. The Kluxers themselves were apparently under no delusions about the position of their Baptist neighbor who went into business with a Jew and hobnobbed with Irish Catholics.

They approached Truman with a suggestion to join the hooded order and Edgar Hinde, postmaster of Independence, has lately told what happened. His story appeared in an article on Truman published in the *Star,* April 20, 1945, just after Truman entered the White House. Hinde said that in the 1922 campaign a Klan organizer came to him with the advice that the cross-burners would support Truman for county judge if he joined up with them.

"I put it up to Truman and he gave me ten dollars for an entrance fee— cash," Hinde explained. "I took it down and then the organizer asked for a conference in the Hotel Baltimore in Kansas City. There he met

Harry and said: 'You've got to promise us you won't give a Catholic a job if you belong to us and we support you.'

" 'I won't agree to anything like that,' Harry said. 'I had a Catholic battery in the war and if any of those boys need help I'm going to give them a job.' "

"The organizer said, 'We can't take you, then,' and he gave back the ten dollars, and that was the end of that."

So Truman saved ten bucks and was out of a job at the end of 1924. He filled in the time working as an organizer for the Kansas City Automobile Club, widening his acquaintanceships, building fences and acquiring useful information on road-building which he put to good account two years later. In 1926, Truman wanted to run for county collector, an office that paid about twenty thousand dollars a year, including salary and fees. Uncle Tom had an older and needier Goat in mind for that rich spot. He suggested that Truman run for presiding judge of the Court, which carried a fixed salary of less than six thousand dollars a year. Truman readily gave up the hope for wealth, and by so doing started up the road that led to the White House. He might have been the most efficient collector in the county's history, but it is highly unlikely that he would then have acquired the reputation and influence he did as presiding judge.

In the eight years while he was the head man in the Courthouse— years when the Pendergast organization's principal attention was concentrated on affairs in the City Hall—Truman had both opportunity and freedom to do the things that established the foundations for his rise to the Senate and the Presidency. The county highway and building program gave him the chance to make a showing as a planner and builder, and he made the most of it. He was favored by circumstances of the time in meeting a minimum of political interference. In 1929, Mike Pendergast died, depriving the Kansas City House of its old supervisor of county affairs, and Uncle Tom was preoccupied with city, state and national affairs. By this time Judge Truman was well established in his own right as the county man with the largest prestige and following in the organization. He had initiated the ambitious improvement program that he was administering, and had impressed the politicians with his forcefulness. The Boss was showing respect for both Truman's personal integrity and his considerable political influence when he let the efficient presiding judge have his own way.

The patronage system on jobs continued to operate in the Courthouse during the Truman administration. It was impossible to eliminate political favoritism entirely, but the record in public services, letting of contracts and delivering the goods has stood up under the closest kind of partisan scrutiny.

There was talk of Truman for Congress and Truman for governor and the presiding judge's ambition first turned toward Congress. His hopes in that direction were raised when the Legislature finally, in 1933, adopted the redistricting based on the 1930 census, dividing Jackson County into two districts, the Fourth and Fifth. Truman's prospects for nomination and election as congressman from the Fourth district were bright until Pendergast decided the place should go to C. Jasper Bell, who had earned the organization's approval with his work as city councilman and Circuit judge. Truman hid his disappointment, which was not prolonged. One day not long afterward he received a telephone call that left him dizzy, for it conveyed the word that Tom Pendergast requested him to file his candidacy for the Senate, and not to waste any time about it. He didn't delay.

Harry Truman had just turned fifty when he reached this surprising and fateful turn in his life. The decision for him hadn't been made by Uncle Tom alone. Jimmy Pendergast went to his uncle in behalf of Truman's candidacy and another large voice in the matter was that of James P. Aylward, chairman of the Democratic County Committee for nearly two decades and the Democratic state chairman in 1934. Famed as a political strategist and a "maker of men" in public life, Aylward acquired wide influence through his ability to work with leaders of both factions of the Kansas City Democracy.

One large factor in the selection of Truman was the renewal of boss rivalry over the senatorship. Pendergast was still smarting from the reversal suffered in the Senate race in 1932, when Bennett C. Clark of Bowling Green downed Tom's man, Howell. He was impressed then with the public's sensitiveness to the machine tag on a senatorial candidate, and reluctant to stir up that issue again. Ordinarily a senatorship was considered largely a prestige affair in boss politics, hardly worth a major fight on the machine's part. That was true in an earlier day, when Federal patronage and influence didn't cut much cake in local affairs, but both Federal power and machine politics had expanded greatly in recent years.

The Kansas City politicians saw that Senator Bennett Clark had begun to build himself up as a Missouri boss with his election in 1932. They became alarmed at the size of his challenge in 1934, when he backed one of his followers for the second senatorship from Missouri. They felt that if he controlled both posts, then Bennett Clark, and not Tom Pendergast, would be the first Missouri boss.'

Actually, the congressional offices always had been more important to a local boss than was commonly supposed. One of the things that made businessmen tolerant of machine politics was the ability of bosses to pick congressmen and senators who appreciated the special interests of business. With the growth of the Federal system through the bureaucracy and the courts, the congressional offices assumed much more importance in the machine. The boys in the precincts might still consider a justice of the peace, a collector's office or a city clerk of more consequence than a congressman, but the boss could no longer view the representative so lightly. And the whole local organization began to look upon the national offices with more respect in the 1930's. The vast Federal government spending program for relief and recovery made influence in Washington a matter of unprecedented concern to the home boys. One of the large items involved in this operation was the office of state director of the WPA, which handled the spending of millions over a period of about five years. This office went to a Pendergast lieutenant, Matt Murray, a year after the Kansas City organization sent Truman to the Senate to challenge the Bennett Clark threat to Goat patronage influence in Washington.

The call to make the Senate race against Clark's man went to Harry Truman because, first, James P. Aylward declined Pendergast's invitation to run and recommended Truman instead. There was a report that Pendergast then tried to interest Joe Shannon, the Rabbit leader, in making the Senate race but Shannon eliminated himself because of his age and failing health. It is difficult to believe that Pendergast dallied over indorsement of Truman after his attention was called to the situation created by the raiding of Bennett Clark, for Truman was the logical candidate in every way. In addition to his admirable qualifications as a Missouri farmer, a war veteran, a Legionnaire, a Mason, a Baptist and a successful county judge, there were two special points that recommended Truman for consideration in 1934: he had established the best record for independence of any office-seeker in the boss organization, and he identified himself as a strong Roosevelt supporter. Speaking a very different language from Senator Reed and some other prominent Kansas City Democrats, Truman praised Roosevelt fulsomely, accepted the whole New Deal program and exhibited a pronounced cordiality toward organized labor. As state director of Federal re-employment in 1934, he had actual contact with some New Dealers and picked up bits of their language. In his opening campaign speech at Columbia, Missouri, before an audience of farmers and small-town tradesmen, Truman boldly acclaimed the Brain Trusters, and declared the Constitution allowed for much more radical measures than any that were undertaken under the program of that "great economist and leader, Franklin D. Roosevelt."

Whether or not he was deliberately selected for that purpose, Harry Truman was Uncle Tom's emissary for a reconciliation between Kansas City and Washington. After Truman's nomination, indication that Roosevelt had been favorably impressed by his new adherent from Jackson County was given when Farley announced that the national party leadership would extend some aid to Nominee Truman. Farley would not say whether this also meant that Roosevelt looked with more favor on Pendergast. For his part, the Kansas City boss would not speak out in praise of Roosevelt, an attitude he maintained to the end. He was too proud to court thus openly the favor of the President whom he had conspicuously opposed and privately criticized. In a discussion of his coldness toward the New Deal reformer, he once explained that he regarded William J. Bryan as the only "sincere reformer." Uncle Tom had lost his interest in reform long before F.D.R. appeared and he couldn't revive it for expediency's sake because, as he described himself, he was "no personal opportunist." His Democratic idealism was summed up in the phrase, "You can't beat five billion dollars," a comment on New Deal appropriations for relief purposes.

None the less, despite the Boss's firm stand on his antireform principles, the Truman nomination was managed throughout in a way to suggest that this was an effort to convince Mr. Roosevelt and his friends that the Kansas City Democrats were good New Dealers. In the process, the Kansas City organization gave a sharp rebuff to former Senator Jim Reed, who had returned to the attack on Roosevelt and was laying the basis for the Anti-Roosevelt Jeffersonian crusade which Reed and a few other Democratic has-beens promoted in 1936.

While Truman gave serious attention to the business of showing that he shared none of the Reed sentiments on Roosevelt, he dealt lightly and pleasantly with the machine issue. In fact, he announced that he was going to make his campaign "just a lot of fun" and he did have some sport answering the charges that he was a boss man. His principal opponents were Jacob L. (Tuck) Milligan of Richmond, Missouri, and John J. Cochran of St. Louis, both of them congressmen seeking larger recognition from the voters. When they branded Truman as a creature of Uncle Tom's, the Independence man smilingly reminded the voters how eager and happy his opponents had been to get the Pendergast indorsement two years earlier in the congressional races. Adding his own bit to the boss picture, Truman warned the voters that Tuck Milligan was a stooge for Senator Clark.

The fact was, of course, that all of the important candidates in all the important races were picked or backed by groups which operated in the manner of machines and contained men with boss ambitions. Senator Clark, contender for the No. 1 position in the Missouri Democracy, was the principal supporter of Milligan. Prominent among the backers of Cochran were Bill Igoe, St. Louis boss, and Mayor Bernard L. Dickmann, who was inflating himself with ideas about running for governor in 1936.

Candidate Milligan invaded Pendergast's home grounds in the last week of the campaign, accompanied by Senator Clark, and raised the boss and ghost vote questions before a large rally in Kansas City. Ridiculing Truman's charge that he, Milligan, was controlled by Senator Clark, Milligan said:

"When we exploded those statements, he journeyed away down to Louisiana to find Huey P. Long and said he would control me.

"You in Kansas City don't have to travel down to Louisiana to find

the man who will control Harry Truman if he ever becomes a member
of the United States Senate. He will be controlled by the same gentleman who has controlled him as presiding elder of the Jackson County
Court. Why, if Harry ever goes to the Senate, he will grow calluses
on his ears listening on the long distance telephone to the orders of
his boss."

Prominent in the gathering were Democrats who figured in the 1934
city campaign against the Pendergast organization. The crowd roared
its approval when the candidate assailed the practice of padded voting
and registration in Kansas City, declaring:

"The dishonest ballot, if continued, will destroy this government. I
believe the man who perpetrates that practice upon the people should
be treated as any other criminal. He not only violates the laws of the
state, but he also violates the Federal laws."

Watching the race was the candidate's brother, Maurice M. Milligan,
then Federal district attorney in Kansas City on an appointment recommended by Senator Clark. Maurice Milligan directed the vote fraud
prosecutions two years later which had such a devastating effect on
the Kansas City organization.

Jackson County Democrats gave Truman some 137,000 votes and
allowed his three opponents together less than 11,000; the vote from
Pendergast's stronghold provided the margin for Truman's victory.
He was nominated by more than 40,000 over the second man in the
race, Cochran. The day after the primary, newspaper political writers
declared that the results established Pendergast as the undisputed boss
from one end of the state to the other.

While the experts studied the returns, Kansas City took a long second
look at the Jackson County man who was going to fill the Senate seat
which had been vacated by Reed in 1929. He didn't have any of Reed's
color—in fact he seemed to be about as neutral as the gray suits he liked
to wear. Despite the dudey effect of his ties and suits, he had the lean,
hard look of a Missouri farmer, a familiar type—except when he smiled,
which was often, and then the wide grin beneath the sharp nose and the
bright eyes flashing through his glasses gave him the air of a gay and
frisky owl. He couldn't orate. He was unable to strike dramatic poses
and didn't seem inclined to try. He didn't roar and beat his breast when

he was accused of being an errand boy for the Boss. He merely smiled and went about his business with an even tread. It didn't seem likely that he would cut much of a figure in the Senate and be talked of for the Presidency, as Jim Reed was.

Harry S. Truman went on to win the Senate seat easily, defeating the Republican incumbent by approximately 265,000 votes. Pendergast's bid for more consideration from the Washington politicians was Truman plus a record off-year vote from Jackson County. The experts on presidential possibilities, surveying the new crop of 1934, passed over Truman without pause while picking out Alf Landon of Kansas, who looked like a new Coolidge and was elected Governor for a second term. The experts are hardly to be blamed for failing to pay more attention to the county judge from Independence in '34, for Mr. Truman wasn't trying to be prophetic in that campaign when he declared: "I intend, as a member of the Senate, to use all of my power to follow Roosevelt to the end of the New Deal."

THE BIG MONEY

ON THE twenty-second of January, 1935, Tom Pendergast met an insurance man in the privacy of a Chicago hotel room to work out final terms in the settlement of a matter that became known as the Second Missouri Compromise. It involved an item of nearly ten million dollars, a fund that was built up during litigation over the fire insurance rates charged Missouri policyholders. As everyone knows, the first Missouri Compromise was the arrangement under which the Show Me State entered the Union in 1821, a complicated deal with a loophole for the extension of slavery which led on to the War Between the States. As quite a few people know, the second deal in 1935 enriched the Kansas City boss by $315,000 and brought him to disaster. However, not many persons have as clear a picture of the second compromise as they do of the first, for the Pendergast operation was a bit more complicated than the 1821 business.

The 1935 meeting in Chicago opened with Charles R. Street, vice-president of the Great American Insurance Company, offering Pendergast $200,000 for a settlement of the Missouri rate litigation. Specifically, what he wanted was to have the State of Missouri abandon the fight on the proposed increase in insurance rates and break up the large pot of disputed premiums that had been collected during the controversy. The issue had started in 1929, under a Republican state administration, when the companies served notice on the then state superintendent of insurance that their rates were being upped sixteen and two-thirds per cent. When the policyholders and the superintendent protested against this large hike the companies went to court to enjoin state interference with the new rates. Pending final decision of the courts the sixteen and two-thirds excess in premiums was impounded and by 1935 this fund amounted to more than nine million dollars. In addition to this prize in the Federal Court, there was a smaller fund of nearly two million dollars impounded in action in the state courts.

Mr. Pendergast was not interested at all in this kind of small change, so Street raised the ante to $500,000 and the Kansas City boss accepted. However, he was slow in getting action started and the Street offer was hiked to $750,000 in the interests of speed when the Chicago insurance executive and the Missouri politician met again in a Chicago hotel, March 28, 1935.

Action was obtained through R. Emmet O'Malley, Pendergast's long-time personal friend and associate in insurance enterprise, who was appointed state superintendent of insurance in 1933 by Governor Park. He was the one who brought Pendergast and Street together through arrangements with A. L. McCormack, St. Louis insurance man, then president of the Missouri Insurance Agents' Association.

Pendergast and O'Malley began to deliver on their part of the bargain immediately after McCormack delivered the first installment of the $750,000 on May 9, 1935. McCormack arrived in a plane from Chicago with $50,000 in cash in a bag, went directly to the Jackson Democratic Club at 1908 Main Street and turned the loot over to Pendergast, who put the money in his safe. Six days later the insurance compromise was put in writing at a conference in the Hotel Muehlebach, attended by O'Malley, McCormack, Street, officials and attorneys of the fire insurance companies. The instrument was signed only after O'Malley personally took a copy of the agreement to 1908 Main Street for Big Tom's final approval.

The second installment was then due and McCormack returned to Chicago, went direct to Street's office, picked up $50,000 and delivered it to 1908 Main Street, Kansas City. Pendergast this time kept only $5,000, directed McCormack to deliver $22,500 to O'Malley and keep $22,500 himself, which he did.

The next payment was not made until after the Federal Court in Kansas City, three judges sitting, February 1, 1936, entered an order to distribute the impounded premiums according to the compromise agreement. Eighty per cent of this fund went to the companies, twenty per cent to the policyholders. The costs, which were large, came from the companies' share and included an unexplained item of five per cent to cover the fix. The original $100,500 bribe money had been assembled by Street from checks made out to him by fourteen companies in the Missouri litigation, and he converted these checks into the currency that was turned over to McCormack. After the court approved the compromise, Street directed each company to issue checks to him totaling $330,-000, which he converted into currency that was handed to McCormack in Street's office for delivery to Pendergast. McCormack put the fortune in a Gladstone bag, boarded the Santa Fe Chief for Kansas City, April 1, 1936, arrived in Kansas City at eight forty-five o'clock that night and went to Pendergast's home at 5650 Ward Parkway. The Boss counted the crisp bills, kept $250,000 and handed $80,000 back to McCormack with the order that he turn over $40,000 to O'Malley and keep $40,000 for himself, which he did.

By this time $430,000 of the agreed price had been delivered, $305,000 to Pendergast and $125,000 divided equally between O'Malley and Mc-Cormack. One further payment, a small one, was made later to Pendergast. Some $300,000 of the agreed price was never delivered.

It was all very slick and high toned. The insurance executives simply made out a check to their trustee for some necessary expenses, and what he did with it was his business. They didn't have to know that the Kansas City boss and an official of the State of Missouri were paid off, they recovered about five million dollars for their companies and the policyholders got a little something. No one had to worry much except the four principals in the pay-off and their number included a protector who appeared to be invulnerable.

Tom Pendergast was not, however, a man at peace. Perhaps he wasn't worried about the well-hidden insurance deal, but he was deeply troubled about something, in fact several things. A reporter who saw him in this period between the campaigns of '34 and '36 was startled by the change in him. He was heavier and grayer, and his eyes carried a sick look. His two hundred and forty pounds made him look shorter than the five feet nine that he measured. When he sat at his desk at 1908 Main Street, giving orders and answering questions, he was still the powerful Boss whose eyes and voice intimidated all others in the room, but the marks of age were painfully visible on him, and within him was a great tension.

Uncle Tom was actually a much sicker man than anyone guessed at the time. In addition to his old intestinal ailment, to the fat, high blood pressure and nervous strain, he was suffering from an acute attack of gambling fever. The destructive force of this last malady was not widely appreciated until several years later, when the government presented some interesting data on the gambling mania together with its detailed account of the insurance bribe and Pendergast's fantastic income tax dodges. The gambling fever reached its highest point in the man most responsible for the rise of the gambling traffic and he became the classic illustration of the development of an ancient social pastime into a major vice. In a community of suckers, he was The Sucker. Some of his friends estimated that he gambled away six million dollars in the last decade of his big play, and the government evidence indicated that in 1935 he actually wagered two million dollars on the horse races and lost six hundred thousand dollars. It was believed that his losses were one of the chief things that decided him to arrange the insurance compromise in that same year. His fascination in the turf game interfered more and more with his business and political affairs. It made him shut himself away from callers in the afternoons while he sat in a room with headphone clamped to this ears following the reports of the ponies. A bet of five thousand dollars on a race was common with him.

As with everything else, Pendergast was very clever about hiding his fever and his losses. He had to hide them from some of his associates, from his wife and children, and from Uncle Sam. He handled everything in cash, and worked out an elaborate system of dummies and fictitious names to cover up the sources of income and outgo. But operations of this size could not be kept entirely secret, and talk about the fabulous Sucker in Kansas City spread over the town, the state and the country. And with the gamblers' gossip, beginning some time early in 1936, went the whisper of a big pay-off in insurance.

The bribe whisper followed Tom Pendergast to Saratoga, to New York, to London and back, to Philadelphia and home to Missouri. It grew very loud in the campaign that immediately followed the Second Missouri Compromise and opened the final assault on the Boss. That last engagement was a protracted affair, however, a series of battles rather than one big smash. Tom Pendergast, cornered, sick and a doomed man, was still a giant in the political arena. His $305,000 from the insurance bribers was soon gone down the same drain with his other bets and the Federal investigation that was to expose every step in this carefully concealed transaction began in the same month that he received the $250,000 installment from Agent McCormack. Events thereafter moved with a rush and Pendergast's rally for the concluding rounds started in the shadow of death.

Uncle Tom's Heart

The bribe rumors got thoroughly mixed up with ghost talk in the August and November campaigns of 1936. This whispering company made a disturbance that reached to Washington and reverberated through election contests and court fights for the next four years. The new addition to this spectral chorus, the ghost votes, was approximately as active and destructive as the pay-off spooks. Between them, the insurance bribe and election fraud scandals of '36 eventually rounded out the Pendergast cycle. Although they figured sensationally in the '36 campaigns, they did not have their grand climax until somewhat later. Meanwhile, the political show out front was dominated by a third factor which probably had as much to do as any one thing with the Pendergast debacle.

This third phenomenon was the entry into the 1936 campaign of the apple man from Louisiana, Missouri, Lloyd Stark, developer of Stark's Delicious, who came forward with Big Tom's blessing and shortly thereafter turned into the Jack the Giant Killer of the reform. Stark won the Democratic nomination for governor with Pendergast delivering another record vote from Jackson County and went on to win the final election with the Democratic ballots in Pendergast's county establishing an all-time high.

This Mr. Stark was strictly an apple knocker despite the fact that he gave a deceptive opening number as an apple polisher. He had first solicited Pendergast's support for his gubernatorial ambition in 1932 and received a cold reception. He came back in 1936 and got what he wanted. This time he was loaded with indorsements, testimonials and pledges of support from Democratic politicians in the state before he called at 1908 Main Street, and it was plain that Mr. Pendergast had to take the Louisiana nurseryman if he desired to avoid a fight against a formidable antagonist. He decided to win the apple man's gratitude.

Stark did not respond naturally to the old 1908 Main treatment. A severe, humorless man with the eyes of a zealot and the mouth of a Puritan, he gave all of the Kansas City boys a chill and they quickly abandoned hope of warming him up. A man with a jaw as ugly as Big Tom's, and something of an eccentric on physical culture, Stark didn't seem to know when he was being intimidated. A former Navy officer and a former Army officer as well, he knew a thing or two himself about the strategy of infiltration and surprise, insinuating himself into the good graces of the St. Louis Democratic machine at the same time he was working the old hocus-pocus on the Kansas City machine. And he was an ingrate. He showed no appreciation at all when the Goats produced the damnedest biggest primary vote ever counted in Jackson County to win the nomination for Stark. He wasn't impressed when Tom followed that with the all-time number in the November election— a vote total which suggested that Kansas City had a population two hundred thousand greater than was allowed by the Federal census, and one which could be interpreted as a profound tribute from the House of Pendergast to the new governor, or a warning to him of the political might of his backer, or both.

In explaining Pendergast's mistake in accepting Stark for governor, it should be noted that the Boss was not his usual self. The deterioration in his health had accelerated in recent months and in June of 1936 his condition became desperate. He hit a big bump shortly after he returned from Europe on the *Queen Mary,* June 2. His homecoming was

noted by Treasury agents and one link that connected him with the
Missouri insurance bribe was closed.

He had returned in time for the Democratic National Convention,
which was held in June, 1936 in Philadelphia. Pendergast took a suite on
the twenty-ninth floor of the Waldorf-Astoria, New York, and received
Missouri politicians and national party figures there while waiting for
the convention to open, June 23. He commuted from New York to
Philadelphia the first day of the Convention and returned to his hotel in
the evening. During the day he ate something or heard something that
violently disagreed with him and that night he suffered a digestive upset,
which was eased when he took a bicarbonate of soda. The next day he
was desperately ill. New York physicians were hurriedly summoned and
it was found that the Kansas City boss was suffering from coronary
thrombosis. For a time his recovery was doubtful.

The doctors ordered complete rest and quiet, a period of perhaps six
months without excitement of any kind. The New York doctor attending him shook his head gravely, then added hopefully: "Although Mr.
Pendergast is a stranger to me, I can see that he is a man of great energy
and forcefulness, physically and mentally."

That spirit which the physician observed produced a rally in the Boss,
and after the first scare was past he began to take a hand in the Missouri
battle that was raging in his absence.

"I guess the people at home are saying I have stayed back here to dodge
a fight," he remarked to a *Star* reporter who interviewed him in the New
York hotel in August, shortly before the primary election. He still looked
like a very sick man, he had lost thirty-five pounds during his illness, the
flesh hung loosely on his bulldog jaws and his whole body sagged, but
the voice and the eyes told that he wasn't licked. He defied the doctor's
orders to rest and prepared final instructions for his followers in Kansas
City which he sent in care of his son, Tom, Jr., who returned by plane
on the eve of the primary election.

Although Lloyd Stark had not yet come out into the open with his
opposition to Pendergast, the emergent insurance scandal created a large
agitation in the primary campaign. Stark's opponent for the gubernatorial nomination, William Hirth, veteran head of the Missouri Farmers' Association, made Pendergastism and insurance his principal issues.

He denounced O'Malley's disposition of the millions of impounded insurance funds, describing it as "the buzzards' feast which the machine lawyers are obtaining from these funds." He also raised a great hue and cry about an item of five million which O'Malley wanted the state to collect from fraternal insurance companies, saying this represented back taxes and interest due. The fraternals replied that O'Malley's action was harassment designed to drive them out of business in Missouri in favor of private companies, and also served to make more fat fees through more litigation.

The attack on Pendergast opened from another quarter when Uncle Joe Shannon took advantage of Uncle Tom's absence and weakness to support a St. Louis Democrat for a place on the state Supreme Court against the candidate favored by Pendergast. Fight for control of the Court mounted in intensity as the litigation over insurance and other matters approached a showdown, and the Shannon defection from the Boss in this instance was a curtain raiser to the great struggle over the court in which Governor Stark played a leading role two years later.

Uncle Joe, like Uncle Tom, was a sick man at this time, but the primary contest over the Supreme Court judgeship had a galvanizing effect on him, and he ended the campaign feeling better than he had for years. That is, he felt fine until the votes were counted. The first to cry fraud was not the *Star* or District Attorney Milligan but Congressman Shannon, whose candidate for Supreme Court judge was downed by a better than two to one count. It seemed that the heated campaign oratory had brought out the election ghosts in a parade of unprecedented proportions.

Uncle Joe was not complaining on the basis of hearsay evidence. On primary day he circulated among the voting booths of the Twelfth Ward and observed the ghosts and their assistants operating in various startling ways. Among other things, he saw two of his women workers slugged by roughnecks for protesting against illegal counting and stuffing. He collected data on numerous other instances in which Rabbit election judges were intimidated or ejected from the premises for protesting the tallying of nonexistent voters. His eyewitness accounts were supported by Mitchel Henderson, judge of the Probate Court, and Sheriff Tom Bash, two other Rabbit leaders.

This election was "so corrupt it was a disgrace to American civilization," said Mr. Shannon. "The Democratic Party cannot exist with this sort of outrage," said Judge Henderson. "I wonder how much of this Kansas City can stand," said Sheriff Bash. The *Star* echoed the charges in a page one editorial entitled "Shame."

For one day it appeared that an important rift in the Kansas City Democratic machine had been made. Jimmy Pendergast and other Goats expressed their contempt for the crybaby tactics of the losing Rabbits. Governor Park pooh-poohed the fraud reports. Then there was some scurrying and whispering behind the scenes, Congressman Shannon came out with a statement praising Uncle Tom's governor and the election board chairman, and a ghostlike silence fell over the Jackson County front.

Lloyd Stark, the new nominee for governor with the Pendergast label, was certain of election in the fall. He had been very restrained up to this point, saying nothing to alarm the machine boys outside of promising to give the fraternals a "fair deal," but he hadn't missed a thing.

A week after the primary election, Tom Pendergast in New York suffered a relapse and his children were called hurriedly from Kansas City to be at the bedside. He rallied again and it was found the latest disturbance was centered in the stomach rather than the heart. The shock of the first heart attack, combined with the excitement of the campaign and the tension under which the Boss was laboring, caused a recurrence of Pendergast's old intestinal disorder. Late in August he was rushed to Roosevelt Hospital in New York for an emergency operation to remove an intestinal obstruction, and the family had another bad day. While Pendergast was fighting for his life, his younger daughter, sixteen-year-old Aileen Margaret, was under observation in the hospital for appendicitis.

The Goat leader rallied again and by mid-September his doctors announced it would be safe to move him to Kansas City, where he was to be taken to a hospital for another operation. He returned to his home town in a special car. Great secrecy covered the movement but his train was observed when it stopped at night at the state capital, Jefferson City, where one passenger boarded the Pendergast special. He was recognized as Emmet O'Malley, the Boss's faithful friend and partner in the insurance bribe.

O'Malley was ordered by Pendergast to collect more on the pay-off as he needed money for hospital and doctor bills. The insurance superintendent passed the word on to Agent McCormack, who obtained ten thousand dollars from Street and delivered it to Pendergast in his hospital bed one morning late in October. It was the last payment on the bribe account and the total was $310,000 below the agreed price. It was a bad deal all around and worse was to follow soon, but by this time Uncle Tom had demonstrated that he could take it and that there was enormous vigor still left in his wrecked body.

Ghosts

When Tom Pendergast came home in the fall of 1936 the fireworks for the final election in November were already popping. Opening the last round, the *Star* set off one of the heaviest barrages it had ever directed against the machine, and the ghosts were the newspaper's particular target. A ghost was a name fraudulently registered and voted.

Since the August primary, the editors had been preparing the attack. The *Star* instigated its own investigation of registration frauds, assigning two of its ablest reporters—Charles W. Graham and Paul V. Miner—to the work. They developed an efficient spy and tipster system and took full advantage of political rivalries and treacheries to get the material they wanted. It was a dangerous assignment, for the newspapermen risked manhandling from hoodlums and rough interference from police. However, throughout most of the investigation, they had the benefit of heavy protection that was said to have been ordered by the Boss himself after a couple of Democratic partisans had made threatening gestures at the reporters. A serious incident obviously would have added fuel to the *Star*'s campaign.

The *Star*'s disclosures were published in a series of stories that appeared in the last two weeks before the election. The newspaper published the photograph of one ghost who was a stranger to the wife of the man whose name he had assumed for registration purposes. A circuit judge

S. J. Ray in The Kansas City Star

Out-Ghosting the Ghosts

The ghost vote scandals of 1936 were recalled by tactics used to prevent a Recall election in 1939.

was embarrassed when reporters produced evidence that two individuals whose petitions for registration he had upheld were ghosts. The reporters found from two to eight ghosts in the homes of many city and county employees. Some of these jobholders were not aware that the goblins had moved in on them. An interesting point in the investigation was the finding that quite a few of the government employees risked the wrath of the fraudulent registration operators by refusing to accommodate the ghosts in their homes. The reporters encountered the highest proportion of honesty and fearlessness in the poorer homes, whose position should have made them the easiest victims of corruption and intimidation. The higher the investigation went, the more indifference and resistance it met.

The exposé agitated the Goat leadership to the extent that it had the Election Board order a canvass of the registration. The *Star* declared that this was a gesture designed to head off the demand for a real canvass of the vote lists. A few thousand names were dropped from the registration books by the machine-controlled Election Board and the ghosts found other ways to get on the list. The newspaper's crusade was not an unqualified success. It succeeded in eliminating only a fraction of the illegal registration. But it was extremely useful in focusing attention on the corruption of the ballot, building up the case for the greater action that was to follow soon from the Federal government quarter.

Two days before the general election of 1936 the *Star* summed up the results of its investigation with the declaration, "An honest election here Tuesday is absolutely impossible." That statement was based on information showing that in "numerous precincts and probably one entire ward, ghosts outnumber the legitimate voters."

The Democratic victory was so complete that no one had the wind to raise the usual cry of robbery and fraud the morning after. For the next five weeks the public was allowed to forget the whole thing. So profound a silence was unnatural and, as it turned out, significant. However, the people needed this time in which to muster all of their strength for the shock of the romance of the ages, the Edward-Wally affair, which "at long last" reached its dénouement December 10, 1936, with the abdication of Edward VIII. The Kansas City gamblers exhibited their sentiment and usual acumen by betting that the American Woman would win over Prime Minister Baldwin and the British Cabinet. For one beautiful half-hour near the close of 1936, the Playboy King and the Baltimore Divorcée restored Twelfth Street's faith in humanity.

District Attorney Milligan waited four days for the abdication excitement to subside before he opened his well-prepared case against the election ghosts. Then Judge Albert L. Reeves in Federal court instructed a new grand jury to go into the vote frauds in all sixteen wards.

"When a man casts a dishonest ballot, he cocks and fires a gun at the heart of America," the Judge told jurors and spectators in a courtroom charged with tension.

"Gentlemen, reach for all, even if you find them in high authority. Move on them!"

The special nature of this investigation was suggested by the range of the instructions, the Court's choice of rhetoric and the presence in town of numerous mysterious individuals who turned out to be F.B.I. agents, sent by Washington to make this the greatest hunt for election crooks in American history.

Thirty indictments were returned in the first report of that jury, but that was only a modest beginning. The last election fraud case was not disposed of in the courts until two years later and the succession of jury reports marked stages in the machine's plunge to ruin.

BALLOTS, JUDGES AND MEN

THERE WERE between fifty and sixty thousand illegal votes from Kansas City in the election of November, 1936, a conservative estimate based on the disclosures in the election fraud investigations and the sharp decline in registration that followed the Federal prosecutions and election law reform. Registration dropped from nearly 270,000 in the landslide year of 1936 to 216,033 for the city campaign in the spring of 1938, the first election held after a new permanent registration law had been enacted and put in force under direction of the Election Board appointed by Governor Stark in 1937.

Kansas Citians had been accustomed to hearing of election thieves for fifty years without getting a good look at them until the long parade of vote fraud defendants was staged in the Federal courts in 1937 and 1938.

They were then startled and disturbed by the appearance of this piratical crew, not because they were more grotesque than they had been pictured in the lurid imaginations of newspaper cartoonists, but because they looked so much like ordinary citizens, which for the most part they were. The underworld types among them were greatly outnumbered by citizens who never before had been in trouble with the law.

Besides the surprising character of the election crooks, there was one other element in the ghost vote that puzzled many people, and that was the fact that this greatest of election frauds occurred in a contest that was not even a close race in the beginning. The machine hadn't needed all or any of those fraudulent votes to win. Why had the organization ordered them produced, or permitted them to be tallied? This phenomenon was noted by Arthur Krock, Washington correspondent of the *New York Times,* who made a study of the Kansas City situation several months after the trials started.

"The frauds revealed and expected to be revealed had nothing to do with the result of any contest for offices in Kansas City last November," he wrote. "There the Democratic majorities are naturally large, and the popularity of the New Deal plus the efficiency of the machine have made them larger. Why, then, was there stealing by 'the boys?' Any observer of city politics knows the real answer. Each party worker of the professional type is an office seeker. From him results are demanded in exchange for jobs. The better showing he makes, the higher his standing over rival precinct, ward or district workers. This competition has led 'the boys' to be what the boss calls 'overzealous.' "

It was very easy to figure these things out if you were an old hand in the Washington political game, but the operation appeared to be a little more complicated if you lived in Kansas City. The Federal investigators, the prosecutor and the judges trying the cases were impressed by the evidence that the boys—or rather the men and women—who appeared before them were directed by orders from above. On one occasion, Judge Reeves interrupted his sentencing of a group of defendants to invite the higher-ups to surrender themselves. He offered this suggestion with the comment that the maximum penalty for the crime committed was only ten years in prison and a five-thousand-dollar-fine and by accepting their responsibility the managers of the ghosts would "rid literally hundreds

of poor people of being humiliated and punished for doing their bidding."

The Judge wasn't trying to be funny.

"There should be some gallantry and chivalry," he added, "but so long
as the higher-ups remain in the background, the only thing for the judge
to do is impose sentence on those who have followed their orders."

The frauds were so extensive, so varied in nature and so marvelously
thought out that it is impossible to believe they were not part of a concerted and well-rehearsed plan. Besides giving little indication that the
boys were out of control, the ghosts served more of a political purpose
in 1936 than was commonly supposed. They weren't needed to win an
election, but they were useful in increasing the Boss's reputation as the
premier vote producer in Missouri, helping him to overwhelm the opposition within his own party, to override and intimidate factional opposition outstate and to keep his prestige soaring.

Anyone who believed that the organization command was not responsible for the wild ride of the ghosts must have been touched by the
way the higher-ups went to the defense of the wretched citizens caught
in the Federal roundup. The machine gave one of its most impressive
demonstrations of "caring for its own people" in this emergency, providing money for bail, legal staff and other purposes, in fact doing everything that was possible except following Judge Reeves's suggestion to
surrender the men behind the scenes.

The grand rally did the defendants no good in court for they were up
against an efficient prosecutor, two uncommonly energetic judges and
an outfit of G-men conducting a kind of investigation that was entirely
new to the politicians in these parts, and all representing the full power
of the Federal government, applied with unrelenting pressure from
Washington. The jurors as well as the investigators were protected from
local influence, for the juries were selected from panels made up predominantly of men from counties around Kansas City in the Western
Federal district of Missouri. Result: an almost complete shutout for the
defense. District Attorney Milligan didn't have a chance to catch his
breath and tally the score until almost two years after the first trial began.
Then, at the conclusion of the thirty-ninth conspiracy case he reported
the prosecution had involved a total of 278 defendants, 259 of whom

were convicted by pleas or trials by jury, and the remainder discharged. There were thirteen jury trials at which sixty-three were convicted, none acquitted. Unlucky 13 appeared again in the number of cases appealed to the higher courts but the side representing the gamblers had slightly better fortune that time, drawing one reversal. Total fines assessed exceeded sixty thousand dollars, and a large number of the principal offenders, including women, went to jail or to prison for terms ranging up to four years. There were thirty-two penitentiary and forty jail sentences.

Federal jurisdiction in the Kansas City vote cases was established under the Constitutional protection of the voter's rights in balloting for presidential electors and congressional candidates in the general election of 1936. Investigation at first centered on registration applications, which turned up such interesting evidence as vacant lots for addresses of hundreds of supposed citizens, and small houses each occupied by a hundred and more alleged voters. In many precincts the registration far exceeded the total population and, as one of the Federal judges remarked, the total registration of almost 270,000 for the city indicated a population of 600,000, or about 200,000 more than the 1930 census allowed. Beginning there, the investigation broadened out to cover all varieties of false registration, padding, miscounting, stuffing, intimidation and interference.

Main weapon for the prosecution was found in an old civil rights' statute, sometimes called the Ku Klux statute, enacted after the Civil War to protect citizens whose voting rights were violated by the Klan. District Attorney Milligan and his assistants discovered this neglected law shortly before the vote fraud investigations started. Under this old statute, which provided heavy penalties for conspiracy to deprive voters of their rights of franchise, election judges and clerks who took part in the frauds were hauled before the courts in batches.

The defense conducted both a legal and a political attack in behalf of the erring election judges and clerks but was handicapped somewhat by the fact that the district attorney was a Democrat and the national administration supporting the prosecutions was Democratic. However, the two Federal judges who called the various grand juries and presided at the trials were distinguished Republicans, whose vigor in pushing the investigations and passing out sentences reminded numerous Goats and Rabbits of the judges' devotion to the party of Harding and Hoover and moved them to cry persecution.

Chief target of this protest was Judge Reeves, who set off the whole thing, carried the main burden and showed no signs of weariness two years later, when he found another way to attack the Democratic machine. The Judge asserted that he received numerous threats by telephone, that some unidentified messenger informed him the "trigger men" were eager to go after him and on one occasion in this period an effort was made to trap him with a lady in a Springfield, Missouri, hotel room secretly wired for sound effects. The lure, he said, was a "sweet-voiced woman" who called him on the telephone one night and asked to see him. The Judge was, of course, too cagey to fall for a routine plot like this. And personal abuse or intimidation efforts merely served to make him more energetic in the cause of righteousness.

Reeves, the flinty Christian, had distinguished himself in public life with his work for the Lord and the Republican faith. His Honor's dander had been stirred to a high point over election frauds long before the ghost scandal of 1936. Nearly twenty years earlier, when he was pursuing political ambitions of his own, he was nominated as the Republican candidate for Congress in Jackson County. After he was defeated, he declared he had been counted out illegally and went to Washington to press his charges before Congress. A congressional committee "viewed with deepest concern" the evidence he presented and then found a way to drop the contest, discovering that Reeves had neglected to raise the issue within the required thirty days after the election of November, 1918.

Judge Reeves's efficient partner in the election fraud cases was Judge Merrill E. Otis, who looked less solemn than his Calvary Baptist colleague on the bench but was not any easier on election frauds. Judge Otis also was a Baptist and a man of great piety, but he hid his severity under an amiable exterior.

The judges pointed out that they tempered justice with mercy, handing out penalties that were, with few exceptions, a third of the limit fixed by the law. Of course, many Democrats considered them excessive. Agitation over the inevitable persecution complaint reached a high-point when Senator Harry S. Truman made a direct attack on District

Attorney Milligan and Judges Otis and Reeves in the United States Senate.

"The Federal court at Kansas City is presided over by two as violently partisan judges as ever sat on a Federal bench since the Federalist judges of Jefferson's administration," Truman asserted.

"Convictions of Democrats are what they want," he added. The junior Missouri senator buttressed his case with the charge that grand juries were hand picked and the attitude of jurymen was ascertained by the court in advance.

"A Jackson County Democrat has as much chance of a fair trial in the Federal District Court as a Jew would have in a Hitler court or a Trotsky follower before Stalin," Truman shouted.

He drew a thunderous retort from Judge Reeves, along with a loud chorus of denunciation from the press. Reeves declared the Truman blast "was a speech of a man nominated by ghost votes, elected with ghost votes, and whose speeches probably are written by ghost writers."

The Truman outburst coincided with a fight on the renomination of District Attorney Milligan for another term. Senator Truman explained that his objection to Milligan antedated the election fraud prosecutions, as indeed it did. Milligan was named district attorney in the first place with Senator Clark's backing and Roosevelt's approval over the objections of Tom Pendergast. Then, in 1934, came the Senate race between Truman and District Attorney Milligan's brother, ending with the brief flurry which the District Attorney created over alleged election frauds in the 1934 primary.

Asserting that "Mr. Milligan has been made a hero by the *Kansas City Star* and the *St. Louis Post-Dispatch,*" Truman challenged Milligan's capacity for the office he held and his conduct in Federal bankruptcy proceedings. The Department of Justice upheld the District Attorney on both counts.

Truman returned from Washington to Kansas City to confer with Pendergast and started back to the capital to continue the effort to block Senate confirmation of Milligan's renomination. He was interrupted on the way in Chicago with a call from the White House conveying President Roosevelt's request that he abandon the fight on Milligan.

"Since the President wants this, I shall not oppose the confirmation, although politically and personally I am opposed to Mr. Milligan because I do not think and never have thought he was fit for the place," Senator Truman asserted.

When the confirmation came to a vote, he did not exercise his Senate prerogatives to demand that his colleagues reject Milligan as "obnoxious" to him, but he took the floor to express his criticism of the Federal judges and district attorney and cast the one vote that was entered against Milligan.

Not long after the excitement over the Truman stand died down, the Federal court announced it would modify the penalties in cases where pleas of guilty were entered. In all, thirty-six guilty pleas were entered. It was explained this offer was made to expedite handling of the congested court docket and also to reduce the number of appeals. Some individuals already convicted by juries returned to the courtroom with guilty pleas and had their sentences reduced from two, three and four years in prison to six, eight and nine months in jail.

There were many incidents in the trials which made it clear that in these cases the courts were not dealing with the ordinary criminal class. Most of these people were individuals from small homes who supported themselves in little jobs and were regarded as good citizens before their involvment in the vote-fraud prosecutions. Many of them were women. There were, however, some tough customers in the lot along with the pathetic offenders and the crime for which they were collectively responsible represented a major violation of the American democratic order.

Not all the defendants were small-time figures in the political organization. Curiously, the principal in the case who attracted widest attention was a woman, and the whole sad complication produced by the ruthless struggle for political power was revealed in her experience. She was Mrs. Frances Ryan, the Pendergast Twelfth Ward leader, daughter of a veteran Pendergast lieutenant. At the time of her indictment and trial, she was superintendent of the Jackson County Parental Home. The vote frauds in her ward were of a sensational extent and character, and she was given two terms of three years each in prison. Judge Otis remarked in court that she had many good qualities, intelligence, strength of character and a reputation for charitable activities, but he added that the frauds in which she was involved were so serious that he could not grant her application for probation.

So the great ghost hunt proceeded to its conclusion, showing in many disquieting ways that political corruption was not the simple thing it sometimes seemed. Costs of the vote fraud cases to the boss machine were beyond calculation. Lawyers' fees, bail and appeal bonds, court costs and fines and the expense of caring for the families of the imprisoned ones ran the bill into the hundreds of thousands. Other costs were harder to estimate. The expense of the defense forced the organization to increase the heavy lug on the joints, upping the gambling syndicate's take to forty-five per cent and even more in some cases. In order to meet the increased overhead, the joints engaged in phenomenal activity, which provoked an unfavorable public reaction calling in turn for more investigations of crime conditions and more prosecutions. A cycle was set in motion that spiraled rapidly toward disaster and its operation was most spectacularly illustrated in the case of the Boss himself.

Pendergast left his sick bed with a tube in his side that kept him alive, and plunged into the thick of the battle. The excitement of the Federal court challenge and other opposition had a rallying effect on him and within seven months after his collapse he completely ignored his doctors' advice to give up business, political and gambling activities. The rise of his gambling fever was manifested in both his betting and his political affairs. Like his organization, he gave a deceptive impression of strength and vigor. Only a few persons besides Uncle Tom himself had any intimations of how fast time was running out.

THE INGRATE

BY THE SUMMER of 1937, Tom Pendergast had recovered sufficiently to feel able to deal directly with the new Missouri governor, Lloyd C. Stark. It was high time that an understanding be reached with the Louisiana apple man, who since his inauguration had shown no consideration for the powerful Kansas City organization that supported him and had been rather too eager in pushing through the General Assembly the new registration law that was designed to prevent a repetition of the ghost-vote carnival of 1936. Governor Stark was about to appoint a new election board of four members to administer this law and he exhibited no inclination to consult Pendergast concerning these appointees.

The Boss summoned, or rather invited, the Governor to visit him in Colorado Springs, Colorado, in July 1937. The call reached Stark while he was returning from a vacation tour in Alaska, and he stopped on his way home to pay his respects to the Kansas City boss. This social and political occasion was well attended by representatives of the Missouri press and the results of the meeting, which became historic, were almost immediately known to the public. Neither Stark nor Pendergast was reticent in telling reporters what happened.

By all accounts, Governor Stark was as remote and cold as one of the snowclad peaks in this delightful vacation land, and Pendergast exhibited his most engaging manners. The Governor later spread the word around that the Boss was almost abject with his requests in this interview, but a picture of Big Tom conducting himself in this fashion when asking anybody for anything was something you had to see personally to believe.

Pendergast's requests were not too modest and he didn't waste any time in coming to the point. He asked Stark to re-appoint his friend O'Malley as state superintendent of insurance for a four-year term and he asked for the selection of an Election Board that was "friendly" to him. Governor Stark bluntly turned down the Election Board request and compromised on the O'Malley matter by agreeing to permit O'Malley to remain in office for a year as a holdover. He let Pendergast understand that he wasn't satisfied with O'Malley's conduct of the Insurance Department and his continuance in office depended on his good behavior.

Showing his displeasure over this response, the Boss insisted that he deserved at least one important appointment in view of his organization's work for Stark in the primary and general election, and Stark finally agreed that he could select the state liquor control supervisor, a new office created by the revised liquor laws, but stipulated that the man chosen must meet Stark's approval.

Keeping the promise he made in Colorado, Stark named Thomas F. Fitzgerald, a Kansas City man, to the liquor control office on the Goat boss's recommendation. This Kansas City Irishman had a line of blarney that impressed the Governor along with a reform technique that baffled him. Mr. Fitzgerald was efficient and energetic but had an unconventional sense of direction. The Governor suggested that he start cracking down on Kansas City. Fired with the Stark spirit, Fitzgerald headed toward Kansas City but landed in St. Joseph.

Governor Stark congratulated his new assistant on his vigorous beginning and suggested again that he investigate enforcement in Kansas City, where the sounds of merriment in the dives were again so loud that they could easily be heard 175 miles away in Jefferson City. Mr. Fitzgerald informed the Governor that the liquor regulations were being observed in model fashion in Kansas City and everything was under control. Before Stark could figure his way around that one, Mr. Fitzgerald was back in the field carrying on his crusade, heading for St. Louis. His reform ran on about seven months before Stark fired him.

Long before the Fitzgerald affair ended, the battle line between Pendergast and Stark was drawn. Shortly after the Colorado meeting at which he brushed aside the Boss's request for a friendly Election Board, the Governor appointed a board consisting of two Republicans, one anti-Pendergast Democrat—Edgar Shook, who had been prominently identified with the Citizens revolt—and one other Democrat who was acceptable to the Kansas City factions.

Pendergast angrily remarked that the Governor had ignored the provision for a bipartisan board. "He has appointed three Republicans and one Democrat," the Goat leader growled.

This action was quickly followed by a more explosive disturbance when Governor Stark ordered Insurance Superintendent O'Malley to withdraw from litigation over a second impounded fund involved in the rate compromise negotiated by O'Malley. This proceeding was an outgrowth of the same controversy that produced the ten-million-dollar fund which was impounded by the Federal Court. At the same time that one group of fire insurance companies sought aid in Federal Court, another group filed action in a state court to prevent interference with their rate increase. The excess insurance premiums impounded during the second dispute amounted to nearly two million dollars. It had reached the Missouri Supreme Court when Governor Stark ordered O'Malley to withdraw from the fight to get his compromise accepted.

O'Malley defied the Governor and, in October, 1937, Stark fired him from the post of state insurance commissioner.

The ousted official called the Governor a polecat and returned to Kansas City, where he was given a city job with a seven thousand five hundred dollar salary. The Kansas City Democrats stormed and talked darkly of reprisals against Stark. City Manager McElroy called him a polecat, just to make sure he hadn't misunderstood O'Malley. The Judge created other opportunities to show his contempt for the Governor. His stellar performance was given on an occasion when he ostentatiously refused to eat a Stark's Delicious apple that was offered him. "I'll take it home and give it to a dog," he explained.

As the year approached its close, the Missouri Supreme Court, in a four-to-three decision, rejected the insurance compromise in its entirety—the second time that this tribunal had ruled against this settlement. Policyholders recovered all of the impounded premiums under this decision—a total of $1,786,481—but this didn't affect the much larger sum involved in the other settlement approved in Federal Court. Distribution of the ten-million-dollar melon went ahead on the eighty-twenty basis that Pendergast and O'Malley had arranged for the companies.

Entering the new year, a review of 1937 showed that the Annapolis-trained strategist in the governor's office had scored a victory on virtually all counts. The blows he delivered were heavy ones and he had made a large contribution to the machine opposition for the city election campaign in the early months of 1938. The boss regime was actually in a state of acute crisis, but curiously there was a widespread impression that the machine was at the height of its power and Uncle Tom was in fine fettle. In some important respects, this was not an illusion, for in its final run before the smashup the machine turned on all the lights and shot the works.

Freedom Begins at Home

It took a surprising amount of time for the Pendergast decline to manifest itself at the polls. The new trend was hardly visible in the city campaign in the early part of 1938. There were many reasons for this phenomenon, some of which have never been satisfactorily analyzed **by** earnest political students. Fortunately for the reader's pleasure, the ordinary experts in this field had at this time the assistance of an ex-sports columnist, who still is remembered by some in Kansas City as the outstanding interpreter of the political follies of February-March, 1938.

This study began with the visit to town of Westbrook Pegler, the syndicated writing fellow, who arrived from New York late in February, 1938, when the campaign was swinging into high. That was early in the period when Mr. Pegler developed a sense of mission, a change that came over him after being impressed that the eccentrics in the political arena were more wonderful than pugilists and ball players, and that statesmen of the press earned more dough than sports writers. Kansas City had reached the zenith of its national notoriety as the Paris of the Plains, and Mr. Pegler came to tell the nation of the fine points of the Pendergast razmataz. He stayed four days, which qualified him as an authority, for that was by far the heaviest study that any newspaper expert devoted to the machine riddle in this period.

Perhaps the most interesting thing in Pegler's four-piece essay on Sinful Kansas City is the impression it conveys of the curious atmosphere that prevailed over this community in the days when the Coalition citizens were attempting to down Uncle Tom. Mr. Pegler was but dimly aware that a campaign was in progress and he picked up no suspicion whatever that the Pendergast victory in the forthcoming election was to be the last for Uncle Tom. The people he saw and moved among were not steeped in gloom over the state of the world or the condition of their souls or the shape of their municipal enterprise. They were, if anything, too joyous. Anyone reading the Pegler reports must conclude that the Kansas Citians were simply too hardy to feel the depression which corruption, crime and wickedness inevitably produce. The writer apparently didn't meet anyone who wasn't on the make or on the loose. If he did, he neglected to mention it.

There was, Mr. Pegler found, both an economic and a historical explanation for the high development of the Kansas City taste for gambling and hell-raising at night. The historical reason, the columnist wrote, was that the city had always been an open town and the economic factor was the livestock industry. Some cattle market man told him that

on the few occasions when Kansas City had the lid on, the cattlemen
shipped the stock to Chicago and went along for the fun in the Windy
City casinos and brothels. This explanation took no account of the way
that livestock men figured the margin on freight rates and shrinkage in
marketing their product, and it slighted the hardware dealers, dyers
and cleaners, undertakers and representatives of several other lines of
business who for years had overshadowed the cattlemen in the production of rip-snorters.

Although the many light diversions offered in the evening explained
why many citizens tolerated and even took pride in their notorious
machine government, Mr. Pegler recognized the fact that there was a
deeper explanation for Pendergast's success. He got it by consulting City
Manager McElroy and several other people in the know. What it
amounted to was the standard justification for machine rule. It was what
Mr. Pegler called "good, rotten government." It protected business
against strike violence, kept tax rates at a moderate level, reduced robbery and motor theft rates and diverted the energies of the criminal element into the vice rackets. And all of these achievements were made possible by the organization's tie with the underworld and the revenue
from gambling and vice.

Mr. Pegler himself was so favorably impressed with this justification
that he took vigorous exception to the comments of a fellow publicist
who was agitating for Kansas City reform. The critic was William
Allen White of Emporia, whom Pegler referred to derisively as "Branch
Water Bill of the hair shirt state of Kansas." He called attention to the
unreasonableness of the White position when the Kansas editor admitted that "businessmen and labor, as well as crooks and officeholders—
in all a great multitude—were beneficiaries of the Kansas City system.
Nevertheless he yearned out loud for a political judgment on the old
saloonkeeper from whom these blessings flow. Always a-wantin' is
Branch Water Bill. Give him good government by a rotten machine and
he wants to risk rotten government by a good one." *

With the delightful vulgarity that characterizes his style, Pegler dismissed the questions of moral tone, civil humiliation and the city's self-

* From a copyrighted article by Westbrook Pegler, 1938; reprinted by permission of the
New York World-Telegram.

respect as "mere mayonnaise," things for the luxury trade. In view of
the fact that the columnist later delivered the most righteous judgment ever passed on Pendergast—after Uncle Tom was down and his
machine in ruins—one must suppose that Pegler was being whimsical
in 1938, or conclude that the four days in Kansas City had a demoralizing
effect on him.

All of this blather about the city's tolerance and indifference took no
account of the battle that had been waged with increasing vigor since
the Mayerberg uprising in 1932. It left out of the picture the Page and
Southern attacks, the agitation in the churches, the struggles in the
Federal courts, the *Star*'s crusading, the Stark challenge and the opposition from Washington. The comparatively small amount of crime which
Pegler noticed in his report was actually the most extensive operation in
history with the police working hand in hand with the crooks, which
accounted for the pretty statistical showing. The impression of machine
efficiency in city services and taxes was equally deceptive.

Mr. Pegler was a busy man, and had to hurry on to the next assignment,
so he missed a chance to see just how disturbed the citizens were over
"good, rotten government" in the campaigning that followed his brief
visit. Although the contest was orderly by comparison with some past
performances, the fight was not lacking in intensity. The antimachine
forces selected the rambunctious Colonel Whitten, survivor of the 1934
debacle, as their hope for mayor and named a bipartisan ticket of five
Democrats and four Republicans. Name of the reform movement was
changed from Citizens-Fusion to Coalition but the interests and personalities in the leadership were virtually the same. Heroes of the 1932 and
1934 wars with the boss organization, Rabbi Mayerberg and the principal figures of N.Y.M., again went into action, but their efforts under
the Coalition lacked some of the spirit that had characterized the
Mayerberg Charter League and the New Youth Movement in their
early days. There was, however, a notable increase in opposition coming
from two sources—the businessmen and the *Star*.

Strategy of the *Star*'s assault was directed along two main lines. The
first was a drive to make certain that the new election machinery designed to produce a reasonably honest vote count would function effi-

ciently. The stage for achievement of this goal was set by the state and Federal governments, with Governor Stark appointing the new election board occupied by Republicans and anti-Pendergast Democrats to supervise the permanent registration law that was pushed through the Legislature in 1937, while the Federal courts in Kansas City kept the vote fraud issue before the public with the prosecutions dating from the 1936 election.

The Election Board appointed by Stark had completely reorganized the registration and voting system in a four-month period before the election. Personnel in the Election Board offices was changed and a new system of records set up. Efforts to circumvent the new law were checkmated at almost every turn.

The second main objective in the *Star*'s campaign was the rallying of business to open defiance of the organization. An interesting thing about this incitation to revolt was that it was not based on an appeal primarily to the pocket books of the merchants, grainmen, stockmen, manufacturers and bankers. Emphasis on costs and taxes was much less pronounced than it was in 1934. Above the usual cry for frugality and efficiency in municipal administration, there arose a demand for freedom. It appeared that some of the commercial interests were seeing democratic rights and responsibilities in a new light as applied to their businesses and homes after twelve years of machine rule.

This agitation reached its height when one hundred prominent citizens signed and issued a declaration of principles. Several representatives of labor were included in this group, but the statement was significant chiefly for the names of the business leaders it contained, and for the declaration that the supreme issue of the campaign was not taxes, patronage, boodle and the customary list of municipal problems, but the question "whether free, democratic government shall endure."

In addition to the new interest in democracy, and the old complaint over the growing costs of machine control, there was another large factor in the 1938 difference between the business community and the organization. The control of labor wasn't working so well as it had in the past, a fact that manifested itself in two labor-management struggles that had rocked the city in the last year. These issues brought City Manager

McElroy into open conflict with two of the city's most important individuals, Builder J. C. Nichols and Banker James M. Kemper, both Democrats, and caused T. J. Pendergast himself to intervene.

In the first of these disputes, the building trades strike in the summer of 1937, McElroy had drawn the fire of the employers when his police failed to stop flying squadrons of union men who went raiding on a wide scale, pulling unorganized workers off of jobs. A committee of builders and other businessmen demanded the police take more energetic action. When the City Manager defied them, they called a mass meeting at which some unkind things were said about Uncle Tom and his organization. That was followed by a meeting with the Boss, who talked to the employers like a Dutch uncle. After that all parties in the dispute exhibited more restraint, but it finally ended with the unions winning wage concessions.

The unions involved in this controversy belonged to the American Federation of Labor, the largest labor organization in Kansas City and one whose membership was predominantly in the Democratic Party. However, the Boss's spectacular championing of their cause in this instance did not signify either an old or a recent conversion to the labor movement, but rather an intensification of political pressure on business, and retaliation for opposition coming from that direction.

Mr. Pendergast exhibited much less enthusiasm for the new and less numerous C.I.O. in the second large labor struggle of the year, but even here the administration angered the business leaders with its slowness in cracking down. The issue came to a head when Ford's labor regulator, Harry Bennett, delivered an ultimatum to the effect that the Ford plant in Kansas City would be permanently abandoned unless the police co-operated to his satisfaction in discouraging C.I.O pickets who were resisting an effort to break up their new union. The businessmen's committee again called indignation meetings to make McElroy more co-operative and the pressure became so intense that Pendergast finally suggested that McElroy should visit Detroit and interview Mr. Ford himself on his employment policies. The Judge made the trip by plane, and the press reported that the Detroit motor magnate and his union-busting director were charmed by the McElroy manners and political views. Mr. McElroy for his part was delighted with what he heard from them, and he returned from Detroit announcing blithely:

> Everything's lovely, and the goose hangs high,
> Soon you will see the Fords rolling by.

The Fords didn't roll from the assembly line as soon as expected, for it took some time to soften up the pickets, during which there were hundreds of arrests, shotgun play, tear-gas attacks, stonings and various other disorders. This struggle was still going on when the citizens prepared to go to the polls in March, 1938.

So the forces and issues involved in the new movement for democracy were not so clear as they might have been when the *Star* summed up the campaign in an editorial on "the issue of the machine over Kansas City." The editorial carried a note of despair, which was understandable. It appeared on the same page with a campaign roundup forecasting the Pendergast victory two days hence.

On the last Tuesday in March, 1938, the citizens went to the polls in dignified fashion and rolled up a majority of more than 43,000 for the head of the Democratic ticket, or about 8,000 above the most optimistic predictions. The Democratic candidates took all except one of the council seats. It was the machine's most remarkable election triumph, deserving that rating on several counts. It was the quietest, most orderly and most nearly honest election held since the conflict entered its major stage. Fighting in the shadow of the vote fraud trials, the party in power showed that it had lost none of its hold on honest voters. Although the Democratic vote totals did not establish another record, the Pendergast showing was the most impressive ever recorded because it was made in the face of the most formidable combination yet arrayed against the ghosts and Rabbits.

Naturally the Boss was elated and he quickly issued a statement to the press proclaiming four more years of organization rule and gently mocking the opposition. Said Mr. Pendergast:

"If it is true, as the *Kansas City Star* and the Coalition speakers reported, that the Democratic President of the United States was against us, that the Attorney General of the United States was against us, that the Governor of the State of Missouri was against us, that the independent *Kansas City Star* newspaper was against us—I think under those circumstances we made a wonderful showing.

"The only further thing I have to say is that the Democratic office-holders elected yesterday will go on doing their duty to Kansas City business interests and to Kansas City generally.

"There never has been and there never will be any reprisals, as was stated by the Coalition speakers, and the Democratic organization which I represent will do its utmost for the best interests of Kansas City now, and for all times in the future."

While the citizens were pondering the implications of this statement from a power outside the regularly constituted government openly asserting his sovereignty, and while the opposition politicians digested the meaning of that final phrase—"for all times in the future"—the City Hall announced the first fruits of the election would be the retention of Judge McElroy in office and a cleanup of bawdy Fourteenth Street.

Uncle Tom's exultation over the confounding of all of his enemies was heightened by a message of congratulation from Jim Farley in Washington. Then he got indirect word of Governor Stark's reaction and his feeling of joy and peace lasted less than one day.

Show Me

APRIL FOOL'S DAY, 1938, was a time of great indignation at 1908 Main Street. Uncle Tom Pendergast saw no humor at all in the roundabout greeting he received from Lloyd Crow Stark, who expressed his congratulations over the party victory at the Kansas City polls in these words: "Of course, as a lifelong Democrat, I am always pleased when the Democrats win." This mealymouthed acknowledgment of his recent defeat was buried in the news that Governor Stark had started an energetic effort to revive the crusade that was interrupted by the Kansas City vindication of the machine, and was beginning with a cleanup through the liquor supervision department. This was accompanied by reports that the Governor and other important figures in the Democratic Party outside Kansas City had laid the basis for another assault on Pendergast in the August primary campaign coming up next.

The Boss had taken all of this sort of punishment that he could stand and the Stark expression of partisan satisfaction over the stunning Pendergast triumph in the city election was the kind of political sophistry that slashed the Goat soul to its depths. T. J. Pendergast's immediate response was a statement delivered to the press which was a declaration of war against Governor Stark and William Hirth, the farm leader who had been Stark's opponent for the gubernatorial nomination in 1936 but since then had joined forces with Stark in the fight on bossism in the party.

There were no subtleties or evasions in the Pendergast retort.

"Now, in reference to the Governor of this state," the statement read, "when he was a candidate for the nomination he had at least five hundred people in Missouri and Kansas City seeing me from day to day asking for my support. Amongst them were fifty outstanding Democrats of Kansas City, whom I could mention except that time will not permit.

"I finally met the Governor, who was then a candidate, with my nephew [James M. Pendergast] and W. Ed Jameson [president of the Board of Managers of the state eleemosynary institutions] in my office. After a few remarks of no consequence, I consented to support Mr. Stark for the governorship. I gave him every ounce of support in the primary and general election, and after the election in the legislative bodies of Missouri.

"I have never done a thing in my life except support Democratic officeholders to the best of my ability. I have not received that kind of consideration from Governor Stark.

"In conclusion," he said, "let me say that Stark will have to live with his conscience the same as the rest of us. If his conscience is clear—I know mine is. I now say, let the river take its course."

Governor Stark remained cool and collected.

"I am perfectly willing to let all the Democrats and all the people of Missouri be the judge of my honesty and integrity, my actions and my democracy," he asserted.

Pendergast caught the emphasis on "all the people" and retorted:

"I am perfectly willing to let the Democrats of Missouri who voted for him be the judge."

All observers understood this to mean that the issue between them would be decided in the Democratic primary four months hence. The battle shaped up over the Missouri Supreme Court, with the Boss and the challenger slugging it out over the nomination of one judge. The contests for the judicial places traditionally had been conducted along lines that kept them aloof from the main partisan struggle, and the candidates in this race tried to keep up appearances by personally taking no part in the heated oratory but their campaign was the stage for one of the fiercest political struggles in Missouri history.

Stark took the initiative with his support for Judge James M. Douglas of St. Louis, a young St. Louis man, whom Stark had appointed early in 1937 to fill a vacancy on the Supreme bench. Judge Douglas voted with the majority in the four-to-three court decision which threw out the fire insurance rate compromise arranged by O'Malley. The Judge's partisans declared that the boss organization sought to punish him for that decision at the same time it buried Stark for his action on the election commission and other matters. Pendergast had some difficulty finding a candidate to oppose Judge Douglas, but the lines finally were drawn when the organization announced its support for Judge James V. Billings, a Circuit judge from a quiet section of the state near the Arkansas line.

As his comment on Pendergast's declaration of war indicated, Stark's one hope rested in "all the people of Missouri." The governor had important allies in Kansas City in the *Star,* District Attorney Milligan, leaders of the Coalition and reform groups and a minority of the legal fraternity who had formed the Lawyers' Association to oppose machine domination of the Kansas City Bar Association, but it was clear that the battle would have to be won outstate and in St. Louis. The St. Louis assistance for Stark's candidate included such potent forces as the *St. Louis Post-Dispatch,* spearhead of liberalism in Missouri, and Charles M. Hay, veteran of the Democratic wars. It did not include Senator Bennett C. Clark, who got Pendergast's support for renomination and successfully played both ends against the middle, returning to the Senate with what he deemed to be a mandate to continue his sabotaging of the New Deal. With the Democratic support in nominally Republican St. Louis less than enough to balance the Jackson County majority for Tom's man, it was seen that the final decision rested in rural Missouri.

William Hirth of Columbia, fiery head of the Missouri Farmers' Association, was so confident that rural Missouri would rise against the Boss that he predicted a victory for Stark's side a month before the primary election. He coupled this forecast with an analysis of Pendergast's situation which led him to conclude that T. J. had "overplayed his hand." Speculating on the reasons that guided the Goat leader in deciding to risk a do-or-die stand, Hirth concluded that he had acted in a moment of blind rage rather than on the basis of a careful survey of his chances.

Perhaps Mr. Hirth was right, but it did seem that the governor was the one who actually issued the challenge and made it difficult for the Boss to ignore it without overtly surrendering. Time was running out for both the machine and its great operator. Even if Pendergast had not elected to launch a major counteroffensive at this stage, the weakening attack would have gone on and the organization—as events proved —would have found itself in a worse position if it had waited to make its stand at a later date.

Viewed in this light, Pendergast took the course that was dictated both by his personal feeling and by a realistic appraisal of the situation. That he appreciated both the immensity and the inevitability of this undertaking was suggested by the tone of his command to "let the river take its course."

Apparently no one appreciated more than Governor Stark how little choice the Boss had in this matter, and no one had a greater suspicion that Pendergast had but a short time left for political campaigning before facing judgment himself in the courts. It was left to the Missouri governor to state in the clearest tones the nature and significance of the issue on the courts. Despite the Hirth confidence that Missouri hadn't changed fundamentally from the faith, independence and pride it expressed in the days of old Tom Benton and Vest, Blair and Schurz, a giant was needed to carry the revival to the people, and Lloyd Crow Stark was the nearest approximation to that stature in the summer of 1938. His qualities as a campaigner were not rated particularly high when he entered the contest. He had not had to extend himself to get elected when Pendergast was behind him and his subsequent forceful performance as an administrator did not necessarily mean he could arouse the citizens to do their duty on election day. The governor was not a polished orator. He didn't inflame audiences and he couldn't unbend easily enough to suit the Missourians. But he had great energy and determination and won the respect due a fighter. He didn't have much color but his lantern jaw was impressive. And when he spoke in the summer of 1938 his words carried conviction and an urgency that held attention. They sent out waves that spread over the state—east into the Mark Twain country along the Mississippi, south into the green Ozark hills, west along the Missouri through the rich farmlands of Little Dixie to its terminus at Kansas City, northwest into the tall-corn counties. Stark stumped the state tirelessly and everywhere he went the crowds turned out to hear him. They listened with an earnestness that bespoke more than the usual interest or excitement of campaign time. The Missourians had not been moved in this way since the Rid Us of Reed battle of 1922.

The great campaigns of the past were recalled by scenes like that of the Douglas rally in Sedalia, home of the State Fair. Three thousand men, women and children gathered in Shaffer's Grove for the speakin' and a fish fry. Neighbors visited happily together under the trees. Crowds stood before the refreshment booths and hurried through the eating to rush for the best seats arranged in tiers before a lighted speakers' platform. The speaking began and gradually the throng settled down. A full moon shed glory on Shaffer's Grove and a voice, amplified to unnatural volume and quality by loud speakers, charged the night air with a feeling of alarm and calamity. The people stirred restlessly and then were quiet for a long period. They did not seem to be in a hurry to leave when the meeting ended. Watching them, the politicians knew that a ground swell was coming.

"A sinister and ominous shadow is raising its ugly head in an attempt to destroy the sanctity of our highest court," the Governor said in the speech that gave the keynote for his campaign. The shadow took definite shape and grew as he went along, repeating charges, amplifying, drawing the whole Boss picture in his effort to convince the voters that this battle was a test between the super-government at 1908 Main Street and the people of Missouri rather than a dispute over the qualifications of two candidates for a judgeship.

The campaign reached its zenith a week before the primary election when Governor Stark invaded Pendergast's home city and spoke before a crowd that jammed into the Hotel Muehlebach ballroom at a meeting

arranged by the Democratic Club of Kansas City, newly formed rival
to the Boss club. Stark pulled no punches in the citadel of the machine
power.

Judge Douglas was nominated by a majority of 120,000, most of it
produced by the farms and small towns. Jackson County delivered a
total of 104,000 for Tom's candidate, a majority of 87,000, which represented a decline in Pendergast voting strength at home but not enough
of a one to inspire any loud cheering over the imminent doom of the
machine. For this reason veteran political writers were inclined to view
the machine setback conservatively. The *Star* interpreted the results as a
reduction of Pendergast to third place among the state powers. Stark,
the producer of this miracle, was allotted no better than second place.
The *Star*'s designation for No. 1 man in the Missouri Democracy went
to that famous anti-New Dealer and expert fencerider, Bennett Clark.

The morning after election Pendergast went to his offices at 1908 Main
Street as usual. He appeared to be calm and unworried. Asked to comment on the election, he wanted to be quoted to the effect that the Republican press and the Republican voters had decided the Democratic
contest, and it was true that a considerable number of Republicans voted
for Douglas. Asked if he would support Douglas in the November election, Pendergast said bluntly that he considered that an impertinent
question. He closed the interview with a sentence on which he probably
had spent much thought.

"In conclusion, let me say that the Democratic Party of Missouri will
need the Democratic Party of Jackson County as it has needed it in the
past, much more than the Jackson County Democracy will ever need the
outstate Democracy."

The formidable threat in this statement was well understood in Jefferson City and elsewhere, and nothing more disturbed the Democratic
peace until after the November election, in which the Kansas City Democrats voted for Douglas along with the rest of the ticket, contributing to a
rousing Democratic victory in Missouri—which was in contrast to a
sharp Republican trend in numerous other states.

The next day Colonel E. J. McMahon, the new liquor office supervisor, fired three of the principal officials in the Kansas City division for
failing to do their duty in a manner satisfactory to Governor Stark. The

Kansas City spooks came out again, for the heat was on throughout the city. It would not lift this time until the Kansas City machine was destroyed.

Rumblings of the coming disaster must have been very audible to Uncle Tom but he was powerless to arrest the course of events or change his own line of conduct. Evidence that was made public a little later shows that he turned more feverishly to his gambling books, probably to seek escape from his other worries as well as to recoup his financial losses. In the last days of the year he had a run of luck with the ponies. Records discovered by the government showed a series of daily winnings in amounts from several hundred dollars to nearly five thousand dollars, and there was a rumor that in one race he plunged with $20,000 and won $248,000.

The New Year's celebration on Twelfth Street was the noisiest and one of the gayest in the memory of Kansas Citians. Governor Stark's snoopers were among the crowds that packed the street and churned slowly in and out of the joints. The investigators already had assembled a surplus of evidence and all the other preliminaries had been attended to in the operation that made this night the farewell to the Pendergast Free and Easy.

6 *Pay-Off*

THE LUG

JUDGE ALLEN C. SOUTHERN, veteran dispenser of justice in the criminal division of the Jackson County Circuit Court, was not a gambling man but he knew when and how to call a bluff. He set about doing this with a grim look on his poker face in the first month of the year 1939, taking the lead in this momentous game in co-operation with two other non-gambling men who were experts in reading the cards—Governor Stark and Federal Judge Reeves.

The bluff that protected the gambling racket had grown immensely more forbidding since the last time anyone had been so foolhardy as to oppose it. The earlier grand jury investigations in the courts of Judge Southern and Judge Page depressed the vice traffic for only a brief period. Shift in the Kansas City police command from Reppert to Higgins and the violent removal of Johnny Lazia, regulator of the syndicates, had the effect of enlarging rather than decreasing the racket operations. Until Stark, Southern and Reeves teamed up for the final round, no one had dared to come out openly against the business in the dives, except some ministers and a forlorn band of P.T.A. ladies. In this period when the gyp enterprise was making its greatest expansion the only important challenge to the racketeers came from a pleasant, motherly woman by the name of Mrs. A. J. Dahlby, and the results in her case were disagreeable enough to discourage any more agitation along this line until Stark, Southern and Reeves started working together.

Some of the obstacles which Judge Southern faced in 1939 were illustrated forcefully in the Dahlby experience in the fall of 1935. Mrs. Dahlby's husband was pastor of the Broadway Baptist Church and she helped him in the pulpit while managing their home and four children. She was filled with the evangelistic spirit of her Swedish forebears, from whom she also inherited a rugged constitution. Mrs. Dahlby went with her husband to India, where they spent a year and a half in missionary work. Soon after they came to Kansas City, Mrs. Dahlby herself became a licensed minister and teamed with her husband to make the Broadway Baptist Church a center of activity that was disturbing alike to the ungodly and the defenders of the status quo. Husband and wife placed equal emphasis on preparation for the perfect life hereafter and work for a better order in Kansas City in the twentieth century. The Reverend Mr. Dahlby startled conservative pillars of the congregation by declaring that "it is the church's place to protest against social injustice."

Mrs. Dahlby produced more excitement when she turned the discussion to Kansas City gamblers. She was so eloquent that she started a movement to boycott all places of business that operated gambling devices, and drew a great hosanna from the Kansas City ministers at the same time that she frightened the businessmen with the suggestion that the churches employ the economic reprisal weapon in the service of the Lord.

The Executive Committee of the Council of Churches and the Ministerial Alliance adopted resolutions approving the Dahlby idea and demanding action by the city government to suppress the games. Frank H. Backstrom, Fusionist member of the City Council, introduced a resolution authorizing Mayor Smith to name a committee to investigate crime conditions. The resolution was promptly tabled, and killed a week later. This emergency was not one requiring Mayor Smith's attention. It needed Judge McElroy's attention.

The Judge gave a very cagey performance, showing his remarkable versatility and utter cynicism. Dropping his usual bluster, he reverted quickly to the role of a simple, benign country fellow from Dunlap, Iowa. His courtesy, kindliness and sincerity won the hearts of the delegation from the P.T.A. and women's clubs, headed by Mrs. Dahlby, which called at the City Hall to get action on the reform.

McElroy singled out Mrs. Dahlby for attention, praising her work for public morals and offering to engage Convention Hall for an immense rally to be addressed by the lady preacher. Mrs. Dahlby glowed and accepted.

"You know," she said, "I'm glad I came down here. You are a grand man. You look like my dad."

The Judge blushed, tossed his silver mane and went on to talk intimately of conditions that shocked a sober country boy like himself, who never took a drink, or smoked, or gambled. He told how the gambling fever had spread among the best people of the town, mentioning the University Club, the Kansas City Club and the Mission Hills Country Club, popular retreats of wealthy citizens who publicly deplored the morals of machine government.

"Gosh," said the Judge, "I guess I am the only highbrow here today. Just take a look at this card. The Kansas City Club is announcing that a series of keno games is to start at the club, for members and their families and friends."

He showed the ladies a pile of petitions from owners of buildings protesting against police interference with "recreation."

Concluding his little sermon, he asserted: "I could take you to the Kansas City Club, where I've been a member thirty-five years, and you probably would find about one hundred members gambling, including many leading business and professional men. Some of these men are of such standing you might hold them up as patterns for your boys."

The ladies nodded and blinked their eyes in confusion. They departed still under the charm of the City Manager. When they got out in the fresh air and analyzed the import of the Judge's propaganda that the town's social leaders and businessmen wanted gambling conditions as they were, a few of them were disheartened. Mrs. Dahlby was not deflected from her purpose. By this time she had collected evidence that the masses wanted to be saved from the gambling evil if the classes did not. She was deluged with letters, most of them from the lower social orders, praising her good work. One came from a boy in prison saying he might have been directed to a useful life if the Baptist crusader had appeared on the scene earlier. Another came from a housewife who said she was planning to commit suicide after hocking her wedding ring for money which she lost in a tango game.

"I had planned to commit suicide in their horrible place Thursday, the seventh, which is their bank night," she wrote, "but it seems the merciful Lord has intervened by putting it in your heart to start this crusade. I hope it is on the level, and will wait till the fifteenth, and if it is not closed by then I will know that the Good Lord wants me to sacrifice myself to free a money-mad crazy people from this horrible blood-sucking devil game—tango."

It is not known if the lady carried out her threat to die on the fifteenth. Mrs. Dahlby unfortunately had to leave town two days before that date, dropping her campaign in midflight. Instead of getting a chance to speak in Convention Hall, as the City Manager had promised, Mrs. Dahlby received a call from a strange woman who visited her home, alarming her with warnings and offer of money to change her interests. This messenger was followed by a man who represented himself as a lawyer working along the same lines. When these maneuvers failed to silence Mrs. Dahlby, the goon squad went to work, employing the technique developed by gangsters and blackmailers to break the nerves of strong men. For two days the telephone in the Dahlby home rang steadily with calls from the ghostly agents of terror. Members of the family who answered the phone heard a sepulchral voice—never the same twice— saying, "Prepare to be taken for a ride," or "We'll get you," or "We'll drive you out of town." Mrs. Dahlby wilted when the threats were directed at her children as well as her husband and herself. Thirteen days after her crusade started, she left Kansas City with her children to be gone for several weeks.

The incident provoked great indignation, a general feeling of insecurity and helplessness, and no police action.

Judge Southern encountered the same kind of resistance, with variations on a wider scale, when he entered the January offensive against the gamblers. The Judge had as much determination as Mrs. Dahlby and considerably more skill and resources. His action coincided with the drive by Governor Stark, who marked 1939 as the cleanup year for Kansas City by ordering his attorney general to proceed to this front on the first day of January. Southern's co-operation with the Stark investigation was signified in mid-January when the sheriff staged surprise raids and the Judge issued search warrants for two of the syndicates' principal gambling resorts—the Fortune Club for bingo and the Snooker Club.

This was a blow at the heart of the racket, for the Fortune was the special property of the machine's collector of the gambling lug.

A day later the Judge called a panel of twenty-four citizens for a grand jury investigation, ordering a secret session to guard the jurors from intimidation and danger. Southern then found that popular sentiment against interfering with gambling and fear of the underworld were still high, for only twenty of the grand jury panel appeared in court and ten gave various excuses to get out of the duty. Proceedings were continued a week and meanwhile the conflict over the Fortune Club went forward. That action took two sensational turns when Charles V. Carollo, successor of Lazia, was brought into the picture as the secret owner of the club, and Judge Southern excluded the county attorney, W. W. Graves, Jr., from the investigation.

A week later the grand jury panel was completed and notice was finally served that this was the bear cat of all investigations undertaken in the state courts. Alex S. Rankin, a pioneer of the N.Y.M.-Fusion reform, was named foreman of the jury which the *Star* called the People's Jury in recognition of the fact that it contained no one who was likely to be friendly to the machine interests. Judge Southern and Governor Stark worked together to arouse the jurors and the public to the nature of the battle ahead. The Judge kept County Attorney Graves and Attorney General McKittrick at arm's length in the proceedings, pointing out that neither of these officials had exhibited any awareness of crime conditions in Kansas City that needed investigation. The jury had the assistance of three special aids to the attorney general, appointed at Governor Stark's insistence, and of a staff of investigators engaged by the governor with a fifty-thousand-dollar crime fund which he jammed through the Legislature.

"You will need no one else in the grand jury room, gentlemen," Judge Southern explained.

It was then that the intimidation squad started to work on Judge Southern. This was a major tactical error, accounted for by the fact that the Kansas City gangsters did not know as much about Independence and the Southerns as they should have. Judge Southern was at all times prepared to take care of himself and one notable exhibition of that fact had occurred in the building strike emergency of 1937, when word

reached Independence that one of the union flying squads was going out
from Kansas City to take nonunion workers off construction jobs in the
old county seat town. The Judge, who owned property on which building work was under way, oiled up his shotgun and went on sentry duty.
No flying squadrons paused in the neighborhood where the rugged
jurist held forth, two loaded shotguns close at hand.

Kansas City was apprised of the full measure of the Southern temper
a few days after the grand jury session started when the Judge quietly
interrupted proceedings long enough to hand out a statement which he
had written in his own hand and which he asked reporters to deliver to
their editors. It read:

At the beginning of this term of court two public officials importuned me
not to call a grand jury at this time because it would hurt the Democratic organization. Since that time I have received covert threats and warnings, the
last yesterday, to the effect that if I did not call this investigation off certain
public officials and police, who may be under investigation by the grand jury,
would frame or have framed evidence with assistance of denizens of the underworld which attacks my character and personal moral integrity.

You will understand that the purpose is to frighten and intimidate me for
its effect upon this investigation, and that, of course, if such framed evidence
comes to your attention it is false and malicious and libelous.

Please notify your superiors of this communication and oblige,

                                        JUDGE ALLEN C. SOUTHERN.

The Democratic judge from Independence then turned back to his
work with the grand jury, but the investigation was interrupted two
days later when County Attorney Graves filed application for a writ of
prohibition before the Missouri Supreme Court, contending the Southern
investigation was an irregular proceeding because the prosecutor was
barred from the grand jury room. Judge Southern went to Jefferson City
to testify at the hearing on the writ of prohibition, and the Supreme
Court, which so recently had figured in the Stark-Pendergast battle for
control, quickly settled the issue by rejecting the Graves application.

Back in Kansas City, Judge Southern assembled the grand jury to hear
his instructions for an unlimited investigation, a dramatic charge in
which it was clear that Prosecutor Graves, Big Charley Carollo and
the gambling syndicate were the main targets. Governor Stark had demanded action against the county attorney at the outset of the inquiry,

with the statement: "His continued failure to prosecute ghastly felonies justifies his immediate removal from office." The grand jury complied by indicting the prosecutor on three counts and the attorney general later instituted ouster proceedings against him.

The first count against Graves was based on his failure to prosecute Charles Gargotta, Lazia lieutenant, for his attempt to kill Sheriff Bash in the Armour Boulevard battle of 1933. Gargotta was the beneficiary of numerous continuances and a dismissal after he was acquitted on perjured testimony at his first trial. The Southern grand jury revived the charge against him by indictment, and he pleaded guilty and went to prison at long last.

Counts two and three against Graves alleged that he was present in the Oriental Club when liquor was sold on a Sunday in violation of the state law and present when it was sold without a state license, and that he did nothing about these violations. Graves closed his career as prosecutor with his most vigorous action, spending the last year resisting the state's effort to remove him from office. He won a directed verdict of acquittal in a Jackson County Circuit Court, when the Judge sustained a defense demurrer to the state's evidence in the cases initiated by the Southern grand jury indictments, but he finally was ousted from office along with the Jackson County sheriff in an action before the state Supreme Court showing that there had been a breakdown in law enforcement.

Evidence produced in the various investigations and prosecutions showed that the gambling racket had grown to the proportions of a major industry in Jackson County. A commonly accepted estimate was that it did an annual gross of twelve million. Judge Southern estimated it at twenty million.

The Southern effort was supplemented and enlarged by Federal Judge Reeves, who roared into action with a charge to a new Federal grand jury at the same time that Southern was directing the Circuit Court attack. Reeves gave a longer and much more fiery charge than any he had offered in the vote fraud investigations, for he was after bigger fish— the higher-ups—this time.

"Kansas City today is a seething caldron of crime, licensed and protected," he thundered in an address that aroused the grand jury to unprecedented action.

The Calvary Baptist crusader on the Federal bench placed his finger on Carollo in his instructions and coupled this with a fascinating explanation of "the lug" as it operated in the gambling racket. From this assessment for protection from police interference, the syndicate annually raised hundreds of thousands of dollars to finance underworld operations and political activities. Judge Reeves was unable to compute the total revenue realized from this source, but he presented enough evidence to indicate that it was a figure of staggering proportions. In this connection he gave the jury an exposition of the income tax law and the weapons it offered for prosecution of the syndicate collectors.

The Reeves charge revealed how much spadework for this assault on the machine had been done by Federal operatives working out of Washington. The Judge quoted at length from an official government report covering the findings of witnesses and agents who had probed into the Kansas City racket. This report was filled with records of big daily payoffs, hints of murder and frequent mention of the Big Man who ruled the underworld. The government agent quoted by Reeves identified this individual only as the Big Man or "the subject," commenting: "I never saw any one individual, in all the years I have been connected with the United States government, who seemingly had so much power as the subject."

To give the grand jury some idea of the extent of the traffic they were challenging, Judge Reeves read some details on the operation of just one resort, described by him as "the least dreadful of the places of crime in Kansas City . . . located within a residential district, within a stone's throw of some of the biggest and most important churches of Kansas City"—obviously Carollo's Fortune Club. The government figures showed that this place paid one of the partners controlling it $30,500 in 1937 and $35,000 in 1938 and, as Judge Reeves remarked, this was but one of hundreds of resorts in the city.

An interesting sidelight on the "partnership" principle in the gambling syndicate was given a little later when Carollo was called to judgment for income tax evasion. Then it was shown how he got control of the Fortune. A couple of chumps from Los Angeles had started the club in

S. J. Ray *in The Kansas City Star*

Short Memory

The Roosevelt administration's part in the cleanup was recalled by this cartoon in the city campaign of 1940.

June, 1934. Six months later Carollo notified them he was cutting himself into a half-interest, figuring his protection was worth that much to his new partners. In March, 1938, he had grown so fond of the Fortune that he sent a letter to his partners advising them he was taking over the other half, enclosing a bill of sale and five thousand dollars each for their interest in a business that by conservative estimate was earning sixty thousand dollars a month.

In the government report read to the jury by Reeves, there were several instances in which this partnership device was worked, but the principal account had to do with the lug. This assessment usually started at twenty per cent of the take when a dive was established and immediately began to climb. It amounted to forty per cent and more in some cases during the vote fraud prosecutions when overhead costs were heavy. Witnesses quoted in the report told of the efficiency of the system in protecting the Big Man, mentioning two incidents in which informants were put on the spot and stating that "None of the persons contacted by me were willing to appear in open court, stating that it was their firm conviction that if they did so—or if it ever got out that they had 'talked'—these men would see to it that they were taken for a ride or killed inside twenty-four hours."

Satisfied that the jurymen were sufficiently impressed with the gravity of the situation, Judge Reeves concluded:

"Every citizen ought to be eager and anxious for his country's welfare to move upon a situation that is as startling as the one that I have given you today. Gentlemen, you have a great responsibility."

At the time that this investigation got under way it was generally believed that Carollo, Lazia's former bodyguard, was the chief figure of the underworld. However, Federal authorities later disclosed information that indicated Carollo was but the front for an even bigger man, another Italian who was named by the agents but was not brought into court. But Charles Vincenzo Carollo—born in 1902 in Santa Ristino, Italy, and never naturalized as an American citizen—was sufficiently important to show that the Federal government was striking at the heart of the racket in its great assault of 1939. That impression was heightened later in the year, when Carollo was brought into court for sentencing for income tax violation and District Attorney Milligan declared:

"According to the records, Charles Carollo was an intimate friend and companion of one John Lazia, who met his death violently at the hands of unknown gunmen July 10, 1934. Accompanying Mr. Lazia was the defendant, Carollo, at the time he met his death.

"John Lazia at the time of his death was reputed to be the vice lord of the underworld of Kansas City. The investigation into the background of this defendant reveals the fact that after the death of Lazia this defendant took over the authority exercised by Lazia in his lifetime, relative to gambling and rackets carried on in Kansas City, Missouri; that he grew in power even greater than his predecessor; that he had a full entree into the offices of the high officials in the city administration. According to the testimony, he was seen going into and out of the private office of the former city manager; that he had full entree into the police headquarters, and almost daily was a visitor at the office of the director of police.

"The testimony reveals that the defendant became the collector of the lug that was imposed on the gambling rackets of Kansas City who paid large sums of money monthly for the privilege of carrying on gambling games unmolested by the police officers of the city."

It was later admitted that the reports of Carollo's actual authority in the underworld were exaggerated at this time, and that his chief function was as collector of the lug and contact man with city officials. Total income from the lug could not be estimated, but District Attorney Milligan's statement gave an idea of its size, showing that annual collections on only nineteen of the joints had jumped from $53,161 in 1935 to $103,275 in 1938. Carollo finally admitted that he collected the lug for Pendergast, among others, making direct payments to the Boss or his secretary. It was estimated that Pendergast got forty per cent of the collection, the remainder being divided among five or six others in the syndicate.

These revelations, and more, were made public in the months following the dramatic charge to the Reeves grand jury.

While the Reeves grand jury proceeded to lay its great siege, the Southern grand jury drew in its net filled with big and little fry. When the jury brought in its final report March 11, it raised the total number of indictments to 167 and announced that it had done no more than lift the "edge of the curtain." In addition to the Graves, Gargotta and Carollo indictments, the haul included indictment of the presiding judge of the County Court and a former judge of the Court for corruptly allowing a claim for $9,781.33 to pay for remodeling and repairing Gil P. Bourk's Jeffersonian Democratic Club, Inc.; indictment of a cleaners' and dyers' union business-agent for two bombings; and indictment of numerous liquor law violators along with the gamblers. The blows were so impressive that, contrary to expectations of Twelfth Street old-timers, the city police decided to keep the lid on the dives after the Southern grand jury recessed. Police Director Otto Higgins ordered a surprise raid on the one spot that defied the order—the horse book retreat managed by Benny Portman, the racketeer who had unwillingly acted as a go-between in the kidnaping of Mike Katz nine years earlier. Benny was constitutionally unable to believe in a reform order. He continued to operate until several years after the 1939 shutdown, and then he was the last of the big-time veterans to be slain in the usual manner.

Popular attention was diverted from the Southern jury's work by reports on the progress of the Reeves jury. Early in March it was reported that the Federal investigation had broadened beyond the gambling racket to include insurance graft, with the jury inquiring into the disposition of a mysterious $447,000 fund. A subpoena was issued for A. L. McCormack, a stranger to most Kansas Citians. A second subpoena was issued for Walter H. Eckert, Chicago attorney for the trustees of Charles R. Street, the insurance executive who figured in the Missouri Compromise pay-off. In mid-March the jury issued subpoenas for a group of Eastern insurance executives, and they came to tell what they knew of the "mystery fund."

Entering April, exactly a year after Boss Pendergast had commanded the river to take its course, the air was filled with rumors and reports of developments in Kansas City and Washington which said that the Reeves investigation had caught a bigger man than the Big Man the grand jury was charged to bring in.

DAY IN COURT

THE STORY of T. J. Pendergast's last days of freedom is scattered in government reports, court records, newspaper stories, private letters and recollections of friends. This material has never been brought together in coherent form, but the main outlines and details of the picture created by the public record are sufficiently clear to leave a lasting impression. It shows the magnitude of the nightmare of deception, conflict and alarm in which the Boss lived for weeks, months and even years before the final reckoning in the spring of 1939. Among other things, it compels respect for the massive staying powers of Tom Pendergast.

The struggle began at the height of his success, long before his decline became evident to observers. He must have known he was overreaching himself, but he exhibited no disposition to yield. A statement presented at his sentencing by District Attorney Milligan shows that in 1935 the Pendergast horse-race bets and losses had attained proportions which meant he had to seek income outside his normal sources. The $315,000 insurance graft he obtained in 1935 and 1936 represented but a fraction of the amount he needed to finance his gambling operations and support himself in the style to which he had become accustomed.

A report that the Boss put the bite on intimates for a million dollars or more was published in the *Star* not long after his crash. In that account Pendergast's old associate, John J. Pryor, was reported to have confided to a friend his misgivings over the way the Boss was handling his affairs in the spring of 1938. He related that Pendergast's calls for large gifts from friends started in 1937 and mentioned that his gambling fever had grown progressively worse since 1934.

William D. Boyle, Pryor's partner, was said to have issued numerous checks or drafts for Pendergast for suspiciously large amounts which he requested Pryor to countersign. On several occasions, the *Star* story added, he even called Pryor from his bed at night with requests to withdraw sums from ten to a hundred thousand dollars for the Boss.

"I told Boyle that T. J.'s craze for betting was going to get us all in trouble," Pryor was represented as saying by his unnamed friend. "Boyle said we had to come through. I told Bill several times that giving T. J. all that money would ruin us and T. J. both."

It was estimated that the Pryor & Boyle companies dug up a million dollars in this manner and that the Old Man had blown between five and six million dollars on the horses since 1933, "a million a year at least."

The bookkeeping system for this amazing operation required the services of a wizard. How T. J. Pendergast managed to keep going at all is something of a mystery. A large staff of Treasury experts spent years trying to run down the transactions, but there were some details that baffled them. The Boss rarely used his bank account. Currency, drafts, telegraph money orders and express vouchers in the names of other persons were the forms in which he was paid. When he was in other cities, money was transmitted to him from Kansas City under assumed names. A part of his income was reported to the Federal government on the returns of associates or trusted employees. An ordinary individual could have spent a large part of his working time figuring up this scheme, yet T. J. was able to do it on the run while attending to his multitudinous other affairs.

Despite the secrecy, the worry and the bother which grew increasingly more complicated, Tom Pendergast managed to present a fairly serene face to the world and to most of his friends.

When the net closed around him in March and April of 1939, Pendergast faced the emergency with perhaps less than his usual calm, but he was still very much in command of himself and his organization. The attack against the machine was proceeding on four fronts—from the Federal government, from the Criminal Court of the Jackson County Circuit, from Governor Stark, and from the local political opposition—but there was no relaxing anywhere of the organization's resistance and the moves reflected the touch of a knowing and steady guiding hand.

While the Reeves grand jury was calling witnesses in the insurance graft "mystery fund," T. J. was sending emissaries back to Washington to plead his cause with the national party leaders. One of his chief envoys was Otto P. Higgins, the police director, himself about to be drawn into the Federal income tax dragnet. Higgins spent a week in the national capital futilely trying to see President Roosevelt. The chief result of his mission was a demonstration on every side that the Roosevelt administration was one hundred per cent behind the efforts of Governor Stark and District Attorney Milligan. Higgins was followed to Washington by the Boss's nephew and heir to the Goat crown, Jimmy Pendergast, who got more bad news.

Signal that the long hunt had reached its end was given April 4 when Attorney General Frank Murphy and J. Edgar Hoover, head of the bureau of investigation, Department of Justice, flew to Kansas City to confer with District Attorney Milligan and the large F.B.I. staff that had been assembled there. The trip drew national attention and some political experts immediately announced that it was a New Deal grandstand effort to publicize the Kansas City cleanup as a counterattraction to Thomas E. Dewey's racket-busting show in New York.

Thus ended the Federal investigation that had begun three years earlier, in April, 1936, with a casual inquiry into the income account of Ernest H. Hicks of the Chicago law firm of Hicks & Felonie. Hicks had died the previous October and the Bureau of Internal Revenue discovered, in a routine examination of the partnership books, an item of $100,500 that required explanation. This was a clue to the first installment on the Missouri Compromise pay-off, but that fact was not known at the time or for some time afterward.

Robert J. Felonie, the surviving partner of Hicks & Felonie, had been chief counsel for the fire insurance companies. The Federal investigators learned that the $100,500 on the partnership books was the record of a transaction with Charles R. Street, the insurance executive who represented the companies in the Missouri Compromise deal. The figure was the total amount of fourteen checks from various insurance companies which Street had deposited in the partnership account May 9, 1935. On the same day the partnership had repaid by checks to Charles R. Street the entire $100,500. The investigation then moved to Street, who said that the money did not represent taxable income for him as it had been turned over to someone else. He refused to identify the recipient but finally intimated that the money went to an important political figure in Missouri though not a public official. Under pressure from the Bureau, he later explained that he could not reveal the name of the person involved until the liner *Queen Mary* arrived in New York on her maiden voyage in June, 1936. Federal agents checked the *Queen Mary*'s passenger list and found Tom Pendergast.

The investigation at this point was still far from its goal, however. After Pendergast's return on the *Queen Mary*, Street again refused to divulge the name of the man in the deal or to discuss the nature of the transaction. He filed an amended tax return on March 8, 1937, and paid the tax on the mysterious $100,500. It appeared for a time that the bribe had been successfully covered up and the investigators encountered a further handicap when Street died in 1938. But by this time the Federal agents had taken a large interest in the case and knew where they were headed. One of the untold stories in the long search, and one that may never be told until he is ready to tell it, concerns a Missouri newspaperman in Washington who has been credited by some authorities with reviving the Treasury intelligence unit's interest in the case after Street closed the door. It is said that he provided leads and information which convinced the agents that the $100,500 was part of a larger pay-off connected with the Missouri insurance settlement.

Further help from Missouri was given by District Attorney Milligan in Kansas City and by Governor Stark, who was reported to have conferred on this matter with both President Roosevelt and Henry Morgenthau, Jr., Secretary of the Treasury. The hunt quickened with the accidental discovery of a special fund of $317,000 which Street maintained. Checks from Street to A. L. McCormack, Missouri insurance man who figured in the case, opened another trail. Elmer L. Irey's men of the Treasury Intelligence operated in many cities winding up their extraordinary search in the Pendergast financial labyrinth. Final break came when District Attorney Milligan called the insurance executives before the grand jury and prevailed on them to use their influence to get Agent A. L. McCormack to tell the inside story. After a long sweating, the agent went to Milligan's office and haltingly told the tale which filled in the missing pieces of the Missouri Compromise riddle.

Three days after Attorney General Murphy and G-man Hoover made their flying visit to Kansas City, the Federal grand jury returned its first indictment of Pendergast for violation of the income tax law, along with an indictment of R. Emmet O'Malley under the same law. The Boss went to his arraignment with a dignified step and a placid air. His blue

eyes were bright and his powerful hands steady when he stood in the
United States marshal's office. A detailed and dramatic account of the
Boss in this scene was written for the *Star* by Paul Fisher, who reported
that Pendergast's only show of emotion occurred when his fingerprints
were about to be taken. One of his lawyers attempted to help him take
off his overcoat and Pendergast shrugged him away.

"I'll take it off," he said audibly enough to be heard by Reporter Fisher.
"There's nothing the matter with me. They persecuted Christ on Good
Friday, and nailed him to the Cross."

It was April 7, 1939—Good Friday—and on this day Emmet O'Malley,
visiting in the East, went into the Catholic Cathedral in Baltimore, Mary-
land, to pray for his soul.

Pendergast's good humor returned immediately after he had taken off
his overcoat without help. He flashed a smile at his lawyer. His son, T. J.,
Jr., and his nephew, Jim, stood near by.

A deputy marshal inquired if Pendergast wanted the newspaper
photographers to photograph him having the prints taken.

"Hell, they have a million," Pendergast growled.

"You are five feet nine, aren't you?"

"I was," the Boss replied with a chuckle. "I've grown shorter. They
say, you know, that age shortens a man."

"Your hair is gray?"

"What's left of it is gray."

Then the Goat leader and his party went before the commissioner of
the court, where Pendergast was released on a ten-thousand-dollar bond
and told to appear in Federal Court April 24 to have his trial date set.
There were numerous friends of T. J. in the group that watched when
he turned to leave, and hands reached out to pat him on the back. He
walked out with impressive dignity.

Later in the month the Federal grand jury indicted Pendergast on a
second count for income tax evasion and this interval was filled with
the lightning and thunder of the storm that was toppling the machine.
District Attorney Milligan was in charge of five Federal agencies on
special Kansas City assignment. United States agents uncovered a narcotics ring that was taking an estimated twelve million dollars a year
from addicts, and the Reeves grand jury returned thirty-three indict-

ments in that case. City Manager McElroy resigned and Mayor Smith seized his powers. O'Malley took a leave from his post as City Water Department director and Police Director Higgins resigned. Governor Stark directed an intensive offensive in the General Assembly for a new bill designed to end Home Rule in Kansas City and restore control of the police to the governor.

Mayor Smith got the Council to order an audit of the city books, and a second audit was started by the Civic Research Institute while pressure was put on the County Court for a county audit. The *Star* did not wait for the audits but started a series of disclosures based on the analyses and findings of reporters working with records made available by the new Smith regime at the City Hall and the Federal investigation.

The Federal grand jury lifted the lid on the garbage scandal with the revelation that members of Pendergast's family held two fifths of the shares in the Sanitary Service Company. Examination of City Hall records uncovered the $356,000 water leak scandal, involving Pryor and McElroy. There was something new every day.

On May Day, Pendergast and O'Malley went before Federal Judge Otis to enter formal pleas of not guilty and have their trials set. They were followed immediately by Charley Carollo, indicted for using the mails to defraud in the Fortune Club operation, and he also pleaded not guilty. Following him were three ringleaders in the narcotics racket, who also pleaded not guilty. The defense still held tight all along the line.

The next day brought a sign of the frantic disturbance within the organization when it was learned that Edward L. Schneider, secretary-treasurer of seven of Pendergast's companies, had mysteriously disappeared. His motor car was found empty in the middle of the Fairfax Bridge over the Missouri River, and inside it were two suicide notes of farewell to his wife and daughter. Investigation disclosed that he had made a full statement of his transactions for Pendergast to the grand jury three days before this incident. One of the last persons to see him alive was Otto Higgins, the former police director, who visited him at his home less than two hours before the Schneider car was driven on the bridge. Higgins shed no light on the mystery. Schneider's body was recovered from the river five days later and the case remained unsolved.

In the days that followed, the political attack grew, the Federal grand jury widened the scope of its income tax investigation, and the Boss finally decided to surrender. On the twenty-second of May, T. J. Pendergast went to the Federal Court to plead guilty to both indictments against him. A large part of the hearing was devoted to testimony from his physician giving a detailed report of the Boss's state of health. He had been a very sick man. Following the heart attack in New York in 1936, he had undergone three operations for the correction of an intestinal obstruction and this had been managed by the construction of an artificial device in his side. His physician would not say whether his life expectancy was good for five years.

The total tax due on Pendergast's evasion was $830,494.73, with penalties, and the government agreed to settle the bill for $350,000. Judge Otis sentenced Pendergast to serve fifteen months in Federal prison and fined him $10,000 on one count. The court set the sentence at three years on the second count but suspended it with probation for five years. There was an immediate outcry from antimachine quarters over the seeming mildness of this punishment. Judge Otis defended his judgment, pointing out that in assessing the penalty the court could not give special consideration to the source of the money that was hidden from the tax collector. The judge obviously gave some weight to consideration of the prisoner's health but it soon thereafter became evident that his sentence was not a mild one. Examination of the terms of the probation showed that this amounted to exile for the political boss, and it was in effect a life term.

Five days after Pendergast's day in court, O'Malley entered a plea of guilty to income tax evasion and was sentenced to a year and a day in prison and fined five thousand dollars. Of the four principals in the insurance compromise pay-off, Pendergast and O'Malley were the only ones who went to prison. Charles R. Street, the insurance executive who raised the money, was dead. A. L. McCormack, the agent who was the go-between and later served as a government witness, finally got off with probation on a two-year sentence based on a contempt of court charge covering his part in the corrupt settlement.

The Federal investigation continued and resulted somewhat later in the sentencing of several other important figures in the machine. Contractor John J. Pryor was given a two-year term for income tax evasion and the investigation revealed his earnings were the highest in the boss-favored company. Matthew S. Murray, who had served as Missouri director of the WPA and also director of public works in Kansas City, drew a two-year term for failing to pay taxes on about $90,000. It was estimated that two hundred and fifty million dollars was spent on the projects under his supervision in the Missouri WPA and the Kansas City Public Works Department. His defense in the income tax case was highlighted by his contention that some fifty thousand dollars he received was nontaxable income because it represented gifts from Pryor and Pendergast.

Another who took the trail to the Federal prison at Leavenworth was Otto P. Higgins, who was indicted not long after he resigned as police director. He pleaded guilty to evading payment of taxes on $65,170 of unreported income received during the great part of his term in office and was given a two-year term. He was followed to Leavenworth penitentiary by Big Charley Carollo, collector of the gambling syndicate, who drew sentences totaling eight years—one year for using the mails to defraud in a lottery, three years for failing to report a large part of $654,391 income over four years, and four years for perjury in an effort to conceal his operations as the machine's collector of the lug on gambling houses. After arriving in Leavenworth, he was involved in a conspiracy to smuggle contraband articles into the prison and was transferred to Alcatraz.

These were the major actions of the cleanup that started in 1939 and they required many months for completion. Meanwhile, the assault on the machine proceeded along many other lines, with audits, grand jury investigations, court trials and general agitation that resulted in the retirement of numerous city officials, the resignation of the presiding judge of the County Court and the removal of the county prosecutor and the sheriff. The actions that were to bring about those changes had been initiated or foreshadowed by the time that the Boss departed for prison.

The two old partners in politics and insurance, Pendergast and O'Malley, made the short trip to the Federal prison at Leavenworth, Kansas, the same day, May 29, 1939. Following his usual custom, T. J. Pendergast arose early and left in a car, accompanied only by his son and nephew.

The party arrived at the east prison gate at eight-forty o'clock in the morning and Uncle Tom, bag in hand, walked quietly to the entrance without looking back. Throughout this long ordeal he had shown no weakening of his iron nerve. He didn't break until after he was dressed in and saw the photograph of himself in convict's uniform. Then the heart of T. J., for a second time, almost stopped forever.

Coup and Double Cross

MAYOR BRYCE B. SMITH, the big little bakery man, realized his ambition to take over City Manager McElroy's office and run Kansas City in the last nine months of 1939. Puffing on his fat cigar and glowering in a manner nobody had seen before, the diminutive mayor served notice on McElroy to quit his post six days after the first indictment of Boss Pendergast. The Judge put on his hat at a rakish angle and took his bean-pole figure out of the City Hall with great dignity shortly before the lunch hour of April 13, leaving behind a piece of paper which said simply: "I hereby tender my resignation as city manager, H. F. McElroy."

The resignation was dated the day before the mayor staged his successful coup against the man who had humiliated him for eight years. Smith's action was made with the explanation that he had decided to step beyond the powers granted the mayor by the nonpartisan charter, to preserve order and peace in the town during the interim period between the Pendergast blowup and the reorganization of the city government. Almost everyone was surprised by this sudden show of energy on Mayor Smith's part and the ease with which he seized control from McElroy. It was never explained whether Mr. Smith originated this move all by himself, but if he did he is entitled to credit for more political initiative than he is commonly allowed. It was a well-timed maneuver, coming before anybody besides Mr. Smith had a chance to recover from the excitement of the last few days. The new regime started with the majority of the Council supporting the mayor and a vast majority of the population wishing him good luck.

The Mayor seemed to feel that his sudden elevation to the front office had changed everything.

"Kansas City is clean now and is going to stay clean," he proclaimed in a statement to the press.

Reached at his home by telephone and asked to comment, McElroy said: "I am as cool as a cucumber but I am saying nothing, not a thing." It was his last word to the people he had managed for thirteen years.

In the days and weeks that followed, it was difficult at times to follow the direction of the Bryce Smith reform and make out who was running the mayor. The trouble was not caused by lack of earnest effort and good will on the part of Mr. Smith. He was naturally such an amiable individual that he wanted to please everybody, with the exception of Governor Stark and a few extremist ministers and the Republicans. He welcomed the advice and co-operation of the *Star* and the leading businessmen, and he let his friends and associates in the organization know that he had their interests at heart. The result was that half the time Mayor Smith appeared to be carrying on a reform and the rest of the time it was clear that his administration was working to save the remnants of the Democratic organization.

In order to keep the reins in his own hands and still observe the charter provisions that limited the mayor's authority to that of president pro tempore of the City Council, Mr. Smith picked a city manager he could trust. His choice was Eugene C. Zachman, Mr. Smith's secretary. Mr. Zachman was a handsome young man who wore his clothes stylishly, and the businessmen and politicians regarded him glumly at first. Outside of his association with Mayor Smith, his only known preparation for his difficult new role had been obtained as a newspaperman when he was a reporter for the *Kansas City Journal-Post*. Everyone was surprised at the talent which Mr. Zachman displayed in administrative work and the political life.

The team of Smith and Zachman made many changes in the City Hall, reducing expenses, cutting the payroll, ordering an audit, shifting personnel, firing some department heads, reorganizing here and there and getting more efficiency on all sides. In the first few months of the Smith regime, eight important department heads—all of them pillars of the machine organization—were removed from office, a process that was hastened somewhat by the urging of a businessmen's committee and the action of the courts.

Chief pressure on the reform mayor came from a formidable group of self-appointed advisers known as the Forward Kansas City Committee. This outfit was dominated by influential bankers, realtors and manufacturers who had been conspicuous in the latter-day opposition to the machine. Their Forward Kansas City Committee drew up an elaborate program that Mayor Smith was expected to follow. The Committee closely checked every move of the city administration and was quick to issue critical statements when things didn't go forward fast enough to suit the leading citizens. The businessmen's "ideal city manager" had turned sour on them in the experiment with party machine government and they made sure that the reform would turn out to their liking.

Mayor Smith's moves were neither eager nor extensive enough to satisfy all the Forward men but the main criticism of the interim government at first came from outside the business circle. The ministers of the old Mayerberg Charter League movement wanted more action. Governor Stark, in the state capital, exhibited no confidence whatever in the Smith crusade. The Governor was about to present Kansas City with another major reform measure in the form of a new law that ended Home Rule for the police. He roared at Smith when the Mayor and his new city manager went to Jefferson City to lobby against the police bill.

"It may surprise some of my listeners to learn that Kansas City has a mayor," Stark said. "That fact has come to light in recent weeks in a most peculiar manner. It is an adequate measure of the desperate straits in which the Pendergast organization finds itself that it feels impelled to produce this hitherto obscure gentleman and push him to the front with the sign Civic Virtue pinned to his coattails."

The police bill was rushed through the Legislature, with Stark's following mustering the votes to overwhelm the organization die-hards, and Home Rule for Kansas City ended in July, 1939. Imbued with the Stark crusading zeal, the new Police Board appointed by the Governor looked far and wide for a fanatic in law enforcement and found their man in the extraordinary Lear B. Reed, G-man; and with his selection as police chief the reform started toward an extreme which confounded even some of the rabid agitators for a change.

Meanwhile, public sentiment for a complete change at the City Hall was kept alive by disclosure of various details of the Country Bookkeeping system which McElroy had operated with no interference from the City Council or the Ten-Year-Bond advisory committee. In nine years, twenty-six millions of the thirty-three million Ten-Year bonds had been sold, a large part of this money being spent without competitive bidding for contracts and a substantial share of the business going to the Pendergast companies.

The city entered 1939 with an admitted deficit of $1,500,000 in the general operating fund, and city employees were informed there was nothing in the till to cover their salaries for the last four months of the fiscal year.

One of the interesting items turned up in the investigations was an estimate of the size of "Cut and Lug," as the citizens called the system that was used to spread the expense of machine government among the small fry in the ranks. The Cut was a kickback from City Hall salaries, which varied from twenty-five to fifty per cent a month through several months of each year, depending on how much the city administration needed in order to make ends meet. This cut was imposed without Council authorization or ordinance, and the Country Bookkeeper got around that charter requirement by having employees sign slips of paper requesting the reduction in pay, with the understanding that the amount withheld was to be repaid later when the city was again in clover, which it never was so long as McElroy was in the City Hall. In addition to these special pay cuts, the city employees had taken a twenty per cent reduction in base pay by Council ordinance in 1933. The Lug was the assessment placed on the pay of city and county employees to raise campaign funds for the party, and this collection grew in size each year until it was admitted to have exceeded $200,000 in 1938, but may have been double that figure, as a full accounting was never made. Cut and Lug between them were estimated to have taken more than ten million dollars from the rank-and-file over a decade.

Total amount squandered and illegally diverted through the long period of machine rule was beyond computation but when the various audits and investigations were completed, the bill included these items:

A deficit of $19,453,976 in claims and accounts.

Funds for retirement of $11,000,000 water sinking-fund bonds due July 1, 1942, unlawfully diverted to other purposes.

S. J. Ray in The Kansas City Star

The Ark Springs Another Leak

The "water leak," discovered in 1939, was a bookkeeping operation that cost the city $356,000.

Expenditure of $11,445,009 from Ten-Year-Bond funds without contracts as required by law.

Operating fund deficit of $2,733,185.

Diversion of $3,263,623 of improvement bond money to pay wages of city employees.

Unrecorded liabilities of $1,200,000.

An additional sum of $2,692,126 diverted to unauthorized uses.

The boss regime also left a large bill for back pay of city employees and the succeeding administration found that claims and judgments in this account totaled $6,825,250.

It was estimated that the delinquent tax bill totaled another ten million dollars and the size of the tax favoritism racket was suggested by the report that tax abatements in 1938 totaled $684,005.

Money squandered by the device of payroll padding was beyond calculation. When Mayor Smith opened the records, it was found that the number on the city payroll was 5,200 against the 3,200 or 3,500 indicated by McElroy. The Smith regime immediately dropped 700, but the search for the pads was still incomplete.

In the final count, total number of city employees was put at 6,500 (as against the 3,500 currently on the city payroll) and many of these did no work other than cash their checks.

One of the more sensational items turned up in the City Hall investigation was the big "water leak." This was an arrangement by which the Rathford Engineering Company was paid five thousand dollars a month to look for water leaks, a service that required hardly any effort outside of the bookkeeping but took $356,500 of the taxpayers' money over a period of years. Rathford was the front in this business for Boyle and Pryor. Rathford performed most of the easy labor required in looking for leaks and most of the money went to Pendergast's associates. One of Rathford's assistants for a time was W. E. Burnett, Jr., son-in-law of Pendergast. McElroy and Pryor were indicted on conspiracy to defraud charges. Pryor, the only one brought to trial, was acquitted but he and the Boyle estate later paid back $40,000 in a settlement with the city.

A mystery that intrigued the public's fancy throughout the spring and summer was the McElroy emergency fund. This was the prime exhibit of his Country Bookkeeping system, the fund he invented to have cash on hand at all times. Several unsuccessful efforts were made to force McElroy to surrender his records on the handling of this fund, but he was preoccupied with a more important judgment than the one his successors were preparing.

The auditor's report established that the emergency fund amounted to $5,843,643.56 over a period of seven and one-half years. It was assembled by ignoring the charter regulations to draw on the Ten-Year Bond money, the city treasurer and the funds of other departments. The report showed that nearly four million dollars was returned to sources which had made the advances and the remainder covered a wide variety of payments to people and corporations with claims against the city.

McElroy was dying when the Smith reform reached a crisis in September. A recall movement, started by various individuals and groups, grew to the dimensions where it couldn't be controlled by the conservative members of the Forward Kansas City Committee. Mayor Smith, who had promised to resign if recall petitions were signed by as many as forty thousand citizens, suffered a lapse of memory on this point. He angered the Forward men by his failure to restrain organization stalwarts in the City Hall who took elaborate measures to discourage and obstruct the recall movement. A break between the committee and Smith was imminent on September 15, when Judge McElroy died at the age of seventy-four, after weeks of illness from eye trouble and heart disease. At the time that death released him from the struggle he faced indictments in the water leak deal and was under Federal investigation on his income tax account.

The battle for control of the City Hall did not pause while the Judge was being buried. Mayor Smith broke with the Forward Committee late in September and the main battle shifted to recall and to a fight for control of the city manager's post for the remainder of the interim period.

Mayor Smith was caught in a crossfire in the final stages of the contest. The Forward Committee turned against him because of the Democratic maneuvers to block the recall movement. The recall campaign struck a bump when three Councilmen resigned and the Council elected their successors, who were not subject to recall for six months under the law and who could not easily be charged with responsibility for the McElroy administration, in any case. A further complication was provided by the city clerk, who played a game of hide-and-seek with the recall petitions and employed other devices to delay or prevent the recall election.

While the Forward Committee assailed Smith over these tactics, certain organization leaders found that the Mayor was growing too independent and this difference inside the Democratic Party reached a climax over two important offices in the City Hall. The office of city manager was vacated when Smith's man, Zachman, evidently sensing the approaching showdown, resigned to take the post of director of the Municipal Auditorium. Then Sam C. Blair stepped out of the office of city counselor. Blair, a young man who had distinguished himself as one of District Attorney Milligan's brilliant assistants in the vote-fraud cases, had taken the city counselor's office soon after Smith seized McElroy's powers. A Democrat from Cole County, he seemed happy to remove himself from the Kansas City imbroglio when Governor Stark appointed him to a circuit judgeship.

In the competition over these two offices, Mayor Smith gave perhaps his outstanding exhibition of independence. He succeeded in getting the Council to appoint a temporary city manager of his choice, J. V. Lewis. Meanwhile, he conducted a vigorous agitation for employment of a trained municipal administrator from out of town. His selection was L. P. Cookingham, the expert who became the city manager of the highly successful administration that was established in 1940, and who still holds that office. But Mayor Smith was too advanced in this matter for the Democratic powers in 1939. They wanted to keep the city managership in the hands of one of their faithful followers and the result was an action which Mayor Smith denounced as a double-cross engineered by members of the Council who had been the first to call on him to save the administration after the McElroy retirement.

Working behind the Mayor's back, leaders of the Goat and Rabbit factions got five-to-four control of the City Council and selected William M. Drennon, retired insurance executive and a friend of the late H. F. McElroy, to be city manager. Bryce Smith rebelled and his last effort to outwit the opposition produced a comic opera scene in the City Hall. The Mayor hurried to put an independent man in the city counselor's office before the Drennon regime could take over. Smith's choice for this post was Jerome Walsh, son of the late Frank P. Walsh, and he had retiring City Manager Lewis appoint Walsh before incoming City Manager Drennon was sworn in. Walsh was in the mayor's office waiting to take the oath, but the ceremony was held up by a suspicious sort of delay in transmitting the commission from the city clerk's office. Then the door opened to admit Councilmen Garrett and Clark and Mr. Drennon. Informed that Mr. Walsh was about to be sworn in as city counselor, Councilman Garrett bellowed:

"Who appointed him?"

"The city manager, Mr. Lewis," Smith replied.

"Well," Garrett roared again, "Mr. Lewis is not city manager. Mr. Drennon is the city manager."

The boss majority on the Council had sworn him in twenty-five minutes earlier.

Jerry Walsh snorted:

"Here goes the city counselor with the shortest record in the history of Kansas City."

Resigning in protest, Mayor Smith stepped out of office at the year's end with a statement reviewing the achievements of his administration in the last eight months. It was a list of thirty-one points, all of them covering important improvements. The Smith farewell in politics was climaxed by an ovation which he received when he appeared at the annual Fathers-and-Sons' luncheon of Rotary. Taking the bows and smiling happily, the little mayor showed that he had emerged from the battle with his amiable disposition intact. "I've kept my sense of humor and that's a big help," he said.

The Drennon maneuver came too late to save the machine, for by this time the recall movement had cleared the road for the final drive. Obstructed by illegal interference with recall petitions against individual members of the council, the reform groups decided to seek an amendment of the charter which would shorten the terms of the councilmen from four to two years. This amendment would bring an election early in 1940, at which the citizens could vote to change the entire administration. The charter amendment election was set for February 13 and its approval was confidently forecast. There remained on the calendar only one more tragic occurrence before the next test at the polls.

Mary's Answer

It was left to Mary McElroy to say the last word for the Judge. Late in June of 1939, when she was guarding her father from interviewers and investigators while he lay ill, this comment was attributed to Miss McElroy in an item printed in the *Star:*

You know that during the last few years unusual conditions have prevailed and emergencies have arisen that had to be met. Dad's nature is to meet, not dodge, any situation.

He has done certain things that, technically, can be criticized but he has not done anything that is economically unsound or ethically wrong. All of this will be made clear to the people of Kansas City. In the meantime my greatest concern is for my father's health.

The things that Mary saw in the Judge's vindication have never been made entirely clear but Mary was, none the less, a most eloquent witness for the Judge and her story is remembered whenever there is talk of H. F. McElroy, his work and his time.

Mary McElroy was thirty-one years old in the summer of 1939 when she watched over her father at St. Mary's Hospital, where he went for an operation to remove a cataract from one eye, and at their home at 21 West Fifty-seventh Street, where he lived in a wheel-chair and in bed until his death in September of that year. Miss McElroy had been watching over the Judge throughout most of his thirteen years as city manager. The popular notion was that she was so often in the Judge's company because he wanted to keep her close under his eyes, but the fact is that Mary was as much responsible for this arrangement as her father.

McElroy had two children—Mary and her brother, Henry. The illness and death of their mother placed upon the father the full responsibility for their rearing, and he discharged this task with a rare devotion. Mary was his favorite, his special concern. When she entered young womanhood, Mary made the widowed Judge her exclusive responsibility. McElroy was an indulgent father who allowed his children wide personal freedom. He encouraged Mary to engage in activities outside the home, but she never strayed far or long. She was the Judge's persistent shadow. She went with him to the City Hall to observe Council meetings and followed him when he traveled about town on official business. She stood beside him at dedication ceremonies and when he welcomed important visitors to Kansas City. Her pictures appeared in the newspapers in countless poses at affairs graced by the presence of the City Manager and his daughter. They walked together on Sunday morning strolls, chatting happily and smiling on passersby, some of whom were startled by this rare view of the testy City Manager.

Mary McElroy seemed unsure of herself and never entirely happy when she was out of her father's company. She was a tall, big-boned and rangy girl whose most conspicuous features were her large, generous mouth and her wide, haunted eyes. She had little of her father's arrogance and seemed to be shy and self-conscious even when she was putting on airs. She tried hard to be smart and gay but the pose was painful. She wore bright colors, decorative jewelry, big hats and the newest extremes in style but her plainness was always evident.

The Judge taught Mary to be proud, independent, self-reliant. One of his favorite stories was of the time he let her travel alone to Chicago when she was a young girl. In her excitement she left her purse behind and when the train was under way she discovered that she had no ticket and only twenty-five cents in change. She efficiently explained the situation to the conductor and had him telegraph her father to make the proper arrangements. Arriving in Chicago, she sent her father a gay message telling him she had more fun riding without a ticket than she would have had if she had one. When Mary finished high school the Judge sent her to a college for girls at Rockford, Illinois, where she exhibited the McElroy forcefulness by getting herself elected president of the student body. Her father was elated when he heard that she had challenged the college authorities with her defense of a girl who was about to be expelled for infraction of the rules.

Mary's pride and self-reliance drew their strength from her intense regard for her father, whom she called Old Boy. The few things that she did to win distinction and impress her personality on others were things that accorded with her conception of what was required of Judge McElroy's daughter.

Mary took huge amusement in the tales of the Old Boy's crotchets and tempers and was not disturbed by the popular impression that he was mean, vindictive and tyrannical. She saw that his enemies exploited the incidents when he cracked heads and called names. They remembered the time when he sent a cut-glass bottle full of castor oil to the Republican Police Board in response to a plea for the policemen's wages; when he built a spite fence against a restaurant on Twelfth Street that defied his order to vacate the property for a public project; when he butted a slow automobile in traffic; when he refused to repair the paving on Wornall Road for property owners who wouldn't pay for a new concrete slab he wanted to build; when he harassed J. C. Nichols and the South Siders who obstructed his building program. They didn't talk about the McElroy who stopped his car in traffic downtown to help an old beggar woman across the street, who maintained a soup kitchen on the North Side and gave handouts to many obscure callers at the City Hall, or if they mentioned these things they spoke of them derisively as cheap gestures for political favor. It was easy for a loyal daughter of the City Manager to feel that he was a deliberately misunderstood and unappreciated man. She never doubted that the heads he cracked needed cracking, and no one exhibited more appreciation of the exuberant performance he gave in carrying out the work he was so admirably designed for.

The idea that the Judge was the City Council's Hired Man was a great joke to the McElroys. Their attitude was shown in humorous fashion at the inauguration of 1938 when the Judge was elected city manager for the last time. His name was put in nomination and the Old Boy took the floor to give his acceptance speech, and then paused when he realized that no seconding motion had yet been made and no vote taken. Mary McElroy's soprano was the merriest sound in the gale of laughter that greeted this *faux pas*.

This scene at the City Hall typified the relationship that existed between father and daughter but beneath the girl's acceptance of domination by the powerful individuality of her parent there was a clash of wills, interests and purposes that found expression in Mary's growing restlessness and finally produced a crisis in the bizarre episode of the Mary McElroy kidnaping in May, 1933. That affair had lasting consequences for both of the McElroys but the crime and the chase and capture that followed produced so much excitement that the public obtained only a confused impression of the main effect. The abduction was a matter of political moment, for it demonstrated the inability of the machine to discipline the underworld through Home Rule, but its significance in that respect was entirely secondary. In retrospect, the chief interest is in the mood and spirit of the time as reflected so fantastically in this case. For the people as a whole, it was a vast crime sensation played out in the manner of a B movie. The majority accepted it as an Adventure and a Romance, involving the Judge's daughter and one of her abductors. Only a few saw it as a personal tragedy and a social catastrophe, which it was.

The romantic implications were based on Miss McElroy's successful efforts to save the leader of the kidnap band from hanging and on her frequent visits to prison to call on three of the men who held her captive for thirty hours on May 27 and 28, 1933. Inevitably the popular mind concluded that this interest betokened Love and this legend persisted until it was included in a book which appeared in 1945 under the name of Alan Hynd. That volume, entitled *The Giant Killers,* contained a collection of stories on the exploits of the intelligence men of the Treasury in running down criminals and corrupt politicians. The chapter on Kansas City, called "Dark Metropolis," carried a brief account of the McElroy kidnaping which was notable for the author's interpretation of the love motif. Mr. Hynd went the whole way, even quoting Miss McElroy in a theatrical speech to her father declaring her love for the fascinating bandit chief. Since both of the McElroys were dead by this time, the reader must be grateful to Mr. Hynd for finally revealing a secret which the family divulged to no one else.

Mary McElroy frankly discussed the love rumor with intimate friends, and always insisted it was preposterous. Her disclaimer is good enough for the writer of the present account, who has no disposition to settle the burning love question.

In fairness to the romantic school of crime writers, it must be admitted that the kidnaping was a very unorthodox operation. It had some of the aspects of a game and the victim and her captors established a spirit of camaraderie almost from the beginning. After her first moment of fright, Miss McElroy played her part in a lighthearted manner that disarmed the kidnapers and made them her partisans. There were four men in the gang but two of them remained in their hideaway while the actual abduction was managed by the others, Walter McGee and Clarence Stevens, who gained entrance to the home by posing as delivery-men with a package for Judge McElroy's "little girl." They did not know that she was a big girl of twenty-five, and they hadn't planned to kidnap her until shortly before they invaded the home. Mary's brother, Henry, was originally their intended victim. They waited outside the home for him to appear. After a long watch, they concluded they had missed him and abruptly decided to take his sister instead, and supposed they were dealing with a child.

McGee's deliveryman trick deceived the McElroy cook, Heda Christen-sen, into opening the front door for him. He produced a revolver, an-nounced his mission, and he and Stevens forced Heda Christensen to show them the way upstairs where Miss Elroy was taking a bath. She screamed after she first heard their command but quickly recovered her poise, put on her bath robe and opened the door to face the men calmly. She asked permission to dress in privacy and the kidnapers stood guard outside her room while she dressed in a becoming pink cotton frock, tan hose and white summer shoes. She put on a hat, picked up a pair of gloves and a purse containing seven dollars, and walked from the house with her strange escort. The kidnapers left a message for Judge McElroy with Heda Christensen, notifying him that they would get in touch with him by telephone to arrange ransom negotiations. Their price was sixty thousand dollars, later reduced to thirty thousand dollars.

Seating Miss McElroy on the floor of the rear of their car, the kidnapers drove across the Kansas line to a hideout near Shawnee, less than ten miles from the McElroy home. Mary was chained to the wall of the room in which she was held, with a handcuff on her left wrist. Then she began to get acquainted with the four men who kidnaped her—Wal-ter McGee, twenty-eight years old, leader of the band, his younger brother, George McGee, Clarence Click and Clarence Stevens. She had talked with Walter McGee and Stevens on the drive to the hideout and she found herself among an attentive and talkative company in the house near Shawnee. They brought her clean sheets, an electric light and a radio. They apologized for the service and the food, which they brought her on a large tray. Her prison was a basement garage in a small frame dwelling.

The men called her Mary and she noticed that they had good faces. They smoked cigarettes constantly and drank some in her presence, but their manner was deferential and friendly.

"It would be foolish to say that I felt no fear at all," Mary explained after she was released. "At the same time I felt sure that any one of the four men I saw would have been ready to protect me against any other person or danger. It is because I know that and felt that they were not bad at heart that I would hate to see them sent to the penitentiary. I would fight to keep them from such a fate."

Miss McElroy gave police and reporters a detailed account of her experience, an account that is striking for its revelation of the affinity that immediately developed between the lonely girl from a sheltered home and four men at loose ends—five people who found a common bond of sympathy in the oddity of their lives and this strange situation.

"We talked a good deal," Mary explained. " 'I suppose you hate us,' said the dark one. I told him I felt no malice at all toward them, and understood perfectly how they felt. I really can see their side of it, you know. I even told them I might have done the same thing.

"We talked about prison reform for one thing. One of them told me he was sorry he hadn't finished his medical course. I was sorry, too.

"They told me they could recommend me as a kidnaping subject and before I left they asked me to suggest some prospects for kidnaping. They didn't say which they preferred, men or women. No, I didn't give them any."

The men did some swaggering and boasting to show they were professionals, speaking of the Lindbergh kidnaping as a crank case. The gang leader, Walter McGee—the one who was supposed to have made Miss McElroy's heart flutter—impressed her more with his considerate manners than his swashbuckling charm. Time and circumstances did not permit him to exhibit the romantic attraction which is indicated in his police record. His divorced wife informed authorities that he had won her with his fierceness. When she resisted his advances, he seized her and held a razor blade to her throat and she knew then that it was a case of true love.

In her conversation and statements covering the experience, Mary referred oftener to George McGee than his dynamic brother. George was her guard in the room. She listened sympathetically to the tale of his interrupted medical studies and called him Doctor.

The prisoner had trouble going to sleep in her dungeon. At midnight she sat on her cot listening to the radio which brought in the voice of a girl singing "The End of a Perfect Day." That sweet elegy was followed by a new hit number, "You'll Never Get to Heaven That Way," repeated four times.

She fell asleep at three o'clock in the morning and was awakened at nine o'clock and told to prepare for her release, which followed the payment of thirty thousand dollars ransom. Mary was set free near the entrance of the Milburn Golf Club early in the afternoon of Sunday. She waved goodbye to her friends of the strange Saturday adventure, then walked resolutely to the clubhouse where she identified herself and waited until her father and brother arrived in a motor car for her.

The kidnapers, unaware that she had money in her purse, had given her one dollar to pay her way home. "I forgot to ask them for an address to send the change to," she quipped to a *Star* reporter who interviewed her at her home. A large crowd was waiting at the home, overflowing the yard, and her first comment upon her return was: "If the kidnaping brought all my friends together, it was worth the results."

Three of the kidnapers were quickly rounded up in the furious hunt that followed. Clarence Stevens, who aided Walter McGee in the actual abduction and ransom collection, got away. Quick and hard justice was dealt out to the other three. A muffler was placed on Mary's pleas for the men and everything done to expedite the prosecution, for the organization, the state and the press were after blood. Judge McElroy overcame his daughter's resistance and she went obediently to the stand to tell her story quietly. She was a grave, hollow-eyed figure in the courtroom, a young woman obviously working under a great strain to do what had been impressed upon her as her duty.

Clarence Click, on whose farm she was held a prisoner, was given an eight-year sentence. George McGee, the dark one who wanted to be a doctor, drew a life term in prison. Walter McGee, the daring and considerate one, was sentenced to death. It was the first time that this extreme penalty had been assessed for kidnaping in the United States.

The Judge took Mary on a trip to the West Coast for a vacation and returned with the report that she was greatly improved by the change of scenery. He took her to Europe and they had a grand time together. In Rome, the City Manager complained to the authorities about the racket made by horn-tooting motor car drivers and Mussolini's celebrated decree against careless or excessive honking was said to have resulted from the McElroy protest. In Ireland, where he visited the home scenes of his parents, the Judge told De Valera how he ran American municipal government efficiently. In Dublin, he and Mary were guests at a ceremony arranged by the Lord Mayor. They returned looking refreshed. Mary wore a black shirt and gave the Fascist salute.

At home, other diversions and more trips were arranged for Mary, but she fell into dark moods that alarmed her father. He complained bitterly that the kidnaping had ruined her health but it wasn't her treatment at the hands of the bandits that troubled her. She visited the condemned men in their cells and returned to her father in agitation over the course that the law had taken. When the sentence was upheld in the Supreme Court and the time for Walter McGee's execution approached, her brooding became more intense and brought her to open revolt against the Judge.

She disappeared from her home the night of February 10, 1935, immediately after telling her father good night. She was missed fifteen minutes later but was not found until shortly before noon the next day, when she was taken from a bus at Normal, Illinois. She had boarded a bus at Kansas City with a ticket, twenty cents and a tin of cigarettes, wearing a long fur coat, a smart black hat, gray blouse and long black skirt. She was traced from Springfield, Illinois, where she sent a telegram to her father, saying: "Sorry, but am so frightened. Don't know what I am doing."

Mary returned to Kansas City by plane, accompanied by an uncle. One of her companions in the plane was Conwell Carlson, a *Star* reporter and a personal friend of Miss McElroy's. She talked to him as an old and trusted acquaintance and the story he wrote of their conversation in the clouds was the most moving and illuminating piece of reporting on the McElroy affair in this period.

Why had she made this wild flight?

"To get away," she said. "Not to have to see people and face people who know me as the City Manager's daughter and the girl who was kidnaped by a man who now faces a death sentence, and by two other men sentenced to prison. I guess that was the reason, or at least part of the reason. Did you ever feel as if you just couldn't stand it a minute longer and must do something or go somewhere?"

Mary talked for a few moments with interest about her trip to Europe the previous fall with her father, and the places and things she enjoyed seeing in Italy and England. Yes, that was nice, she told Carlson. She could forget a lot of things there for a while, for a few hours or days. But then the old thoughts came back.

"It was my testimony," she said, "that convicted those men. It was the right thing to do. Their sentences were just and I still believe capital punishment is merited for kidnaping as well as murder. Yet I came to know the McGee brothers and Clarence Click in a sort of way. We talked and kidded together when I was held prisoner. I decided to deal with the situation realistically, then make the best I could of it. I hold no personal hard feelings against them, and I am sure today that they do not hold hard feelings against me. That's what makes the situation all the worse. I have nightmares about those men and the fates they brought on themselves. I was a part of the drama that fixed their destiny."

She was silent a moment and hesitated before answering the next question.

"Have I seen them since the trials? Do I try to forget them? Yes, I have seen them, and no, I cannot forget them. I have visited all of them in person. I have tried to help their relatives. Something drives me to do this. I cannot let them go."

Describing the scene in the plane, Carlson wrote that Miss McElroy turned to look out the plane window, watching the first star appear in the sky that was so blue and cold above the fleecy carpet of clouds. "This was fairyland up here. Yet Mary was curiously unmoved by it. Her thoughts were still on the men in the cells."

Miss McElroy lighted a cigarette, took a few puffs, smiled wanly, and continued:

"We seem to want to live our own lives. Why should I feel boxed up and so useless when there are so many things I might do? I want to be just Mary McElroy, an ordinary girl, and yet here I am attracting more attention to myself by a foolish stunt like this.

"I can't get away from a feeling for the underdog. Did you know that George McGee is taking a high school correspondence course in prison? He's a hotheaded boy but he wasn't the leader of the kidnapers. He once hoped to study medicine, he told me. There was a time, a short time, in Leavenworth, when George was on top. He lived there, you know, but now the poor fellow is way at the bottom of the heap."

When Mary alighted from the plane, pallid and weary, she saw her father and walked quickly to him. They were both under restraint. "Did you have a good flight?" he asked. "Oke doke," said Mary.

. The Judge surrendered then. Two months later he went with Mary to Jefferson City to ask that the life of Walter McGee be spared. The Judge and his daughter were guests of Governor Park at luncheon in the executive mansion. McElroy told the Governor that he believed the law had been vindicated and the execution of McGee would cause Mary more suffering. Miss McElroy stated the case more eloquently in her formal appeal.

"In pleading for Walter McGee's life, I am pleading for my own peace of mind," her statement said.

"Through punishing a guilty man, his victim will be made to suffer equally. He would even have this advantage: He would not have to think about his execution afterwards.

"I do not forget the suffering this has brought in many ways to many people. Walter McGee's death will not erase nor ease the suffering. Rather, I believe the mercy shown him, and the feeling of warmth and hope any act of mercy brings, will serve as a balm to us all."

Miss McElroy argued that McGee's trial was "primarily important as a test case," in which "the State of Missouri was trying to prove the possibility of giving the death sentence for kidnaping. The sentence passed by the jury has been confirmed by the Supreme Court. I believe that the full force of the law has been emphasized and that it is clear that Walter

McGee has no legal means of escaping the gallows. I hope and believe that this has served to warn men like him that kidnaping is a serious and dangerous crime to contemplate."

Governor Park commuted the sentence to life in prison with the declaration that justice should be equal, a principle that had carried less weight with the politicians a few years earlier when Rabbi Mayerberg tried to save the life of Joe Hershon.

Miss McElroy recovered rapidly in both health and spirits, though she was a much more serious young woman than she had been before. She set herself to the task of working for the welfare of her friends in prison, visiting them, sending them gifts, arranging correspondence school studies for them, and planning for the job that Clarence Click would get when he left prison. She did this unostentatiously, trying to avoid attention, but not going about it secretly or apologetically. Once when a reporter questioned her about this work, she said:

"I am not trying to be benevolent. That's such a lofty word. Anyway, it doesn't fit at all. In fact, I am not sure exactly what I am trying to do. I only know I want to help those McGee boys find themselves."

Mary's interest in reform did not extend beyond her efforts to improve the convicts' minds and their opinions of society. Friends who discussed politics with her found her very emphatic in rejecting the suggestion that she entertained any serious criticism of the existing political system and social order. She was thoroughly versed in the conventional argument of the organization and she was a good talker, speaking with the Judge's bluntness and some of his wit. She seemed to have no doubts that the boss system was inevitable and the best thing all around, men and institutions being what they were. If Pendergast didn't exist, some other boss would be in his place, perhaps a much less efficient boss than Pendergast.

It all seemed very simple to her, yet she was deeply troubled and she grew increasingly sensitive to the criticism heaped on her father. Although she effected casualness in discussing the evils of machine government, admitting that many things were wrong, she called them necessary evils and became very vigorous in her answers if anyone indicated any reservations on her father's personal integrity. Her three articles of faith were the Old Boy's honesty, efficiency and vision. She regarded all the building achievements in the Ten-Year-Bond Program as his particular feats. The massive six-million-dollar Municipal Auditorium was his monument for the ages.

Mary grew enthusiastic in discussing her father's work to bring the air age to Kansas City and she herself took a hand in the work of making the town air-minded in the period when the municipal air terminal was being developed at Kawsmouth. Some aviation experts complained that the airport site, in the great bend of the Big Muddy where it has its confluence with Kaw, was inadequate as to size and exposed pilots to unnecessary hazards of wind currents and fogs. Other critics protested at the price paid for the land. McElroy ignored all opposition and bulled it through. Perhaps the critics were right but at least two classes of citizens —travelers and rubbernecks—benefited from the McElroy vision or obstinacy. The site he selected places the arriving or departing air passenger within five minutes' ride from the heart of downtown Kansas City. It gives loafers and kibitzers of Kansas City a magnificent daily spectacle to watch.

The best place to watch the airport, and the whole West Bottoms show for that matter, is from the crest of West Bluff, or Quality Hill. Here too the McElroy enterprise is in evidence. One of the last things he did was to arrange for a lookout point, with parking accommodations for numerous cars and a parklike effect, at the highest point on Quality Hill. He was not able to accomplish this without exhibiting some more of the old McElroy temper. He got in a quarrel with a woman who owned a home on the lookout site. She said it was worth more than five thousand dollars and Mac said he wouldn't pay much more than one thousand dollars, for values on Quality Hill have been sadly reduced in the thirty years since Kansas City quality moved out south, leaving their fine old red-brick houses to be occupied by a new class of people who are accustomed to living with decay and ghosts. The quarrel over the house went on for some time, holding up the project, until one day the owner happened by and found the house was gone. It vanished just like that, and no one knew where or why. Just another mystery of the machine days.

However the injured house owner may feel about it, the sitters and watchers get a lot of pleasure out of the civic improvement on her lot. From the lookout they see one of the finest views of the might of industrial America offered anywhere in the land. Judge McElroy had a particular feeling for this scene, which may explain his impatience with the lady with the house and lot. It is said that he decided to make Kansas City his home after sampling the view from Quality Hill, for it combines industrial and pastoral effects to a rare degree, certain to appeal to any man who likes both land and machines. The construction of the airport in the Missouri bend on the North Kansas City side of the river unquestionably added something to the view from the bluffs, where people have been sitting for a century watching a large part of the history of the West roll by.

Mary had numerous instances like the airport deal to justify her faith in her father as a doer, a builder, who resorted to ruthless tactics to get things done for the town he loved. She completely accepted his businessman's creed as the only realistic one for the time and place—she was a great realist, as were all the people she knew and respected. Her father's idea of social usefulness was having something to sell. His job was selling boss government and, in his daughter's opinion, the results justified the means. She gloried in the fact that he operated openly for the organization. He was no hypocrite.

Not in so many words but in essence, Mary said that the town was corrupt, the machine vicious, everybody was on the make, life was mean but the Old Boy was as straight as a string—the only good man in a lousy world.

Her sympathies were plainly with the oppressed and the misfit, but she believed that the only practical way to help was through individual kindness. She continued her work for the three men in prison in the few years that remained of the McElroy regime after Walter McGee's life was saved. This interest could not completely occupy her and she filled in the time with civic activities, with work for the Philharmonic orchestra and social doings. She attempted to join in the standard pleasures of the period, going to cocktail parties, being seen in the night spots. She was a solemn, detached figure in the crowds except in rare intervals of animation. She narrowed the circle of her intimates. She was seen frequently with a male escort but seemed to be avoiding the company of women.

She had entered spinsterhood and there was no one man for her.

When the crash came and the Judge went home to die, Mary was his nurse and constant companion. She politely but firmly turned away officials and newspapermen who wanted to bother him about records and city affairs. She was seen outside the house infrequently. A month before the Judge died, when the recall movement was gathering momentum, a practical joker called at the McElroy home with a recall petition and asked Mary to sign it. She invited him in, explained that she believed the people were entitled to express their preference in this way, and signed the paper.

After her father died, she took a trip to the South for rest and sunshine. When she returned she looked tanned and fit but found loneliness and unhappiness waiting for her. She seldom left the house except for errands and for brief appearances among her father's old friends, when she tried to show that she was not impressed or disturbed by the disclosures that impeached the integrity of the Old Boy. Neighbors who caught glimpses of her were startled by the misery in her face and eyes.

In January, 1940, she made an effort to shake off her depression. On Saturday, January 20, she decided to have a few friends in for the evening. The ones she called had made other arrangements and expressed their regrets. Mary decided to have her party alone. She fixed herself a drink and some food and sat down in the sunroom to read. It was a cold night, with a moaning north wind bringing two below zero. Some time in the early morning watch Mary got a pistol and shot herself. There was no one else in the house except the maid, and Mary's body was not found until late Sunday morning. The news of her death overshadowed for a day the accounts of trials for various figures in the boss regime and reports of progress in the campaign for the charter amendment election three weeks away.

Perhaps no one knew more of the sickness and hollowness of her time, and no one uttered a more anguished protest than the one contained in this brief note she left:

My four kidnapers are probably the only people on earth who don't consider me an utter fool.

You have your death penalty now—so—please—give them a chance.

MARY McELROY.

Vox Populi

Since the Tom story entered its final period, various other types besides politicians have been competing for attention. Preachers, club ladies, businessmen, newspaper editors and collegians have stepped into the picture for brief but sometimes important appearances. There were others representing different elements of the population. In fact, the agitation was so widespread and profound that it produced a new political consciousness in the whole population which may prove to be the most significant long-range result of the disturbances of the 1930's.

At intervals throughout this period, the citizens were reminded that the Kansas City storm was not entirely a local phenomenon but rather an acute manifestation of the universal disorder. They were, however, fairly successful in discouraging agitators who sought to interest them in broader reform than the suppression of Tom Pendergast.

A notable illustration of the attitude toward radicals in Kansas City's upper circles was given in the case of Tom Benton, the celebrated muralist, whose demonstration that art constitutes a threat to social stability provided a long and exciting distraction in the final years of machine rule. Thomas Hart Benton, a native Missourian, came to Kansas City to make his home in 1935, after many years of wandering, including long stays on the Left Bank of Paris and in New York's Greenwich Village. He had associated with almost every known variety of revolutionary, and although he quarreled bitterly with Communists, he boldly identified himself as a collectivist just before leaving New York to get acquainted with the rugged individualists of the Kansas City Chamber of Commerce.

Mr. Benton came to Kansas City to be head of the painting department in the Kansas City Art Institute but he left the East partly because of a political objection and returned to his home state with a political hope. In an interview in St. Louis, on his way west, he said:

"I'm sick of New York. It's full of talking, radical 'intellectuals.' I say talking because they never do anything else. This part of the country is going to dominate the coming social change and I desire to be here to see what happens, not just to hear about it. The Middle West is going to dominate because you've got the manpower, the votes and you raise the groceries for the remainder of the country."

Mr. Benton, son of a Missouri Democrat who had served in Congress, obviously was eager for political action and he got it in the next two years with the magnificent mural he painted on the walls of the Missouri Capitol in Jefferson City, a commission for which the Democratic-controlled General Assembly appropriated sixteen thousand dollars in an unguarded moment.

The artist at this time was in his late forties, a pint-sized figure with a large head, tousled hair, a weathered, seamed face that was shaped for ribald laughter, and a squirrel-hunter's eyes. He had the spirit if not the bulk of his illustrious grand-uncle and namesake, Missouri's first senator. There is a legend that the Senator kept himself in fighting trim by having his Negro servant curry or rub him down with a horse brush every morning, and he stirred things up for a half-century and more with his duels and debates. Artist Benton played the harmonica and smiled often, but he agitated the Missourians with his brush, his pen and his voice, for he had talent as a writer as well as a painter.

On the walls of the Missouri Capitol, in vivid colors, remarkable technical detail and dynamic form, he painted the whole Missouri story as it had never been presented before. Here was the Missouri of Daniel Boone, the pony express, prairie schooner, stage coach and steamboat, of the turkey shoot and the courthouse square, of prairie and woodland. This was the Missouri of Mark Twain and Tom Pendergast, the border state, Mother of the West, scene of constant commotion, strife and much misery along with the adventure. Here were Huck Finn, Nigger Jim, Jesse James and his boys in a train robbery, a plantation overseer whipping a slave, an Indian being rooked by a white trader, brother murderously pursuing brother in the border wars, the Mormons being driven from Independence with fire and club by their intolerant neighbors. And here was the Missouri of the cities, the brothels and the honky-tonks, Frankie and Johnny, the industrial smokes rising from the Bottoms, the hardfaced tradesmen, the figure of Boss Pendergast, in the foreground, seated in a chair on a platform and next to him the rump of a prominent local Babbitt.

The guardians of the sacred fiction that everything is lovely under the established order traveled to the Capitol, took one look at the mural and left in shudders. Former Senator James A. Reed gave it a hurried examination and said: "Now I am going home and pray for the soul of Michelangelo." A demand arose that the mural be obliterated and Tom Benton be fired from his post in the Art Institute. The fight reached its height in Kansas City with a cleaning and dyeing man and a realtor, Thomas Dods and Howard Huselton, leading the opposition. These veterans of the stereopticon school of art carried their campaign before businessmen's associations, and Benton personally entered the argument, making a forceful statement for an art that portrayed the true and important facts of life regardless of their effect on the political thinking of the people. He did not bother to defend himself against the charge that he was lacking in Missouri patriotism. He asserted that he had a large interest but no vainglory in his native state. Asked to explain why he painted Jesse James rather than General Pershing, both native Missourians, he said:

"In the development of Missouri, General Pershing was not as important as an ordinary old bucksaw and my granduncle, Senator Benton, was of less importance than a common Missouri mule."

Fresh fuel was added to the controversy after Realtor Huselton read Benton's newly published autobiography, *An Artist in America*. Wielding a red pencil, Huselton underlined passages in the book which he denounced as "sensual, gross, profane and vulgar," and this narrow view of a rich piece of literature found wide support. The Art Institute Board seriously considered Huselton's demand that it refuse to renew Benton's contract in 1938, an action that was announced in the press but later reversed.

But Tom Benton continued to irritate the important people with his paintings, his talk and his ideas. His "Susanna and The Elders," acclaimed by art critics, brought an outcry from the opponents of nudity. South side tempers were ruffled by an incident at a Beaux Arts Ball sponsored by the Institute, when Benton and two of his noted compatriots, Grant Wood of Iowa and John Steuart Curry of Kansas, were named as judges to select the prize-winning costumes. Under Tom's guidance, they offended the dowagers' sense of pure art by awarding the women's first prize to a harem dancer in a few green beads and the men's first prize—a case of whisky—to a guy dressed in the lower half of a pair of pajamas, representing a eunuch.

Benton brought the fight on himself to a head in 1941 with his agitation against what he called the conventional or effete administration of art museums. He provoked a crisis on a visit to New York City, when he aired his views over a bottle while surrounded by appreciative newspapermen. They quoted him in interviews which provoked angry sounds back in Kansas City. Mr. Benton declared he was opposed to art museums and wanted to sell his stuff to "saloons, bawdy houses, Kiwanis and Rotary Clubs and Chambers of Commerce—even women's clubs." He described a typical museum as a graveyard run by "a pretty boy with delicate wrists and a swing in his gait." The Art Institute Board decided he had overstepped the bounds of propriety, Tom lost his job and his students picketed in futile protest. He decided to stay on in Kansas City but the citizens thereafter heard little from him, and their conservative leaders encouraged them to forget that one of the nation's foremost artists and clearest social minds resided in their midst.

Another interesting disturber of the public peace in this period was Dr. Logan Clendening, who represented both the medical and literary professions. Unlike Artist Benton, he was not an agitator by nature and he was drawn into the political struggle against his will, performing in a fashion that made the Clendening affair a semicomical or poignant matter. However, the incident was important, as it revealed the depth of the disturbance among people who had long supposed that they had nothing to do with politics and it actually served as the tip-off of the campaign which reached its climax in 1940 with the downing of the Democratic organization.

Dr. Clendening, Kansas City's famous columnist doctor, was a man of civilized pursuits, opposed to athletics, politics and anything else that interfered with eating, drinking and laughter. After writing his popular book, *The Human Body,* he kept up literary labor in a syndicated column for newspapers while continuing his work as a teacher in the University of Kansas Medical School. As a columnist, Dr. Clendening was primarily concerned with man's wonderful capacity to enjoy good food, and he devoted more attention to the nuances of the burp and the marvels of the alimentary canal than he did to the latest medical discoveries. He was chary with advice on how people should regulate their lives, and his only crusading was done against the American sport of football.

To a rare degree, Logan Clendening exemplified the common and soundly based notion that political activities and interests were unnatural and degrading tendencies. He lived among the rich Republicans on the South Side, but his was a free spirit and a bold mind, and he thought that by standing aloof he could do his bit to discourage the whole miserable enterprise of organizing humanity into factions, parties, blocs and denominations. But the political interference pursued him with relentless logic and finally set up a stand outside the window of his large home at Fifty-sixth Street and State Line. It broke in upon his studies in the form of the State Line sewer project which City Manager McElroy had ordered over the protests of the homeowners and without formal Council authorization. For four months the WPA workmen had been engaged in this project, tearing up the pavement and boring in the earth with drills. For days Dr. Clendening listened to the clatter of the air compressor operating the drill outside his home. The machine became a hammer beating on his mind, giving him no peace from the political problem.

Dr. Clendening's irritation over the drill was no exceptional thing and the issue it represented was no small matter. It was an incident in a struggle that had been going on several years between the South Side and the McElroy administration. Considerable commotion had been created earlier by the Brush Creek and Brookside sewer projects, which South Siders protested as being unnecessarily elaborate and expensive, and declared they were designed primarily to make profitable business for Pendergast concrete and the Boss's contractor associates, Boyle and Pryor. This difference produced a personal feud between Judge McElroy and Jesse Clyde Nichols, champion of the South Side and builder of the Country Club residential district. The crusty Judge threatened to build a viaduct over the Country Club Plaza to spite Mr. Nichols and for a time the quarrel was diverting to the onlookers, for the common man found it difficult to choose between Judge McElroy and J. C. Nichols, and many did not realize the deep significance of this struggle.

The contest reached a crisis over the State Line sewer in February, 1939, when Dr. Clendening decided he could stand the drill no longer. He called City Manager McElroy and the Pryor Construction Company to protest. Denied relief in these quarters, he walked a long block to the home of Boss Pendergast and spent a half-hour on the steps and the ground of the home vainly trying to attract attention. By this time he was ready for more direct action, moving with the speed and in the same mood of another victim of machine oppression who had created a furor at the City Hall some time before this. That other agitator was the wife of a city fireman, who called on Judge McElroy to protest his actions in cutting the wages and breaking up the union of the firemen. Armed with a leather whip, she was swinging lustily on the Judge when his attendants went to the rescue. They attempted to explain the woman's action by charging that she was intoxicated, and she admitted that she had had a nickel beer, which was all she could afford on her husband's salary of $67 a month.

Fortified with something better than beer, Dr. Clendening obtained an ax, concealed it under his coat and started toward the offending air compressor. The WPA workmen paused to watch the agitated approach of his portly figure, attired in a dark suit with a flower in lapel and wearing a Homburg. While the startled workmen looked on, Dr. Clendening silenced the drill with lusty blows of his ax. He was booked at a police station for intoxication, destruction of federal property and disturbing the peace. He amused himself in a cell for four hours, singing songs, reciting from Shakespeare and behaving like the Pickwickian that he was. Released on bond, he later paid a fifty dollar fine on two counts and the intoxication charge was dropped.

Of all the blows struck by an individual against political oppression in this time, the Clendening protest was by all odds the most disquieting. In the revolt that became general several weeks after the doctor staged his march, the State Line sewer was closed down for good, along with a lot of other things. Dr. Clendening found that he had made himself a hero of the reform, but he wanted no more of the political life, and retired to the background while the conflict ran its course. In the intolerable days of the global struggle he declined in health and spirits until he came upon complete despair, when he removed himself from this politicians' world by committing suicide.

In the campaigns of February and April, 1940, which ousted the Democrats and brought in the Nonpartisan regime, the South Side realized its supreme political moment. This was a victory in which the whole city participated but the leadership, the passion, the spade work and the big majorities came principally from the Eighth Ward, the section where the economically and socially important people were concentrated.

The actual management was handled through the *Star* and the businessmen. The paper had established itself as the organ or the antimachine movement by its action in the Mayerberg, New Youth, Fusion and Coalition struggles of 1932, '34 and '36. It was in the position and it had the initiative to fill the vacuum created by the fall of Pendergast in April of nineteen hundred and thirty-nine. In two editorials published in that month, entitled "Forward Kansas City" and "Opportunity," the *Star* provided the name and the idea for the organization that actually ruled Kansas City in the brief Smith interim period. That was followed quickly by the formation of the Forward Kansas City Committee under the leadership of R. J. DeMotte, president of the Chamber of Commerce; Vincent O'Flaherty, Jr., president of the Real Estate Board; W. T. Grant, insurance executive, and J. W. Perry, a retired banker. The *Star* had called for a businessman's organization to guide Mayor Smith and the council in this emergency and, with the old bosses on the run, the executives hurried to take over all the key spots. The Executive Committee of the Forwards was composed of Perry and Grant, Republicans, O'Flaherty, Robert L. Mehornay and Robert B. Caldwell, Democrats. Banker Perry was made chairman.

The size of the businessmen's revolt was shown when the Forward Committee expanded its membership to 339, its list being a roster of financially important names, both Republican and Democratic.

Conspicuously missing from the list of Forward subcommittees was one for labor.

There was such an amplitude of opposition by this time that the Forwards faced a large problem in amalgamating the various groups. In addition to the businessmen's own committee, these included the Republican organization, two independent Democratic outfits, the Ministerial Alliance and the Charter Party, headed by Hal W. Luhnow, director of the enterprises owned by the city's leading philanthropist, William Volker. They were all brought together, under the name of the United Cam-

S. J. Ray in The Kansas City Star

Only the First Round

Celebrating the results of the Charter Amendment election of February 13, 1940, which foretold the cleanup victory of April 2.

paign, for the charter amendment election in February and the election of new city officers in April.

The Democratic organization made only a modest effort to defeat the charter amendment, which cut the councilmen's terms from four to two years and thus served the purpose of a recall by bringing the next election in April. The boys at the City Hall had shown immense resourcefulness in blocking the original recall petitions, employing such devices as having councilmen resign and appointing successors who, under the law, weren't subject to recall for six months. Recall petitions mysteriously disappeared at the City Hall and other things happened to them. When the recallers wearied of this contest and turned to the charter amendment device, the Democrats contented themselves with offering four other amendments to confuse the voters. The citizens were not misled, voting 95,683 to 17,316 for Amendment No. 1 and rejecting the others.

Squaring away for the final test, the United Campaign people named a ticket composed of five Democrats and four Republicans for the Council places, headed by John B. Gage, Democratic lawyer and cattle raiser, who served as mayor of Kansas City for three successive terms. Among the successful Council candidates was Joseph C. Fennelly, leader of N.Y.M. in the 1934 battle. This bipartisan group took its stand on a nonpartisan platform, a point of higher strategy and political philosophy which has been fiercely debated for six years. There are many arguments for the nonpartisan approach, but the only practical one seems to be that it provides a cloak for the bipartisan character of the ticket, divesting the candidates of their proper party labels and confusing some voters as to how many Republicans are on the ticket. Under this device, the Republicans have regularly taken four out of nine places, which may be more than they would get under honest proportional representation based on actual voting strength if the situation were one that permitted a straight test between the two major parties, which it isn't. In other words, a way had to be found to weld the rump Democrats and the Republicans in the only combination that seemed capable of challenging the Democratic organization, and the nonpartisan fiction effectively served that purpose, but it took a powerful lot of propaganda from the *Star* to make it stick.

The regular Democrats used the nonpartisan trick as one of their chief talking points in the 1940 campaign, warning that nothing but trouble would come from "the political monstrosity of nonpartisanship . . . a political will-o'-the-wisp, which in the past had led only to political extinction."

For their main argument, the assault on the *Star,* the Democrats called out their ablest orators, who warned that if this battle was lost, "then Democrats of this city must recognize that no Democrat can hereafter be elected to office without the apostolic blessing of the *Kansas City Star.*" Women were reminded that if the Nonpartisans won, then none of their husbands could rise to office "without the benediction of the *Kansas City Star.*"

Uncle Joe Shannon, in the tenth year of his service in Congress, returned from Washington to assist the salvaging effort, and the touch of his smooth hand was discernible in the strategy that followed. He did not, however, take a position up front in the speaking and he was a rather bemused figure in the midst of the storm. He looked in on some of the United Campaign rallies, watching, listening, smiling benevolently on all.

Congressman Shannon was particularly interested in the United Campaign's women, for they were the sensation of the election melodrama, introducing a refinement that was completely bewildering to veteran wardheelers. Among those responsible for this innovation was former Senator Reed, ex-champion of the Goats but a hero of the Republicans since his bolt from the Roosevelt ticket in 1936, which he repeated in 1940. Appearing publicly at one of the Forward Kansas City Committee rallies, he drew cheers with a call for a cleanup and a suggestion that the women be given a large role in this campaign. Three women were admitted to the inner council of the Forward Committee and the special division they organized for the campaign included an estimated six thousand ward and precinct workers. They adopted the broom as their symbol and wore it with great style. Their leaders were the darlings of the *Star* and the South Side.

Heading the women's division was Mrs. George H. Gorton, credited by the Nonpartisans with being one of their foremost vote getters. Her main assistants were Mrs. Williston P. Munger, head of the finance committee, Mrs. Russell C. Comer, chairman of the Charter Party women, and Mrs. Louise Stewart, vice-chairman of the Republican County Committee. Mrs. Munger praised Mrs. Gorton for "her sure-footed wisdom and capacity for facing dark facts." Mrs. Gorton called Mrs. Comer "a lovable little dynamo" and praised all of her lieutenants. They were all extremely efficient and the men looked on in admiration mixed with some trepidation.

Mrs. Gorton grew angry over a Democratic pamphlet libeling the United ladies as "pinknailed, cocktail-drinking, cigarette-smoking South Siders." She singled out Uncle Joe Shannon at a noonday rally in the women's headquarters to assure him that she was a true Democrat from Alabama. This Alabamy Democrat campaigned vigorously against Roosevelt in the fall of that same year but in April her nonpartisan appeal won thousands of votes, with her assistants manning 4,500 telephones and driving 5,000 motor cars to carry citizens to the polls.

The returns showed 94,192 for John B. Gage for mayor, 74,033 for his Democratic rival, a majority of 20,159. The United ticket carried seven of the other eight Council places, the Democrats retaining control in the First District, the old river ward precincts where Alderman Jim Pendergast had started all this.

The victory celebration reached its height in the women's headquarters, where a crowd of 1,500 excited partisans were packed like sardines. A band struck up, "Happy Days Are Here Again." Somebody started a cakewalk and the throng joined in.

Mrs. Gorton shouted to make herself heard above the clamor.

"Tea?" she cried. "We aren't going to serve tea. It's going to be punch, fruit punch, with a brass band."

Thus Good Government came to Kansas City.

THE PUBLIC PEACE

THE LORD works in mysterious ways and one of the larger reforms in Kansas City was well advanced even before Mayor Gage and his bipartisan Nonpartisans took over the City Hall. In fact, this particular clean-up was so far along that it had produced a major reaction, creating a crisis for the new administration in the first years of Nonpartisan rule.

This political disturbance was the work of Lear B. Reed, G-man, Minute Man, author and hero of the book *Human Wolves,* who became police chief of Kansas City in July, 1939. Mr. Reed combined in his person the more formidable characteristics of Fearless Fosdick and Paul Revere, and he was equally energetic in efforts to save Kansas City from criminals and the nation from Reds, whom he regarded as much more of a threat to America than the British Redcoats ever were.

A crusader of Chief Reed's range and temperament was bound to kick up a row in any community, but the situation in Kansas City was one that enabled him to get the maximum effect. He reformed, intimidated, irritated or angered so many different kinds of citizens that he distracted attention from other important phases of the new order in town. Besides suppressing criminals and scattering Reds, he antagonized workingmen and union officials, Negroes, liberals and a wide variety of ordinary individuals who began to wonder if democracy could stand the strain of absolute rectitude.

Chief Reed was drafted from the Federal Bureau of Investigation by the new Police Board that Governor Stark appointed at the end of Home Rule, and his particular sponsor was the Board chairman, Edgar Shook, lawyer and one of the South Side's early champions in the fight on the Pendergast organization. Reed had served in the F.B.I. fourteen years and was familiar with the Kansas City situation from many assignments in this area.

When he became the Kansas City police chief he was thirty-nine years old, in the prime of phenomenal vigor. He wore eyeglasses which didn't make him look studious, for he had been a two-hundred-pound tackle at Richmond University and grew more athletic with age. A native of Georgia, he spoke with a Southern accent which didn't sound like a drawl. His heroes were J. Edgar Hoover and the F.B.I., to whom he devoted a glowing chapter in *Human Wolves,* the breathless narrative of his adventures as G-man and police chief. When he was not preoccupied with the organizational details and laboratory work of modern scientific investigation, he was out in the field charging around in a manner that would have impressed the Revolutionary hero who aroused the Minute Men.

Before his first month in office elapsed, Chief Reed staged his most spectacular performance in crime suppression. He summoned to his office Big Charley Carollo, the collector of the gambling syndicate, and enforced the invitation with the kind of threat that Carollo understood. This unnaturalized Italian gangster was soon to be sentenced to Federal prison but before he departed he spent thirty minutes in the intimidating presence of Chief Reed. Carollo was informed that his days of dictating to the police were over.

Whether Carollo was more discouraged by the Reed talk than the Federal sentences is a question that has never been settled but the available evidence is that he was properly impressed with the forcefulness of the new chief. Lear Reed himself gave the press a dramatic account of his effect on the big gangster. He described how his powerful eyes bored in while he told Big Charley that he would engage a hundred ex-marines if necessary to work on the gangsters and that he would throw the entire mob into jail for twenty-four hours if they didn't show the right respect for cops.

"If it's necessary to bring your kind in on a slab, that's the way we will do it," Chief Reed said that he said.

Big Charley Carollo withdrew into the North Side background until he left for prison, Chief Reed turned to other work and the Kansas City cleanup began to attract national attention, with Chief Reed serving as his most efficient press agent. He wrote chiefs in other cities telling them of the change in his territory. "The underworld here has been getting a cleanup the like of which it never dreamed," he explained.

The Reed crusade ran on for two years, giving conclusive proof of two important points: One, that police provide a higher degree of public safety when they are fighting against rather than working with the underworld. Two, it is impossible to deal adequately or permanently with the police problem by using authoritarian methods in an American community. The demonstration on the second point filled the Lear Reed episode with political controversy. Labor representatives and Negroes protested against some of the police methods. Reed's Red hunt provoked wide agitation. He set up a file of subversive activity reports and started a campaign for the wholesale fingerprinting of private citizens. Labor unions stormed that their members and organizers were being forced to give their prints in violation of their civil rights. They filed suits and called on the Police Board to stop the fingerprint practice. One of Reed's main supporters, the *Star,* warned that the crusade was going too far when the Chief ran a Communist speaker and his wife out of town, and again when Reed sought to organize a semi-military "civil defense" organization allied with the police.

Chief Reed remained under fire from Kansas City's Negro community, an agitation that extended over many months. The chief regarded himself as a great friend of the colored man, remarking once that he knew precisely how Abraham Lincoln felt when he first saw the slaves on his trip down the Mississippi River. The Negroes were unable to see evidences of this attitude in the measures Reed's police took to keep order on Vine Street and in other parts of the Negro quarter. Their indignation flared high over the slaying of a colored man by a police officer in a night club and several other violent incidents. They carried their case to the Missouri governor, a Republican who had succeeded Lloyd Stark, listing eighteen instances of alleged police brutality against Negro citizens.

It is possible that Reed might have weathered these storms, or at least have delayed his leave-taking, if he had not muffed the investigation of the principal crime that occurred in his two-year reign—a murder mystery that involved one of the most gruesome crimes in Kansas City annals, and one that had sharp political repercussions. This was the slaying of Leila Welsh, twenty-four years old, granddaughter of a well-to-do pioneer Kansas City realtor, an heiress and a popular and attractive young woman who had been a beauty queen at the University of Kansas City a few years before her death. She was slain in her home in the dark hours of a Sunday morning in March, 1941, not long after she returned at 1:30 A.M. with her escort, Richard Funk, with whom she had been keeping company for five years. After bidding Funk goodnight, she stopped in the bedroom of her mother, Mrs. Marie Welsh, for a brief talk. Her brother, George Welsh, twenty-seven years old, was dozing on the davenport in the front room in their one-and-a-half-story bungalow at 6109 Rockhill Road, and she passed him on the way to her rear bedroom. She was brutally murdered in bed not long after she retired, but her body was not discovered until after nine o'clock Sunday morning. Her mother told the police that she entered Miss Welsh's room to close the bedroom window which her daughter always left open at night, and had crossed to the window before she noticed that anything was wrong. The brother, George, was not in the house then, having arisen earlier and gone to keep an appointment with people who were looking over a house for which he was agent.

The city was terrorized by the ghastly nature of this murder in the center of one of the town's most respectable residential areas. Leila Welsh's head was bashed in with a hammer, her throat cut with a knife and a piece of flesh was cut from her hip. The missing piece was later found in the yard of a neighbor, where it was picked up by a dog. There was a confusing plenitude of clues inside the girl's room and outside the first floor window through which the killer apparently had entered. The knife, the hammer and a blood-stained pair of cotton gloves, among other things, were found. The knife was traced to the dealer who sold it and he described and identified the young man who bought it. The man who sold the hammer was found but his description of the buyer did not tally with the description of the knife purchaser except in one detail, and he was unable to identify the suspect picked out by the trades-man who sold the knife. Fingerprints were found on the windowsill of Leila's bedroom which matched the prints of George Welsh. He stoutly denied any knowledge of the crime and conducted himself coolly throughout the investigation. His mother expressed absolute confidence in him and all the evidence made public indicated that a bond of rare affection existed between brother and sister.

Along with the bewildering array of clues, the police were bothered by the number of people who wanted to confess the murder but couldn't establish their claims, together with the advice of psychiatrists and a series of letters from cranks, including a thirty-seven-page "Complete Solution of the Welsh Case." Chief Reed took complete charge of the investigation and his performance was distinguished by his quarrels with the Democratic sheriff and county prosecutor's office, who tried to horn in on the inquiry, and by his series of announcements that the mystery was about to be solved or was virtually solved. His most interesting contribution to public enlightenment was his discovery that the killer had spelled out an initial in blood on one of the victim's legs. The Chief regarded this as the murderer's calling card, marking him as an egotistical type, but the clue yielded nothing more than some fancy Hawkshaw speculation.

Partisan differences over the case continued for some time after Reed quit as police chief, and the mystery was hopelessly involved in the dispute. A grand jury called by Circuit Judge Marion D. Waltner indicted George Welsh for the murder and issued a sensational report on Reed's alleged conduct of the original investigation, charging, among other things, that the chief had positive identification of George as purchaser of the knife thirteen days after the crime. The indictment of Welsh was set aside by Circuit Judge Emory H. Wright, who upheld a defense plea in abatement and declared that the grand jury's actions in interviewing witnesses outside the jury room, employment of detectives and use of county funds by jurors in carrying on their investigation were violations of the statutes. Welsh later was brought to trial on a murder charge filed by the county's prosecuting attorney and was acquitted by the jury that tried him.

Chief Reed resigned in August, 1941, to take a job in Chicago, stepping out of office at a moment when the sounds of derision from unregenerate Twelfth Street, the protests of Negro delegations to Jefferson City and criticism from other quarters were giving the Nonpartisan politicians chills over the future of the reform.

After his departure, the Police Board picked as Reed's successor Harold Anderson, a Reed man who had exhibited an engaging personality and pleasant voice as leader of the police quartet. While the politicians watched to see if adequate law enforcement could not be had in a more routine manner, the citizens were permitted to look around and study some of the other things that the Nonpartisan reform was accomplishing.

Good Government

THE LADIES with the brooms, their leaders and admirers generated so much enthusiasm that six years later their movement was still going strong, at the end of which time they had triumphed over the Democratic opposition in three more elections. So much attention has been attracted by the success of the Nonpartisans in municipal administration and political campaigning that insufficient notice has been given to the comeback efforts of the Goats and the Rabbits under the command of the old bosses' successors, Jimmy Pendergast and Frank Shannon.

With Tom Pendergast forcibly restrained from participation in politics and Joe Shannon removed by his death in 1943, many observers proclaimed that an era had ended and confidently looked for the speedy disappearance of the old Democratic factions as they existed and operated in the heyday of Tom and Joe. They were, in fact, demoralized, but the retreat was neither so extensive nor so fast as was generally supposed.

However, the proclaimers of a new era had much more than the rout of the old organization to support them in the impression that the Kansas City reform was permanent. Changes that have been effected in these few years are so extensive that a whole book could very well be devoted to the new development. National attention has been called to the Nonpartisan experiment in newspapers and magazines during this period, but nothing like an adequate appraisal has yet been made. The change already has endured longer and accomplished more than any similar effort in the past. It is certain to have lasting effects and is likely to continue in its present form for some time, even though it is not yet clear that there will be no important political interruptions before the decade of 1940 runs out.

One distinguishing feature of the Nonpartisan administration is that it is a businessman's government, just as surely as the McElroy regime was a businessman's government during a large part of that enterprise. This aspect of the Kansas City change is perhaps most striking when it is compared to earlier reform efforts. In his investigations of the battles against the great city machines of forty and fifty years ago, Lincoln Steffens found that the do-gooders invariably encountered major resistance from the dominant economic interests, and that the machine in fact was the instrument of the business community, leading to the conclusion that private economic interests by their very nature required corrupt politics. Another Steffens is needed to study the implications of the Kansas City crusade in which the economic powers took over the reform at the last and made it their own, doing the things that have made possible its consolidation.

On the score of administration the Nonpartisan scheme has thus far justified all the hopes of old Colonel Nelson, the *Star* editors, Walter Matscheck and others who campaigned so long for this innovation in

municipal government. Achievements to date have been confined mostly
to improvement in the routine services, but there has been a gain all
along the line, a change that has been large in some departments such
as financial management, personnel and social welfare and recreation.
Along with a broadening conception of the government's functions in a
modern city there has been elaborate planning for well-rounded development of the civic plant. The war interrupted construction, but the city
now is on the threshold of the greatest civic undertaking in its history,
combining a large public building program with extension in regular city
services. How well this is promoted and carried out by the present occupants of the City Hall will have a large bearing on the length of their
tenure.

Whatever comes, even if the Nonpartisans should be replaced at the
next election in 1948, the city may count some permanent gain from the
changes made and the new methods and techniques introduced. A new
administration would be slow in abolishing many of the things that have
brought so much luster to the Nonpartisans. That an important part of
the business community will fight hard to prevent a change may be
safely predicted on the basis of the dollars-and-cents record of the reform.
Increased efficiency under the direction of City Manager L. P. Cookingham has enabled the administration to reduce the size of the payroll and
effect other economies, to increase wages, to retire many of the obligations
left by the last regime, to place the city on a sound financial basis, to cut
the tax rate on real and personal property and lower real estate tax
valuations by $30,000,000, and to create a large surplus. The change in
the financial picture was humorously illustrated in the last campaign
when the Democratic opposition had to make an issue over the surplus,
accusing the city government of hoarding, a departure from the old cry
over deficits which didn't make any votes for the outs.

The present city administration closed the 1946 fiscal year with the
statement that Kansas City was better off by $22,000,000 than it was six
years ago. Among the achievements listed in the report were permanent
improvements costing $9,125,527; a reduction of $6,322,054 in the bonded
debt, payment of $1,982,749 on backpay claims and unpaid bills from
the previous administration and a cash surplus of $3,049,300.

Unlike most past reforms, the Nonpartisan movement does not depend entirely on its record in office and its personalities to sustain it. It has no personalities like Golden Rule Jones of Toledo or Tom Johnson of Cleveland. In place of strong individuals who dramatize the reform, the Nonpartisans have a political party, or rather an organization that possesses some of the features of a party. This is called the Citizens Party, and it represents the various groups that were combined in the United Campaign ticket in the 1940 battle that overthrew the Democratic organization.

The history of reform failure is written largely in terms of the inability of the uplifters to form a real political organization or to seize control of one of the regular parties, so the Citizens Party may represent an important forward step. For example, Mayor John B. Gage, who came in with the reform in 1940, was able to retire at the end of his third term without jeopardizing the popular appeal of the Citizens cause, which has been signally successful in not identifying itself with one individual. Gage's place was taken by William E. Kemp, former city counselor, who became the second Citizens mayor of Kansas City.

It is difficult, however, to form a true political party that is confined to activity in the local field, and particularly one that is composed of such disparate elements as the Citizens attract. Internal differences, factional and partisan, keep it from going beyond the local level and create difficulties for it even in this restricted field. It is not a party but a campaign device that brings together the reform or independent Democrats and the Republicans. It is held together chiefly by the businessmen and the *Star,* and, of course, by the women with the brooms. So the Citizens Party is not without some substantial support despite its curious political structure.

This question is now the most important issue in the Kansas City reform and before long there must be an answer, showing whether the Citizens Party has much of a future or whether there has been or is liable to be anything like a regeneration of either or both of the major parties. It may turn out that the Citizens Party and the nonpartisan approach are not an answer to the breakdown in the American political system in the city, but rather a stopgap, and also a symptom of the depth of the political crisis. The Citizens Party has no traditions, no state or national connections and no social philosophy of the kind that gives life and stability to a party. The Nonpartisan organization was brought into being, nourished and enabled to prevail by the corruption and demoralization of the real political parties. Under the American democratic order, the true remedy for the collapse of the political system lies in the reformation and rehabilitation of the Republican and Democratic parties. The nonpartisan idea can be used to obstruct and delay the work of party revitalization, assuming that such a revival in the local field is either feasible or desired by the citizens at this late date. Thus far there has been no broadening of the base of political organization to give a larger voice to other elements of the population besides business, and the significant thing about all this is the small part the public actually plays in the selection of candidates and the formulation of policy.

Because the routine services do represent a large part of municipal administration, the idea grew up that city government is a business operation, largely divorced from policy-making, legislation, social planning and political thinking. The experience of the Kansas City Nonpartisan venture is that the political element is still the chief factor, and will continue to be as long as we have free elections and democratic forms. No reform will be safe for long unless it restores the health of the political parties.

While the Nonpartisan administration has flourished, the Citizens Party gives no indication of becoming anything more than a sterile hybrid. On the other hand, the regular Democrats gave vigorous signs of a revival after a couple of years, suggesting that Jimmy Pendergast and Frank Shannon inherited more political savvy than they were allowed in some circles. Jim seems to be a mild and cautious individual in comparison with his uncle and his father, the pugnacious Tom and Mike, and Frank is regarded as but a small chip off the old Joe Shannon block. Both of the new factional leaders are lawyers. Both like to stay in the background but they have gradually been drawing more attention.

When the smoke cleared from the United Campaign battle of 1940, the Democrats had one Council seat in the City Hall, from the First District, and retained a hold on the Courthouse. The reformers at first made a spirited effort to change the order in the Courthouse and in the county Democratic organization. They made some gains with a new presiding judge, George S. Montgomery, and with the co-operation of Mayor Roger T. Sermon of Independence, personal friend of Harry Truman and leader of the Democratic faction of Eastern Jackson County. The offensive did not achieve its goal, however, and the failure was due to the fact that the Citizens Party could function only in city contests and the reform Democrats had no program, no ticket and no strong party leaders to rally the faithful in the county contests.

Low point for the regular Democrats was reached in the city election of 1942, when the Citizens majority passed beyond thirty thousand and they again captured eight of the nine Council seats. It appeared then that the old organization might break up into various small factions, with Pendergast being eclipsed in importance by ward leaders who had acknowledged Uncle Tom's leadership but couldn't be held in line by Jim. The decline in relative voting strength was arrested by the Democrats in the city election of 1944, and in the August primaries of that year, the Pendergast leadership was reasserted in the county organization in the election of committeemen, as well as strengthened in the Courthouse through the selection of successful candidates for county offices. Jim Pendergast's prestige was further increased by the nomination of a candidate for governor who had the indorsement of his faction and against whom the old boss-control issue was vigorously raised by the *Star*. In the primary he eliminated two rivals who were identified with the Kansas City and Jackson County anti-Pendergast offensive, Edgar Shook and Roger Sermon, and went on to win the final election. Things were looking up for the regulars.

The organization Democrats obviously were waiting for the Citizens amalgamation to fall apart, and they decided the time for this had come in the spring of 1946. The result was the most spirited campaign since 1940. In the last two city campaigns, the Democrats had been beaten each time by the same tactics that won for the coalition in 1940, with the *Star* and the Nonpartisan orators fastening the machine label on the opposition. The Democratic leaders endeavored to overcome this handicap in 1946 by employing a new method of naming the ticket. An advisory committee of twenty-five was appointed, and it named a nominating committee of one hundred which conducted public hearings. This subterfuge did not long prevent the *Star* from crediting selection of the ticket to Pendergast and associates, and again working the old boss bogey to the limit.

In retaliation for the plastering they got with the machine tag, the Democrats went all out with a parade of their favorite bogey—domination by the *Star*. Robert K. Ryland, the Democratic candidate for mayor, railed against the newspaper monopoly and oppression in a colorful manner that was reminiscent of Jim Reed in his early fighting days. He succeeded in reminding everyone that Kansas City now has but one daily newspaper, and convinced all who were not already convinced that the *Star* is the main force in the Citizens combination; but again a majority decided that the Republican newspaper and the Nonpartisan will-o'-the-wisp produced the kind of government they wanted. However, the Democrats picked up one more Council seat, making it two to seven, and reduced the Citizens voting lead sharply outside the rock-ribbed Republican Eighth Ward. Showing the new trend, the Citizens majority of some twenty-four thousand in 1944 was cut to less than twelve thousand in 1946. The Citizens got 49,166 in the light vote in 1944 and 63,780 in 1946; the Democrats polled only 25,135 for the head of their ticket in 1944 but doubled the figure to deliver 51,906 in 1946.

A stronger show of Pendergast power was made in the 1946 congressional primary, when Jim Pendergast complied with President Truman's publicly expressed request to "purge" Congressman Roger C. Slaughter, recalcitrant Democratic representative from the Missouri Fifth District. While this work was being done, Pendergast and his allies swept the field, nominating their candidates for county offices, winning firmer control of the county committee and temporarily burying Frank Shannon, the new Rabbit faction leader, who had backed Congressman Slaughter. Observers were startled at the size of the Democratic vote rolled up on the North Side, recalling the top-heavy majorities of Tom Pendergast's heyday.

The fight gained momentum in the campaign for the November election, turning into something of a revival of forces and personalities that had figured conspicuously in earlier Kansas City politics. Albert L. Reeves, Jr., son of the Federal judge who had presided in many of the sensational court actions of the 1930's, was nominated for Congress on the Republican ticket, and later elected in a campaign that was highlighted by his verbal blasts against the "Pendergast machine." Another familiar name had reappeared in the primary when the Democratic congressional nomination was sought by Jerome Walsh, son of the late Frank P. Walsh, the party agitator of other days. Pursuing his father's liberal line, Jerome Walsh took a strong pro-Roosevelt stand and went down to defeat when the Truman-Pendergast support went to a third and less New Deal-ish man in the race, and the P.A.C. played along with the organization.

Following the primary, the *Star* opened one of its heaviest antimachine offensives, conducting a private investigation of vote frauds in the recent primary that was even more elaborate than the newspaper's ghost hunt of 1936. This inquiry drew the attention of the Federal district attorney, and brought the F.B.I. and agents of a congressional committee into the field. The agitation grew with the formation of a Jackson County Committee for Honest Elections, and with the return to action of Rabbi Samuel S. Mayerberg, leader of the Charter League crusade of 1932. A new element entered the conflict with the organization of a veterans' committee that did effective work for the Republicans.

The general Republican trend of 1946 completed the work, and when the storm cleared, the Jackson County Democrats found they had lost a seat in Congress, two key posts in the Courthouse and a majority of the county delegation in the legislature. It was a severe jolt, and there was much speculative talk of a continued Democratic decline, with the outlook being made darker by the revival of Democratic factional warfare in the primary. However, the size of the Democratic vote and the number of offices retained were impressive in comparison with Democratic performances elsewhere outside the Solid South, and in view of the many depressing factors besides the national G.O.P. trend.

Meanwhile, business goes on at 1908 Main Street. Many things have changed in Kansas City, but the Goats and the Rabbits and the *Star* have not yet ended their long contest and the road to reform still has many strange turns.

THE FINAL STAKES

IN THE FALL of 1944, Tom Pendergast witnessed his last political campaign. He had been out of prison since late in May, 1940, after serving
a year and a day of his fifteen-month sentence, but he was still not entirely a free man under the terms of the rigid five-year probation which
Federal Judge Merrill E. Otis fixed for him. Until May, 1945, he was
prohibited from engaging in any form of political activity, even from
discussing politics or granting interviews. He was not permitted to
go to his old headquarters at 1908 Main Street. And he was under
strict orders to eschew all gambling interests. He reported regularly
to a probation officer and moved in a limited circle between the office
of the Ready-Mixed Concrete Company at Twenty-fifth and Summit
streets and his modified Italian style mansion at 5650 Ward Parkway,
where he lived alone in three of the many rooms in that imposing three-
story affair. Mrs. Pendergast moved away to an apartment in the Country
Club Plaza, and while there was no divorce or legal separation the gossip
was that she had left Uncle Tom because he had broken his promise to
her to give up gambling before the crash in 1939. The retired Goat leader's loneliness was broken by visits from his children and a few cronies,
and his only amusements were reminiscing, taking motor car rides and
watching the trains go by his office adjoining the Union terminal yards.

Rumors that Pendergast was eager to return to political life were preva-
lent throughout this period and in 1943 he made a determined but unsuccessful attempt to obtain executive clemency to end the strange exile
that was imposed by the Otis probation. Pendergast's petition for release
from the probation was recommended by a group of prominent citizens,
including the town's leading banker, its foremost real estate man, a
Protestant minister and a Catholic priest, but Judge Otis and Roosevelt's
Department of Justice quickly squelched the Boss's hope for a pardon.

Although he was still not entirely free, Pendergast in this same year,
1943, finally was relieved from the threat of further punishment for his
part in the insurance compromise bribe. Since his return from Federal
prison, he had been fighting bribe conspiracy and contempt charges that

were filed in state and Federal courts some time after the income tax actions. The state case collapsed when A. L. McCormack, the insurance man who delivered the money, refused to testify. In the Federal Court, Pendergast and O'Malley were sentenced to two years each in prison on contempt charges growing out of the insurance settlement. McCormack, who appeared as a government witness, was granted probation on a two-year sentence. The contempt sentences were set aside in 1943 by the United States Supreme Court in a six to one decision, Mr. Justice Jackson dissenting from the ruling that a three-year statute of limitations barred prosecution. The contempt occurred February 1, 1936, with the foisting of the fraudulent insurance settlement upon the Federal Court, and the contempt prosecution was not instituted until July 13, 1940, more than a year beyond the statutory limitation discovered by the defense.

Judge Otis had taken the initiative in this prosecution, which was accompanied by a successful effort to recover for the policyholders the money which the fire insurance companies obtained under the Pendergast-O'Malley compromise that gave the companies eighty per cent of the ten-million-dollar impounded fund. A three-judge Federal Court directed that all of this fund must be turned over to the policyholders, and the companies carried the issue to the United States Supreme Court, which refused to review the decision. In July, 1944, the Federal Court's custodian of the impounded millions began to mail out checks to policyholders.*

In that same July, T. J. Pendergast observed his seventy-second birthday anniversary. He found his desk had been decorated with flowers when he went to his office in the Ready-Mixed Concrete Company building. His friends remarked that he looked better than he had in years.

The old Boss lived to see the Goats start their recovery in the courthouse and the county organization, an action that gained headway in the campaign of 1944. He also was privileged to see in that campaign the defeat of a couple of figures in the antimachine crusade who believed that their just reward was the governorship. And he was drawn into the glare

---

* For their part, the 122 fire insurance companies involved in the corrupt settlement were to find that justice was slow but sure and severe. Instead of getting possession of the nearly eight million dollars which they would have received under the settlement, they were assessed fines totaling $2,090,000 by the Missouri Supreme Court in December, 1946.

S. J. Ray in The Kansas City Star

Here Come the Boys!

In the primary campaign of 1940, when Harry S. Truman was nominated for his second term in the Senate.

of the national spotlight again with Harry Truman's nomination and successful race for the Vice-Presidency in the summer and fall of 1944.

Newspaper commentators generally have acclaimed the Truman promotion over Henry Wallace in the Chicago Convention of 1944 as a supreme achievement of the big city bosses, Kelly and others, working with the Southern and congressional organization leaders against the purposeful C.I.O. strategists and the starry-eyed New Dealers. They did not include Tom Pendergast in this intrigue, for Uncle Tom was carefully observing the terms of his probation. However, the retired Boss had had a hand in Truman's preparation for this key role at a decisive stage of his career. Truman's nomination in Chicago climaxed a comeback in public life that has few if any parallels, and one that would not have been possible without the Pendergast support.

Senator Truman's career was generally believed to be over in April, 1939, when his principal political sponsor was indicted. Truman received the news of Tom Pendergast's fall with the comment: "I am sorry this happened, but I am not going to desert a ship that is in distress." Some persons were offended by this statement but many were favorably impressed by the spunk and personal loyalty displayed by the man from Independence. None supposed then or for some time afterward that he was the man destined to fulfill the old Pendergast hope of some day producing a President of the United States from Jackson County.

Truman's first term in the Senate expired in 1941 and he came home in 1940 to check the prospects for re-election. He found them better than most observers imagined. One of the large factors in his favor was the support of organized labor, particularly the railroad brotherhoods, whose good work for Truman was recalled repeatedly in the press after he cracked down so hard on the engineers and trainmen in the 1946 railroad strike.

A more important factor was the Jackson County Democratic organization, which provided Truman with a large block of votes from his own county and gave him the power and the connections for some profitable trading on the opposite side of the state. This was a decisive factor, for it gave Truman the inside track with the St. Louis organization headed by Bernard Dickmann and Robert E. Hannegan, who needed

Jackson County votes for their candidate for governor, Lawrence McDaniel.

A third large factor was a situation of a kind that had developed with interesting consistency in the past to help out a Kansas City organization man in a tight race. That was the three-way contest, repeating the vote-splitting procedure that figured importantly in Truman's first nomination as senator. It happened again in 1940 when the two Democratic heroes of the reform, Governor Stark and District Attorney Milligan, decided at the same time that they were entitled to the senatorship. Although it was certain that these two would divide the outstate and antimachine vote to an extent that greatly improved Truman's chances, Stark still looked like the winner until he became preoccupied with a Stark boom for Vice-President and a Stark hope for a place in Roosevelt's Cabinet. His political opponents encouraged this inflation at the same time that they derided him for big-headedness, declaring that Stark was running for everything.

The potent Jackson County organization figured further in the consideration that kept Senator Bennett C. Clark from giving Milligan the support he expected. Clark had received the Pendergast backing in his re-nomination fight in 1938 and was going to need it again in 1944. He was, moreover, a close personal friend of Truman's by this time. He delivered the nominating speech for Truman at Chicago in 1944 and received a presidential appointment to a judgeship after Truman entered the White House.

The Stark forces looked for a large majority from St. Louis in 1940 but could get no final commitment from the bosses there, who put off the deal until Stark could make up his mind what office he was running for. Milligan's backers meanwhile were quieted with the secret word that the St. Louis organization actually intended to divide its votes between Truman and Milligan. At the last moment, in a coup engineered by Hannegan, the organization went down the line for Truman, delivering an 8,311 lead from St. Louis for him. When all the ballots in the state were counted, he had won the nomination by 7,476 votes, with Stark in the runner-up position.

Returning to Washington in the third Roosevelt landslide, Senator Truman stepped to the forefront of the national picture with his committee to investigate wartime contracts and production. In this he employed a technique in which all representatives from the Jackson County school were thoroughly grounded. Senator Reed had built himself up for his presidential bid in 1928 with his Senate campaign funds investigating committee. Congressman Joe Shannon was endeavoring to draw the national spotlight with his committee to discourage government competition with private business and his bill to place government on a cost accounting basis, before Mr. Roosevelt's economists made all this very quaint. Representative C. Jasper Bell picked a likely publicity medium with his committee to investigate the Townsend Movement. Congressman Roger C. Slaughter follows the tradition with his committee to investigate surplus property sales.

From this point on, the advancement of Truman was an affair managed entirely by himself, the other bosses in the party and the American press. The commentators who gave major credit to the old bosses for the maneuver that put Truman on the ticket with Roosevelt were much too modest about their own endeavors. Numerous powerful publishers and their trained seals had been preparing the way for Truman for some time before he arrived in Chicago. It was clear to every reporter, editor and politician who got a good look at President Roosevelt in this period that the Vice-President would stand a good chance to finish out the fourth term. It was clear to all that the outcome of the 1944 convention struggle over the Vice-Presidency might determine the direction of the Democratic Party and the national government for many years to come. The selection of Truman as a possible compromise man for the anti-New Deal stand in Chicago is clear in the lines of his build-up, in the volume, the tone and the effect of the publicity he received in the work of the Senate Wartime Investigating Committee.

Senator Truman deserves much credit for that work; and while a committee chairman customarily reaps all the personal glory, the fact cannot be ignored that his favorable press had the proportions of a concerted campaign and his principal pluggers were magazine and newspaper editors who were praying for a Democratic leader who knew the New Deal routine and yet was safe. Harry Truman met the specifications almost to a unique degree. Jimmy Byrnes was a good conservative in the inner circle but he had been out of the traditional line of advancement for some time, he was intimately identified with the Southern Bourbons and un-acceptable to labor. Senator Truman had the best New Deal voting record in the Senate next to Joe Guffey; he was solid with labor, he had risen to his present eminence in the elective field, and yet he was essentially a conservative.

Truman's appointments since he became President, and his perfunc-tory efforts to get action on Rooseveltian measures he has called for, have impressed the fact of his conservatism on the nation. But long before the C.I.O. and the brilliant New York leftist observers began to understand the man from Missouri, many practical politicians, businessmen and newspapermen had correctly placed Truman and were not confused by his voting record. President Roosevelt did not admit him to the New Deal inner circle, and rarely saw him personally. Truman's intimates in Washington were not Ickes, Wallace and Hopkins. Senator Bennett Clark of Missouri, Senator Burton K. Wheeler of Montana and John Nance Garner, Vice-President until 1937, were among the men in the Senate with whom he was closest.

Commenting on Truman's reputation as a liberal, Roy A. Roberts, managing editor of the *Star,* wrote in 1944 that Truman had not seen F.D.R. personally more than five or six times, adding: "The Senator's close friends, and especially his colleagues, knew that at heart he was an old-fashioned Missourian—not a pink or a reformer."

The quality of convention generalship was very high in the Truman-Hannegan camp in 1944. It was particularly adroit in the important busi-ness of rumor-spreading, and Mr. Hannegan exhibited an uncommon grasp on the art of publicity. His chief contribution, which was the thing that clinched the vice-presidential nomination for Truman, was the famous letter from President Roosevelt, stating that he would be pleased to accept either Justice Douglas or Senator Truman as his running mate.

Politicians and editors had worked together to make one other large contribution to this situation. That was the business of the Southern re-volt against Henry Wallace, led by the Texas Bourbons. For weeks the anti-Roosevelt press played up the maneuvering of the rebels, producing much smoke and clamor but little fire. New Dealers countered by having Roosevelt put the squeeze on Jesse Jones, the Texas businessman in his Cabinet, and when the Southern hotheads assembled in Chicago for their anti-Wallace demonstration they made a pathetic show, which the press charitably played down. But the purpose had been served of impressing on the absent Roosevelt that it would be impolitic to press for Wallace as hard as he did in 1940. At the climax of the struggle, Wallace took the convention floor with the speech that made it clear to all that the Democrats would accept or reject the New Deal crusade in their decision on his candidacy, and for a moment it appeared that the popular demonstration for him would stampede the convention his way. But the city bosses and the old line practical politicians from Washington were prepared for this emergency. The convention chairman quickly adjourned the convention to protect the delegates from the roar of the crowds and permit the negotiations in the hotel rooms to be completed. The amateurs had nothing more in their bag of tricks and the next day the nomination went to Truman. He stood before the convention, giving a convincing impression of a modest man overwhelmed by his good fortune. It was said that he hadn't asked for the nomination and didn't want to be Vice-President, but there was no hesitancy in his acceptance, and the record showed that he had moved unerringly toward the main chance.

Senator Truman came home and was the honor guest at a massive reception given by the business leaders, at which he found himself the hero of numerous prominent Willkie Democrats and Republicans. The air of rejoicing among the Republicans was so pronounced that it seemed this was being celebrated as the G.O.P. victory of 1944. Mr. Truman also found himself the object of flattering attention from the *Star*, and a popular local gag of the period was that the Republican newspaper was trying to elect Truman Vice-President and Tom Dewey to the Presidency at the same time. While the old Boss's faithful friend was being thus honored, the reform paper hauled out the machine stainer for use against a couple of other Democrats who were running for state offices. This new agitation over the machine scandals grew intense but didn't defeat the candidates against whom it was aimed. When the election smoke finally cleared, Missouri had gone Democratic again and Roosevelt was in for the fourth term. However, the Republicans found some consolation in an upset victory in the senatorial race. And, of course, everybody in Jackson County was happy that Harry made it all right.

Tom Pendergast had little time left in which to put his final affairs in order. He declined rapidly in the final months of 1944. Perhaps he was depressed by the revival of the boss scandals during the campaign. Certainly he had some reason for supposing at this time that the machine skeleton would be rattled forever over the Goats, and he would never know peace again on this earth. Doubtless he derived considerable satisfaction from the vindication of Harry Truman, but the conduct of the campaign could have left him under no illusions that there would be any forgiving and forgetting for T. J. Pendergast himself.

Pendergast's thoughts were on the judgment of the people, and he broke his long silence late in October, 1944, two weeks before the general election, to speak up in his own behalf. He must have realized the end was near for he welcomed the opportunity to justify himself before the public and say a word of farewell. He was interviewed by Harry Wohl of the *St. Louis Star-Times* in his Ready-Mixed Concrete office.

"At seventy-two," he said, "it is too late to get back into politics, to start the day's work at five or six o'clock in the morning, to see my friends from morning until night. No. I am too old for that.

"But if I were a young man I would engage actively in politics again. Politics is a great game and I have enjoyed every minute of it.

"All I want to do is go ahead with my business here, to provide for my family and to take care of any poor friends as I did in the past. I'd like to do this for a long time to come.

"I've had a good life. I got into trouble, but I am not blaming anybody but myself.

"I've done a lot for Kansas City—for the poor of Kansas City. I've done more for them than all the big shots and bankers, all of them put together. We used to take care of our poor, with coal and wood and food and rent, and we helped them in their trouble. We never asked the poor about their politics.

"And I've never broken my word. Put this down: I've never broken my word to any living human being I gave it to. That is the key to success in politics or anything else."

He died three months later, at nine-forty o'clock the night of January 26, 1945, still an exile in his home town, leaving a debt that took virtually all of the one hundred and twenty thousand dollars in personal holdings to which his once large estate had shrunk. All the rest had gone to his wife, his children and lawyers, and to pay the costs of his illness and his settlement with the government.

A crowd filled Visitation Church to overflowing and extended to the street at the Pendergast funeral services. The priest spoke quietly, saying the things that properly could be said about a man who had charitable instincts and overpowering ambitions, who did some good things and made some mistakes. "Some always look for the evil," the priest said. "They never look for the good. Mr. Pendergast never maliciously injured the character of anyone. We all know he was a man of his word. I have heard men say they would rather have his word than his note. We all have faults. We are all human beings."

The theme of a sermon ran through the priest's words. "A man who tries to find happiness through money or power never finds it," he said.

There were numerous prominent citizens and former public officials among the mourners, but all attention was centered on Vice-President Harry Truman, who flew from Washington to attend the services. He could easily have found an excuse to stay in the capital but he hurried to Kansas City in an Army bomber, arriving shortly before the funeral.

After the services Vice-President Truman chatted briefly with friends who crowded around him. There were a few final words between Jimmy Pendergast, the new head of the Jackson Democratic Club, and the club's vice-president who had become the Vice-President of all the American people. Mr. Truman was in a hurry to get back to the Army bomber which was waiting for him at the airport in the industrial West Bottoms, where this story began more than sixty years ago. He had an engagement to fill in Philadelphia before returning to Washington and events were rushing on him. It was seventy-three days before he was called to the White House to take the oath of office as the Thirty-third President of the United States.

Index